Human Rights and Statistics

Human Rights and Statistics

Getting the Record Straight

Edited by Thomas B. Jabine
and Richard P. Claude

UNIVERSITY OF PENNSYLVANIA PRESS   Philadelphia

Library of Congress Cataloging-in-Publication Data

Human rights and statistics : getting the record straight / edited by Thomas B. Jabine
and Richard P. Claude.
    p.   cm. — (University of Pennsylvania Press Pennsylvania studies in human
rights)
  Includes bibliographical references and index.
  ISBN 0-8122-3108-2
  1. Human rights—Statistical methods. 2. Human rights—Statistical services. I.
Jabine, Thomas B. II. Claude, Richard Pierre, 1934– . III. Series: Pennsylvania
studies in human rights.
JC571.H76885 1991
323'.072—dc20   91-25079
                                                                   CIP

For activists and monitors who have given their lives in the service of human rights

Contents

Preface

In February 1977 Carlos Noriega, a former director of the Argentine Statistical Office, was abducted in the presence of his wife and three small children while vacationing in Mar del Plata.[1] Word of Noriega's disappearance reached U.S. statisticians, including Fred C. Leone, the executive director of the American Statistical Association (ASA), who had been beneficiaries of Noriega's official and personal hospitality during a visit to Argentina in May 1976. Largely because of Leone's efforts, in 1978 the American Statistical Association (ASA) established an Ad Hoc Committee on Scientific Freedom and Human Rights, following the lead of other professional and scientific societies that had begun to respond to widespread violations of the human rights of their professional colleagues throughout the world.

The ASA Committee (which soon became a permanent committee), with important help and counsel from staff of the American Association for the Advancement of Science (AAAS), began to monitor the cases of Noriega and other statisticians who had been victims of human rights abuses and to make formal appeals on their behalf. These appeals did not benefit Carlos Noriega, whose fate is still unknown, but the committee believes they were effective in bringing about better treatment of some other victims. Progress in some areas of the world is accompanied by new outbreaks of repression in other areas, and the ASA Committee continues its casework.

Working on behalf of one's professional colleagues is imperative but is not enough to ensure significant progress toward worldwide realization of the rights set out in the United Nations Universal Declaration of Human Rights. Members of the ASA Committee and others began to ask themselves how statisticians, using the tools of their profession, could work with others to promote the assurance of human rights for all. Prominent among the ASA members who raised this question was Professor I. Richard Savage who, in his 1984

Presidential Address to the association, challenged statisticians to explore the application of statistics to human rights issues.[2]

This book is meant to provide some answers to the question of how statistical methods and the statistical profession can contribute to the advancement of human rights for all. Our intended audience is not restricted to statisticians: We hope that this collection of papers will prove to be useful and provocative to anyone interested in human rights—government officials, scientists, members of human rights advocacy groups and others—whether they are presently active in the field or merely curious to know more about it. In consideration of this hoped-for audience, the inclusion of statistical formulas has been held to a minimum, and the authors have been urged to focus on goals and results, rather than on any advanced statistical techniques that they may have used.

Lest there be any misunderstanding, we need to point out that "statistics," as used in the title of this book, is meant to cover all aspects of the production and use of statistics. Margaret E. Martin, in her 1981 Presidential Address to the ASA, made an important distinction between statistics as a product and statistical methods:

In one sense, producing statistics as an end product is a narrower concept than applying statistical methodology across a whole range of problems . . . in another sense it is broader. It encompasses not only statistical methodology as a tool, but the whole gamut of activities that must be performed in producing statistics for the use of others—planning, collecting, analyzing, and disseminating data. The practice of many of these functions is not based primarily on statistical science or methodology, but is an art based on a mixture of intuition, experience, and judgment, as well as scientific evidence or procedures—in other words, the practice of a profession as well as the application of a scientific discipline.[3]

The relevance of statistics to human rights may also be clearer if we think of the origin of the term. The root traces back to the Latin word for state, and in German the word *statistik* referred to the study of political facts and figures.

The enjoyment of full human rights for all may seem to many to be an over-ambitious, unattainable ideal. We prefer to think of it in the spirit of Martin Luther King Jr.'s "I Have a Dream"—clearly a distant goal, but one that can help us to identify present problems and to know where to expend our efforts. For this purpose, it is not enough just to know that individual human rights violations occur. We need to know which rights are being violated, how frequently, and who the victims and violators are. To evaluate efforts to advance human rights, we need to know how patterns of violations change over time. An important function of such statistical information on human rights is to let the world community know what the problems are, so that deliberate abusers of human rights can be held responsible. This is what we mean by "getting the record straight."

Effective use of statistics in all fields, but especially in the area of human rights, requires the careful, objective application of sound techniques and procedures to collect, analyze, and present statistical information. No matter how strongly we may feel about human rights violations, in the long run it will not help to present data that lack credibility. The chapters in this volume have been selected as illustrations of good statistical practice in the field of human rights: this was a much more important consideration than the recency of the data presented. However, for readers who may be interested in locating the latest available data on various aspects of human rights, the final chapter in the volume, "A Guide to Human Rights Data Sources," includes a listing of 29 important data bases, with emphasis on those that provide international comparative data.

Progress in human rights requires that people with a variety of skills and knowledge work together toward common goals. The two editors of this work represent the fields of statistics and political science. Each has learned much from the other. We hope that the individual chapters and the overall result will illustrate the benefits of cooperation between disciplines.

Thomas B. Jabine
Richard P. Claude

Notes

1. Committee on Scientific Freedom and Responsibility, *Human Rights and Scientific Cooperation: Problems and Opportunities in the Americas*, AAAS Workshop Report prepared by Eric Stover and Kathie McClesky (Washington, DC: American Association for the Advancement of Science, 1981): 95–96.
2. I. Richard Savage, "Hard-Soft Problems," Presidential Address, *Journal of the American Statistical Association* 80 (1985): 1–7.
3. Margaret E. Martin, "Statistical Practice in Bureaucracies," Presidential Address, *Journal of the American Statistical Association* 76 (1981): 1–7.

Acknowledgments

This volume was produced under the sponsorship of the American Association for the Advancement of Science (AAAS) with support from the Ford Foundation. It is one of many products of AAAS's Science and Human Rights Program (formerly the Clearinghouse on Science and Human Rights) which, in addition to its work on behalf of scientists, engineers, and health professionals who are victims of human rights abuses, develops and applies scientific methods and techniques to the documentation and prevention of abuses.

Five of the fifteen chapters in this volume appeared originally in a symposium issue of *Human Rights Quarterly* in 1986.[1] Most of those five have been substantially revised and updated. The remaining chapters are new. A project steering committee established by the AAAS was responsible for the selection of papers for the symposium issue and for this volume. Members of the steering committee also reviewed several of the papers. Committee members were Thomas B. Jabine, Chair, Murray Aborn, Richard P. Claude, David Forsythe, Kari Hannibal, Denis F. Johnston, Douglas A. Samuelson, Eric Stover, and Ronald W. Wilson.

The editors are indebted to all of the steering committee members for their valuable assistance. Four of them deserve special mention. Eric Stover, AAAS human rights program director when the project was initiated, along with Stephen Marks, the project officer for the Ford Foundation, provided much of the impetus for expanding the activities of the AAAS Science and Human Rights Program to include applications of scientific methods and techniques in support of human rights. Kari Hannibal, senior program associate with the Science and Human Rights Program, provided invaluable staff support and substantive contributions throughout the process of soliciting papers, arranging for reviews and revisions, and preparing the final manuscript for the publisher. Murray Aborn, recently retired from the

National Science Foundation, did more than his share of reviews, including much of the introductory material for both the symposium issue of *Human Rights Quarterly* and this volume and, with his broad knowledge of measurement in the social sciences, provided wise counsel throughout.

In addition to Eric Stover and Karl Hannibal, other present or former AAAS staff who assisted the editors were Ann Clancy, who did the difficult job of readying the manuscript for copy edit by taking materials from diverse sources and putting them in a standard format, and Carol O'Hallaron, who assisted in the preparation of the symposium issue.

In addition to the indispensable support of the AAAS staff, the editors received useful advice and encouragement from the AAAS Committee on Scientific Freedom and Responsibility and its Subcommittee on Human Rights. Several members of the American Statistical Association's Committee on Scientific Freedom and Human Rights participated in the project as authors, steering committee members, and reviewers. We would also like to thank Pieter van Dijk and Peter Baehr, of the Netherlands Institute of Human Rights, for helping us to establish contacts with European researchers in this field. We gratefully acknowledge that publication of this volume has been supported in part by a grant from the Friends of Raoul Wallenberg Foundation.

All the chapters were refereed, most of them by two or more persons chosen from relevant disciplines. Many of the reviewers prepared detailed comments and contributed suggestions leading to substantial improvements. In addition to the members of the steering committee listed earlier, reviewers include: Carl Baar, Albert D. Biderman, Michael L. Cohen, Patricia Davis-Giehrl, Stephen E. Fienberg, Margaret E. Galey, Joseph L. Gastwirth, Jo Marie Griesgraber, Jon R. Kettenring, Donald P. Kommers, Joseph B. Kruskal, Fred C. Leone, the late Eli S. Marks, Juan Mendez, Han S. Park, Robert Parke, Patricia L. Rengel, Richard C. Rockwell, Barnett Rubin, Andrew L. Rukhin, John P. Salzberg, Wayne S. Smith, Piotr Swistak, Alexander von Cube, and Laurie S. Wiseberg.

In developing the Guide to Data Sources (Chapter 15), we prepared a tentative list of data bases and asked several human rights researchers to review it and suggest additions. In addition to some of the authors, steering committee members, and other reviewers already listed, we received helpful responses from Ernst Haas and Charles L. Taylor. We are grateful to the persons who reviewed the draft listings for each of the data bases included in the Guide. In most instances they are listed as the contact person for the data base.

Finally, the editors would like to thank the authors who, after all is said and done, deserve the lion's share of the credit for whatever success this volume may achieve in helping to further the application of sound statistical methods in human rights reporting, research, and advocacy. Although many of them received a modest honorarium, it in no way compensated for the substantial effort they devoted to writing the papers and responding to comments of the reviewers and editors. We hope that they will be able to take satisfaction from the fact that their work is helping to advance understanding of human rights issues and to achieve the long term goal of full human rights for all. Their names and affiliations appear in the list of contributors.

Notes

1. Richard P. Claude and Thomas B. Jabine, eds., "Symposium: Statistical Issues in the Field of Human Rights," *Human Rights Quarterly* 8, No. 4 (November 1986): 551–699.

Part I
Overview

INTRODUCTION

Most of the chapters in this volume focus either on the development or on the analysis of human rights data. Those chapters appear in Parts II and III respectively. Part I consists of three chapters which are broader in their scope and which, taken together, set the stage for the remainder of the volume. They define the subject and goals of the volume, trace the emergence of human rights as a subject for statistical treatment, and identify both the opportunities and limits for exploring human rights questions with the aid of statistical data gathering and analysis techniques.

In the opening chapter, the editors first try to answer the question: why statistics? We explain why we see a role for statistics about violations of human rights, even though the documentation of individual cases is and must be the primary concern of the many organizations that work on behalf of individual victims. We discuss the importance of the Universal Declaration of Human Rights as a conceptual framework for human rights statistics. We explain why we have focused on civil and political rights and rights to integrity of the person, and we trace the development of data sources, from statistics on lynching in the late nineteenth century up to the 1990 congressional legislation requiring the U.S. Department of Justice to collect statistics on hate crimes. Clearly, much more needs to be done, and that is the reason for bringing together in this volume diverse examples of the development and analysis of human rights data.

The other two chapters in Part I, by Robert Goldstein and Douglas Samuelson and Herbert Spirer, are also wide-ranging, touching on a variety of questions related both to the development of human rights data and to their interpretation and use. In addition, both chapters deal with all of the major categories of human rights, whereas most of the chapters in Parts II and III focus either on civil and political rights or on rights related to the integrity of the person, to the exclusion of economic and social human rights.

The purpose of Goldstein's chapter on "The Limitations of Using Quantitative Data in Studying Human Rights Abuses" is, in his words, "to caution about the difficulties of developing adequate definitions in the human rights area, in obtaining reliable quantitative human rights data in both historical and contemporary studies (especially for the worst regime violators), in relying excessively or exclusively on such indicators and in interpreting such data in an intelligent manner." He provides numerous examples of these difficulties.

Goldstein does not argue that statistics should never be used in the analysis of human rights questions. He does argue forcefully that they should be used in combination with nonstatistical information, and by users who have sufficient understanding of the issues to put the data in context. One suspects that none of the authors represented in this volume would dispute this dictum; indeed, the same idea is expressed in various ways in most of the other chapters, even though most of their authors tend to be more optimistic about what can be done to exploit existing sources of human rights data and to develop improved measures.

Optimism, combined with a sense of urgency about the need to exploit all potential sources of information about violations of human rights, characterizes Chapter 3, by Samuelson and Spirer. There is an old story about a drunk who was confining his nighttime search for his lost wallet to the area around the streetlamp because that was the only place where he could see anything. Samuelson and Spirer argue that we should look at the dark areas, and that we can learn something by asking why they are dark.

The intriguing idea presented in their chapter and liberally illustrated by examples is that inferences about a country's human rights situation can be drawn from indications such as the absence or suppression of data on a phenomenon known to exist or anomalies, which can be detected with statistical techniques, in the data that are available. Their ideas are in keeping with the underlying objectives of the branch of statistics called statistical inference: to draw conclusions or reach decisions in the presence of uncertainty. A citation that appears in their chapter bears repeating here: "The person who must have certitude, who cannot embrace conclusions tentatively, should not be engaged in social science research."[1]

Note

1. Norvall D. Glenn, *Cohort Analysis*, Series on Quantitative Applications in the Social Sciences, 07-005 (Beverly Hills, CA: Sage Publications, 1977), p. 17.

Chapter 1
Exploring Human Rights Issues with Statistics

Richard P. Claude and Thomas B. Jabine

Goals

The objective of this volume is to explore the possibilities for improving the analysis of global human rights with the assistance of statistical and other quantitative tools. The application of such methods is not limited to scholarly or scientific pursuits; it can also help to strengthen governmental policy making, advocacy, and education. The challenge of promoting better methods for assessing human rights is one which should be shared by all persons and all professions concerned with building a more humane international community.

Why Statistics?

Each violation of human liberty deserves universal condemnation. However, those who work in the field of human rights know that fixing the responsibility for violations requires an assessment of how, how much, and why human freedoms are curtailed or endangered. It is the thesis of this volume that statistics applied to human rights issues can make a difference.

This view was borne out long ago. A striking example of early human rights statistics was the periodic data on lynchings in the United States, first compiled and published by the *New York World* in 1885 and, starting in about 1900, by the Tuskegee Institute. The statistics, which soon received wide attention in media, classified victims by race, date of execution, jurisdiction, location, and the offense reportedly causing the lynching, such as "insults to white persons." These so-called "legal homicides" overwhelmingly victimized African-Americans, according to the *Negro Alamanc*.[1] Nearly 2,000 African-Americans were lynched in the two decades from 1890 to 1909. The number for 1910–29 fell to 875 and for 1930–47 to 146. Effective response to these flagrant violations of human rights was slow in coming—advancing first at the level of state and local anti-lynching legislation. But regular publication of the statistics undoubtedly provided effective evidence of the problem for use by those who worked tirelessly and eventually succeeded in doing something about it.

Statistics like the lynching data, which show clear patterns of human rights abuses directed against certain groups, can often be used to demonstrate that these abuses are parts of political strategies employed or encouraged by governments, military, or paramilitary forces. An individual case, although irreducible in its importance, does not evidence a pattern or policy. But in combination with other cases, it creates a moral imperative, for those conscientious enough, to respond by exposing and censuring human rights violations, locally if possible, and internationally as well, so as to call to account persons responsible and to prevent further abuses.

Statistics can make a difference in many ways: they can help people to understand and publicize the extent and character of human rights violations, to identify the groups most affected, and to clarify responsibility for violations. Participation in the process of developing reliable data can lead to better understanding of the issues. To open up a wide range of possibilities, we have taken a broad view of statistics in defining the scope of this volume. As indicated by the citation from Margaret Martin in the Preface, we are concerned with the practice of statistics as a profession, covering all aspects of the production and uses of statistics.[2]

Martin's distinction between "statistics as a product" and "statistical science" has proven helpful to us in organizing the essays included in this volume. Consistent with her distinction, Part II focuses on the production of human rights data, and the essays there are principally concerned with the processes identified by Martin as planning, collecting, and disseminating data. For example, the chapters by Dueck (Chapter 5) and by Reiter, Zunzunegui, and Quiroga (Chapter 4) are about classification, which is one of the elements of statistical production. Although the primary interest of these authors is in the use of violations data to help individual victims, the development of the standard classifications they advocate is a necessary prerequisite for nongovernmental organizations and other groups around the world to produce comparable statistics of human rights violations. Chapters 6, 7, and 8, by Gurr and Harff, Bollen, and Lopez and Stohl are also about the processes of developing statistics, with emphasis on the planning (conceptual formulation) and collection phases. This is also true, to a considerable extent, of the chapters by Innes and Pritchard concerning U.S. State Department and Norwegian country reports on human rights practices.

By contrast, Part III is more concerned with statistical science applied to the analysis of human rights data. Overall, our thematic goal is to illustrate how the practice of the statistical profession, in Martin's broad sense, can contribute to better understanding of human rights issues and to increased respect for and implementation of human rights by all countries. Clearly, we are concerned with much more than the application of the tools of statistical science, such as descriptive statistics, hypothesis testing, experimental design, analysis of variance, regression analysis, probability sampling, and the like. However, the first four chapters in Part III (Chapters 11–14) draw heavily on the tools of mathematical statistics and illustrate their use.

The chapters in Part I also fit into a broad conception of statistics and should help to orient the reader to various problems that are inherent in the application of statistics to the field of internationally defined human rights. Samuelson and Spirer, and Goldstein cover, respectively, the opportunities and limitations of using the tools of statistics to analyze human rights problems and issues. Samuelson and Spirer identify some applications that might not occur to people who take a narrow view of statistics. Goldstein emphasizes the practical difficulties of compiling and analyzing human rights data and makes the important point that analyses must be informed by an understanding of substantive issues.

A Human Rights Case Study

By producing statistics on any subject, we seek to set the record straight. This task is of primary importance in the human rights field, because reliably produced data may supply the key to securing a remedy for violations. Human rights monitors and activists are acutely aware of the urgent need for developing verifiable information about transgressions concerning human rights. Below, we detail a case study from Southeast Asia which highlights the fate of one human rights victim in the context of a wide-ranging effort to profile the pattern of victimization throughout an entire nation. The resolution of this case did not require sophisticated levels of statistical science, but it demonstrated the effectiveness of responding to tragedy at the grassroots level by launching a process of planning, collecting, analyzing, and disseminating information. That the process of statistical production, in this instance, linked reliable data with an internationally generated remedy should provide encouragement to professionals in the areas of human rights and statistics.

A year after President Ferdinand Marcos suspended civil liberties in 1972, church leaders known in the Philippines as the Association of Major Religious Superiors canvassed their members throughout the 7,000 island nation "to gain an objective picture of the effects of martial law." The Catholic Church survey revealed that political detention without criminal charges and the practice of torture were pervasive in all regions of the country.

In January 1974, ecclesiastical authorities established the Task Force Detainees of the Philippines (TFDP) "to provide moral and spiritual support through regular detention camp visits." Under the leadership of Sister Mariani Dimaranan, the Task Force consulted with cooperative attorneys and statisticians and created a network of national, regional, and local units to gather information systematically on torture and other aspects of political imprisonment in the over 100 detention centers throughout the archipelago. TFDP reports, denounced by the Marcos government as subversive, were distributed locally to relatives of the victims and circulated internationally through church channels and human rights networks. By 1976, nearly 6,000 persons were identified as imprisoned without the benefit of habeas corpus or other legal recourse, according to the Task Force.[3]

One of the TFDP reports details the tragedy of Mrs. Trinidad Herrera. As she was walking down Chico Street, Quezon City, in April 1977, she noticed some men in a car following her. One of them called out her name. When she turned to acknowledge them, she was hustled into the car and arrested on grounds of illegal assembly. Herrera had led protest meetings against government plans to relocate squatters in order to make way for the construction of tourist-oriented hotels. Mrs. Herrera was the president of the Zone One Tondo Organization (ZOTO), an umbrella organization for several hundred small groups throughout the Tondo slum area. She had accompanied Pope Paul VI on the occasion of his historic visit to the Tondo area in November 1970.

On the day of her arrest, Herrera was taken to Camp Crame for interrogation. There she denied that she was a member of the Communist party; acknowledged knowing two priests about whom she was interrogated; gave her correct address; and explained the relationships among several groups within ZOTO. Nevertheless, one of the interrogators suddenly shouted, "You are not cooperating!" Thereupon all but two interrogators quietly left the room. The remaining officers uncovered a box containing an army crank telephone with clipped wires. Mrs. Herrera was stripped of all her clothing. Wires were attached to sensitive parts of her body. She was asked various questions. Each time the uniformed men did not like the answer, and even when they seemed to believe the response, they turned the crank on the field telephone, imparting electric shocks. She could not help urinating from the intense pain and finally agreed to sign any confession put before her.

On May 5, 1977, Mrs. Herrera was transferred to the Bicutan Rehabilitation Center, where inmates and religious visitors smuggled out reports to her family that she could not feed or bathe herself and would merely sit and stare blankly with tears in her eyes. At that time, Lieutenant Ladislao Dialo, a medical officer, filed a report confirming the existence of scars from electrical abuse. On May 14, Trinidad Herrera was released on orders from President Marcos.[4] Circumstances which may have contributed to this outcome were revealed in United States Congressional Hearings in 1977, where it was noted:

The instances of torture have increased so rapidly that even the World Bank threatened postponement of a $15 million resettlement loan to the Philippines at the suggestion of Canadian Director Earl Drake. Drake was concerned with the arrest of Trinidad Herrera, a Manila slum leader. Ms. Herrera had been detained by authorities after having expressed some concerns about aspects of the World Bank project in Manila's Tondo slum district.[5]

The detention and torture of Trinidad Herrera was poignant and tragic. But as Congressional Hearings make clear, it alone would not have been sufficient to spark Canadian, American, and World Bank concern. Yet seen as representative of a consistent pattern of gross violations of human rights under the Marcos regime, the Herrera case prompted a high-level policy response. Were it not for the careful documentation of thousands of such cases by the TFDP, substantially relied upon as well by Amnesty International and International Commission of Jurists reports, the case of Trinidad Herrera might have gone unnoticed at the international level and unremedied in the Philippines.

Statistics based on carefully documented cases can be used in several ways to show how abuses represent policies rather than individual aberrations. One is to demonstrate the absence of government efforts to eliminate and remedy abuses. Another is to analyze patterns of numbers and trends over time. Thus in addition to documenting each individual case, it is important to establish the number, frequency, distribution, and pattern of cases—all matters that are basic considerations in careful statistical presentations. The analysis of cases involves other dimensions as well. Reports of human rights violations should include not only descriptive accounts of cases, but also an accompanying reference to the internationally defined standards that are violated. In addition, political analysis of the national and international situation is necessary if we are to interpret the numerical data on human rights violations. Thus, documentation skills like those developed by TFDP are of primary importance. Generally, groups collecting human rights data should provide contextual interpretation, but where they are unable to do so—perhaps because of political risks or deficient resources—others in the international community should undertake the necessary social, legal, and political analysis, improved, where possible, by careful statistical expertise. At least, that is the challenge if statistics are to play a useful role in constructing a more humane international world order.

Responding to the Challenge in a New Global Environment

The prevalence of human rights violations everywhere makes the process of reporting such tragedies morally imperative, but changing technologies also make such action feasible. Today we live in a world served by satellite dishes, super-radio transmissions, computer networking, inexpensive worldwide fax services, and improved jet age travel. In short, we now live in a global environment that exponentially expands opportunities to disseminate information, including information about gross violations of human rights.

As an example of how these media can be used to disseminate information, in 1989 the French newspaper *Actuel* conceived the idea of a globally coordinated "Fax-in" to help the Chinese people learn the truth about what happened in Tiananmen Square in June of that year. A simulated issue of the official Chinese Communist party organ *People's Daily* was prepared, with articles in Chinese describing the massacre, subsequent arrests and executions, and the continuing repression since the government crackdown. The material was printed in 13 publications in Europe and North and South America, along with instructions about how to fax it to China and a long list of fax numbers in "universities, bureaucracies, trade associations and workplaces" in China. *Actuel* also sponsored "a 'pirate' radio station, a boat sailing in the international waters off the coast of mainland China, beaming information and culture into the country."[6]

These technological tools of the information age should give tyrants much to fear. Means of communication that defy frontiers can readily expose abuses of internationally defined human rights. In that sense technology can be "human rights friendly," advancing the prospects that international norms will be used to judge political acts of barbarism. Repressive states thereby shape their own punishment. Those who would seek the benefits of global interaction are learning that they must also accept responsibilities, not only toward foreign powers, but to their own people who are also global citizens.

Through technological changes, the "international community," invoked so often in rhetoric, is becoming a reality and a challenge. It is a challenge shaped by the new global environment and a challenge to an ever broadening circle of conscientious professionals concerned with human rights everywhere. If adherence to human rights is to be the foundation for the international community, new patterns of cooperation must be developed. For example, cooperation among professionals across the boundaries of many disciplines is needed to make progress in so broad a field as international human rights. Human rights workers need the combined counsel of lawyers and scientists in the documentation of rights violations. Interdisciplinary cooperation is not without difficulties. Lawyers, social scientists, statisticians, medical specialists, humanists, and lay activists use quite different professional vocabularies and often employ incompatible methods of analysis. Still, when all concerned share a determination to make progress on problems of global importance, there is inducement for specialists and professionals to find ways to work together in assessing the status of human rights worldwide and to direct quantitative approaches to specific problems of human rights observance. In his Presidential Address to the American Statistical Association in 1984, Professor I. Richard Savage set a goal for statisticians when he alerted them to the possible contributions of statistical science and asked them to attend to the quantitative features needed to understand and help eliminate the causes and results of human rights deprivations.[7]

The Human Rights Menu from the Statistician's Perspective

For statisticians no less than for lawyers and social scientists, complex topics must be understood in terms of their component parts. Human rights, covering many topics, must be disaggregated. Appropriately enough, an essential first step toward this objective was taken by the United Nations in its Universal Declaration of Human Rights, adopted by the U.N. General Assembly in 1948.[8] With its listing of internationally defined standards, this document underlies most human rights reporting today and identifies possible objects of measurement. The many objectives of the Universal Declaration are predicated on the view, set out in Article 1, that "all human beings are born free and equal in dignity and rights." The overarching principle of equality of rights and freedoms is extended in Article 2 to everyone "without distinction of any kind." The remaining twenty-eight articles of the Declaration are divided into three categories: security and integrity of the person; civil and political rights; and socioeconomic rights, such as an adequate standard of living, medical care, and financial security in the event of unemployment.

The concept of equality, which pervades internationally defined human rights standards, implies comparison and measurement. However, the Universal Declaration and other international instruments, in spite of their great significance as a foundation for worldwide agreement on the importance of rights relating to specific aspects of life and society, do not themselves define each right in sufficient detail to provide a basis for international measurement and comparison. To collect and analyze quantitative information on a particular human right requires careful examination of all its ramifications, in various ethnic and cultural settings, and a lengthy process of developing and testing suitable measurement instruments and data processing procedures.

One does not have to look far to find data-based research undertaken to monitor large-scale social change in areas such as education, health, and welfare. Indeed, a leading feature of the literature that emerged from the social indicators movement of the 1960s has been its focus on the development of data that bear on problems of discrimination and maldistribution.[9] If we think of Morris's work, *Measuring the Conditions of the World's Poor, the Physical Quality of Life Index*,[10] if we consider the operations of such United Nations units as the International Labor Organization and the World Health Organization,[11] if we review the environmental reports of the Worldwatch Institute,[12] and the health, food, housing, education, and labor force indicators compiled by the World Resources Institute,[13] then it becomes clear that statistical and measurement efforts have concentrated on the cluster of Declaration articles pertaining to socioeconomic rights. Relatively little, by contrast, has been done (at least until recently) to measure and monitor personal security, civil rights, and political freedoms. This uneven development is not surprising, but it is ironic. Eleanor Roosevelt, who chaired the Drafting Committee on the Universal Declaration of Human Rights, said that the purpose of each of the thirty articles was to serve as a common standard by which to assess "the achievement of all peoples and all nations."[14] Insomuch as the statistical description of human rights already is well established in areas of environmental quality, food, health, education, and employment, the challenge now arises to improve statistical description addressing personal security and political rights.

Means

Having defined a set of goals, we turn in this section to the question of what has been done to date to achieve them. What kinds of statistics on human rights are presently available? What are their main strengths and weaknesses? How are the statistics being produced and by whom? We will see that national governments and international organizations cannot do the whole job; consequently, an important role devolves on nongovernmental advocacy groups. We will note the relative scarcity of data on public opinion about human rights issues, which is both surprising and unfortunate, given the substantial influence of public opinion on the human rights policies and practices of governments and international organizations. Subsequent sections will spotlight some encouraging recent developments and address the question: What next?

Gathering and Analyzing Information

Most national governments make a reasonable effort to gather, analyze, and publish data relevant to the achievement of economic, social, and cultural human rights by the people of their countries. National governments and international bodies, such as the United Nations Statistical Office, have collaborated on the development of concepts, definitions, and operational procedures for the production of statistics on income, expenditures, health, education, housing, labor force activities, and other aspects of the welfare of their citizens. Censuses, sample surveys, and program data provide a broad array of information. Sometimes governments withhold data or tinker with the results in attempts to improve their images, but on the whole nations provide enough data of moderate to good quality on these subjects so that anyone who wants to can determine how well the citizens of a country are faring with respect to the economic, social, and cultural rights included in the Universal Declaration and, at least roughly, how they compare with people in other countries. Governments that have any concern at all for the welfare of their citizens need this kind of information to guide their economic and social policies.

For the other categories of human rights—personal security and civil and political rights—national governments are much less likely to provide relevant data. When governments commit wholesale violations of provisions of the Universal Declaration, and of international instruments to which they are a party, they do not want the facts known to the world community. Some relevant data may be kept internally, but such data are much less likely to be available to the public, especially from countries with repressive styles of government. Consequently, the reliable information needed for effective work in the field of human rights must be elicited from diverse sources.

The description of events involving abuses of human rights conventionally originates with the national and international news media. Information also comes from single-issue organizations and specialized private groups interested in various aspects of human rights. It is disseminated by political solidarity and refugee groups with diverse motivations. Direct reporting, occasionally at great risk, comes from victims and their families as well as from human rights workers with various support groups, all of whom may be vulnerable to government interference. For example, during the last year of the Pinochet regime in Chile, a military prosecutor attempted to seize the medical files of the Vicaría de la Solidaridad, a human rights organization of the Catholic church in Santiago. When Prosecutor Sergio Cea arrived at the Vicaría on February 15, 1989, Auxiliary Bishop Sergio Valech informed him that the files had been removed from the premises and refused, on grounds of conscience, to say where they had been taken. Even after the Supreme Court issued a ruling upholding the government's seizure order, Bishop Valech said that compliance with the decision "violates one's conscientious duty to safeguard the moral and legal rights protected by professional secrecy [confidentiality]." The documents presumably contained medical evidence of torture by government officials of the Pinochet government.[15]

Governments sometimes report on the human rights records of other countries, as in the case of the U.S. State Department *Country Reports on Human Rights Practices*. The premise for U.S. government human rights reporting was explained in 1979 by Deputy Assistant Secretary Warren Christopher. Testifying before the House of Representatives Committee on Foreign Affairs, Christopher said: "The assessment of human rights conditions is not an exact science. There are inevitably some questions of judgment on which reasonable people will differ." Nevertheless, Christopher concluded: "I believe we can have confidence in our overall appraisals and in our identification of trends. And that is an essential predicate for an effective human rights policy."[16]

The main motivation for the United States and other countries that have attempted to produce standardized assessments of international human rights has been to provide an objective basis for relating foreign assistance to human rights performance in recipient nations. Thus, the U.S. State Department *Country Reports* which covered 170 countries in 1989 does not include an entry for the United States. Indeed, it is perhaps unrealistic to expect any nation to provide an objective evaluation of its own human rights performance relative to that of other countries. It is difficult enough to be objective in presenting information about other countries, some of them long time allies and friends and others antagonists.

Information on human rights is also generated by regional institutions, such as the Inter-American Commission on Human Rights. But these institutions must rely on governmental permission for on-site visits to countries under investigation. The United Nations Human Rights Commission since 1965 has sponsored a triennial system of self-reporting by governments, resulting in reports which are little-used because the governments which supply information are too often defensive in their presentations. More recently, however, the U.N. Human Rights Commission has shown initiative and independence in speaking out on violations of human rights in Afghanistan, Chile, Iraq, South Africa, and others, particularly when prodded by nongovernmental organizations and when relying upon investigative reports assigned to special rapporteurs. Component units of the U.N. Human Rights Commission have also recently set an improved record in obtaining information on problems of discrimination and consistent patterns of gross violations of human rights, such as genocide and "disappearances." The International Human Rights Committee, which operates under the terms of the U.N. Covenant on Civil and Political Rights, receives and comments confidentially on government reports, a technique that has become more effective by inclusion of a feedback process of criticism and queries.[17]

The Roles of NGOs

To date, the chief antidote to unreliable information in the field of human rights reporting and fact-finding derives from the multiplicity of independently published assessments by nongovernmental organizations (NGOs). Such voluntary groups include: Amnesty International, Survival International, the International Commission of Jurists, Physicians for Human Rights, the World Council on Religion and Peace, the International League for Human Rights, the Minority Rights Group, the Ligue international des droits de l'homme, the Human Rights Watch Groups, the Lawyers Committee for Human

Rights, and scores of others. Human rights NGOs are proliferating worldwide and hence the sources of information are increasing. In the 1980s, the Human Rights Internet, then a project of the Harvard Law School, published directories enumerating and profiling NGOs active in international human rights throughout the world. In Western Europe, the Internet listed about 800 such groups; over 500 in the United States and Canada; nearly 400 in Latin America, Africa and Asia; and in excess of 200 unofficial as well as "approved groups" in Eastern Europe and the Soviet Union.[18] Many others remain unlisted for fear of political reprisals. Following the dramatic political transformations of 1989–90 in Eastern Europe and the Soviet Union, the number of indigenous human rights monitoring groups has increased sharply in the 1990s. All of these organizations greatly increase the number of people who are engaged globally in monitoring international human rights. In other words, the international law of human rights has an attentive global constituency.

While the reliability of the reports of such NGOs is often reputed to be very high, taken in their entirety they do not provide systematic and comprehensive coverage of human rights violations. Each group operates under the constraints of its respective mandate and resources, leaving lacunae in geographic, topical, and temporal coverage. This adds to the haphazard rather than systematic nature of public reporting on human rights abuses. The resulting gaps in human rights data collection impede the goal of systematically and, when appropriate, statistically measuring change in human rights observance over time.

The users and uses of human rights data are many and varied. Nongovernmental organizations—significant gatherers of events data on violations worldwide—employ the facts they collect and analyze for monitoring, advocacy, and educational purposes, consistent with the mandates of the groups. For example, the London-based Minority Rights Group (MRG) develops qualitative information on oppressed ethnic, linguistic, and religious groups worldwide: ethnic Koreans in Japan, Tamils in Sri Lanka, and the religious Baha'i of Iran. MRG occasionally collects its individual reports and publishes them in paperback volumes used for educational purposes in British universities and elsewhere. Its *World Directory of Minorities* is an important contribution to standardized information on problems of discrimination.[19] Because MRG has consultative status in the United Nations, it is also positioned to present its findings to the Human Rights Commission and subsidiary units for review and assessment. Whenever the item "Violations of Human Rights" is taken up within the Commission on Human Rights, the most courageous and outspoken champions of human rights prove to be a few NGOs, including the MRG.

The Role of Public Opinion

By gathering and disseminating reliable information, NGOs hope to influence public opinion, which in turn will affect governments and international organizations. Jerome Shestack, former representative to the U.N. Human Rights Commission, acknowledged in 1988 that United Nations implementation of human rights has not always lived up to expectations, "but at least progress is being made." Quipping that "human rights is not a sport for the short-winded," Shestack argued that NGOs help to shape public opinion, and, in the long run, improved implementation of international norms depends on world public opinion. The reason, he said, is that: "World opinion stirs the yearnings of people. It encourages dissent. And repressive nations are always worried about being overthrown."[20]

Public opinion regarding human rights issues is greatly influenced by the work of human rights nongovernmental organizations. Such groups, whether testifying in diplomatic fora or before international organizations, are not bound by the norms of non-intervention applicable to states. They can maximize the free flow of information across borders, spreading the word on human rights violations. While governments dally with "quiet diplomacy," NGOs turn up the volume on complaints to mobilize shame and to enlist world public opinion regarding egregious rights violations. By framing complaints in human rights terms, even indigenous groups can realistically hope to win the concern of receptive groups overseas. A successful international media-based campaign can bring embarrassment to the offending regime, calling its legitimacy into question. This is a new phenomenon in international politics.

James N. Rosenau has argued that contemporary theories of international relations do not "do a good job in accounting for the possible impact of global television on the conduct of world affairs." Speaking of the power of global media reporting on human rights, Rosenau argues that "image-building" is not some regrettable aberration of political processes. Rather, we are beginning to learn from the uses of the media that it is becoming an integral part of global political processes, the part that enables people to assess governmental performance, test reality, and evaluate the activities that are central to their responsiveness to and acceptance of their leaders. He asserts:

The decline of traditional bases of legitimacy may well be accelerating as a consequence of the growing capacity of publics to observe directly, through global television and other microelectronic breakthroughs, their leaders in action. . . . [A]ble to watch domestic and world politics unfold before them, publics seem bound to evolve criteria of effective performance that they apply to officials who previously were accorded a presumption of competence.[21]

Where there is a positive valuation of the state—its identity, coherence, its political and general "way of life"—there is legitimacy. Regime legitimacy is secure when there is a broad sense among the inhabitants of a state that they control their destinies and that government operates for their welfare and security so as to establish what John H. Herz, a political scientist, has termed "a popular image of legitimate rule."[22] The formation of regime legitimacy is no longer the preserve of diplomats and other state actors. It is increasingly a matter of domestic public opinion and, according to Herbert C. Kelman, may become problematic if the regime becomes oppressive or unrepresentative.[23]

Given the importance of public opinion regarding human rights issues, it is surprising that relatively little has been done in terms of polling on human rights. An exception was a 1977 multicountry study involving stratified random national samples of adults (age 18 and over) conducted simultaneously in West Germany (959 persons), Italy (944), France (970), and Great Britain (1716). The surveys were conducted by the Emnid-Institut (Bielefeld), Machie Femmine (Milan), Demoscopie Sondages (Paris), and NOP Market Research (London). The study questions were attached to national opinion samplings designed in each country to represent an adult cross section. Identical questions were asked which, in complex ways, probed human rights related values, attitudes and priorities, and in simpler and straightforward ways, explored European reactions to U.S. human rights policies. Analyses of the data were published in 1979 by Steven F. Szabo and Richard P. Claude.[24] Among other findings, these authors presented three conclusions of broad general interest.

First, human rights activism at the international level was viewed approvingly by a broad spectrum of West Europeans. American human rights activism during the Carter administration was applauded by West Europeans, neither out of admiration for American sincerity of purpose—a negligible consideration—nor on account of any firm conviction that international human rights would somehow improve East-West relations and prospects for détente. Rather American activism reflected in Carter diplomacy was viewed favorably because it resonated well with indigenous European values and was seen as consonant with the strong sense of approval Europeans direct toward their own progress in human rights protection—progress seen to be in advance of that in the United States.

Second, the social bases of both support for and concepts of rights confirmed established theory in the field of political sociology. Those in Western Europe with the highest level of education, and those in the middle and upper classes (often the same people) are the most supportive of political rights, and they are most likely to believe that rights are inherent in human nature rather than state-granted privileges. These segments of society were also much more aware of rights developments and more supportive of action on rights violations than their less educated, working class countrymen. Education is the single most powerful variable in shaping rights responses, negating generational differences and the degree of urbanization; and, as hypothesized by Lipset and others, education also strongly dilutes the impact of class.[25]

Third, the more people hear about and discuss human rights, the more they want them acknowledged. The correlation found between awareness of human rights activism and respect for the importance of human rights suggests the validity of a phenomenon termed by C. Wilfred Jenks as "the sparkplugging effect." In an essay entitled "Law and Opinion in the International Protection of Human Rights," Jenks argued that the transition of human rights from "acknowledged rights into established facts" requires that "the fullest opportunities should be afforded for the widespread diffusion and completely free discussion" of the adequacy of human rights remedies in any given case. He called for "interaction of international opinion" as part of a strategy for further progress in the international promotion and protection of human rights.[26]

What does this speculative suggestion mean in concrete terms? When Colchester Labourites read about racism in the United States, they are likely to recognize the symptoms in their own English neighborhood behavior regarding the treatment of Jamaican blacks or exiled Ugandan Asians. When Cubans read an indignant article in the government press about Chinese communists being denied jobs in the Hong Kong civil service, they can hardly fail to think of non-communists or expelled communists who are refused jobs in their own country. Finally, the more Americans hear of U.S. sponsored criticism of human rights problems abroad, the more they are sensitized to the need for attention to human rights problems at home as well. Comparisons do not always have a one-way effect.

Some human rights polling has been done in the United States, but less than one might expect, and with less consistency than would be helpful for analytical purposes.[27] One line of interrelated but not wholly consistent questions was used between 1977 and 1981. The data may be interpreted to show sustained positive concern of the U.S. public for factoring human rights into foreign policy. A Yankelovich, Gallup question in 1977 centered on American views about aid to South Korea in the following terms.

President Carter says that he is trying to bring more morality to our country's foreign policy. Some people feel he is doing the right thing, others that he is making unwise decisions. Do you personally feel that President Carter should or should not: Continue to give aid to countries like South Korea because they are essential to our defense—even if they suppress human rights in that country?

	3/77	9/79[a]	5/81[b]
Should give aid	29%	26%	23%
Should not give aid/make conditional	50	49	67
Not sure/don't know	21	25	10
	N = 1004	N = 1065	N = 1221

a. Would you favor or oppose making the U.S. security commitment to South Korea conditional upon an improvement in the human rights situation?
b. Now, I'd like to know how you feel about a number of important issues that face the country. Do you favor or oppose: Giving economic and military support to anti-communist allies such as South Korea even if they violate human rights?

Although the three questions noted above use related language, their variation could have influenced the reported results. For survey researchers, the consequent problems of comparability of data weaken the prospects for analysis. In their article "The Polls—A Report on Human Rights," Anne E. Geyer and Robert Y. Shapiro conclude that "strikingly few questions about human rights have been repeated verbatim in national surveys," making it extremely difficult to track opinion trends.[28] They suggest that many existing survey items be replicated, rather than new questions created, each time human rights becomes a front-page issue.

Monitoring Progress and Explaining Change

In 1973 the journal of the Strasbourg International Institute of Human Rights, *Revue des droits de l'homme*, published a symposium reflecting diverse views on "The Methodology of Human Rights."[29] It acknowledged some uneven development in human rights research but noted that the literature on all categories of rights was beginning to expand rapidly. The symposium issue called for a "science of human rights" to explain developments in this field, but throughout its discussion of sociological and historical perspectives, there was little consideration of measurement and statistical approaches. One might justify this orientation on the view that the essential nature of human rights is qualitative, not quantitative. The argument is that a single human rights violation is one too many. Its full significance can never be adequately expressed by a number. A pattern of human rights violations shown by cold statistics is insufficient to communicate the context of fear or the regime of repression debasing the dignity of those associated with such violations.

While the importance of qualitative perspectives on human rights cannot be denied, the selective and discriminate use of statistical approaches to the topic is useful. Though the phrase "a science of human rights" may seem pretentious, it was invoked in the French symposium by some scholars to draw attention to the need to enlist systematic analytical techniques, including statistics, in the effort to assess progress in human rights performance and to explain change over time.

We argue that measurement, although it might not represent the central feature, must play a role in studying, assessing, and planning for human rights. Numbers cannot substitute for judgment, but judgment based upon imprecise information is risky. For example, if U.S. security assistance to El Salvador is tied by congressional resolution to human rights progress in that country, then we need to assist those attempting to assess progress by developing and applying objectively verifiable methods. It becomes a cause for concern when the State Department tells us El Salvador is making human rights progress, and Americas Watch, an independent nongovernmental organization, tells us that "serious fallacies inherent in the embassy data on human rights and some bias in investigation make the U.S. information weak at its base."[30]

Getting the facts straight and analyzing them carefully is a serious matter in the field of human rights because lives, integrity, and regime legitimacy, as well as money and government assistance, are all at stake. Whether we are talking about freedom of association in South Korea, political repression in Albania, starvation in Ethiopia, spying on students in China, or labor force discrimination in South Africa, the urgency of these and other issues linked to human rights now suggests that every technique that can better inform judgment is needed. We will know more precisely whether the observance of human rights standards in any given country—Cambodia, Kenya,

Turkey, Iran, or Northern Ireland—has improved or deteriorated when such evaluation is enhanced by objectively quantified reports, which are explicit in the evaluative criteria used and can be checked, replicated, and corrected if erroneous. In short, there is an important place for measurement and refined statistical approaches to the subject of internationally defined human rights.[31]

Human rights monitoring is more likely to produce the desired condemnation of violations (or to track changes in policy) when there are quantifiable standards to present data on the attainment or abuse of rights. These may take the form of rating scales based on expert knowledge and judgment, produced, for example, by Freedom House,[32] and by Charles Humana's *World Human Rights Guide*.[33] In its annual *Country Reports on Human Rights Practices*, the U.S. Department of State explicitly cross-references its findings with those of Freedom House and Amnesty International.[34] Likewise, the Ministry of Foreign Affairs of the Netherlands has explicitly relied upon (and sometimes differed from) human rights assessments by Amnesty International when making allocation decisions for foreign aid to Third World countries.[35] A wide variety of sources of systematically developed human rights data, some longitudinal, are profiled in the final chapter of this volume.

The processing of human rights complaints by regional and international bodies supplies a rich field for data gathering and statistical analysis designed to monitor progress and change. The increasing dockets of the commissions and courts of the inter-American and European human rights systems supply obvious opportunities for quantitative research testing theoretical perspectives. For example, Clovis C. Morrisson, Jr., has placed his statistical work on Europe in the context of "functional integration" theory. In his studies of the annual trends in the petitions to the European Human Rights Commission, Morrisson used longitudinal data on applicants filing petitions against states other than their own. He assessed the steady increase in such "alien petitions" to represent changing patterns of interdependence and to indicate integration among members of the Council of Europe.[36] The data sources for such analyses are readily available in the annual tables of statistics published by the European Human Rights Commission.[37]

Some Promising Developments

As the bases of information on international human rights proliferate and become more reliable, new opportunities emerge for the constructive use of case studies and the statistical analysis of human rights data. Three such significant opportunities involve efforts at: (1) building theory; (2) enhancing NGO communications; and (3) improving governmental and U.N. functions.

Building Theory

Aside from human rights, there is precedent for statistical approaches being linked to theoretical issues in international relations in which the objective is to explain change and to identify its causal components. For example, the late Lewis Fry Richardson, a conscientious pacifist and expert on mathematical modeling, turned his attention to the causes of war during the 1940s.[38] International relations scholars such as Anatol Rapoport have usefully sought to examine whether Richardson-type processes describing the dynamics of arms spirals can in fact be observed empirically and analyzed statistically.[39] Dina A. Zinnes, editor of the *American Political Science Review*, concluded that although data-based research on the causes of war has been characterized by ad hoc hypothesis testing, "there is growing concern for putting the pieces together for the construction of explanatory theories."[40] Human rights, like peace, is beginning to draw the concern, attention, and expertise of professionals in quantitative disciplines. True, the study of "man's inhumanity to man," war, and rights abuses remains theory-poor. But the need for the application of measurement skills, even if unguided by any grand theory, is becoming increasingly evident to those with the capacity to contribute usefully and practically to the resolution of problems of public policy affecting international human rights. The search has barely begun for theory supported by data.

One constructive effort to build theory has been inaugurated in the Netherlands: "The Interdisciplinary Research Project on the Root Causes of Human Rights Violations." PIOOM (The Dutch acronym for the Project) is a privately funded program to promote academic research analyzing the circumstances and processes which facilitate and inhibit gross human rights violations. The strategy of PIOOM is to develop theory on the "determinants" of torture, political killings and "disappearances," and to do so within the framework of conflict studies, cross-national comparison, and studies of the role of the police, military, death squads, and secret services, as well as the judiciary. Alex P. Schmid, research director of PIOOM, says that such studies, especially conflict studies, are "strongly influenced by quantitative statistical correlation methods." He urges others to search for the origins of human rights violations because: "The field is wide open for research for those wishing to take up the challenge."[41]

The first research project of the Dutch group seeks to discover regularities in the course of various kinds of conflicts. To this end, a global mapping of gross human rights violations is underway. The scholars involved have critically examined the sufficiency of existing data bases and seek to develop a new set of case studies based on rigorous definitions, improved information, and uniform data collection formats and procedures.

Ardent advocates of human rights will not be satisfied with after-the-fact analyses of what happened and why. Too often, such analyses are literally post mortem. One of the authors[42] has challenged statisticians and social scientists to turn their attention to the development of an early warning system for human rights violations. If theory can be developed to explain change and identify its causal components, the logical next step would be to apply that theory in ways that can quickly focus worldwide attention on new "outbreaks" of attacks on the rights and liberties of particular groups of individuals. The techniques and mathematical models used in epidemiology and statistical process control may be helpful. Theory, aided by good data management, offers the prospect of forestalling suffering and irreparable harm to many of those who are at risk.

Enhancing NGO Communications

There are good prospects for the development, in the 1990s, of a global NGO information system that can enable the member organizations to become a countervailing power to that of violators. This vision was the impetus in Oslo, Norway, for the creation of the Human Rights Information and Documentation Systems, International (HURIDOCS). Recently, the organization's international computerized information-sharing system has become operational. It facilitates information exchange among the community of human rights advocates. With the advent of computers and modern information technologies, HURIDOCS can format, electronically store, and transmit bibliographic and other supporting information needed for human rights documentation.[43] As the Norwegian-headquartered group creates coordinating and training structures in Europe, Latin America, Asia, and elsewhere, it aims to achieve a multiplier effect through trainees' sharing of their techniques with others involved in documentation and information handling. As this opportunity expands, human rights groups everywhere should develop improved capabilities in rapid global communications such that people throughout the world may participate in constructive efforts to influence international relations.

A new perspective on the international flow of information is suggested if one takes into account PIOOM's global mapping project, the HURIDOCS program, the previously noted clearinghouse functions of the Human Rights Internet, as well as the new Paris-based "hot-line" for up-to-date information on major human rights issues, sponsored by the League of Human Rights.[44] It is a perspective on international relations labeled the "global society model" by the Australian scholar John W. Burton.[45] He and his followers reject the conventional notion of world politics focusing exclusively or largely on the behavior of states. Rather, in an increasingly integrated process of international politics, states constitute an important subsystem in the global social community, but they are by no means the only, or even the principal, actors. Non-state actors, such as human rights NGOs, also become significant on the international scene.[46] Because of modern communication and transportation technologies, territorial boundaries, however bolstered by doctrines of sovereignty, are no longer impregnable to the flow of information and its capacity to influence public opinion and diplomacy.

Improving Governmental and U.N. Functions

Occasionally governments and international organizations take action designed to improve the use of statistics bearing on human rights. Three groundbreaking examples of general interest are notable, involving (1) constitutional developments in the Republic of the Philippines; (2) new federal legislation in the United States; and (3) initiatives in the United Nations.

(1) The Philippine Constitution of 1987 seeks to remedy fraud and deception in the reporting of statistics on basic human needs and rights. Article III, Section 6 of the Bill of Rights provides that:

The right of the people to information on matters of public concern shall be recognized. Access to official records, and to documents and papers pertaining to official acts, transactions, or decisions, as well as to government research data used as basis for policy development, shall be afforded the citizen, subject to such limitations as may be provided by law.

This constitutional guarantee, unique among democratic systems, proffers a serious basis on which to hope that statistical reporting on public policy affecting human needs and human rights will be reliably compiled and accurately published.

Consciousness of the need for the "right to information" grew out of experience with the yearbooks *Philippine Health Statistics*, from 1965 to 1985, during the regime of Ferdinand Marcos. According to

Dr. Michael L. Tan, M.D., government health indicators during those years were "doctored because of [their] politically volatile nature."[47] The premise underlying Dr. Tan's critical view was articulated by a World Bank analysis in 1984 reporting that, "while poverty is generally a politically sensitive subject, it is even more sensitive in the Philippines than in most borrowing countries."[48] According to the international lending institution, such sensitivity is due to the fact that the Marcos years of martial law (1972–1982) had been "justified considerably on the basis of their benefits to the poor." In short, *Philippine Health Statistics* since 1972 were "doctored" to show annual progress so as to legitimize martial law and the supposed "trade-off" of economic and social "gains" at the expense of suspended civil and political rights.[49] The melancholy result of the Marcos policy of self-serving reporting is that there is no reliable data base to profile health conditions in the Philippines before President Marcos was driven from office in the Revolution of 1986.

(2) In 1990, the United States Congress enacted the Hate Crime Statistics Act. The purpose of the legislation is to require the U.S. attorney general to acquire data about certain crimes which manifest evidence of prejudice based on race, religion, sexual orientation, or ethnicity. According to Senate hearings on the law, Congress expected that the systematic collection of hate crime statistics would provide federal and state governments with comprehensive information about the national incidence of hate crimes.[50] While legislative deliberations on the new law made clear that identifying crimes motivated by prejudice can sometimes be difficult,[51] a few state and local agencies that already collect such data have been able to develop practical working criteria to make accurate assessments. For example, a racial epithet uttered in the course of a fight is not always evidence that the offense was motivated by hate, but it is equally clear that there are obvious cases of bias-related motivation such as a swastika on a synagogue or a cross-burning on the lawn of an African-American family.

Support for the law derived from congressional interest in sending "an important signal to victimized groups everywhere that the U.S. Government is concerned about this kind of crime." Moreover, it was recognized that systematic data about hate crimes would be useful not only to law enforcement agencies to know where and how to focus their resources, but also to policymakers at every level of government to better gauge the extent of the problem and to local community groups to direct their educational and other preventive efforts. The Senate Constitution Subcommittee heard testimony from Colonel Leonard Supenski of the Baltimore County Policy Department, who developed and implemented procedures on data collection, that several important benefits were derived from data collection.[52] Specifically, he testified that precise information enabled police to develop long-term nonreactive strategies to combat hate violence, and it helped the department to plan more effective responses to such violence.

(3) In recent years, the U.N. Commission on Human Rights has initiated an approach to violations which concentrates on the types of abuses, not solely on the countries said to be perpetrators. For example, the Working Group on Enforced or Involuntary Disappearances was established in 1980. Several Special Rapporteurs on thematic concerns followed: Summary or Arbitrary Executions (1982), Torture (1985), Religious Intolerance (1986), and Mercenaries (1987). Two experts on international organization and law, Reed Brody and David Weissbrodt, say that the thematic procedures associated with the Working Group and Rapporteurs "do the most important concrete work of the Commission in protecting human rights in specific cases by saving lives, stopping torture, resolving 'disappearances,' etc."[53] Moreover, the thematic procedures since 1980 have also given birth to the human rights units of the U.N. most concerned with improving the quality of statistical reporting and analysis.

The problem of "disappearances" became widespread in the 1970s and persisted into the next decade in Argentina, Brazil, Chile, Guatemala, the Philippines, Afghanistan, Cambodia, and Ethiopia. "Disappearances" involve the officially unacknowledged capture and detention of prisoners by government authorities whose agents allegedly have been directly or indirectly responsible for the extralegal action. In effect, governments assume the power to end lives, criminally, without cause or responsibility. The U.N. Working Group has dealt with reports of human rights violations from 38 countries, receiving information on "disappearances" from various governments, nongovernmental organizations, and from private individuals. The annual reports of the Working Group are an integral part of its work. In reporting a clear picture of situations in named countries, the Working Group has succeeded in giving accused governments an incentive to cooperate so as to redound more to their credit than mere general denials or attacks on the sources of information. Nigel Rodley, Director of the Amnesty International Law Department (London), reports that "some evolution in the form of the reports is evident." He concluded approvingly that beginning with its third annual report, the group gave:

statistics, country by country, of cases transmitted to governments, answers which solve the cases, and other responses. The reports generally tend to bear out the Group's view: "The older cases continue to create difficulties. There is no lack of dialogue but there is a lack of results. . . . Current cases tend to be solved or no new 'disappearances' are reported."[54]

The U.N.'s efforts to investigate disappearances revealed the importance of accurate registration of vital events by governments of their own citizens and residents. Few obstacles to international statistical reporting and analysis are so fundamental as the failings, worldwide, which beset the registration of vital events, including live births, deaths, marriages, and divorces. As observed by the late vital statistics expert, Nora P. Powell, "The fundamental relationship between human rights and registration of vital events was forged when the International Covenant on Civil and Political Rights proclaimed that 'Every child shall be registered immediately after birth and shall have a name.' "[55] An important perspective underlying this requirement is that the collection, analysis, and dissemination of information concerning population matters can materially aid efforts to clarify, systematize, and more effectively implement human rights. If states are obliged through civil registration procedures and reports to account for their populations, then state officials may more readily be called to account for the violation of those human rights dependent upon appropriate population records.

Very few countries have failed to enact basic legislation requiring the compulsory, nationwide registration of at least births and deaths. Nevertheless, according to Powell, "Examination of the degree to which virtually universal registration laws have been implemented reveals that systems covering some 70 percent of the world's population do not operate effectively."[56]

What Next?

A broad review of events in the decades since the end of World War II provides some basis for optimism about the future of human rights for all the peoples of the world. The Universal Declaration of Human Rights, adopted in 1948, provided a clear set of goals. Since then, the scope of the rights enumerated in the Universal Declaration has been clarified and expanded in scores of international and regional instruments, such as the International Covenant on Economic, Social and Cultural Rights, the International Covenant on Civil and Political Rights, and a large number of conventions and declarations on specific topics such as genocide, racial discrimination, forced labor, asylum, refugees, children, and the rights of workers, women, and prisoners. None of these agreements has been ratified by all the member countries of the United Nations, but enough countries have subscribed to most of them so that the rights enumerated therein can properly be said to have widespread acceptance in the international community.

Formal definition of human rights does not, in itself, guarantee that they will never be abridged, denied, or violated. Although the geographic location and the nature of human rights violations shift, they continue at a discouraging rate. The realization of economic human rights is hampered by the pressures of increasing population and dwindling resources. Nevertheless, we feel that the movement for worldwide human rights is slowly gathering momentum. The very phrase "human rights," which was seldom heard a generation ago, is now common in the media and is widely understood and favorably received. The information revolution of the postwar period means that people living under repressive regimes can no longer be completely barred from learning about the more favorable treatment of citizens of other countries. Recent years have seen a spreading of democratic institutions in Latin America and Eastern Europe that has some of the features of an epidemic expanding by contact and contagion.

However, waging the struggle for human rights intelligently requires more than general feelings or impressions of what is happening. To marshall resources effectively, one needs to know which rights are being violated, where, and how frequently. For responses to violations that threaten the lives or physical safety of persons, the information is needed quickly. In short, there is a need for information, both in the form of data that permit action on behalf of individuals or groups and in the form of statistics that guide and measure effectiveness of initiatives to reduce the level of human rights violations.

The chapters in this volume offer many examples of how statistics and statistical methods can assist this enterprise. The difficulties of obtaining high quality information on violations of human rights are alluded to by several of the authors. However, most of these difficulties are not new to statisticians. They apply to the collection and analysis of statistical information relevant to any of today's major issues: drug use, global warming, AIDS, crime, and many others. For all of these topics, the statistician must deal with conceptual ambiguities, reluctance of informants to provide information on sensitive subjects, measurement errors of many kinds, and limited resources for data collection, processing, and analysis. The existence of such difficulties is regarded not as a deterrent but as a challenge.

The development of statistics relevant to civil and political rights and the right of security of the individual does involve two difficulties that are not as commonly found when dealing with other issue-oriented data. First, as mentioned earlier, the data collectors or human rights monitors are frequently themselves threatened with physical harm because of their activities. As has been systematically documented by Human Rights Watch,[57] several of the monitors have paid with their lives for their work on behalf of victims of human rights abuses. The evident risk attached to this role has not deterred other courageous human rights workers from taking their places.

The other special difficulty is the scarcity of resources for information gathering and analysis. Governments, according to their abilities, are willing to provide the necessary personnel and facilities for the production of data on health, education, income, and other topics relevant to economic and social human rights. But for data on illegal killings, torture, denial of rights to travel or emigrate, press censorship, and like subjects, the work is left primarily to nongovernmental organizations, most of which lack the technical and financial resources needed to sustain statistical programs that meet professional standards. Under the circumstances, the achievements of these organizations are remarkable, but they need additional support for the important task of informing the world about progress, or the lack of it, in responding to the challenge.

Notes

1. Harry Ploski and James Williams, *The Negro Almanac: A Reference Work on the Afro-American*, 4th ed. (New York: John Wiley, 1983).

2. Margaret E. Martin, "Statistical Practice in Bureaucracies," Presidential Address, *Journal of the American Statistical Association* 76 (1981): 1–7.

3. Association of Major Religious Superiors in the Philippines, *Political Detainees in the Philippines* (Manila: Task Force Detainees, Philippines, 1977).

4. Bicutan Rehabilitation Center, "Prisoners' Newsletter" (August 18, 1977), cited in Richard P. Claude, "The Decline of Human Rights in the Philippines: A Case Study," Essays in Honor of Myres S. McDougal, *New York Law School Law Review* 24 (1978): 215–216.

5. *Congressional Record* H 11211 (daily edition), October 18, 1977, remarks of Representative Burke.

6. "Fax Power: The Great China Fax-In Begins," *L.A. Weekly*, 10–16 November, 1989. See William M. Evan, *Knowledge and Power in a Global Society* (Beverly Hills, CA: Sage Publications, 1981); David P. Forsythe, *The Internationalization of Human Rights* (Lexington, MA: Lexington Books, 1991).

7. I. Richard Savage, "Hard-Soft Problems," Presidential Address, *Journal of the American Statistical Association* 80 (1985): 5.

8. Universal Declaration of Human Rights, adopted 10 December 1948, G.A. Res. 217A, 3 GAOR at art. 5, U.N. Doc. A/810, at 71 (1948).

9. Michael Carley, "Value Weighting and Distributional Equity," in *Social Measurement and Social Indicators: Issues of Policy and Theory* (London: George Allen and Unwin, 1981).

10. Morris David Morris, *Measuring the Conditions of the World's Poor: The Physical Quality of Life Index* (New York: Pergamon Press, published for the Overseas Development Council, 1979).

11. David M. Trubeck, "Economic, Social and Cultural Rights in the Third World: Human Rights Law and Human Needs Programs," in *Human Rights in International Law: Legal and Policy Issues I*, ed. Theodor Meron (Oxford: Clarendon Press, 1984), Chap. 6.

12. Lester R. Brown et al., *State of the World 1990* (New York: W. W. Norton, 1990).

13. International Institute for Environment and Development and the World Resources Institute, *World Resources 1986* (New York: Basic Books, 1986).

14. Quoted in Louis B. Sohn, "A Short History of United Nations Documents on Human Rights," in *The United Nations and Human Rights* (New York: Commission to Study the Organization of Peace, 18th Report, 1968), p. 70, n.3.

15. "Vicaría Records Under Legal Siege," *Record*, Physicians for Human Rights 2, No. 2 (1989): 4. Regarding political risks involved in collecting and disseminating human rights data, see Richard Morin, "Why Kill a Pollster," *Washington Post*, 9 December 1989. Ignacio Martín-Baro, Central American University Institute of Public Opinion (along with five other Jesuits, and two others) was murdered the day before he planned to release Salvadorean opinion surveys finding that the army "didn't enjoy a very good reputation."

16. "Statement of Warren Christopher, Deputy Secretary of State," *Human Rights and U.S. Foreign Policy*, Hearings before the Subcommittee on International Organizations of the Committee on Foreign Affairs, House of Representatives, 96th Cong., 1st Sess., 2 May 1979, p. 15.

17. Howard Tolley, Jr., *The United Nations Commission on Human Rights* (Boulder, CO: Westview Press, 1988).

18. See *Human Rights Directory: Western Europe* (1982), *North American Directory* (3rd ed., 1984), *Latin America* (1990), *Africa* (1989), *Asia* (1981), and *Eastern Europe and the USSR* (1987)—all available from Human Rights Internet, c/o Human Rights Centre, University of Ottawa, 57 Louis Pasteur, Ottawa, Ontario K1N 6N5, Canada.

19. Minority Rights Group, *World Directory of Minorities* (Chicago: St. James Press, 1990).

20. Jerome Shestack, "The Agenda for Action: A Summary," in *An Agenda for Action in 1988, Eleanor Roosevelt and the Universal Declaration of Human Rights* (Hyde Park, NY: Franklin and Eleanor Roosevelt Institute, 1988), p. 38.

21. James N. Rosenau, "Subtle Sources of Global Interdependence," paper presented at the Conference on Conflict in the International System, Polemological Institute, Grøningen, The Netherlands, November 19–22, 1986, p. 19. See Rosenau, *Turbulence in World Politics, A Theory of Change and Continuity* (Princeton, NJ: Princeton University Press, 1990).

22. John H. Herz, "Legitimacy and International Politics," in *International Politics and Foreign Policy*, ed. James N. Rosenau (New York: The Free Press, 1969), p. 84. See also Kenneth E. Boulding, "Social Change Dominated by

the Dynamics of Legitimacy," in *Three Faces of Power* (Newbury Park, CA: Sage Publications, 1989), pp. 113–115.

23. Herbert C. Kelman, "Patterns of Personal Involvement in the National System: A Social Psychological Analysis of Political Legitimacy," in Rosenau, *International Politics and Foreign Policy*, p. 277.

24. Stephen F. Szabo, "Social Perspectives and Support for Human Rights in West Germany," *Universal Human Rights* 1, No. 1 (January–March 1979): 81–88; and Szabo, "Contemporary French Orientations Toward Economic and Political Dimensions of Human Rights," *Universal Human Rights* 1, No. 3 (July/Summer 1979): 61–76. Richard P. Claude, "Western European Public Opinion on American Human Rights Advocacy," in *International Human Rights: Contemporary Issues*, ed. Vera M. Green and Jack L. Nelson (Standfordville, NY: Rights Publishing Group, 1980), pp. 97–117.

25. Seymour Martin Lipset, *Political Man: The Social Basis of Politics* (Baltimore: Johns Hopkins University Press, 1981; orig. Garden City, NY: Anchor Books, 1963), Chap. 4 on "Working Class Authoritarianism." Cf. Lewis Lipsitz, "Working Class Authoritarianism: A Re-evaluation," *American Sociological Review* 30 (1965): 109.

26. C. Wilfred Jenks, "Law and Opinion in the International Protection of Human Rights," International Institute of Human Rights, *René Cassin Amicorum Discipulorumque Liber*, I. *Problèmes de protection internationale des droits de l'homme* (Paris: Éditions A. Pédone, 1969), pp. 114–120.

27. Herbert McClosky and Alinda Brill, *Dimensions of Tolerance: What Americans Believe About Human Rights* (New York: Basic Books, 1983). See also David P. Forsythe and Susan Welch, "Foreign Policy Attitudes of American Human Rights Supporters," *Human Rights Quarterly* 5, No. 4 (November 1983): 491–509.

28. Anne E. Geyer and Robert Y. Shapiro, "The Polls—A Report on Human Rights," *Public Opinion Quarterly* 52, No. 3 (1988): 386–398, at 388–389. Cf. Kathleen Pritchard, "Human Rights: A Decent Respect for Public Opinion," *Human Rights Quarterly* 13, No. 1 (February 1991): 123–142.

29. Jean-Bernard Marie, "Une methodologie, pour une science des droits de l'homme," *Revue des droits de l'homme/Human Rights Journal* 6 (1973).

30. Americas Watch, Helsinki Watch, and the Lawyers Committee for International Human Rights, *Critique: Review of the Department of State's Country Reports on Human Rights Practices for 1984* (New York, 1985), p. 6. See also Dirk Eisen and Berth Verstappen, "Counting Human Rights Violations: El Salvador in Statistics," *SIM Newsletter* (Netherlands Institute of Human Rights) 6 (May 1984): 3–4.

31. See Barnett R. Rubin and Paula R. Newberg, "Statistical Analysis for Implementing Human Rights Policy," in *The Politics of Human Rights*, ed. Paula R. Newberg (New York: New York University Press, 1980).

32. Raymond D. Gastil, ed., *Freedom in the World: Political Rights and Civil Liberties, 1978–1980* (Boston: G. K. Hall and Co., Freedom House Books, 1978, 1979, 1980); (Westport, CT: Greenwood Press, Freedom House Books, 1981, published annually, to date).

33. Charles Humana, *World Human Rights Guide* (London: Hutchinson, 1986).

34. U.S. Congress, House Committee on Foreign Affairs and Senate Committee on Foreign Relations, *Country Reports on Human Rights Practices for 1985*, Appendix A (Washington, DC: U.S. Government Printing Office,

1986), published annually, 1976 to date. See also data analysis prepared for U.S. Congress by Stanley J. Heginbotham and Vita Bite, "Issues in Interpretation and Evaluation of Country Studies," in U.S. Congress, House Committee on International Relations, *Human Rights in Selected Countries and the U.S. Response* (Washington, DC: U.S. Government Printing Office, 1978).

35. Peter R. Baehr, "Concern for Development Aid and Fundamental Human Rights: The Dilemma as Faced by the Netherlands," *Human Rights Quarterly* 4, No. 1 (1982): 39–52. More recently, see Manfred Nowak and Theresa Swinhart, eds., *Human Rights in Developing Countries 1989 Yearbook* (Arlington, VA: N. P. Engel, 1989); cf. Sigrun I. Skogly, "Human Rights Reporting: The 'Nordic' Experience," *Human Rights Quarterly* 12, No. 4 (November 1990): 513–528.

36. Clovis C. Morrisson, Jr., "The European Human Rights Convention System as a Functional Enterprise," in *Universal Human Rights* 1, No. 4 (October–December 1979): 81–92.

37. Council of Europe/Conseil de l'Europe, *Yearbook of the European Convention on Human Rights*, for the Human Rights Documentation Centre, Strasbourg (Hingham, MA: Martinus Nijhoff Publishers, imprint of Kluwer Academic Publishers, 1989).

38. Lewis Fry Richardson, "Variation of the Frequency of Fatal Quarrels with Magnitude," *Journal of the American Statistical Association* 43 (1949): 523–546.

39. Anatol Rapoport, *Fights, Games and Debates* (Ann Arbor: University of Michigan Press, 1961).

40. Dina A. Zinnes, *Contemporary Research in International Relations, A Perspective and a Critical Appraisal* (New York: Free Press, 1976), p. 15. For an example of hypothesis testing using human rights data, see Conway W. Henderson, "Conditions Affecting the Use of Political Repression," *Journal of Conflict Resolution* 35, No. 1 (March 1991): 120–142.

41. Alex P. Schmid, ed., *Research on Gross Human Rights Violations*, 2nd ed. (Leiden, The Netherlands: Center for the Study of Social Conflicts, Interdisciplinary Research Project on Root Causes of Human Rights Violations, 1989).

42. Thomas B. Jabine, "An Early Warning System for Tracking Human Rights Violations," in *Challenges for the '90s* (Washington, DC: American Statistical Association, 1989), p. 39.

43. Bjorn Stormorken, *HURIDOCS: Standard Formats for the Recording and Exchange of Information on Human Rights* (Dordrecht: Martinus Nijhoff Publishers on behalf of HURIDOCS, 1985). See also *A Guide to Establishing a Human Rights Documentation Centre*, ed. Laurie S. Wiseberg (Tokyo: United Nations University, 1988).

44. See "French League Establishes Human Rights Hotline," *Human Rights Internet Report* 11, No. 5/6 (Winter–Spring 1987): 38.

45. See John W. Burton, *Global Conflict: The Domestic Sources of International Conflict* (London: Wheatsheaf Books, Ltd., 1984). See also Michael Banks, "The International Relations Discipline: Asset or Liability for Conflict Resolution?" in *International Conflict Resolution, Theory and Practice*, ed. Edward A. Azar and John W. Burton (Boulder, CO: Lynne Rienner Publishers, 1986), pp. 18–19. See also R. J. Vincent, *Human Rights and International Relations* (London: Cambridge University Press, 1986).

46. Christopher Hill, "Implications of the World Society Perspectives for

National Foreign Policies," in *Conflict in World Society: A New Perspective on International Relations*, ed. Michael Banks (New York: St. Martin's Press, 1984), pp. 174–91.

47. Michael L. Tan, M.D.,. "The State of the Nation's Health," unpublished paper (Manila: Health Action Information Network, 1986), p. 6.

48. World Bank, "Philippines—Working Level Draft Country Program Paper" (Washington, DC: World Bank, August 29, 1984), p. 17.

49. Alicia de la Paz, "A Second Look at the Philippine Health Statistics," *MAG Bulletin* (Manila: Medical Action Group) 3, No. 1 (January–March 1986): 22–27. See also Robert E. Goodin, "The Development-Rights Trade-Off: Some Unwarranted Economic and Political Assumptions," *Universal Human Rights* 1, No. 2 (April–June 1979): 31–32.

50. "Hate Crimes Statistics Act," Hearings before the Subcommittee on the Constitution of the Committee on the Judiciary, U.S. Senate, 100th Cong., 2nd Sess., June 21, 1986, signed by President George Bush, 23 April 1990.

51. Steven R. Schlesinger, Director of the Bureau of Justice Statistics, U.S. Department of Justice, testified that the bill would "set out a task which professional statisticians familiar with the criminal justice system believe would be extremely difficult and expensive to perform." Ibid., p. 116.

52. Testimony of Leonard Suprinsky, Ibid., pp. 207–213.

53. Reed Brody and David Weissbrodt, "Major Developments at the 1989 Session of the U.N. Commission on Human Rights," *Human Rights Quarterly* 11, No. 4 (November 1989): 586–611, at 602.

54. See David Weissbrodt, "Country Related and Thematic Developments at the 1988 Session of the U.N. Commission on Human Rights," *Human Rights Quarterly* 10, No. 4 (November 1988): 544–558, at 546.

55. Nora P. Powell, "Human Rights and Registration of Vital Events," Technical Paper No. 7 (Bethesda, MD: International Institute for Vital Registration and Statistics, 1980), p. 1.

56. Ibid., p. 2.

57. Human Rights Watch, *The Persecution of Human Rights Monitors, December 1986 to December 1987: A Worldwide Survey* (New York: Human Rights Watch, 1987). For information on subsequent reports, see Human Rights Watch profile below, item (05), page 408 of this volume.

Chapter 2
The Limitations of Using Quantitative Data in Studying Human Rights Abuses

Robert Justin Goldstein

The most significant addition to the methodological toolbag of social scientists since the days of Aristotle has no doubt been the increasingly widespread use of quantitative data and techniques during the post-World War II era. The explanations for the quantitative revolution involve a mixture of the academic equivalent of the sacred and the profane, of motivations scientifically sound and those less so. Certainly the strongest and most scientifically sound motivation behind the quantitative revolution has been the strong and often justified feeling that without "hard data," social science often consists of no more than the subjective impressions of individual scholars, which are reported without any clear standards or procedures and which cannot be tested, replicated, or compared in any methodologically sound way across time or space with other findings on similar subjects.

Good quantitative data are often enormously useful in disproving what is regarded as common knowledge. For example, the general impression given by the mass media in the 1985–86 period was that Americans are at high risk from and the prime targets of international terrorism; however, a different perspective emerges when one learns that in 1985 more Americans drowned in their bathtubs than were killed by terrorists; that the chance of an American dying in an automobile accident in 1985 was 300 times greater than the chance of dying at the hands of a terrorist; and that only 23 Americans were among the 982 worldwide deaths attributed to terrorists during the 1985–86 period. Widely circulated news reports of the mid-1980s suggested that tens of thousands of American children are kidnapped every year by strangers. These cases, when subjected to close scrutiny, collapse into at most a few thousand cases in which children are missing for more than a few hours at the hands of abductors; most "abductions" turn out to involve runaway children, child-custody disputes, or brief absences (some of which involve attempts at or actual molestation), after which the child is found or returns home. The enormous public focus in the late 1980s on the danger to health posed by illegal drugs calls for a different interpretation in light of the 1989 U.S. surgeon general's report that, while such drugs cause or contribute to perhaps 10,000 or so deaths per year, tobacco helps to kill 390,000 Americans annually, and alcohol abuse is implicated in 100,000 deaths each year.[1]

Sometimes statistical information can document in startling ways phenomena, including those clearly related to human rights questions, that are extremely important to know for public policy purposes. For example, in early 1989, news reports indicated that scientific studies have found that, even with socioeconomic class held constant, blacks in need of kidney transplants were only half as likely to receive them as were whites. A 1989 analysis of the outcomes of 10 million home mortgage applications indicated that blacks were twice as likely to be rejected for such applications as were whites, and that in much of the country high-income blacks are rejected at the same rate as are low-income whites.[2]

Sometimes statistical information is reassuring, such as data that only half as many Americans were killed by police in the nation's largest 50 cities in 1984 as in 1971, suggesting real gain in police professionalism. Sometimes the news is alarming, such as the 1986 report of the National Highway Traffic Safety Administration that odometers are rolled back in 93 percent of rental cars. Even where good quantitative data merely confirm "common knowledge" or common sense—as in a 1986 study which reports that doctors who gain a financial benefit from ordering medical tests order 50 percent more cardiograms and chest x-rays than doctors who are paid fixed salaries and do not gain financially—it is a benefit to have confirmation not only for academic or popular knowledge but also often from a public policy standpoint.[3]

While the dominant motivation for the rise of quantitative methodology is no doubt scientifically sound, sometimes other motivations are less so. Thus, any reasonably aware academic social scientist must notice that the prospects for funding and publication and often for promotion and professional mobility increase with the use of quantitative methodologies. To the extent such motivations drive the adoption of methodology, the social sciences are likely to be swamped with poorly conceived or trivial studies, or research based on supposedly quantitative data that do not meet methodological standards. Another unsound motivation is that the social sciences collectively have something of an inferiority complex in comparison with the "hard" sciences. This largely results from their inability to describe social and political behavior with the precision of scientific statements, such as the law of gravity, or to predict future events with the kind of assurance that allows astronomers to predict the return of Halley's comet every seventy-six years. Such feelings of inferiority often translate into a collective social science orientation that a more rigorous methodology alone would solve the problem. Another possibility, however, is that human motivations and behavior, especially en masse, are simply not susceptible to the same kind of measurement and predictability as are the rocks and the stars. As political scientist John McCamant has noted, compared to the relatively "neat repeatability of copper atoms," the "inconstancy of societies begins with the inconstancy of their basic parts, individual human beings—none of whom are like any other and each of which is always learning and adjusting," creating "infinite" combinations and permutations with "structures and processes . . . never the same in any two places or at any two times."[4]

Whatever the precise motivations, given the general rise of quantitative methodology in the social sciences it is certainly not surprising to find that the burgeoning literature in human rights studies is filled with attempts to use such methods, accompanied by calls for their improved applications and development.[5] The purpose of this essay is not to suggest in some turn-back-the-clock Luddistic manner that quantitative approaches in general, or with regard to human rights studies specifically, are without value, but rather to express some warnings with regard to overreliance on quantitative data and approaches. In particular, this essay will seek to caution about the difficulties of developing adequate definitions in the human rights area, in obtaining reliable quantitative human rights data in both historical and contemporary studies (especially for the worst regime violators), in relying exclusively or excessively on such indicators, and in interpreting such data in an intelligent manner.

Although this essay is primarily concerned with academic social science research, in some cases, as will be noted in the conclusion, quantitative data which might not meet scholarly standards, particularly in terms of cross-national or longitudinal research, can still be useful in terms of general education and public policy concerns. The reader should also keep in mind that many of the problems which bedevil the use of quantitative data for human rights studies are common to other topics. Thus, the 1969 presidential address to the American

Economic Association featured a warning against a general tendency to perform "sophisticated statistical analysis" on grossly unreliable data. Twenty years later, statisticians A. J. Jaffe and Herbert Spirer made the same point, warning that "making precise statistical calculations from imprecise data" is "misuse of statistics" and that "hairy and even well-shaven statistical procedures may only be a disguise, camouflaging the subjective and imprecise judgments which give rise to the basic data."[6]

Problems of Definition

Quantitative data collection requires a clear definition of the subject under study, but defining what are human rights poses enormous difficulties. Typically, the U.S. government and many Western-oriented human rights organizations have concentrated almost entirely on political and civil rights (e.g., the rights to vote and to freedom of speech) and rights of personal security (e.g., freedom from torture and arbitrary arrest), while communist regimes and Third World countries have stressed social and economic rights (e.g., the rights to employment and to decent and adequate food and shelter). Further, the Western stress has been almost exclusively on individual rights within defined nation-states. Non-Western approaches, however, have often stressed group rights associated with economic and cultural autonomy and freedom from ethnic-racial discrimination, sometimes on a worldwide basis, as in demands for freedom from alleged Western global cultural-economic hegemony.[7] A small sample of this "talking past each other's definitions" can be grasped from the comment of an American delegate to an international human rights conference held in Canada in 1985, who noted, "We talk about human [i.e., political and civil] rights and they [the Soviets] talk about unemployment and racism."[8]

Many scholars have endorsed the 1947 United Nations Universal Declaration of Human Rights and subsequent convenants as formulations which encompass a broad variety of rights and have broad international support, but such support is greater in theory than practice. Clearly the U.S. government and many conservative scholars do not really endorse the Universal Declaration's assertion that everyone in the world is entitled to enough "food, clothing, housing and medical care" to provide a living standard adequate for their "health and well-being"; clearly the Soviet government did not really accept the Universal Declaration's assertion of a right to own property, at least not until the changes of the 1990s.

Regardless of the general concept of human rights that is adopted, from the standpoint of quantitative data collection the definition of specific types of violations is far more important, since no one has suggested any way in which human rights can be measured as one monolithic concept. The variety of types of possible human rights violations is so large that no comprehensive list of what to measure seems possible, however. Human rights abuses may be as diverse as "banning" in South Africa, congressional antisubversive investigations in the United States, house arrests in South Korea, or detention of political dissidents in psychiatric institutions in the Soviet Union. Even defining relatively widespread types of violations has proved extremely difficult. For example, the definition of torture used by Amnesty International (AI) includes state-induced "severe pain or suffering, whether physical or mental," which constitutes "an aggravated and deliberate form of cruel, inhuman or degrading treatment or punishment."[9] The inclusion of "mental" suffering, while quite reasonable, makes this concept largely subjective. One scholar has noted "what is torture for one generation may very well be minor inconvenience for another."[10] In practice, interpreting such otherwise undefined terms as "cruel, inhuman or degrading punishment" poses such difficulties that charges of British use of torture in Northern Ireland in 1971 were unanimously confirmed in a 1976 decision of the European Commission of Human Rights but rejected by a thirteen to four vote in 1978 by the European Court of Human Rights.[11]

Others' terms have been no more adequately defined. For example, AI defines political killings as "unlawful and deliberate killings of persons by reason of their real or imputed political beliefs or activities, religion, other conscientiously held beliefs, ethnic origin, sex, color or language, carried out by order of a government or with it's [sic] complicity."[12] This definition is too narrow since it excludes "lawful" killings of persons for their political beliefs, yet many clearly politically motivated executions in Russia, South Africa, and Nazi Germany were "legal," as was the entire basis of the Hitler dictatorship. As political scientist Franz Neumann has written, "there can be a legal system that is nothing more than a means of terrorizing people."[13] Historian Michal Belknap offers a definition of political trial which literally collapses under its own complexity:

Any trial or impeachment that immediately affects or is intended to affect the structure, personnel, or policies of government, that is the product of or has its outcome determined by political controversy, or that results from the efforts of a group within society having control of the machinery of government to use the courts to disadvantage its rivals in a power struggle which is not immediately political or to preserve its own economic or social position.[14]

The area of social and economic rights lends itself to much easier definition and operationalization than the political, civil, and personal security rights area. Thus, there is general agreement on the definition of terms such as infant mortality, life expectancy, and caloric intake. Yet many concepts in the social and economic rights area still pose great difficulties. For example, the U.S. Census Bureau, using a definition of literacy as the completion of a fifth grade education, reported in 1979 that fewer than 1 percent of Americans over age fourteen were illiterate. In 1986 the U.S. Department of Education reported that 13 percent of adult Americans are illiterate, defining illiteracy as the inability to score twenty or more correct answers on a twenty-six question test of reading ability. (If the cutoff were twenty-one answers, the illiteracy rate would have been significantly higher.) Other estimates of American illiteracy, defined in terms of the functional ability to perform simple tasks requiring comprehension of written materials, have ranged from 20 percent to over 50 percent of adults, depending upon the level of competency required.[15]

Any discussion of a definition of poverty raises a question concerning human rights measurement and definition more fundamental than any raised so far: does it make sense to apply the *same* definition of poverty to countries at varying stages of development? Poverty is defined by the Organization of Economic Cooperation and Development as the percentage of national population falling below two-thirds of the average disposable income in each country; this definition will produce a different absolute cutoff level for each country. Such a floating definition of poverty unquestionably has many merits, since people typically compare their standards of living with their fellow nationals, but human rights definitions that vary from country to country pose enormous conceptual difficulties for comparative measurement purposes. (In this case, comparative income distribution figures could help somewhat.) Yet sociologist Rhoda Howard and others have made compelling arguments stating that, in effect, measuring all countries by the same definitional standards is grossly unfair to developing nations. Howard concluded that human rights studies should compare countries "at similar levels of social evolution or development, and must take into account different cultural traditions." Africa of the 1980s, therefore, should not be held to the standards of contemporary Europe but should be compared to nineteenth century Europe, which was marked by "massive violations of what we would now consider elementary human rights."[16]

Another relativist argument often made is that state actions that might be considered repressive in one context might not be considered so in another. Thus, Professor George Lopez suggests that one cannot categorize state use of coercion without determining if the actions are "unilateral and unprovoked" or justified by terrorist incidents or other "de facto reasons" in invoking "extraordinarily harsh and repressive measures."[17] (This of course is the flipside of the "one man's terrorist is another's freedom fighter" argument.)

Problems in Obtaining Reliable Data

Even if definitional problems can be satisfactorily resolved, data must still be obtained. However, reliable and comprehensive data in the human rights area, especially in forms that lend themselves to either longitudinal or cross-national studies, are often not available due to lack of collection or to governmentally imposed barriers. Where data are available, they will often be extremely difficult and expensive to obtain and are likely to be fragmentary, controversial, or of dubious reliability.

Some distinctions can nonetheless be usefully drawn between difficulties involved in obtaining different types of human rights data: (1) historical data, particularly for the period before World War I, are far less available and reliable than are data for the post-World War I period; (2) data in the social-economic rights area are far more available and reliable than are data in the political, civil, and personal security rights area; (3) data for the latter areas are available and reliable, in general, in inverse relation to the level and seriousness of violations; and (4) data for the developed countries are far more available and reliable than are data for the developing areas. Thus the most available and reliable data are recent data on economic and social rights in the developed world (e.g., infant mortality statistics for Sweden, while reliable data on such topics as political killings and torture in highly repressive Third World nations [Guatemala, Uganda, Cambodia] are largely unobtainable or highly unreliable).

Historical Studies

An insistence upon relying heavily on quantitative data rules out or strongly limits significant scholarly pre-twentieth-century analysis of human rights problems. Cross-nationally comparable and longitudinal quantitative data for entire countries, as opposed to small geographic regions, are scarce for any area before 1800. When available, the data are often of dubious reliability until well after 1900. Much of what reasonably reliable data exist before the late nineteenth century are available only for Europe; even then, the vast bulk of them are aggregate economic data such as agricultural and industrial output. Data useful for social and economic human rights studies such as information on infant mortality, life expectancy, standards of living, literacy, and unemployment become available for Europe around 1850 but are far more fragmentary and unreliable.[18]

Measures of political human rights violations such as numbers of political prisoners and killings of protesters by the police and military (there were many such violations) simply do not exist in any systematic form for pre-twentieth-century Europe. Although large-scale massacres and executions presumably would be easiest to measure, invariably one must rely solely upon gross estimates of those killed or upon government figures which scholars agree are serious underestimations. For example, although the "Bloody Sunday" massacre of 9 January 1905, which touched off the Russian Revolution of that year, has been extensively studied, all that scholars can agree upon is that the official government count of 130 killed is a ludicrous underestimate.[19] The most thorough attempt to calculate casualties resulting from American labor disputes in the 1873–1937 period produced a tally of over 700 deaths and thousands of serious injuries but also a warning that the data are gross underestimates. The authors state that the United States has had the "bloodiest and most violent labor history of any industrial nation in the world"; however, as there are no comparable studies, this conclusion may be quite misleading. Depending upon the definition of labor dispute, casualties may well have been higher in France, Russia, Spain, and Italy.[20]

Obtaining human rights-related data, aside from deaths for the pre-1900 period, is usually even more difficult. For the United States and Europe, data on such subjects as politically motivated arrests, police brutality, incidents involving censorship, numbers of political exiles, and so forth, are generally either not available or are accessible only in highly decentralized police archives or in hundreds of newspapers (which, at least in Europe, were often censored). Outside of Europe and the Anglo-American lands, even basic population data are unavailable, and data concerning political, civil, social, or economic rights before 1900 are for all practical purposes nonexistent.[21]

Contemporary Studies

The availability and reliability of various forms of quantitative data for the twentieth century far exceed those for the pre-1900 period. This is markedly less so, however, for the underdeveloped world where statistical reporting procedures are often embryonic; embarrassing information is also often deliberately suppressed. Thus, there has never been a complete national census conducted in either Chad or Afghanistan. Although it is widely believed that the highest concentration of AIDS disease occurs in central Africa, African governments have refused to cooperate in releasing statistics for fear of bad publicity. Also, surveillance systems for communicable diseases in the region are inadequate. Much data on world hunger and malnutrition (including those for the United States) are inadequate; estimates of the number of persons who starved to death in the Ethiopian famine of 1984–85 range from several hundred thousand to over one million.[22]

As in the case of U.S. hunger statistics, even in the most advanced countries quantitative data are sometimes severely limited in availability and reliability. This may result from lack of interest, difficulties in obtaining data or defining terms, or in some cases, from deliberate manipulation or suppression. The U.S. Census Bureau estimates that in 1970 it failed to count over 6 million Americans, or about 3 percent of the total population.[23] Due to apparent lack of interest (at least until recently) and practical difficulties in conceptualization and data collection, nobody knows how many people in the United States were homeless in the mid-1980s, with estimates ranging from 250,000 to 3 million.[24] The same holds true for Europe, where one social worker noted bitterly in 1985 that the homeless are the segment that has no statistics. "Everything else is counted—every cow and chicken and piece of butter."[25] The official U.S. unemployment rate in March 1986 was 7 percent, but if this were to include those so discouraged about finding work that they had stopped looking, and the six million part-time workers unable to find full-time jobs, the rate would have been 13 percent.[26]

Social and economic human rights data. Contemporary quantitative data are clearly far more available and reliable in the areas of social and economic rights than in political, civil, and personal security rights. Thus, data on such clearly definable and relatively easily countable subjects as mortality rates, infant mortality rates, and life expectancy are available for almost all countries, although the quality of this data deteriorates for some of the poorest nations (notably those in sub-Saharan Africa). Other data, such as measures of poverty, literacy, unemployment, and homelessness present major problems of conceptualization, interpretation, and measurement. In some cases, data may be unavailable for cross-national comparative purposes, due to definitional differences or lack of compilation, but may be adequate for the purpose of tracking trends within individual countries.

Despite existing difficulties, the availability of a considerable amount of reasonably good and comparable social and economic human rights data can yield results that are useful from the standpoints of both academic knowledge and public policy decisions. For example, despite the widespread belief in the United States that social spending programs are too generous, comparative data reveal that social spending as a percentage of both GNP and total government outlays in the United States lags far behind comparable outlays in Western Europe.[27] Similarly, it is useful to know that while per capita wealth in the United States, defined in terms of the ability to buy a standard basket of goods, far exceeds that of any other Western industrialized democracy, distribution of income in the United States is perhaps the least equitable of all such countries. Therefore, the rate of relative poverty (as defined previously) is far higher than in almost all other comparable nations.[28]

One quantitative indicator which has gained widespread acceptance as a comparative measure in the economic and social rights area is the Physical Quality of Life Index (PQLI) developed by the Overseas Development Council.[29] The PQLI rates each country on infant mortality, life expectancy at age one, and literacy on a scale of one to 100. The three ratings are then added together, divided by three, and thus a single overall PQLI rating on a scale of one to 100 is produced for each country. Although the PQLI is certainly useful in producing an overall evaluative country ranking, it suffers from a number of flaws: (1) there is no methodological justification for either equally weighting or combining together in one index three dissimilar measures; (2) the comparability of literacy data is far less than the other two measures across countries; (3) the PQLI obscures subnational differences;[30] (4) in general, the PQLI fails to differentiate significantly among the developed countries, which typically score highly on all three components but differ drastically on measures of distributive equity and social welfare provisions; and (5) although PQLI data are often interpreted as a measure of government performance, they largely simply reflect differences in national wealth and regional-cultural factors.[31]

Political, civil, and personal security human rights data. The availability and reliability of data for contemporary human rights studies deteriorates markedly when the focus shifts to the political, civil, and personal security areas. This is especially true for some of the worst human rights violations such as torture and arbitrary executions, and for candidates for worst violators, such as, in the 1965–1985 period, Guatemala, Indonesia, Uganda, Argentina, and Cambodia. Occasionally modern governments, especially those in the developed world, which claim to value adherence to legal norms, do publish data related to political human rights violations. South Africa, for example, reports enough data that AI could estimate 238,000 arrests of blacks for pass-law violations occurring in 1984 and could report that South Africa led the world in 1985 with 137 "confirmed" executions.[32] In general, however, the problem is quite simply that governments do not generally publish statistics on how repressive they are (much less in forms comparable across countries or time!), and it is virtually an axiom that the more repressive the regime, the more difficult it makes access to information about its human rights atrocities to researchers (or anyone else).

Thus, it is astonishing, but true, that it was years after the mass executions in Stalin's Russia, Hitler's Germany, Idi Amin's Uganda, and Pol Pot's Cambodia before authenticated information about the extent of the crimes there became available—and then only after the death or ouster of the dictator. Even today, however, what presumably would be the easiest quantitative indicator to gather and verify—the number of deaths—remains a mystery, with estimates varying not only by hundreds of thousands but in some cases by millions. Reliable information about torture is only rarely available when it is occurring, especially since it cannot generally be proved, even through medical examination. Confirmed information about torture emerged in the 1970s only after changes in the regimes of Portugal, Greece, Iran, Nicaragua, Equatorial Guinea, Cambodia, and Rhodesia.[33] A 1979 study that attempted to use the number of political prisoners per capita as a measure of repression was greatly hindered (aside from the problem of comparable definition across countries) by the total lack of such data for many countries; for example, data were available for only half the Latin American countries.[34] Often what data are available for political prisoners vary widely from source to source. Thus, the Rumanian government reported 7,674 political prisoners in 1960 but AI reported 12,000; for 1971, the Indonesian government claimed 45,000, while AI reported 116,000; for the same country the U.S. State Department reported 31,000 political prisoners in 1976 while AI found 55,000.[35] After the fall of the Marcos regime in the Philippines, the new government was for days unable even to find many political prisoners because it could find no single master list.[36]

In general, obstruction is the normal contemporary governmental response to attempts to gather data on human rights violations and has often made it impossible to investigate charges of grave abuses. Thus, Iranian opposition groups have charged the Khomeini regime with over 40,000 executions and thousands of tortures since 1979, but a November 1984 United Nations report could only say such allegations "cannot be dismissed as groundless" since U.N. officials were not allowed to visit Iran and requests for information about 299 persons alleged to have been killed were ignored.[37] Amnesty International, in its October 1985 annual report, stated it could reach no conclusions as to whether more or fewer human rights violations had occurred than in the previous year because, "secrecy concealed many deaths and governments denied responsibility for killings carried out on their orders or with their complicity."[38]

In 1984, AI reported that "government secrecy and intimidation . . . makes it impossible to establish a reliable and consistent basis" for comparing violations in different countries. Human rights lawyers and organizations trying to function within repressive countries are often subjected to arrests, physical threats and assaults, and even murder.[39] Journalists are routinely denied access to many of the world's most repressive regimes such as North Korea, Albania, and Cambodia. Academic researchers are also hindered. For example, sociologist Rhoda Howard, an expert on human rights abuses in Africa, was given research clearance in only three African countries out of the nine she applied to around 1980.[40]

One of the most horrendous and common forms of human rights atrocities today in the Third World, the "disappearances" of tens of thousands of people since 1970 in Chile, Argentina, El Salvador, Guatemala, and elsewhere, seems to have been specifically designed to frustrate human rights workers, journalists, and academics. In Guatemala, where human rights activists and journalists estimate perhaps 50,000 political killings have occurred since 1980, diplomats reported that military officers ordered the killings of soldiers and police involved in death squads and tortures to prevent evidence from emerging after the January 1986 installation of a civilian president. One European ambassador to Guatemala predicted, "The military will take no chances, and there will be no bodies found, no documents, no photos or tapes," while the outgoing military dictator stated many of the "disappeared" are merely "in Havana with a scholarship."[41]

Obstruction of information gathering on human rights violations is by no means limited to the Third World. In the Soviet Union, persons attempting to gather and publicize information about human rights abuses have been repeatedly harassed and arrested on such charges as "anti-Soviet agitation." In the United States, the long-secret "dirty tricks" of the FBI (which included thousands of illegal burglaries, wiretaps, and mail-openings directed against dissident groups over a period of almost forty years) were only revealed in the mid-1970s as a side effect of Watergate. Even then records of the worst abuses were apparently destroyed when J. Edgar Hoover died, were not committed to paper, or were filed separately under a "do not file" procedure.[42] One astounding example of suppressed information about human rights abuses in Europe involves fragmentary reports from Bulgaria in 1985 indicating that several hundred ethnic Turks resisting forced "Bulgarization" of their names were killed by security forces. As the *Economist* noted in a report titled "The Other Side of the Moon," "nobody can establish the true extent of the killings, or whether they took place at all" since Western diplomats and journalists were barred from reported trouble spots.[43]

Even if problems of access and definition can be solved, enormous difficulties remain. Valid longitudinal or comparative work will typically require tediously applying definitions concerning human rights abuses to incident after incident; one cannot work with already processed data available from different sources using different definitions. The amount of work involved will be mind-boggling, especially if, as will often be the case, data must be gathered from scores of newspapers, archives, or police files.

The problems posed for data collected for cross-national longitudinal political human rights studies by the combination of definitional difficulties, problems in obtaining access, and practical difficulties resulting from the massive workload entailed, and other factors (including the intrusion of political considerations) can be deduced by briefly examining four resources commonly referred to in the literature. Three of these resources, the annual reports of Amnesty International and Freedom House and the *Country Reports on Human Rights Practices* of the U.S. State Department are simply not quantitative sources in any normal sense of the word, at least with regard to political human rights assessments.[44]

All of the reports are useful resources for political human rights reporting, especially because they appear annually in a generally similar format with individual country reports, but with occasional exceptions (i.e., estimates or official government versions of numbers of political prisoners) they do not report data in quantitative form. Neither AI nor the State Department gives any summary assessment or comparative ranking for each country (at least partly for policy reasons). Both the Freedom House survey and the State Department reports seem to have a clear bias reflecting American foreign policy interests and/or reflecting an undifferentiated, visceral anticommunism. Thus, the Freedom House reports during the 1980s consistently rated El Salvador and Guatemala, two countries allied with the United States that have been notorious for government-allied "death squads," which murdered thousands of their citizens, as having a comparable or (usually) more favorable human rights climate than Hungary or Yugoslavia, two one-party Communist regimes which were not engaged in the slaughter of their citizens. Similarly, the State Department reports emphasized human rights violations in Nicaragua, a country clearly viewed as an "enemy" of the United States, while downplaying far more murderous conduct by the "friendly" neighboring regimes in El Salvador and Guatemala.

Only Freedom House makes even a pretense of quantitative reporting by ranking each country in both the political and civil rights areas on a seven-point scale and then giving an overall evaluation of "free," "partly free," or "not free." While this quantitative presentation has led to widespread use of the results, as Freedom House boasts,[45] the basis for the assigning of scores seems to be entirely impressionistic; furthermore, the scales are obscure, confusing, and inconsistent and change from year to year.[46]

Even more disturbing than the deficiencies of these data resources is the fact that social scientists have treated them as though they *are* methodologically sound quantitative data. Thus, quantitatively coded assessments of the AI data and the quantitative reports by Freedom House have been correlated with a variety of other factors or otherwise subjected to secondary analysis in a number of papers.[47] As Professors Scoble and Wiseberg have warned, the pressures towards quantification are clearly leading some scholars to adopt "the article of faith that 'some data are better than no data' (which often degenerates into the flat assertion that any data, especially 'quantifiable and quantified' are better than no data at all). An empirical law that seems increasingly operative in the social sciences is 'if data exist, they will be used.' "[48]

The only major longitudinal cross-national contemporary quantitative data set in the political human rights area is the *World Handbook of Political and Social Indicators*, which contains measures of "state coercive behavior" for each country on a yearly basis between 1948 and 1977.[49] Included are data for political executions, defined as involving the killing of a person "under orders of the national authorities while in their custody" but excluding "assassinations, even if known to have been arranged by the authorities." Also included is a summary measure of governmental sanctions, encompassing censorship and "restrictions of social and political behavior" ranging from martial law to banning political parties and arresting, exiling, and deporting political dissidents.[50] Due to the definition of political executions used, not a single event is reported for El Salvador and only thirty-five are reported for Guatemala during the entire thirty years covered.

The sanctions data reported are simply grand totals, with the imposition of martial law apparently counted as one event, thus equivalent to the censorship of one news story. Due to this peculiar orientation, combined with an excessively legalistic interpretation of sanctions and a heavy reliance on Western news media such as the *New York Times*, the United States, West Germany, and the United Kingdom are listed as among the ten nations having imposed the most sanctions during 1948 to 1977, while Albania and Taiwan are among the ten nations having imposed the fewest. (The *Handbook* just lists raw numbers without even any correction for population.) Despite the manifold deficiencies of the *Handbook*, in some cases, depending upon the consistency of the reporting, the data may still be useful for tracing trends over time within countries. This may also be true for time-series data on individual countries found in other sources. For example, one good measure of advancing political rights among blacks in the United States is data charting the steady increase in the percentage of blacks registered to vote as a result of civil rights legislation passed in the 1958–65 period.[51]

Difficulties in Interpreting Data

Even if human rights terms can be adequately defined and reliable quantitative information can be obtained, making intelligent assessments of such data will often be extraordinarily difficult, especially if the data are interpreted out of the context of other, nonquantitative sources, such as interviews, on-the-spot observation, and background reading. Measuring and comparing or assessing the impact of different kinds of human rights violations will be extraordinarily difficult because they come in so many forms. Clearly just a raw count of human rights violations (as in the *Handbook*) or any analyses or correlations based on such raw counts will not be terribly revealing without differentiating among different types of violations, since, as Freedom House notes, it is "the pattern of rights, and not a simple checklist of pluses or minuses, that is critical for evaluation."[52] But any form of weighting different types of violations will be even more problematic than a raw count, suggesting that any single summary measure of political human rights violations will be either impossible or meaningless.

The danger posed by an excessive and automatic quantitative orientation to all problems—a sort of quantitative fetishism—can be clearly demonstrated by referring to several recent publications which have attempted to develop schemes for comparing overall human rights violation levels between different countries. Charles Humana, in his 1983 *World Human Rights Guide*, assigned each country a single overall human rights rating based on his evaluation of their performance on a highly idiosyncratic list of 50 measures, which were all equally weighted in forming the final results.[53] Thus, according to Humana, the right "to purchase and drink alcohol" counted equally in determining a country's human rights climate as did the right to freedom "from torture or coercion" (whatever that meant) by the state. In the 1986 version of his guide, Humana tried to correct this obvious absurdity by weighting the performances on seven of his (now reduced to) 40 measures three times as heavily as the others. However, in the absence of any theoretical justification for creating formulas which express one type of repression in terms of another, it is difficult to understand how Humana has now concluded that being subjected to indefinite detention without charge is three times worse than reading censored newspapers but no worse than being subjected to state torture.

But Humana, a nonacademic, has been equaled or even exceeded in such bizarre endeavors and analyses by several academics. Barnett Rubin and Paula Newberg seriously state that a fundamental "dilemma" in human rights research is to determine "how many reports of torture are equivalent to a murder"; Gloria Valencia-Weber and Robert Weber suggest a formula which answers such a question by equating 70 murders with 100 "disappearances"; and Kenneth Bollen suggests creating a system whereby a hypothetical country might be assigned a baseline score of 100 with regard to, for example, freedom of party organization, and then "a real country judged to have party liberties a fifth of the standard would receive a score of 20 while one 18 times greater would have 1800 as a value." John McCamant reports having actually carried out such an endeavor, and that, for example, with regard to the overall human rights climate, he concluded that East Germany was "probably 200 times more severe in 1976 than was the Federal Republic of Germany, but Uganda was still 100 times worse." Chile under Pinochet was assessed as 10 times more repressive than the Philippines and "100 times worse than India."[54]

How can such determinations even be rationally attempted, much less calculated? What does it *mean* to say that there is 18 times more freedom to organize a political party in one country than in another? Or that one country is 200 times more repressive than another? How can one possibly arrive at a theoretically sound formula for equating a certain number of people injured by police at a political demonstration with one killed? How can one reasonably conclude that one newspaper suppressed counts as more than or less than one person killed or one labor union banned? When Lech Walesa or Benjamin Spock is arrested for antigovernment activity, can this possibly be counted as the same as when John Doe (or Jan Doesky) is? Is there any real point in trying to measure degrees of political repression with such exactness, especially given that the underlying data are almost certainly incomplete and noncomparable across countries?

Even if one avoids trying to create overall "indexes" of repression of the sort just discussed, instead sticking to raw counts of human rights abuses, numerous problems of comparability, context, and interpretation remain that statistical data alone cannot resolve. Thus, examples of the difficulties arising from relying on raw counts of political arrests or detentions can easily be found in American history, even though these detentions are some of the more easily measured and cross-nationally common types of violations. During the Alien and Sedition Acts crises of 1798, only about twenty-five arrests were made, a figure which suggests mild repression indeed. One cannot understand the threat these arrests posed to the fledgling American democracy and the uproar they caused without knowing that many were directed against editors of leading opposition newspapers at a time when newspapers were the central element in organized party behavior.

Does the fact that the federal government arrested about 2,100 people for written and oral opposition to World War I compared to only about 200 arrested for similar opposition to World War II indicate that repression was less (as most scholars suggest) during World War II? Probably it simply reflects the fact that hardly anyone opposed the latter war, although those who did often suffered multiple prosecutions. This suggests the need to somehow quantify and measure protest activity and then construct a ratio of repression to protest, tasks which verge on the theoretically gargantuan and the practically impossible.[55] How would the incarceration (but not formal arrest) of 110,000 Japanese-Americans during World War II affect the equation? One scholar has termed this event "the most widespread disregard of personal rights in the nation's history since the abolition of slavery,"[56] yet it conveyed a repressive message only to those with yellow skins.

How could "McCarthyism" be compared quantitatively with other periods of repression in the United States (much less in other countries)? During the 1948–54 period, generally considered the years with the worst abuses of McCarthyism, less than 300 persons were actually arrested for clearly political offenses, mostly for contempt of Congress and alleged violations of the 1940 Smith (sedition) Act.[57] But such a measure totally fails to capture the atmosphere of McCarthyism. Even adding other data such as over 3,000 persons being called before congressional red-hunting committees or the 11,000 persons fired from governmental and private jobs in "loyalty" proceedings still does not solve the measurement problem, since the data now cannot be compared with countries lacking such forms of repression. Other countries may have their own repressive measures which the United States does not share, such as "banning" in South Africa and "disappearances" in Latin America. It would even be difficult to compare the McCarthy era with other periods in American history which had different types of repression such as the FBI "dirty tricks" of the Vietnam War period.

Can any statistic capture the real atmosphere of McCarthyism as well as the following quotations? A University of Washington professor, placed on probation after admitting past Communist party membership, responding to a question if he might join the party again in the face of a threatened fascist resurgence: "In my present state of mind, something would have to happen to some of the cells of my cerebrum before anybody could persuade me to ever touch politics with a ten-foot pole after what I have been through." Or a government employee, cleared after several loyalty hearings: "If the communists like apple pie and I do, I see no reason to stop eating it, but I would." Or the haunting 1954 statement of Albert Einstein, who had fled the specter of Nazi tyranny to come to the United States: "If I would be a young man again and I had to decide how to make my living, I would not try to become a scientist or scholar or teacher. I would rather choose to be a plumber or a peddler in the hope to find that modest degree of independence still available under present circumstances."[58]

No quantitative calculation can really measure the most significant impact of human rights abuses alluded to in all three of these quotations. There are enormous conceptual and practical difficulties in trying to measure the impact that human rights violations have of frightening people into *not* doing what they might have done otherwise. In some cases, data suggesting few human rights abuses such as few political arrests may actually reflect the success of previous repression or a general but unmeasurable atmosphere of intimidation. This idea is captured in the Chinese proverb, "Kill one, frighten 10,000." Professors Scoble and Wiseberg have noted, however, that in a society with a poorly developed communications network many such actions are needed to attain a "given level of deterrence," while in a more sophisticated setting "the marginal utility of each repressive act is considerably higher."[59] The point is that past repression, as Professor Stohl writes, "seems to radiate a kind of 'afterlife' which lingers and has effects for some time after the observable use of coercion by state agents."[60] Thus, little dissent may reflect either a terrorized or a satisfied society. Statistics alone are unable to tell us which.[61]

To take some concrete examples, low figures for political prisoners being held "may well denote the very opposite of the contented, peaceful conditions they appear to indicate," since "in Amin's Uganda and Pol Pot's Kampuchea, for example, there were less protracted ways of dealing with opponents than confining them to jail."[62] Scholars unanimously agree that the Hapsburg Empire was the leading police state of Europe in the 1815–1830 period, yet there were no political trials or executions during this period because the atmosphere of oppression stifled dissent in the bud. Thus a visitor to Vienna noted, "You can visit public places for months without hearing a single word about politics, so strict is the watch maintained over orthodoxy in both state and church. In all the coffee-houses, there reigns such a reverent silence that you might think High Mass was being celebrated."[63]

The very existence of censorship may obviate the need for its actual implementation. During the 1852–1912 period, only 103 of 19,304 plays submitted to the British theatre censorship were refused a license, but scholars indicate that this reflects not a liberal censorship policy but the practical decision by most playwrights to avoid controversial topics.[64] Thus, the Russian literary giant Leo Tolstoy noted, "What matters is not what the censor does to what I have written, but to what I might have written." A nineteenth-century French writer complained that before writing a word "you had to turn your pen around seven times between your fingers since before the courts you could sin by thought, by word, by action or by omission."[65] A distinguished contemporary South African journalist reports that editors there, unable to be sure what material might lead to prosecution, "[t]ime and again, . . . apply the adage: when in doubt, leave out."[66]

Going beyond the impact of repression on individuals, how can one measure the impact upon the future of crushing or forcing underground dissident organizations such as Solidarity in Poland, the African National Congress in South Africa, or the American Communist Party in 1919–20 and again in the 1947–54 period?[67] Thus, McCamant, in the study referred to above, in assigning weights to martial law in the Philippines after 1972, could only assume that banned left-wing groups "would not have attracted a great deal of support if they had been allowed, an assumption that could be wrong because, as these groups have not been allowed to operate openly for more than thirty years, we do not know how strong they would have been."[68]

One final example will illustrate how to overcome the problems posed by excessive or exclusive reliance on quantitative data, even where data are relatively accessible and a clearly defined and operationalized measure is used. Marianna Choldin's 1985 *A Fence Around the Empire: Russian Censorship of Western Ideas Under the Tsars*[69] makes inventive use of data kept by the tsarist bureaucracy concerning numbers of imported books which were censored in whole or in part or allowed into Russia without changes between 1864 and 1894. Her data show that about 50 percent of foreign books were censored under Tsar Alexander II between 1864 and 1870, compared to about ten censored under his son Tsar Alexander III between 1882 and 1894. The obvious conclusion is that Alexander III was considerably more tolerant than his father, but this is a conclusion no serious Russian scholar (including Professor Choldin) would accept, since Alexander II is known as the reforming "Tsar Liberator" of the serfs, while his son's reign is known as a period of bleak reaction and repression.

Professor Choldin concludes that a much higher percentage of books imported into Russia under Alexander II must have been politically sensitive. She also points out that a higher percentage of books censored under the son were entirely banned while many works censored under Alexander II were allowed with deletions. She concludes that "[t]here is no doubt that the reign of Alexander III was characterized by a more negative attitude toward foreign works than was his father's."[70] This is a conclusion that more rejects than reflects the data she presents, but it reflects a far broader knowledge of the subject than the particular data involved and no doubt is a statement more accurate than the data alone would suggest.

A Concluding Word

Despite all the problems discussed above, it is not my argument that quantitative data should never be used in human rights studies or that they are never helpful. What must be avoided is a dependence on statistics alone in an area such as human rights, where needed data either are not available or are not meaningful unless interpreted within a historical and political context, which alone can tell us the significance of even negative data such as the lack of dissent in Metternich's Austria and McCarthyite America. What must also be avoided is the orientation that suggests "if you can't measure it, you can't study it" and the disease labeled statistical "moreitis" by former American Statistical Association (ASA) President William Shaw, that more statistics are necessarily better.[71] (That can be true of course—if they are relevant and reliable.)

I doubt the orientation which suggests that if enough resources are devoted to obtaining and interpreting human rights statistics the problems discussed in this chapter will be solved. Scholars with such orientation admit, possibly with some exaggeration, that the required resources would be "enormous," equivalent to a "Manhattan Project" in terms of money and man-years and involving codebooks "several hundred pages long" to convert data to usable form.[72] I suggest investing prudently in resources that will yield significant returns in obtaining good quality data, both quantitative and qualitative, but "Manhattan Project" thoughts are a mirage because I do not think that any amount of resources can solve the basic problems of access and conceptualization discussed in this chapter.

Even if I am wrong, I doubt that it would be worth the cost to know, with a kind of false precision, that, for example, Chile has a "human rights score" of 144 and East Germany has one of 150. Human rights specialists and statisticians would recognize such differences as being largely meaningless, but they might be viewed as significant by the press and the lay public. It is much easier and just as useful to know (through a variety of qualitative and quantitative indicators, including journalistic evidence) that both countries have highly repressive regimes. As statisticians Jaffe and Spirer have pointed out, "Numbers need only be as correct as is necessary for the purpose at hand."[73] Given the notorious unavailability and unreliability of human rights data, especially for the more repressive regimes, small differences in human rights "scores" between countries or across time within one country are not ever likely to be very credible as an accurate indicator of real change; on the other hand, large differences will likely be obvious before detailed and reliable statistics are available. Thus, David Banks, a statistician with a special expertise in human rights data, has noted that while the limitations of existing statistics in the field do not "preclude crudely approximate sorts of analysis," most major changes in human rights policy are heralded by a "great variety" of clues "that signal something is afoot," and therefore "the most useful contribution statistical methods can make is to document formally what everybody already knows."[74]

Perhaps Banks is slightly too pessimistic. Statistics can unquestionably be helpful when used in an intelligent way and by a user who can put them in a context. In my own work, to help chart the rise and fall of the red-hunting fervor and fever of the McCarthy period, I have used annual data such as congressional appropriations for "subversive-hunting" committees, numbers of political deportations, and passage of antisubversive laws by state legislatures.[75] And despite all of the limitations which have been spelled out at length in this chapter concerning the difficulty of using and obtaining good human rights data inthe political field for scholarly purposes, in many cases even incomplete data or data which do not lend themselves to comparative purposes can still serve a helpful public education and public policy function. Examples of this would be the publication of data by the Tuskegee Institute on lynchings in the United States in the early part of this century, and the publication by such organizations as Amnesty International, the writers' group PEN, and the periodical *Index on Censorship* of (often incomplete) numbers and names of political prisoners held in various countries.

Even for scholarly purposes, it is probably true that bad quantitative information is better than none, just as it is true that bad nonquantitative information is better than none (within reason, of course, in both instances). I agree with former ASA President Shaw, who in 1972 told his organization that statistics are "a crutch, indispensable, but still a crutch" which "cannot walk by itself," and "if not proportioned to the needs of the user ... can hinder as well as help."[76] I also agree with the maxim that economist Sar Levitan, director of the George Washington University Center for Social Policy Studies, keeps framed on his office wall: "Statistics are no substitute for judgment."[77] What is needed is a combination: statistical information where it is meaningful and reliable, nonstatistical information where it is also meaningful and reliable, and sound judgment.

Notes

1. "Terrorism and Tourism: Americans Alter Their Vacation Plans," *New York Times*, 2 April 1986, 1; "Reagan Leaving for Talks in Asia, Warns Terrorists," *New York Times*, 27 April 1986, 1; "On Being a Nation of Number Numbskulls," *New York Times*, 23 January 1989, 16; Neil Spitzer, "The Children's Crusade," *Atlantic*, 18 June 1986; Joel Best, "Missing Children Misleading Statistics," *Public Interest*, Summer 1988, pp. 84–92; "Does This War Make Sense," *Economist*, 21 January 1989, p. 25.

2. "Race and Sex are Found to Affect Access to Kidney Transplants," *New York Times*, 24 January 1989, 19; "Records Hint at Racial Discrimination by S&Ls," *Ann Arbor News*, 22 January 1989, D1; *Ann Arbor News*, 26 October 1986; *New York Times*, 8 November 1986.

3. "Doctors' Fee Schedules Tied to Ordering of Medical Tests," *New York Times*, 24 April 1986, 14.

4. John F. McCamant, "Governance Without Blood: Social Science's Antiseptic View of Rule," in *The State as Terrorist*, ed. Michael Stohl and George Lopez (Westport, CT: Greenwood Press, 1984), pp. 17–18.

5. For example, see Jorge I. Dominguez, "Assessing Human Rights Conditions," in *Enhancing Global Human Rights*, ed. Jorge Dominguez et al. (New York: McGraw-Hill, 1979), p. 116; John F. McCamant, "A Critique of Present Measures of 'Human Rights Development' and an Alternative" and James R.

Scarritt, "Definitions, Dimensions, Data and Designs," both in *Global Human Rights: Public Policies, Comparative Measures, and NGO Strategies*, ed. Ved P. Nanda, James R. Scarritt, and George W. Shepherd, Jr. (Boulder, CO: Westview Press, 1981), pp. 123–146 and 115–122; Michael Stohl et al., "State Violation of Human Rights: Issues and Problems of Measurement," *Human Rights Quarterly* 8, No. 4 (November 1986): 592–606; Kathleen Pritchard, "Comparative Human Rights: An Integrative Explanation," paper presented at the Southwestern Social Science Association Convention, San Antonio, 1986; Jack Donnelly and Rhoda E. Howard, "Assessing National Human Rights Performance: A Theoretical Framework," *Human Rights Quarterly* 10, No. 2 (May 1988): 214–248.

6. William Shaw, "Paradoxes, Problems and Progress," *Journal of the American Statistical Association* 68 (March 1973): 7–8; A. J. Jaffe and Herbert Spirer, *Misused Statistics: Straight Talk for Twisted Numbers* (New York: Marcel Dekker, 1987), pp. 169, 185.

7. For example, see the discussion in Adamantia Pollis and Peter Schwab, "Human Rights: A Western Construct with Limited Applicability," in *Human Rights: Cultural and Ideological Perspective*, ed. Adamantia Pollis and Peter Schwab (New York: Praeger, 1979), pp. 1–18; Rhoda E. Howard, "Evaluating Human Rights in Africa: Some Problems of Implicit Comparisons," *Human Rights Quarterly* 6, No. 2 (May 1984): 160–179; Rhoda E. Howard and Jack Donnelly, "Human Dignity, Human Rights, and Political Regimes," *American Political Science Review* 80, No. 3 (1986): 801–817.

8. "Reporter's Notebook: A Rights Parley in Ottawa," *New York Times*, 25 May 1985, 2.

9. AI defines torture according to the Declaration on the Protection of all Persons from being Subjected to Torture and Other Cruel, Inhuman or Degrading Treatment or Punishment, adopted December 9, 1975, G.A. Res. 3452 (XXX), 30 U.N. GAOR Supp. (No. 34) at 91, UN Doc. A/1034 (1975). Amnesty International, *Torture in the Eighties* (London: Amnesty International, 1984), p. 13.

10. Malise Ruthven, *Torture: The Grand Conspiracy* (London: Weidenfeld & Nicolson, 1978).

11. Amnesty International, *Torture in the Eighties* (note 9), p. 14.

12. Amnesty International, *Amnesty International Report 1984* (London: Amnesty International Publications, 1984), p. 6, n.1.

13. Franz Neumann, *Behemoth: The Structure and Practice of National Socialism* (New York: Oxford University Press, 1942), p. 440.

14. Michal Belknap, *The Trails of American Political Justice* (Westport, CT: Greenwood, 1981), p. 6.

15. "13% of US Adults are Illiterate in English, A Federal Study Finds," *New York Times*, 21 April 1986, 1; American Survey, *Economist*, 3 May 1986, 36.

16. Howard, "Evaluating Human Rights in Africa" (note 7), pp. 166–167. See also Stanley J. Heginbotham and Vita Bite, "Issues in Interpretation and Evaluation of Country Studies," in *Human Rights Conditions in Selected Countries and the U.S. Response*, House Committee on International Relations (Washington, DC: U.S. Government Printing Office, 1978), p. 351. See generally on nineteenth-century Europe Robert J. Goldstein, *Political Repression in Nineteenth-Century Europe* (London: Croom Helm, 1983).

17. George A. Lopez, "A Scheme for the Analysis of Government as Terrorist," in Stohl and Lopez, *The State as Terrorist* (note 4), p. 63.

18. See generally B. R. Mitchell, *European Historical Statistics, 1750–1970* (New York: Columbia University Press, 1978).

19. See, for example, Sidney Harcave, *The Russian Revolution of 1905* (New York: Collier, 1970).

20. Philip Taft and Philip Ross, "American Labor Violence," in *Violence in America*, ed. Hugh Graham and Ted Gurr (New York: Bantam, 1969), p. 281.

21. See, for example, Fernand Braudel, *The Structures of Everyday Life* (New York: Harper & Row, 1981), pp. 31–46.

22. Nicholas Eberstadt and Clifford M. Lewis, "How Many Are Hungry?" *Atlantic*, May 1986, 34; *New York Times*, 10 December 1985, 15; "Hunger in US is Widening, Study of 'New Poor' Reports," *New York Times*, 20 April 1986.

23. Eberstadt and Lewis, "How Many Are Hungry" (note 22), 36.

24. "Warm Season Masks but Doesn't End Problems of the Homeless," *New York Times*, 3 June 1983, 16; "Homeless in US Put at 250,000, Far Less Than Previous Estimates," *New York Times*, 2 May 1984, 1; "Anguish of the Homeless Outlasts Winter's Cold," *New York Times*, 14 April 1985, 6.

25. Quoted in "The Homeless of Europe: A Scourge of Our Time," *New York Times*, 7 October 1985, 2.

26. "April Unemployment Was 7%, Labor Dept. Says," *New York Times*, 3 May 1986, 33.

27. For example, in 1981, 15 percent of GNP in the United States was used for social spending as compared to 28 percent in the Netherlands and Sweden. Organization for Economic Cooperation and Development (OECD), *Social Expenditure, 1960–1990* (Paris: OECD, 1985), pp. 79–97.

28. For example, 13 percent of the United States population was impoverished in the early 1970s compared to less than 5 percent in Norway and West Germany, *Economist*, 1 May 1984; Arnold J. Heidenheimer, Hugo Helco, and Carolyn Teich Adams, *Comparative Public Policy: The Politics of Social Choice in Europe and America*, 2nd ed. (New York: St. Martin's, 1983), p. 227, table 7.7; US Department of Commerce, *Social Indicators, 1976* (Washington, DC: U.S. Government Printing Office, 1977), pp. 477–478; George Thomas Kurian, *The New York Book of World Rankings* (New York: Facts on File, 1984), p. 104.

29. Morris David Morris, *Measuring the Conditions of the World's Poor: The Physical Quality of Life Index* (New York: Pergamon Press, published for the Overseas Development Council, 1979).

30. For example, in the United States, life expectancy for whites exceeds that for blacks by five years, and black infant mortality rates are almost twice those of whites, in some urban slum areas exceeding those of some Third World countries. "Infant Mortality Rate in US at Record Low," *New York Times*, 12 October 1985, 28; "Increase Reported in Infant Death Rate," *Detroit Free Press*, 17 January 1986, 1.

31. Fifty-one percent of PQLI variance can be explained by per capita GNP alone and 81 percent of the variance is explained if the region of the world is also factored in. Heginbotham, "Issues in Interpretation" (note 16), pp. 365–366.

32. "1,125 World Executions Are Documented in 1985," *New York Times*,

16 April 1986, 11; "Pretoria Rescinds Pass-Law Control on Blacks' Moves," *New York Times*, 19 April 1986, 1.

33. Amnesty International, *Torture in the Eighties* (note 9), pp. 9, 84.

34. James Seymour, "Indices of Political Imprisonment," *Universal Human Rights* 1, No. 1 (January–March 1979), p. 99.

35. Dominguez, "Assessing Human Rights Conditions" (note 5), pp. 97-98.

36. "Aquino Says All Held For Politics Will Be Released," *New York Times*, 1 March 1986, 1; "Manila Delays the Release of Four Jailed Communists," *New York Times*, 2 March 1986, 14.

37. "UN Rights Report on Iran Assailed," *New York Times*, 24 November 1984, 8; "State Department Critical of Iranian Group's Drive to Overthrow Khomeini," *Ann Arbor News*, 25 December 1985, B1.

38. Quoted in "Rights Unit Reviews 123 Nations," *New York Times*, 9 October 1985, 4.

39. Amnesty International, *Torture in the Eighties* (note 9), pp. 2–4.

40. Rhoda Howard, letter to author, 7 March 1986.

41. Quoted in "Controversy Awaits New Guatemala President," *New York Times*, 4 December 1985, 8.

42. See generally Athan Theoharis, *Spying on Americans: Political Surveillance from Hoover to the Huston Plan* (Philadelphia: Temple University Press, 1978).

43. "The Other Side of the Moon," *Economist*, 21 December 1985, 14.

44. For the following discussion I have drawn upon the critiques in Stohl et al., "State Violation of Human Rights" (note 5); McCamant, "Critique of Present Measures," (note 5); and Harry M. Scoble and Laurie S. Wiseberg, "Problems of Comparative Research on Human Rights," in Nanda, Scarritt, and Shepherd, *Global Human Rights* (note 5), pp. 147–171; Kenneth Bollen, "Political Rights and Political Liberties in Nations: An Evaluation of Human Rights Measures, 1950 to 1984," *Human Rights Quarterly* 8, No. 4 (November 1986): 567–591; and Judith Innes de Neufville, "Human Rights Reporting as a Policy Tool: An Examination of the State Department *Country Reports*," *Human Rights Quarterly* 8, No. 4 (November 1986): 681–699.

45. Raymond D. Gastil, ed., *Freedom in the World: Political Rights and Civil Liberties, 1983–84* (Westport, CT: Greenwood Press, Freedom House Books, 1984), pp. 8–9.

46. To get a four ranking for civil rights in 1978, a country was assessed as having "broad areas of freedom" yet "also broad areas of repression," while a five was awarded to countries in which "civil liberties are often denied, but there is no doctrine that denies them." Raymond D. Gastil, ed., *Freedom in the World: Political Rights and Civil Liberties, 1978* (Boston: G. K. Hall and Co., Freedom House Books, 1978), p. 19. In 1984, Freedom House upgraded the rankings of Poland, South Africa, and Yugoslavia because their citizens were assessed as increasingly assertive and because a higher listing would "better serve the educational purposes of the survey" and might encourage "forces of freedom," although the governments were characterized as the "same repressive" regimes as before, Gastil, *Freedom in the World, 1983–84* (note 45), ix, 28–29.

47. These papers include Pritchard, "Comparative Human Rights" (note 5), Seymour, "Indices of Political Imprisonment" (note 34); Conway Henderson, "Military Regimes and Rights in Developing Countries: A Comparative

Perspective," *Human Rights Quarterly* 4, No. 1 (Spring 1982): 110–123; John Boli-Bennett, "Human Rights or State Expansion? Cross-National Definitions of Constitutional Rights, 1870–1970," in Nanda, Scarritt, and Shepherd, *Global Human Rights* (note 5), pp. 173–193, James C. Strouse and Richard P. Claude, "Empirical Comparative Rights Research: Some Preliminary Tests of Development Hypothesis," in *Comparative Human Rights*, ed. Richard P. Claude (Baltimore: Johns Hopkins University Press, 1976), pp. 51–67.

48. Scoble and Wiseberg, "Problems of Comparative Research" (note 44), p. 148. Professor Lars Schoultz has warned that when "data appear to 'be hard,' researchers tend to squeeze them a bit too much, to use inappropriate statistical techniques, to carry calculations too far to the right of the decimal point." "US Policy Towards Human Rights in Latin America: A Comparative Analysis of Two Administrations," in Nanda, Scarritt, and Shepherd, *Global Human Rights*, (note 5), p. 84.

49. Charles L. Taylor and David Jodice, *World Handbook of Political and Social Indicators III*, 3rd ed. (New Haven, CT: Yale University Press, 1983), pp. 61–77.

50. Ibid., pp. 62–63.

51. U.S. Department of Commerce, Bureau of the Census, *The Social and Economic Status of the Black Population in the US: An Historical View, 1790–1978* (Washington, DC: U.S. Government Printing Office, n.d.) is an extremely useful collection of time series data.

52. Gastil, *Freedom in the World, 1978* (note 45), pp. 19–22.

53. Charles Humana, *World Human Rights Guide* (London: Hutchison, 1983); Charles Humana, *World Human Rights Guide* (London: Hodder & Stoughton, 1986). In partial defense of Humana and some similar studies, an examination of his 1983 study found high Spearman correlations (approaching .9) between his human rights ranking of countries and those reported in the Freedom House study published in 1984 (see David L. Banks, "Patterns of Oppression: A Statistical Analysis of Human Rights," *Proceedings of the Social Statistics Section of the American Statistical Association* [1985]: 154–162). Although the rankings of a few countries were highly dissimilar between these two studies, this finding suggests that both the Humana and the Freedom House studies are somewhat useful in that they at least probably accurately reflect the general "informed lay" opinion (which may or may not be accurate) held in the West about overall human rights conditions in various countries. Although both the Freedom House and Humana studies clearly commit statistical "sins" by giving precise numerical assessments based on subjective and imprecise judgments made concerning highly incomplete data, Humana's study is perhaps somewhat less sinful in that the basis for his overall assessment is much clearer, since he gives sub-assessments for each component of his overall index. However, the Freedom House reports only give two overall assessments for "civil rights" and "political rights" (and the Banks study cited in this footnote found these two measures correlated so completely that they were "almost perfectly redundant" [p. 155]).

54. Barnett R. Rubin and Paula R. Newberg, "Statistical Analysis for Implementing Human Rights Policy," in *The Politics of Human Rights*, ed. Paula R. Newberg (New York: New York University Press, 1980), p. 280; Gloria Valencia-Weber and Robert Weber, "El Salvador: Methods Used to Document Human Rights Violations," *Human Rights Quarterly* 8, no. 4 (November

1986): 767; Bollen, "Political Rights" (note 44), p. 590; McCamant, "Critique of Present Measures " (note 5), pp. 136, 144.

55. See J. M. Smith, *Freedom's Fetters* (Ithaca, NY: Cornell University Press, 1956); Robert Justin Goldstein, *Political Repression in Modern America: From 1870 to the Present* (Cambridge, MA: Schenkman Publishing, 1978).

56. A. Russell Buchanan, *The United States and World War II* (New York: Harper & Row, 1964), vol. 2, p. 236.

57. See generally David Caute, *The Great Fear: The Anti-Communist Purge Under Truman and Eisenhower* (New York: Simon & Schuster, 1978).

58. Goldstein, *Political Repression* (note 55), pp. 377, 383.

59. Scoble and Wiseberg, "Problems of Comparative Research" (note 44), p. 152.

60. Stohl et al., "State Violation of Human Rights" (note 5), pp. 594–595.

61. See Richard Rose, *Governing Without Consensus: An Irish Perspective* (Boston: Beacon Press, 1971), pp. 32–41.

62. Michael Kidron and Ronald Segal, *The State of the World Atlas* (New York: Simon and Schuster, 1981), text accompanying table 31 (no pagination).

63. E. Wangerman, *The Austrian Achievement, 1700–1800* (New York: Harcourt Brace, 1973), p. 184.

64. See, for example, Richard Findlater, *Banned! A Review of Theatrical Censorship in Britain* (London: MacGibbon & Kee, 1967), p. 73.

65. Philip Spencer "Censorship by Imprisonment in France, 1830–70," *Romanic Review* 47 (February 1956): 27.

66. Benjamin Pogrund, "How to Cow the Press," *New Republic*, 3 February 1986: 18.

67. For example, I have argued elsewhere that the destruction of radical American political organizations and trade unions during these two periods profoundly influenced subsequent American history due to their absence. Goldstein, *Political Repression* (note 55).

68. McCamant, "Critique of Present Measures" (note 5), p. 139.

69. Marianna Tax Choldin, *A Fence Around the Empire: Russian Censorship of Western Ideas Under the Tsars* (Durham, NC: Duke University Press, 1985).

70. Ibid., 135–136.

71. Shaw, "Paradoxes, Problems, and Progress" (note 6), p. 9.

72. Stohl et al., "State Violations of Human Rights" (note 5), p. 606; Scoble and Wiseberg, "Problems of Comparative Research" (note 44), p. 171; McCamant, "Governance Without Blood" (note 4), p. 144.

73. Jaffe and Spirer, *Misused Statistics* (note 6), p. 3.

74. David L. Banks, "The Analysis of Human Rights Data over Time," *Human Rights Quarterly* 8, No. 4 (November 1986): 667, 669.

75. Goldstein, *Political Repression* (note 55), pp. 308, 332, 343, 349.

76. Shaw, "Paradoxes, Problems and Progress" (note 6), p. 7.

77. "A Defender of the Welfare System," *New York Times*, 31 July 1985, 1.

Chapter 3
Use of Incomplete and Distorted Data in Inference About Human Rights Violations

Douglas A. Samuelson and Herbert F. Spirer

Because of the nature of organizational decision making and the need to justify decisions to outside parties, governmental and non-governmental organizations concerned with human rights find statistical evidence effective. Such evidence is useful in "breaking through the barriers to belief"[1] of members of the public and decision makers of governmental and non-governmental organizations. Unfortunately, such evidence is difficult to obtain. Some of this difficulty is due to problems of definition and the specialized knowledge required for statistical inference. But, as Goldstein and many others have discussed, it is difficult to obtain reliable data because of the deliberate efforts of human rights violators to suppress the evidence of their actions.[2]

Goldstein does not "think that any amount of resources can solve the basic problems of access and conceptualization," but does say that "in many cases even incomplete data . . . can still serve a helpful public education and public policy function."[3] We would go further: the process of withholding, suppressing, or counterfeiting data leaves its mark in the observed incomplete and distorted records. When correctly analyzed, this evidence may be as convincing as the original data would have been.

Since most regimes which violate human rights are aware of the kinds of data which help to determine whether human rights violations have occurred, it is logical to conclude that these are the data which a regime will distort or suppress when attempting to cover up its actions. In this chapter, we review historical cases in which human rights violations have subsequently been proven, categorized by the type of data involved. We pay particular attention to the "footprints" the regimes responsible for violations leave when attempting to hide their activities. Often these footprints are best seen in changes in on-going time series of economic or demographic measures.

We offer guidance in making inferences about current and pro-jected human rights situations and propose tentative hypotheses about the relationship between the type of incomplete or distorted data and the country's human rights situation. We suggest making inferences based on indications such as absence of data on a phe-nomenon known to exist; cessation of reporting data on a particular variable; withdrawal of resources for collection of data; validated re-ports of suppression; absence of appropriate random variation in raw data; overly close fits to expected or desired results; time series values inconsistent with forecasts based on past values; and monotonic im-provements in an important variable over time.

Finally, we discuss the implications of our findings for effective re-porting of suspected human rights violations. Norvall Glenn, author of several books on the status of American blacks, said, "The person who must have certitude, who cannot embrace conclusions tenta-tively, should not be engaged in social science research,"[4] and we do not propose that anyone can get certitude about a nation's human rights status from incomplete or distorted data. However, we believe that incomplete or distorted data can be the basis for a suspicion of human rights violations, or that it can be objective support for uncon-firmable or unconfirmed reports.

Cases of Incomplete and Distorted Data Giving Evidence of Human Rights Violations

Data Availability

When a government believes that knowledge of its human rights vio-lations will work against its interests, that government may use its ability to control the availability of data. Argentine statisticians and economists were among the earliest of "the disappeared" of 1976–77, which may be a clue to the government's fears of the escape of certain data from its control. The U.S.S.R. ceased publishing crime rate data in 1933[5] by Stalin's order, when the rate increased. Similarly, the U.S.S.R. stopped publication of infant mortality data in the 1970s,[6] when the rates, which had been decreasing steadily, began to in-crease. As it turns out, the apparent increase in the infant mortality rate appears to be due to serious errors in the data collection![7] But the reaction of a government sensitive to external criticism clearly shows how suppression can be crudely used to try to avoid such criticism.

In reporting on South Africa's human rights practices, the U.S. Department of State finds that "The country's black majority (73.4 percent of its population) suffers from pervasive, legally sanctioned discrimination based on race in political, economic, and social aspects of life."[8] The Central Statistical Services of South Africa report data from which Paul Campbell of the U.S. Census Bureau has estimated life expectancy at birth of the black majority and white minority.[9] These estimates are a confirmation of the effect of discrimination in social aspects of life; in 1970 the estimated life expectancy at birth of the black majority was 49 years and of the white minority 64 years.

The government of South Africa is more selective in its release of other data. Kwashiorkor is a serious disease of infants and children resulting from long term malnutrition.[10] In 1968, kwashiorkor was a notifiable disease in South Africa. Table 1 shows the racial breakdown[11] of cases and the racial distribution in the population for the reported cases of kwashiorkor in 1968. This high rate for a malnutrition disease among the majority population objectively reveals an underlying human rights problem. Has this problem gotten better? Probably not, since 1968 is the last year that diseases of malnutrition were notifiable in South Africa.[12] The 1968 rate of kwashiorkor for African South Africans was over 300 times as high as the rate for white South Africans. We do not know how great the discrepancy was two decades later, but we think that it is logical to conclude that the continued suppression of these data strongly suggests that kwashiorkor continues to be a disease that mainly afflicts the African and coloured populations in South Africa. For all we know, the rates for Africans and coloured may have decreased, but the government must have a reason for continued suppression of the data.

Mortality Statistics

Data on deaths are a source of evidence on the most egregious violations of human rights. The coincidence of many more deaths than one would expect for over a short period of time—in the aggregate, of certain age groups, of a particular gender or social class, and so forth—should immediately arouse suspicion. If the causes of deaths or the nature of burials are peculiar or not reported, suspicion is reasonable. For example, reports of numerous deaths on the same day from heart failure among Jews deported to Polish labor camps were

TABLE 1. Notified Cases of Kwashiorkor in South Africa, 1968[a]

Racial category	Number of cases	Proportion of cases (%)	Proportion in population[b] (%)
African	9,800	91	70
Colored	1,000	9	9
Asian	12	.1	3
White	7	.1	17
Total	10,819	100%	99%

[a] F. Wilson and M. Ramphele, *Uprooting Poverty: The South African Challenge* (New York: W. W. Norton, 1989), p. 100.
[b] Harold Nelson, ed., *South Africa, a Country Study* (Washington, D.C.: Foreign Area Studies, the American University, U.S. Government Printing Office, 1981), 2nd. ed., p. 377. We use 1970 proportions, as census data are available only for even decades. The proportion of Africans is known to be higher since these figures do not include Africans in certain "independent" areas and because of the known undercounting of Africans.

sufficient grounds for the Dutch ambassador to Germany, in 1941, to make pointed inquiries. These inquiries generated enough discomfort that the Germans discontinued sending death notices, although they continued the deceptive practice of sending postcards from the deportees.[13]

If a government wishes to hide certain violations of human rights, it may suppress the registration of deaths. Famine is used as a weapon in the long term civil war in the Sudan. At the time of this writing (1989), the large number of famine victims, with their similarity to Holocaust victims, has attracted international attention. Thus we should not be surprised to find that in the refugee camp at El Meiram, "The local authorities prohibited the registration of deaths . . ."[14]

Mortality (and other) problems occurring within specific regions or ethnic population groups can be hidden, deliberately or otherwise, by averaging. The reporting of infant mortality rates in South Africa, for example, shows how human rights issues can be hidden in aggregated values. The 1985 overall average infant mortality rate as reported by UNICEF was 78 per 1000.[15] This value is the weighted average of the rates of the African and non-African populations, where the weights are the corresponding population proportions. We estimate the non-African infant mortality rate as 15 per thousand (the U.S. rate for 1985 was 10.6 and the estimated value for whites in South Africa is 12 per 1000).[16] Using the official mid-1987 population proportions of Africans (.7) and non-Africans (.3), our estimate of the South African infant mortality for Africans is $(78 - .3*15)/.7 = 105$.[17]

Using proportions corrected for the undercount of Africans (.73 and .27, respectively), our estimate of South African infant mortality for Africans is about 101 per thousand.[18] Independent estimates for Africans in South Africa range from 90 to 140 per thousand.[19] Thus, it appears that the infant mortality rate for Africans (about 100) is around eight times the value for whites (about 12). We cannot say in this case that reporting only the aggregate rate is deliberate; however, this would be a reasonable suspicion if a government or agency changes from reporting by subcategories to reporting by aggregates.

Time Series

In the case of the disappearances in Argentina, closer attention to an increase in a particular form of incomplete data might have led to faster recognition and possibly an effective offset to denial. Clyde Snow (a forensic specialist from the Office of the Oklahoma State Medical Examiner) and Maria Julia Bihurriet (Subsecretariat of Human Rights, Ministry of the Interior of Argentina) have recently done a superb job of field data collection and evaluation of the Ningún Nombre[20] burials in Buenos Aires province before, during, and after the period of repressive military rule in Argentina.[21]

Snow and Bihurriet give the time series for Ningún Nombre burials of different categories of remains. As they say:

> Minor, (or "chance"), fluctuations in the number of unidentified bodies buried annually in a given cemetery naturally would be expected, but major deviations would excite the curiosity of a statistician. Such major and, presumably "non-chance" deviations, upon closer investigation, might be found to have been caused by transitory events such as a natural disaster resulting in a large number of unidentified victims. Longer-term fluctuations, especially if unidirectional, might be caused by major shifts. . . . [22]

The after-the-fact evidence is overwhelming in showing statistically and practically significant rises in the aggregate Ningún Nombre burials as well as significant rises in many subcategories. If an external observer had access to even limited subsets of the burial data, the observer could have been alerted to evidence which might have helped to break through the barriers to belief. In the next section, we discuss some of the ways in which such data could have been used.

As these examples also show, current data on the whereabouts and condition of persons supposed to be alive and well are also important. Disappearance in Argentina was total in most cases. But in many other situations, the officials, torturers, or kidnappers would release tape recordings, photographs, and even brief live telephone messages from victims to sustain negotiations by showing that the victim was still alive. In other cases, recorded messages were used to achieve the same results after the victim had been killed.

Health Statistics

Information about the health of population groups and about the incidence and severity of injury and disease can be revealing. A sudden change in the numbers of heart failures, burns and bruises, assault cases, or skin disorders could mean the presence of gross patterns of violations. In an effort to prevent the appearance of a rise in numbers which might reveal a violation, reports are suppressed or altered. As we have seen in the example of kwashiorkor in South Africa in the prior section, we can find great potential for inference about human rights from data on the incidence of malnutrition, or of illnesses whose high incidence suggests lack of group access to basic medical care. Also, a significant reduction in such reports could mean the presence of such violations, rather than their absence.

The alleged response of the government of the U.S.S.R. to the possible medical aftereffects of radiation related to the Chernobyl reactor disaster gives us an unusual opportunity to study the deliberate action of such a suppression:

A wide variety of reports from émigré doctors [point] . . . to secret orders banning mention of radiation-related illness. . . . [A] physician from Central Asia also reports that "oral instructions forbidding the use of the diagnosis 'cancer' in medical histories have existed for over three years . . . Even the diagnosis 'anemia' is now taboo. . . . " A Moscow doctor also reports the existence of an order banning mention of death by leukemia in case files.[23]

This suppression should create a conspicuous deficiency: we would expect an increase in reported numbers due to the Chernobyl incident; but if suppression is occurring, we will in fact see a decline or absence of any reports.

Economic Data

Distortions in economic data may reveal the movement, disappearance, or disenfranchisement of population groups. In World War II, British pilots overflying Eastern Europe noticed that scheduled and customary freight train movements either disappeared or decreased in size. This was the consequence of the Nazis' diversion of great numbers of freight cars for the movement of Jews to Poland for the "final solution."[24] Similar sudden mass deportations from the cities to the countryside in Kampuchea are a dramatic recent example of a similar atrocity in the making. These deportations were the prelude to mass killings and to numerous deaths by starvation and exposure in areas less accessible to outside observers.[25] In both cases, massacres were facilitated by the concentration of target populations in areas removed from the outside world.[26]

What statistical indicators or observations might have been good "leading indicators"? Any statistician can hypothesize an ideal situation. Where demographic counts are available, trends can be tracked and evaluated. But even if census data from Third World or totalitarian countries were made public, it would simply not be timely enough. We must look for new forms of basic data to which to apply statistical analysis of missing elements. For example, satellite reconnaissance can give timely but crude measures of population density, abandonment of dwellings and farms, disappearance of cultivation, and reduction in pedestrian and vehicular traffic flow. As discussed in the next section, we can monitor once again for the presence of a process which is "in control" using many of the classical methods of process control. We also need to exploit the newer graphical methods of data analysis: as Tukey says, "The greatest value of a picture is when it forces us to notice what we never expected to see."[27]

Another form of movement is the exclusion of a population group from one or more parts of the national social structure. Examples are limitation or denial of voting rights, exclusion from certain occupations, prohibition of the use of a language preferred by the group, inferior access to medical care, inferior educational opportunities, and exclusion from some public facilities and services. In addition to being human rights violations in themselves, such practices facilitate the commission of worse violations later: indeed, Fein's major conclusion in her study of the Nazis' atrocities is that the victims' degree of isolation and exclusion from a country's social structure was the single most influential determinant of whether Jews in that country escaped or were killed.[28]

Distorted or missing values in crime statistics are also important. A national government may use its internal police forces to repress dissent, execute summary punishment, or otherwise violate the rights of the civilian population. These activities often result in deaths. The governmental authorities of a country may argue that police, militia, or troops are being attacked with deadly force and must respond in kind.

What then are we to make of reports that few police officers are killed while many civilians are killed by the police? In Table 2, we see the ratio of killings of police to killings by police in Jamaica for 1980 to 1985. These ratios undoubtedly are low, possibly by as much as a factor of two, since the counts of police killings are based on newspaper reports and not all such deaths are reported in newspapers.

The Americas Watch investigators were able to get official data on woundings of police for 1985. In that year, 22 police were wounded in shootings, but police received no injuries in 372 reported shooting incidents. Subsequently the investigators made in-depth field studies (reading witness statements, interviews with eyewitnesses, and so forth) and concluded that "The pattern of repetition from case to case . . . lends striking support to an inference that many of the police killings must be deliberate executions, or the result of negligent and indiscriminate use of firearms."[29]

Event Reports

We expect members of a persecuted group to complain.[30] Hence we can get human rights information from both the presence and absence of political protests. Although the nineteenth-century Hapsburg Empire was widely regarded as one of the most oppressive regimes of its time, there were no contemporary reports of riots.[31] Against this we can balance the record of the United States. In the years 1948–1977, the United States had more reported riots (861) than any other country.[32]

Governments, non-governmental organizations, and journalists have had great difficulty getting information about the human rights

TABLE 2. Killings by and of Police in Jamaica, 1980–1985[a]

Year	Killed by police (A)	Police killed (B)	Ratio (A/B)
1980	206	22	9
1981	319	4	80
1982	101	7	14
1983	196	7	28
1984	288	20	14
1985	210	9	23
Total	1320	69	19

[a] *Human Rights in Jamaica: An Americas Watch Report* (New York: Americas Watch Committee, 1986), p. 15.

situation in the People's Republic of China. In the 1970s, the high level of civic order in China was taken by some as an indication of the effectiveness of the regime in satisfying the people's needs. We now know that this order was achieved at an unusually high price in human rights. At that time, a Chinese official told a *New York Times* reporter that 95 percent of the people enjoy rights.[33] This is strange hyperbole; we use this statement (as did the reporter at the time) to estimate the number of Chinese not enjoying their rights as forty million—five percent of the official population estimate of eight hundred million.[34] If this number sounds extreme, consider Premier Deng's 1980 announcement that "according to incomplete statistics, 2,900,000 people have now been rehabilitated . . . and many more [have been rehabilitated who were not on the record]."[35] The absence of civic disorder at any level should have been our first clue to extensive human rights violations.

Thus, data about political dissent and its realization in protest are intriguing raw material for inference. Few today are so naive as to think that the greater the repression the greater the political protest—although, of course, it is reasonable to suppose that greater repression generates more cause for protest. A frequent justification for repression by authoritarian regimes throughout human history has been the maintenance of civic order: for example, when the "hard-liners" in Beijing suppressed dissent in June 1989 their expressed goal was to eliminate chaos. The point for data analysis is that the students' and workers' demonstrations resulted from a loosening of restraints on human rights, and the subsequent suppression of "chaos" was a return to constraints.

This recent experience supports our view that the absence—and especially, the discontinuation—of reported dissent is an early indicator of systematic human rights violations. From Nazi Germany to Stalin's U.S.S.R., from Argentina during the "dirty war" to Kampuchea in the Khmer Rouge period, the disappearance of officially acknowledged protest has coincided with the beginning of systematic repression. As we noted earlier, the nineteenth-century Hapsburg Empire was apparently so effective in repression that no one dared to protest.

In contrast, democracies experience continual dissent and protest from all sorts of individuals and groups. While dissatisfaction is a seemingly universal human attribute, the freedom to express it is not a universal political liberty. We have already mentioned the record of the United States, which has high rates of riots and political demonstrations. Against this we can place the lack of contemporary reports of riots and political demonstrations in other countries, despite their recognized position as oppressive regimes. For example, for 1977, Hudson and Taylor report 51 political demonstrations in the United States and one in North Korea.[36]

Making Inferences

Suppression and distortion leave their own evidence in the data—complementary and concomitant. These incomplete or distorted data can be as revealing as what has been suppressed or distorted when viewed within the larger framework of considered inference.

One method of making such inferences is to use the methods of the analytical phase of statistical process control.[37] The process which generates data is affected by two sources of variation, common and special. Common causes are those inherent in the process whereas special causes are from outside the process. One classical method for monitoring such a series in statistical process control is the use of "control charts," in which the reported values are used to establish a level of variation due to common causes. From this variation, we establish upper and lower "control limits" that set boundaries for signaling the probable presence of a special cause. If we get an observed value outside either of the control limits, we have a basis for suspecting the presence of a special cause. This is a call for further investigation. The Dutch ambassador to Germany intuitively applied these principles when contacting the Nazi government about the apparently excess heart attack deaths of Jews in Poland.

We propose that the statistical process control rationale be used as the basis of a systematic approach to monitoring human rights time series. To continue this example, consider deaths from heart attack to be generated by an ongoing human random process. The time series of individual reports of heart attack deaths will have a variability which is the result of common causes in the absence of any special causes. If a large number of deaths due to oppressive measures are reported as heart attacks, this special cause should produce one or more values outside the control limits. The appropriate control chart for this situation is called an "individual chart," and such charts have been in use in industry for over four decades.[38]

However, the human rights time series may be one which is subject to variation with time due to trends, seasonal, or cyclical effects. In statistical terms, time-series data are characterized by autocorrelation (succeeding values are dependent), which call for different methods of analysis. In any given situation, a particular time series may have its own characteristics. We propose applying the methods of time-series analysis—well known in business and physical science—to human rights time series. As we have discussed in the case of the Ningún Nombre burials in Argentina, the contemporary use of time-series analysis would have given forecasts against which observed values could be compared.

The essence of time-series analysis is that it accounts for seasonal and trend effects, leaving residuals (the difference between observed historical and forecasted values) which should show variation around a mean with a constant standard deviation.[39] We can use this information in two ways. We can compare an observed value to the residual variability. A value which shows statistical significance at a high level (an outlier) may be sufficient evidence to sound an alarm. If such an outlier is then followed by a significant outlier in the opposite direction (which would show an administrative reaction, as in the case of the Jewish deaths due to heart failure), then the evidence is reinforced. Even where the number of observed periods is small, exploratory methods or life tables may provide evidence of problems. In the second approach, we compare a predicted value based on the forecasting model with the observed value to give a turning point error (as discussed earlier) which is a clue to a change in the underlying causal conditions: oppression may have started.

Can we expect that human rights violators will try more subtle forms of suppression and distortion than those we have discussed? In less critical situations in industry and politics we see many examples—usually not recorded in scholarly journals, but the subject of internal action—where records are made to look "too good" in order to cover problems.[40] Thus, we may be able to track human rights violations through the suppression of normal variation, which the violators may try to cover with fake variation. There are a number of statistical tests for randomness which we can use to see if data of different kinds conform to reasonable patterns of variation.[41] At this early stage of statistical monitoring of human rights, we expect to be able to detect counterfeit entries.

One of the mass murderers' major problems is the need for the physical disposal of great numbers of bodies in a short period of time.[42] Mass murderers usually prefer inconspicuous disposal, which further complicates their actions. The many Nazi examples during the Holocaust and the Katyn massacre are well known. One recent example is the disappearances in Argentina in the 1970s; almost all the disappeared were murdered or died in captivity.[43] Evidence survives because of Argentine law and cultural practices regarding the dead. Having disposed of the bodies as unidentified corpses, they entered the Argentine cemetery system as Ningún Nombre (No Name) corpses. As such, they were buried in separate sections of provincial cemeteries. For lack of payment of the grave tax, many of them were transferred to mass graves, which made them easier to find in large numbers when the Alfonsín government began to investigate. The missing are now becoming the known.

Implications for Reporting and Observing

Inferences from incomplete and distorted data can serve as an early indicator of human rights violations. When statistical inference—even if informal—is used, we are subject to Type I and Type II errors. We feel that the Type II error (failing to signal a violation when one is present) is much more costly than a Type I error (signaling a violation when one is not present). We hope, by our presentation of some examples and ideas, to set a challenge to statisticians and others skilled in quantitative analysis to monitor not just for apparent reports of violations, but for the incomplete and distorted data that also can indicate ongoing violations. We have indicated some of the kinds of data in which missing information is especially significant, but our list is by no means complete.

The probabilities of both types of errors is increased in the presence of problems of basic data which continually arise. In our proposals about inference, we implicitly assume that in the absence of human rights violations or deliberate suppression the data are valid and reliable. But data may be flawed in definition, incorrectly gathered, transcribed incorrectly, or tabulated wrongly.[44] If incompleteness or distortions are to have significance, the basic data must be sound or their flaws known. We believe that "just how sound" in any given case is amenable to analysis. While we know of no such analysis for human rights data at this time, in meta-analysis a similar problem is dealt with by using inference to find the "Fail Safe N," which counts how many additional studies confirming the null hypothesis would be necessary to reverse a conclusion.[45]

Those who would search for human rights indicators among missing data must be able to separate out artifacts of data contamination. For example, if a report of a country's alleged violations includes incomplete data on movements of the target population group, we must know whether similar omissions occurred in the best data released by the country. Did similar omissions occur in previous releases of the same or similar data for periods before or after the alleged violations? If it is clear that the omissions are in the original data and that such omissions are atypical for the country, then suspicions of suppression or tampering are credible. If, on the other hand, the omissions can easily be attributed to the carelessness of the reporter, then no useful inference is possible.

As in all other fields, statistical analysis is suspect unless the statistician has a knowledge of the subject or works with an expert who does. We think that statisticians who analyze human rights data have an obligation to seek assistance from subject matter experts, even though such persons are not necessarily their immediate colleagues. We believe that analysts should routinely make available their raw data on which the analyses are based. Today, this is easily done through the medium of computer-readable magnetic disks. Statistical experts have been known to disagree over the choice of assumptions and analytical techniques. If the raw data are available, others trained in quantitative inference can review the analyses and draw their own conclusions.

It is also important to report on and give the background information which helps to assess whether or not the observed data are unusual. For example, in reporting on movements of a population group it helps to know how much these data differ from those on movements of other population groups. For tribesmen in rural Africa to visit the nearest city only a few times a year means something very different from the same statistic for formerly middle class Kampucheans. The discovery of a number of Kurdish peasants near the Iraqi border with burns on their hands and faces has a different meaning from a similar discovery among truck drivers near a chemical plant in New Jersey. The scarcity of the phenomenon of interest strongly affects inference about its possible causes, and that scarcity can only be assessed in relation to usual conditions in the vicinity.

On the other hand, analysts should pay more attention to the routine unofficial reporting of information, which generates a rich, largely untapped source of data from which to make ongoing inferences about human rights. Relevant data appear in scientific and professional journals, news accounts, and commercial records. Many such sources of information continue unaffected while official reports are distorted or suppressed. For example:

Complete data on the incidence of common diseases in South Africa are unavailable because official statistics do not exist for the entire population. The UN has pointed out that the list of reportable diseases—particularly those that have long been preventable but which persist among non-Whites—has been shortened periodically by the health authorities in Pretoria in order to avoid criticism. *Nonetheless the prevalence of certain diseases continues to be reported in medical literature in the country and abroad.*[46] [Our italics]

Great quantities of data flow to U.N. agencies and are regularly analyzed for economic and scientific information. But to our knowledge, these data are not regularly monitored and analyzed for what they might tell us about human rights. The incompleteness and biases of these data are insufficient reasons for the lack of such ongoing analysis.

The analysis of incomplete and distorted data can be a valuable early indicator of human rights abuses and violations. We hope that this discussion is helpful to reporters and analysts of human rights practices and to those all over the world who are working to maintain and improve human rights.

We thank H. Fein, J. Gay, T. Jabine, N. Tec, L. Spirer and two anonymous referees for their assistance.

Notes

1. "From the point of view of preventing genocide—or at least of curbing it—as an ongoing occurrence, not only do we need to seek the truth, but also to search for ways to break through the barriers to belief." Bill Frelick, "Refugees: Contemporary Witnesses to Genocide," paper presented at the Genocide Watch Conference, Institute for the Study of Genocide, John Jay College of Criminal Justice, New York, 22 May 1989.

2. Robert J. Goldstein, "The Limitations of Using Quantitative Data in Studying Human Rights Abuses," *Human Rights Quarterly* 8, No. 4 (November 1986).

3. Ibid., p. 627.

4. Norvall D. Glenn, *Cohort Analysis*, Sage University Paper Series on Quantitative Applications in the Social Sciences 07-005 (Beverly Hills, CA: Sage Publications, 1977), p. 17.

5. Esther Fein, "Breaking Taboo, Soviets Report Big Jump in Crime," *New York Times*, 15 February 1989.

6. Fred W. Grupp and Ellen Jones, paper presented to the Population Seminar of the University Seminar Series of Columbia University. Grupp is with the CIA, Jones is with the U.S. Defense Intelligence Agency.

7. Ibid.

8. *Country Reports on Human Rights Practices for 1987*, report submitted to the U.S. Congress, House Committee on Foreign Affairs and the U.S. Senate Committee on Foreign Relations by the Department of State (Washington, DC: U.S. Government Printing Office, 1988), p. 270.

9. Paul R. Campbell, "South Africa 1960 to 1986: A Statistical View of Racial Differences," paper presented at the 1987 Joint Statistical Meetings, American Statistical Association, San Francisco, August 17–20, 1987, Table 4. Paul Campbell is with the Center for International Research, U.S. Bureau of the Census, Washington, DC 20233.

10. The disease is associated with a diet high in carbohydrate and low in protein.

11. Official South African categories as they appear in South Africa, 1979: Official Yearbook of the Republic of South Africa. Johannesburg (1979).

12. F. Wilson and M. Ramphele, *Uprooting Poverty: The South African Challenge* (New York: W. W. Norton, 1989), p. 100.

13. Martin Gilbert, *The Holocaust: A History of the Jews During the Second World War* (New York: Holt, Rinehart and Winston, 1985), pp. 318, 671.

14. Raymond Bonner, "A Reporter at Large: Famine," *The New Yorker*, 13 March 1989, p. 86, quoting representatives of Oxfam-UK and Save the Children-UK.

15. Wilson and Ramphele, *Uprooting Poverty*, (note 12), p. 107.

16. *U.S. Value from Statistical Abstract of the United States: 1988* (Washington, DC: U.S. Bureau of the Census, 1987), 108th ed., Table No. 116, p. 76. South African value from Wilson and Ramphele, *Uprooting Poverty*, p. 107. (Values obtained from cited primary sources.)

17. *Africa South of the Sahara* (London: Europa Publications Ltd, 1989), 18th ed., p. 937.

18. Adjusted proportions are from Campbell, "South Africa 1960 to 1986" (note 9), Table C.

19. Wilson and Ramphele, *Uprooting Poverty*, pp. 106–112.

20. In Argentina, an unidentified corpse is officially designated as "Ningún Nombre." The literal meaning is "no name."

21. Clyde Collins Snow and Maria Julia Bihurriet, "Ningún Nombre Burials in the Province of Buenos Aires from 1970 to 1984," a report to the Subsecretariat of Human Rights, Argentina Ministry of the Interior, 19 June 1987.

22. Ibid., p. 10.

23. Gabriel Schoenfeld, "A secret Soviet disaster? Chernobyl may not be their only radiation mess," *Washington Post*, 5 March 1989.

24. British intelligence monitored the movements of German trains daily! Walter Laqueur, *The Terrible Secret: An Investigation into the Suppression of Information about Hitler's 'Final Solution'* (London: Weidenfeld and Nicholson, 1980), pp. 85–86.

25. William Shawcross, *The Quality of Mercy: Cambodia, Holocaust and Modern Conscience* (New York: Simon and Schuster, 1984), p. 18.

26. Helen Fein, *Accounting for Genocide: National Responses and Jewish Victimization during the Holocaust* (New York: Free Press, 1979), especially pp. 90–92.

27. John W. Tukey, *Exploratory Data Analysis* (Reading, MA: Addison-Wesley, 1977), p. vi.

28. Fein, *Accounting for Genocide* (note 25), p. 141.

29. *Human Rights in Jamaica: An Americas Watch Report* (New York: Americas Watch Committee, 1986), p. 15.

30. Ibid., pp. 10, 14.

31. This is a valid expectation for many parts of the world. However, where the members of the group are inarticulate, or do not communicate in commonly known languages, or are isolated, or are without confidence the expectation can be unreasonable. French- or English-speaking individuals in, say, Africa, can be expected to make themselves heard and have access to media, NGOs or other agencies. It is no accident that we have such a strong sense of the human rights violations in China and the U.S.S.R. However, who

could have heard from or understood the Ixil tribe when it was eliminated in Guatemala?

32. M. C. Hudson and C. L. Taylor, *World Handbook of Political and Social Indicators*, Vol. 2, 3rd ed. (New Haven, CT: Yale University Press 1983), Table 3.4: Riots, pp. 33–36. The U.S.S.R. reported 70 riot events during the same period.

33. Robert Cohen, "The People's Republic of China: The Human Rights Exception," *Human Rights Quarterly* 9, No. 4 (November 1987): 456–457.

34. This is the Chinese government estimate for 1974 as reported in the *World Almanac* (New York: Newspaper Enterprise Association, Doubleday, 1977), p. 522.

35. Cohen, "People's Republic of China" (note 33), p. 457.

36. Hudson and Taylor, *World Handbook* (note 32), pp. 77–84; Table 2.1, "Political Protest and Government Change," p. 21.

37. We make this distinction because analysis of the data from an ongoing process is only one part of the total control function. For example, in Deming's quality control rationale, the control function includes planning, acting, and doing, as well as checking, which we call analysis. See, for example, H. Gitlow, S. Gitlow, A. Oppenheim, R. Oppenheim, *Tools and Methods for the Improvement of Quality* (Homewood, IL: R. D. Irwin, Inc., 1989), pp. 19–20.

38. Ibid., pp. 322–333.

39. In the terminology of the field, this is the test for stationarity of a series after appropriate measures to remove trend and seasonal effects. If the model is appropriate, the residuals will also be uncorrelated.

40. For an example from appliance manufacture, see Exercise 14, H. F. Spirer, *Business Statistics: A Problem-Solving Approach* (Homewood, IL: Richard D. Irwin, 1975), p. 35. The inspectors faked randomness but were found out because they did not fake a normal distribution as well.

41. For example, the one-sample runs test, as described in S. Siegel, *Nonparametric Statistics for the Behavioral Sciences* (New York: McGraw Hill, 1956), pp. 52–56.

42. In the absence of mass murder, the same number of deaths eventually occur. But since they are distributed in time and space, there is no logistics problem.

43. Nine thousand disappearances have been documented. Estimates go as high as 20,000. See Snow and Bihurriet, "Ningún Nombre" (note 21), p. 1. See also Christopher Joyce and Eric Stover, *Witnesses from the Grave* (Boston: Little Brown and Co., 1991), p. 222.

47. See, for example, A. J. Jaffe, "Some observations on the nature of basic quantitative data," *New York Statistician* 33, No. 5 (1982): 5.

45. Frederic M. Wolf, *Meta-Analysis: Quantitative Methods for Research Synthesis*, Sage University Paper series on Quantitative Applications in the Social Sciences, 07–001 (Beverly Hills, CA: Sage Publications), pp. 38–9.

46. Harold Nelson, ed., *South Africa, A Country Study* (Washington, DC: Foreign Area Studies, American University, U.S. Government Printing Office, 1981), 2nd ed., p. 153.

Part II
Developing Human Rights Data

INTRODUCTION

The chapters in Part II are about the *development* of human rights data. Analysis of the data is covered in Part III. Human rights data may range from simple counts of violations to scale scores assigned to countries on the basis of knowledge gleaned from many different sources. We have chosen the term data development rather than data collection to characterize the scope of the chapters in Part II. The former term is more encompassing: in addition to the direct collection of data from victims or witnesses, it includes, for example, the extraction of data from records of legal proceedings or from newspaper articles and other media accounts of human rights violations.

This volume focuses mainly on data associated with violations of civil and political rights and rights related to the integrity of the person. Data on such violations are hard to come by, as they usually refer to actions that are illegal. Perpetrators are not a likely source of data, since they have no interest in having their personal responsibility for their actions publicized. Victims and their families and friends may feel that informing sympathetic individuals about their experiences will lead to further violations of their own rights.

Producers of human rights data often work with very limited resources. Nevertheless, they must take care to document their sources of data and the methods used to process them. The statistics that they disseminate will not be popular with national governments whose performance with respect to human rights is shown to be unsatisfactory, and they can expect that the authorities will try to discredit their data as being biased or otherwise inaccurate. In spite of their best efforts, the data they produce will contain errors. As many social statisticians phrase it, they will be working with "messy" or "dirty" data.

Our intent, however, is not to discourage the reader. Messiness or dirtiness of the data is characteristic of virtually all information derived from real-world events and behaviors, and social statisticians have developed tools for dealing with the associated problems. Statistics as a science does not consist merely of descriptive or analytical techniques: it is fundamentally concerned with the relevance, accuracy, and reliability of data and provides theories and methods for investigating and assessing the processes used in data development. Thus, the relatively new enterprise of exploring human rights issues with statistics can benefit from the experience and techniques that represent the current state of the art in social statistics. The chapters in Part II illustrate both problems and solutions.

Data Development

Broadly speaking, the process of data development consists of two phases: specification and execution. The specification phase is critical. Without careful consideration of goals and specific data requirements, useful and defensible data are unlikely to emerge. Of course, if the process is designed to produce data at regular intervals, it can be improved over time through feedback from users, as illustrated in the chapter by Innes.

An underlying purpose for many kinds of human rights data is to *monitor* violations of human rights. Are violations increasing or decreasing? What kinds of violations are occurring? Who are the victims and who are the perpetrators? What countries have the worst and best records for guaranteeing the rights of their citizens? Answers to these questions help to guide the policies of international organizations, national governments and nongovernmental advocacy groups and to bring human rights problems to the attention of the public. Monitoring may also include an element of *prediction*. Prediction is much more difficult than monitoring, but preventive action, if at all possible, is certainly preferable to reaction after the fact.

Human rights data also provide inputs to the analytical *research* that is needed to understand why and under what circumstances violations of human rights occur. We hope that the inclusion in this volume of the Guide to Data Sources (Chapter 15) will encourage more researchers to exploit the data bases that are already available.

Sources of human rights data are numerous. Data on individual violations (*events-based data*) are compiled by international organizations; by national governments (see Innes, Chapter 9, and Pritchard, Chapter 10); by nongovernmental advocacy groups (see Dueck, Chapter 5, and Reiter, Zunzunegui, and Quiroga, Chapter 4); and by academic researchers (see Gurr and Harff, Chapter 6). These data may come directly from victims or they may be compiled indirectly from media accounts and other sources, such as records of legal proceedings (see Nowak and von Hebel, Chapter 12, and Dickinson and Fairley, Chapter 11, in Part III).

Standards-based data which measure human rights performance at the national level permit international comparisons and, if the same measurements are repeated at different times, analysis of national and international trends. Such measures, as discussed in Bollen, Chapter 7, and Lopez and Stohl, Chapter 8, are generally developed by advocacy groups and by academic researchers. Survey research provides another source of human rights data. It is important not only to know what violations are actually occurring but to understand public perceptions of these events and the extent to which people feel that some kinds of violations may be justified in certain circumstances.

Whatever kinds of data are being developed and whatever their source, sound statistical practice demands that the study or target population and the data items be carefully and clearly specified. In our editorial role, we have tried to ensure that this was done in each chapter and for each of the data sets included in the Guide to Data Sources, Chapter 15.

The definition of the study population identifies the units of analysis, their geographic location, and the date or time period of interest. Units of analysis may, for example, be events or episodes (the latter is the term used by Gurr and Harff to describe instances of communal and political victimization), court decisions, persons, population groups defined by ethnic religious or political affiliations, or nations. The study population may cover the units of analysis in a restricted area such as a city or province, or it may cover the entire world or a region thereof, as when the units of analysis are nations.

The specific data items that can be collected are even more varied than the study populations. Major considerations in defining data items are specificity, comparability, and operational feasibility. As stated in the general introduction to this volume, the Universal Declaration of Human Rights provides a widely accepted framework for defining various kinds of human rights violations, but its articles are couched in terms that are much too broad to serve as a basis for careful data compilation. Detailed operational definitions are essential.

The work described in Chapters 4 and 5 is aimed directly at filling this gap for individual events data: both chapters advocate the widespread use of standard definitions for types of violations and characteristics of victims and perpetrators. In Chapter 6 Gurr and Harff try to do the same thing for episodes of communal and political victimization. The authors of Chapters 7 and 8 pay careful attention to the variables used to characterize nations with respect to their human rights performance. Chapter 10 examines both the conceptual structure and the actual contents of country human rights reports issued by the United States and Norway to evaluate their comparability.

After the data requirements are clearly specified, attention must be given to the mode of data collection or compilation, the recording instruments (forms, questionnaires, transcription sheets, etc.) and the qualifications, training, and supervision of the persons who will perform the various operations. The extensive literature and experience from the field of survey research can provide many useful insights on these aspects of data development.[1]

If the primary aim of an organization that is developing human rights data is to assist individual victims, then its information-gathering procedures will be designed with this in mind. However, as pointed out in Chapters 4 and 5, some fairly simple features can be built into these procedures to facilitate the use of the same case records to produce statistical summaries. These summaries will be valuable to the organization for evaluating and guiding its work and for telling the public about the extent and character of human rights violations.

The production of credible statistical information on any subject requires that those who collect and process the data have suitable qualifications and receive adequate training and review of their work. However, gathering statistical information on human rights violations has a feature that is not common in most other statistical endeavors: those who compile the data are often at risk themselves. One has only to review the reports issued annually by Human Rights Watch (cited in Chapter 4) to gauge the price that is being paid by those who choose to work on behalf of the victims of human rights violations. However, there is also some good news in this department. As Innes points out in Chapter 9, participation in the gathering of information for the U.S. State Department's annual *Country Reports* has made many of those involved more sensitive to the widespread violations of human rights that are occurring in many areas of the world, and one can anticipate that in the long run this consciousness-raising process will influence official U.S. policy with respect to human rights questions.

The Quality of Human Rights Data

To be of maximum utility, human rights data, like any other kind of data, should be relevant, accurate, and timely. None of these criteria is an absolute requirement: in the real world of statistics there is always a trade-off between the available resources and ideal standards for quality. Keeping these goals firmly in view is, however, essential in order to maintain credibility and avoid wasted effort. Timeliness, that is, quick dissemination of data following the period to which they refer, is essential so that action can be taken to combat emerging trends in the level and nature of those kinds of violations that pose the greatest threats to individuals.

Quality is a major consideration in all of the chapters in Part II. The beneficial effects of using standard concepts and definitions, as advocated by Reiter et al. and Dueck, has been amply demonstrated by the initiatives of the United Nations and other international and regional organizations, over many decades, to develop standards for demographic, economic, and social statistics compiled by national governments. The relevance of such statistics is enhanced if they are comparable with similar data for other countries and accuracy is promoted by adherence to precise concepts and definitions, adapted as necessary to meet the special needs of different countries.

Thus, the statistics that are needed to monitor the fulfillment of economic and social human rights have had the benefit of standards that represent a meeting of the minds among statisticians and data users from the member countries of the organizations that issue the standards. For obvious reasons, it has not been possible to follow the same route to establish standard concepts and definitions for the compilation of data on violations of civil and political rights and rights related to the integrity of the person, so the task has been left to private organizations and individuals. The HURIDOCS Task Force that is working on the development of standard formats for recording event information, as described in Chapter 5, represents the most recent and organized attempt to follow the recommendations put forward earlier by Reiter et al.[2]

The data base for episodes of violations of the rights of communal and political groups described by Gurr and Harff in Chapter 6 is unique, so the issue of comparability with other datasets is of less importance. Nevertheless, the authors are rightly concerned with other aspects of quality, especially the validity and reliability of the data for groups included in their system. An important part of their chapter is concerned with procedures for recording and coding the characteristics of groups and events. For some of the values they record, such as the number of victims associated with a particular episode, multiple estimates are given by different sources, posing a problem of how to use and incorporate such information in their dataset.

In Chapters 7 and 8, Bollen and Lopez and Stohl address quality issues in connection with standards-based data systems used in comparative international human rights analysis and research. Bollen reviews the methodology of existing sets and concludes that relatively little is known about their quality. He recommends fuller documentation of these data sets. This point has been taken seriously in the development of the Guide to Data Sources: we have included a brief description of the methods used to develop and maintain each of the data sets included and, whenever possible, have provided references to more detailed information.

Lopez and Stohl have focused on the first of our three components of quality—relevance—and call for a multidimensional approach to the measurement of human rights violations. They identify three relevant dimensions—scope, intensity, and range—and recommend that existing measurement systems incorporate these three dimensions.

Innes, in reviewing the development over time of the U.S. State Department *Country Reports*, points to improvements in quality such as greater consistency in definition, accuracy in measurement, and comprehensiveness in coverage that have resulted from the intense interest in and scrutiny of the reports by human rights advocacy groups and researchers. She recommends that this feedback process be formalized through the establishment of one or more advisory or user groups similar to those associated with major U.S. statistical agencies. Pritchard, by comparing similar data from two different systems—the U.S. and Norwegian country reports—follows a practice that has proven to be an invaluable tool for evaluation of data quality in other fields. When differences are observed for particular data items, explanations are sought, often leading to better understanding of the strengths and weaknesses of both of the systems compared.

United States Commissioner of Labor Statistics Janet Norwood, in a 1989 address "Data Quality for Public Policy,"[3] said:

Data produced by the Federal statistical system are inextricably intertwined with policy and decision making processes. . . . Government statistical series affect billions of dollars of government expenditure. . . . In such an environment, the maintenance and improvement of the quality of government statistical work is a critical responsibility.

The same argument, perhaps with even greater force, can be made for the importance of efforts to maintain and improve the quality of human rights data. The stakes are human dignity and human lives rather than dollars.

Protecting the Anonymity of Individuals

The success of large-scale statistical programs—censuses and surveys—depends on the cooperation of the individuals who supply information about themselves and their families. To ensure their continued cooperation, governments have established elaborate legal, procedural, and technical safeguards to preserve the anonymity of information about each individual. Legal safeguards forbid the use of individually identifiable information for nonstatistical purposes and establish penalties for unlawful disclosure. Frequently, laws require that persons asked to supply information be fully informed about the purposes for which the data will be used and who will have access to their data.[4] Procedural and technical safeguards minimize the risk of unauthorized access to the information and the risk that disclosure of statistical information could lead to the identification of specific persons.

The sensitivity of data about individual human rights violations makes this kind of protection a matter of special concern. Private human rights groups are especially vulnerable to attempts by unfriendly government authorities to seize their records and use them in ways that harm, rather than help, the victims and others who have supplied information. Both Reiter et al. and Dueck report attempts by government authorities in Latin American countries, successful in some instances, to seize case records from nongovernmental human rights organizations. These experiences spotlight the importance, for such groups, of taking special precautions and explaining clearly to those who supply information how their information will be used and protected from unauthorized disclosure. Reiter et al. and Dueck recognize this problem and suggest several ways of coping with it.

Chapters Included In Part II

Several aspects of the chapters in Part II, particularly the ways in which they all focus on various aspects of data quality, have already been alluded to in this introduction. Here we provide a brief summary of the topics covered by the seven chapters in order of their appearance.

Chapters 4 and 5 portray successive stages in ongoing efforts to develop and promote the use of standard concepts, definitions, and formats for recording information about individual violations of human rights. These efforts are directed at and participated in mainly by nongovernmental human rights organizations, which need the information primarily to support casework on behalf of victims and their families but also use it to provide statistical information about levels and trends in different kinds of violations.

An earlier version of the chapter by Reiter et al. appeared in 1986,[5] and since that time several organizations, mainly in Latin America, have adopted their recommendations concerning the definitions of events and the characteristics to be recorded for different types of events. Dueck describes the work of an international task force organized by the Human Rights and Information System International (HURIDOCS) to develop standard formats for recording and communicating information on human rights violations. A draft of their proposed standards has been widely circulated, and the standards are being field tested by many of the organizations whose representatives participated in their development.

Chapters 4 and 5 address issues related to the compilation of data for violations (events) involving individuals or small groups, such as families; Gurr and Harff in Chapter 6 present two data sets containing information about violations of the rights of large groups (collectivities). The Minorities at Risk study embraces 261 communal minorities in 126 nations who have been subjected to differential social treatment. The Genocides and Politicides study concerns 44 episodes of mass murder against communal and political groups occurring between 1945 and 1987. The chapter describes the conceptual framework and intended uses of the two data sets and the procedures used to develop them. Several analyses based on these data sets have already been published.[6]

Chapters 7 and 8 are about data used in international comparative human rights analysis, where nations are the units of analysis. The sources of data are varied, including a wide range of official statistics, media reports, country reports on human rights, and reports of nongovernmental groups. Particular attention is given to standards-based data, that is, human rights-related scores or rankings of countries, based on expert knowledge or reviews of available information. Both chapters provide a critical appraisal of existing data sets in this category and make some recommendations for improvement.

Finally, Chapters 9 and 10 discuss a category of sources of human rights data that do not qualify as or pretend to be formal statistical compendia, but which do provide a fairly systematic compilation of quantitative and qualitative information on human rights violations. We refer to country reports on human rights. Such reports are issued both by national governments and by private organizations, such as Amnesty International and Human Rights Watch. What they have in common is coverage of several countries and the attempt to present information in a more or less standardized format for each of the countries included.

Innes (Chapter 9) reviews the history and current status of the U.S. State Department's *Country Reports*, which evolved from the passage of 1976 legislation that established the requirement to submit annual reports on human rights status by country to the U.S. Congress. Innes, who served as a consultant to the State Department in 1980, developing indicators and methods for the economic and social section of the *Reports*, sees a parallel between the use of statistics in the *Country Reports* and the earlier development of key indicators such as the unemployment rate and the consumer price index, which gained general acceptance and became influential only after decades of debate over policy and definitions. Her conclusions about the influence of the reporting process on policy making at the State Department and elsewhere will be, we believe, both surprising and encouraging to human rights advocates.

The last chapter in Part II is by Pritchard, who conceived the valuable idea of comparing the U.S. and Norwegian country reports on human rights for 1986. In addition to comparing the general purposes and methodology used by the two countries, she compares entries for particular rights for some of the countries covered by both reports. She finds some interesting examples of differences in definitions of human rights and the data selected to assess their practice. Her conclusions address the impact of the reports and the question of "objective" reporting.

Notes

1. There are many excellent texts on survey research methods, e.g., C. A. Moser and G. Kalton, *Survey Methods in Social Investigation* (New York: Basic Books, 2nd ed., 1972). From 1978 on, current developments have been extensively reported in the annual *Proceedings of the Survey Research Methods Section*, American Statistical Association.

2. See Randy B. Reiter, M. V. Zunzunegui, and Jose Quiroga, "Guidelines for Field Reporting of Basic Human Rights Violations," *Human Rights Quarterly* 8, No. 4 (November 1986): 628–653. Their chapter in this volume is an updated and expanded version of that paper.

3. Janet L. Norwood, "Data Quality for Public Policy," The 1989 Distinguished Lecture on Economics in Government, delivered at the Joint Session of the Society of Government Economists and the American Economic Association, Atlanta, Georgia, December 29, 1989.

4. For a detailed discussion of information privacy laws and their application in several western countries, see Robert F. Boruch and Joe S. Cecil, *Assuring the Confidentiality of Social Research Data* (Philadelphia: University of Pennsylvania Press, 1979) and David H. Flaherty, *Privacy of Government Data Banks: An International Perspective* (London: Mansell, 1979).

5. Reiter, Zunzunegui, and Quiroga, "Guidelines" (note 2).

6   See references in the Guide to Data Sources, Chapter 15, listings 15 and 16.

Chapter 4
Guidelines for Field Reporting of Basic Human Rights Violations

Randy B. Reiter, M. V. Zunzunegui, and Jose Quiroga

In recent decades many governments around the world have en-gaged in the widespread violation of basic human rights of their peo-ples by the practices of killing, disappearances, physical and psychological torture, arbitrary detention, and exile. Such practices, particularly prevalent in undemocratic and repressive military re-gimes of Third World countries, involve varying degrees of state par-ticipation, from active violations by state officials to passive failure to protect citizens from the actions of private or paramilitary groups. In an effort to stop these practices, national and international groups opposed to human rights abuses have mounted a variety of cam-paigns of documentation, publicity, and protection.[1]

The work of national human rights groups has been shaped by the particular political conditions in the countries where they operate and has, therefore, resulted in the development of various methods of human rights documentation. This lack of uniform standards for human rights reporting has been used to discredit such groups by defenders of repressive governments. Other factors that have ham-pered the work of these national groups include a lack of material resources and international contacts and timidity of the media to dis-tribute information on human rights violations in the face of political pressure and possible reprisals. The result has been an underuse of large amounts of information collected by these groups under very difficult, often dangerous conditions. In addition, human rights activists have themselves been victims of arbitrary detention, torture, disappearance, and killing. Their offices have been raided by security forces, and data gathered from years of hard work have been destroyed.[2]

It is urgent for those who believe that human rights are important, including members of the scientific community, to respond to such systematic repression and to contribute to the struggle to expose and stop it. Such a response needs to be coordinated with local human rights groups on the front lines to aid and augment their efforts. Because of the systematic nature of political repression, these efforts should be directed at protecting individual victims and national human rights groups from state terrorism.

In this chapter we argue that a standardized protocol for collecting and reporting data on human rights abuses could contribute to the amelioration of the problems mentioned above. In addition, we suggest guidelines for the development of a reporting protocol based on a review of the experiences of human rights groups reporting abuses from current and past repressive regimes. By protocol we mean a minimum set of data to be collected, along with procedures for collecting and compiling it. Our aim is to promote the establishment of a standard and workable reporting system. We first discuss the context of state repression and the subsequent development of human rights groups, including some short case histories. In doing so, we examine the organizational structure, strategies, security, and reporting schemes of these groups. We then present an illustrative series of definitions and approaches for case handling and data collection. Finally, we discuss the scientific value of standardization, some possible uses of data collected with such a protocol and conclude with comments on the political and human need for such a system.

This chapter is based on documentary evidence and interviews and personal communications with some of the leaders of human rights organizations in Chile, Argentina, El Salvador, and South Africa. It intends to contribute to discussion among human rights activists, statisticians, health professionals, and lawyers toward the goal of establishing uniform and flexible guidelines for data collection and reporting of human rights violations. While human rights can refer to political, social, and economic rights and protections, in this chapter we are focusing on the most basic rights to protection of the life, security, and integrity of the person.

Repression and Human Rights Organization Responses

Context

In recent decades many governments have established policies aimed at repressing the entire population (e.g., Chile, Haiti, Paraguay) or particular population groups (South African blacks). Such governments are often run by the military, but even when they are not, military, police, or security forces play a powerful role in repression. Whatever the nature of the power base, the aim is generally to maintain the existing social, political, and economic arrangements (South Africa, Somoza's Nicaragua) or to reverse a prior administration's socioeconomic reforms (Pinochet's Chile, Guatemala after 1954, Brazil after 1964).

While in such countries some of the trappings of democratic decision making have been allowed, when challenges (legal or extra-legal) to basic arrangements favored by the government have arisen, repressive states have curtailed such processes and (re)asserted authoritarian control. This is often the setting for a military coup and/or the establishment of state terrorism and the restriction of labor unions, political parties, a free judiciary, and generally of rights to organize or act politically—that is, collectively or publicly. The rights of people as human beings and as citizens are severely restricted or abolished. State terrorism is imposed to intimidate opposition, often with active or passive international support for this policy or its agents.

While denial of human rights violations is still the standard practice, during the last twenty years in many countries of Latin America, in the Philippines under Marcos, in South Korea, South Africa, and elsewhere a new doctrine of national security has been put forth to provide theoretical support for those repressive actions that are acknowledged or discovered. National security is typically expressed as the capacity of the state to maintain the vital interests of the nation (sovereignty, independence, Western civilization) against national or international interference. In practice this doctrine claims that to fight international communism and preserve the moral values of Western societies, the state must use all means, including the coercive methods necessary to destroy any opposition.[3] Recent examples include El Salvador, the Philippines, South Korea, and South Africa as well as the military junta in Argentina from 1976 to 1983 and the rule of Augusto Pinochet in Chile from 1973 to 1990.

Implementing widespread repression requires the establishment by the state of a repression apparatus. The national security system is controlled by military or security forces. It develops widespread surveillance, with informers among the population. Numerous secret detention centers are set up around the country, since often large numbers of people are confined and this must be done in relative secrecy from the public and the press. Computer systems store and analyze information about dissidents. Personnel specialized in surveillance, abduction, interrogation, torture, computer use and data analysis, and health care, as well as strategic planners are required to apprehend, imprison, interrogate, and torture, examine and dispose of victims, and to cover these operations with false documents about legal and health status and cause of death. In short, the apparatus of repression involves large numbers of people, including health professionals, and a physical infrastructure. Many of the personnel are trained in military schools teaching counterinsurgency techniques. Often there is assistance from other countries in establishing the torture infrastructure.[4]

In the face of this, groups organize to protect or help victims and to oppose the violence against the government's targets. In each country there is a spectrum of conditions that shapes the way this is done. These conditions include the kind of repression and who it is directed against; the institutional or organizational auspices available to human rights activists (for example, whether the church is sympathetic or collaborationist); the needs and possibilities of security; the services available to be offered; whether the group is well established or newly formed; and the political climate for coalitions or organizations. In each case, the human rights groups operate in an environment defined by the destruction of social and political institutions. These groups are typically needed in conditions of extreme poverty, with few material or health resources available to victims and their families.

Local groups documenting abuses represent the front line of human rights monitoring. The context in which human rights groups operate often involves threats to the human rights monitors themselves. This happens both as part of the general environment of repression and specifically to discourage monitors from documenting or publicizing activities that the repressive apparatus is unwilling to accept responsibility for, or in some cases even to acknowledge as happening at all. Such repression includes campaigns against the existence and activities of organizations, threats and violence to individuals, and threats to the group's capacity to maintain the security of its records. In recognition of the prime need to protect human rights monitors so that other abuses can be publicized, Human Rights Watch (Americas Watch, Asia Watch, Helsinki Watch) has established as a highest priority the monitoring of threats to the existence of human rights monitors. In its annual report of persecution of human rights monitors it lists almost 500 cases in 39 countries, including 10 killings and 2 disappearances, from December 1986 through November 1987. These included 95 cases in Chile, 49 in the U.S.S.R. and 44 in South Africa. Five of the deaths occurred in Colombia and another two in El Salvador.[5]

At the onset of repressive rule, local groups play an especially decisive role in information collection and dissemination and in aiding victims. In turn, international governmental and nongovernmental human rights organizations, often denied access during the early repressive period while the government is using repression to assert and solidify its control, rely heavily on reports from local groups. Therefore, guidelines for human rights data collection and reporting by local groups would facilitate the transfer to and processing of such information by international organizations. These latter groups are in a better position to publicize abuses to a wider audience, which can help bring pressure for an early abatement of patterns of abuses.

Evolution of Responses: Case Histories

A series of case histories and examples illustrate how national human rights organizations have responded to political conditions. From these examples we can begin to formulate general standards for reporting abuses that are broad enough to be widely applicable and at the same time flexible enough to adapt to particular and changing situations.

Chile

Human rights organizations have had an unusually successful history in Chile, during the rule of one of the more repressive military dictatorships in the Western Hemisphere. This has been possible in part because of Chile's long democratic tradition and the strong position on human rights adopted by the Roman Catholic church.

The first human rights institution, created one month after the military coup that brought Augusto Pinochet to power in September 1973, was the Committee of Cooperation for Peace, formed by order of the Archbishop of Santiago on October 19, 1973. Its aim was "to assist persons in need, giving legal, economic, technical and spiritual aid." The committee immediately established relationships with other religious denominations and became an ecumenical agency, with the cooperation of members of Chile's Lutheran, Methodist, evangelical, orthodox, Pentecostal, and Jewish religious communities. On December 19, 1975 the committee was dissolved by special request of the military government, but on January 19, 1976 the Vicariate of Solidarity was founded.[6] Since then, its aim has been to provide legal, medical, social, and economic assistance to victims of repression.

Another ecumenical institution, the Christian Churches Social Aid Foundation (FASIC), has worked in the area of human rights since 1975.[7] It initially worked with the United Nations High Commissioner for Refugees (UNHCR) on behalf of political prisoners, requesting commutation of their prison sentences to exile and family reunification. In 1977 FASIC began a medical-psychological program to help victims of repression and their families. From 1977 through 1986, this mental health program expanded in three levels of action: (1) primary prevention, through publication and denunciation of human rights abuses to the national and international community; (2) secondary prevention, reviewing psychological damage through group work in populations at high risk of repression, such as politically or socially active people or those living in poor dwelling areas; and (3) repairing psychological damage from the effects of repression in torture victims and in families of prisoners and those disappeared, executed, and exiled.[8]

The Chilean Human Rights Commission (CCHDH) was established in December 1978.[9] Its aims are to document, thwart, and denounce violations of human rights. In an effort to avoid duplication, the commission began by using the information gathered by the Vicariate of Solidarity. Since 1979, the commission has acquired its own national and international identity, with community-based organizations in the provinces. The research department of the commission publishes a monthly report using information collected by Chilean human rights organizations. This report provides the most complete information on human rights in Chile.

The Foundation for the Protection of Children Damaged in Periods of Emergency (PIDEE) was organized in 1979 to protect children hurt by the disappearance, death, imprisonment, or other forms of repression of their parents. PIDEE also attends to the needs of children who have returned to Chile from exile.[10] Its work has expanded from Santiago to other cities of Chile.

The Committee for the Defense of the Rights of the People (CODEPU) was founded in November 1980 in response to the military dictatorship's attempt to legitimize itself through the enactment of a new constitution, which was adopted in 1980. A coordinating body of individuals and organizations, CODEPU offers legal, medical, and psychological services to victims of repression; training in health care for volunteers; and training in popular education for members of social organizations of the community.[11] The organization is active throughout Chile.

The National Commission Against Torture was founded in January 1983 with the objective of working for the abolition of torture.[12] The commission's specific objectives include (1) raising awareness about the existence of systematic torture; (2) making known the consequences of torture; (3) educating the Chilean community about the ways in which it can join the struggle to end torture; (4) denouncing the ineffectiveness of the judicial system; and (5) denouncing the participation of health professionals in torture.

These represent the main organizations that have formed since 1973 and the ways in which they have developed specialized clienteles, services, functions, or orientations. Some other organizations have also been founded to defend human rights, but it is beyond the scope of this chapter to describe them here.

Argentina

There are nine human rights organizations in Argentina. They have emerged in response to the human rights violations that occurred for many years, especially in the 1970s. As in Chile, the various groups in Argentina have tended to develop a division of labor as they oriented their work toward meeting specific needs.[13]

The Argentinian League for Human Rights was created in 1930. The oldest organization in this field, its principal original aim was to defend the members of the Communist party persecuted by the government. Its work has extended to cities outside Buenos Aires, and it has international connections.

Service for Peace and Justice is an international movement supporting a philosophy of active nonviolence. It shares activities with other human rights organizations. It was founded in 1974 by Adolfo Perez Esquivel, who received the Nobel Peace Prize in 1980.

The Permanent Assembly for Human Rights was founded immediately before the military coup, in December 1975; disappearances, torture, and killings had already begun. The organization has been able to document more than 7,000 cases of detention and disappearance of prisoners. Management is by a collegiate directorate, with more than 50 affiliate groups in the rest of the country.

The Ecumenical Movement for Human Rights was founded in 1976 by several religious groups. It gives spiritual, legal, and financial aid to victims of repression and has close relations with the World Council of Churches.

The mothers of detained and disappeared people used to go to the government palace to ask for news about them. Later they began to protest in silent rallies every Thursday in front of the building, wearing white handkerchiefs on their heads. This was the origin of the organization the Mothers of the Plaza de Mayo, founded in 1978 by Azucena Villaflor de Vicenti and fourteen others. They became a symbol of courage whose message has spread throughout the world.

The Grandmothers of the Plaza de Mayo is an independent group searching for those children who were kidnapped with their parents. Some of the children are living with families of the same military personnel implicated in the detention and disappearance of the parents. To date at least 196 children have been registered in their files, and 41 have been located. The Grandmothers, with the aid of scientists contacted through the American Association for the Advancement of Science, are using modern genetic and biotechnological methods to identify missing children, including some born after the disappearance of their mothers and so lacking any other means of identification. Such evidence was used in court to identify one girl who was returned to her grandmother in a landmark 1984 ruling.[14]

The relatives of the detained and disappeared in the Commission of Relatives of Disappeared and Political Prisoners denounce the taking of political prisoners, search for them, work for their release, and give assistance to their families.

The Center for Legal and Social Studies (CELS) was founded as a nonprofit organization by lawyers in 1980 with two main objectives: (1) to help relatives in their search for the disappeared, and (2) to take court action against suspected perpetrators of human rights violations.[15]

Because of the extremely repressive conditions during the first years of the military dictatorship, testimonies of victims of repression were collected almost exclusively outside of Argentina from victims who had been able to escape abroad. These testimonies were scarce and did not receive the attention that they deserved. However, those accounts motivated a special investigatory mission to Argentina from the Inter-American Commission of Human Rights in 1979. The findings of this commission exposed the brutality of the military regime in its efforts to wipe out any kind of opposition.

Since 1980, the Center for Legal and Social Studies (CELS) has been collecting testimonies from victims of repression. During the early period, CELS teams studied and filed the information contained in testimonies collected by human rights groups abroad. Slowly but regularly, victims began to come to the CELS offices in Buenos Aires to testify. This was often the first time that victims had narrated their experiences, often after six or seven years of silence.

Even when identification was not required, most of the victims gave their names and addresses. An agreement was made that the victim would be consulted if any identifying information were to be used in public. Most of the testimonies (95 percent) were given by survivors of disappearance—people who had been abducted, subsequently disappeared, tortured and later released. The great majority agreed to public use of their stories.

By 1984, CELS had collected a total of 180 testimonies. Semistructured interviews lasted between one and four hours and focused on three issues: (1) description of experiences in the detention center; (2) description of security forces and other people involved in detention and torture; and (3) data on other detainees. The interviews were taped, and the victim was asked to come back two weeks later to read and sign the transcription. During the past years a computer has been used to build three data bases, covering testimonies, detained or disappeared individuals, and repressors.[16] Computer techniques are useful for cross-validating information and increasing the speed of updating ongoing legal actions and preparing material for searches. By the end of 1985, there were files on 1,350 disappeared persons last seen at any one of the 340 secret detention centers identified as used by the security forces.

Since July 1984, under the new democratic regime that brought Raúl Alfonsín to the presidency, the CELS team of mental health workers has collaborated with the Office of Solidarity with the Argentines in Exile (OSEA) to establish a specific program for those people returning from exile to Argentina.[17] The situation of people returning from exile cannot be isolated from other effects of political repression; those who return often lack jobs and housing, and they need to adapt to their extended families and social environment after the traumatic experience of exile. Moreover, children and adolescents have a different pace of adaptation as they move into a new country and often a new culture. Every member of the family and the family as a whole is affected by exile and return, and they often ask mental health professionals for help in adapting to the new and often hard conditions in their country of origin. The OSEA mental health team responds to the needs of people returning from exile. OSEA is linked with the National Commission for the Return and the United Nations High Commission for Refugees.

South Africa

Political detention without trial is a central legal device to control and suppress black opposition to white control in South Africa. The Internal Security Act of 1982 provided for four different forms of detention: (1) *interrogative*, allowing indefinite incommunicado detention; (2) *preventive*, directed "to any person who may be dangerous for the security of the State";[18] (3) potential state *witness* in political trials, for as long as six months or until the trial is completed; and (4) *short term* (up to 14 days) for persons regarded as contributing to public disturbances. For each of these provisions, the order might be renewed or the person redetained under alternative sections.

Solitary confinement, as prescribed under South African detention legislation, constitutes a human rights violation under the 1984 U.N. Convention Against Torture and Other Cruel, Inhumane and Degrading Treatment or Punishment.[19] Moreover, the general circumstances around security law detentions favor the occurrence of torture under detention. Despite the frequent allegations of torture of detainees, the South African state has failed to investigate officially such allegations.

Even when psychological, psychiatric, medical, and legal professional bodies have been timid or restricted in attempting to combat torture in South Africa, there have been isolated attempts by human rights activists. As a result of this work, the Medical Association of South Africa published recommendations on the treatment of political detainees.

Human rights organizations have become more organized over the last ten years. However, the almost continual states of emergency imposed since 1985 have limited their activities, with many of their activists being restricted or detained and their documentation and reporting activities severely curtailed. Such has been the case, for example, for the Detainees' and the Detainees' Parents Support Committees, which provided services to detainees and their families, information on detainees, and public campaigns.

The Institute of Criminology at the University of Cape Town has completed a project that studied detention and torture in South Africa.[20] The sample consisted of 176 ex-detainees who were approached through community-based organizations and the Detainees' Support Committees. The sociodemographic distribution of these cases was similar to the population of political detainees of South Africa. In this sample, 83 percent of the participants reported some kind of physical torture and 100 percent of them reported psychological torture. This study provides an example of the use of scientific methodology to describe violations of human rights, in particular arbitrary detention, which has been legalized by the current government of South Africa. The study has been subjected to criticism by government officials in an attempt to undermine its credibility. However, the report leaves little doubt that the practice of torture often follows arbitrary detention in South Africa.

The South African case illustrates several important points. First and foremost is the extent to which South Africa has laws which permit many human rights abuses. International human rights covenants are clear in forbidding such practices regardless of their legal status in a country or of threats to national security alleged by the government.[21] Standards included in the covenants may be applicable as a matter of customary international law or as *jus cogens*.

The "lawful" commission of abuses makes documentation more difficult for human rights groups collecting data from primary sources, as groups' activities are also restricted according to South African laws. At the same time, though, this situation also provides the opportunity to report cases through the existence of legal records. Such records, of course, only cover legal proceedings and not other abuses such as occur during public demonstrations. Media restrictions, such as the laws that prohibited media coverage of police actions in public, make all the more important the internal reporting of state abuses to the rest of the world by sources other than the media. As a result, with the suppression of organizations, the most systematic regular reporting of abuses left may be by the *Southern Africa Journal on Human Rights*, which summarizes major cases and publishes an *Annual Human Rights Index*. Press reports, court judgments, and information from lawyers are their main sources of case descriptions. Lawyers for Human Rights also reports cases, from similar sources, and the South Africa Institute of Race Relations publishes an *Annual Survey of Race Relations*, a broad catalog covering race relations and human rights cases, also based largely on press reports.

The Institute of Criminology study is a survey to document abuses, not a population-based surveillance system. While sampling limitations in such surveys may preclude their use for estimating the incidence of abuse in the population, they can establish the existence of abusive practices, especially if they employ standardized data protocols. International acceptance of such protocols could make it harder for states to discredit such studies.

El Salvador

The main human rights groups in El Salvador—Socorro Juridico, Tutela Legal, and the (non-governmental) Human Rights Commission of El Salvador—have had their work continuously jeopardized by attacks on their credibility and by political killings, abductions, and forced exile of their leaders. Reports by Amnesty International have concluded that the current government lacks power to stop human rights violations amidst the civil war.[22] A recent report by Socorro Juridico documents clearly that arbitrary killing, arbitrary detention, and torture are common practices of the armed forces in El Salvador.[23] Reports by Americas Watch demonstrate how the Reagan administration distorted the facts when dealing with human rights in El Salvador in order to claim improvements there.[24]

Tutela Legal is a human rights organization founded in 1982 by the Catholic church. It is under the direct supervision of the Archbishop of El Salvador. Tutela has a Service Department which is in charge of receiving direct testimony from victims, their families and witnesses; investigating the case; and reporting to the court when appropriate. The Information Department produces monthly, annual, and special case reports and statistics, which are printed by the Publication Department for local and international distribution. Tutela publishes only denunciations presented to and investigated by them, using its own legal definitions based on the penal code of El Salvador. It has a head office in San Salvador and a peripheral office in Chalatenango.

The Human Rights Commission of El Salvador (CDHES) is an independent (nongovernmental) human rights organization which has published monthly, annual, and special reports on political killings, disappearances, and arbitrary detentions. It reports cases it investigates and those published by the newspapers. The CDHES has been a target of the Salvadorean Armed Forces which accuse the commission and other humanitarian organizations of belonging to umbrella groups with the guerrillas. Two of the three CDHES presidents have been assassinated by paramilitary groups: Marianela García Villas, a lawyer, killed on March 14, 1983; and Herbert E. Anaya Sanabria, killed on October 26, 1987.

Socorro Juridico has continued publishing reports on human rights abuses and, in particular, surveys describing methods, frequency, and personnel involved in the torture of male and female political prisoners. According to its own definition, "Socorro Juridico Cristiano" (Christian Legal Aid of El Salvador) is a nongovernmental humanitarian institution. Founded in 1975 in San Salvador, it works locally to provide social and legal assistance to victims of human rights violations and to persons with minimal financial resources who require legal counsel. It is not an official Catholic institution. It is a Christian-inspired humanitarian institution that bases its work on national legislation and international laws on human rights and their defence.[25]

The report of Socorro Juridico and our personal communications with some of the leaders of the human rights movement in El Salvador illustrate several points that would be useful in the development of a broad surveillance system for human rights abuses. Since El Salvador is undergoing a revolutionary war, the government can claim its security is more clearly threatened by an opposing military force, and its actions are military, or directed against an army. However, widespread and systematic bombings of civilian populations by the government[26] still constitute human rights abuses just as do the abduction and killing of urban individuals by death squads. While such practices are difficult to document due to the prevailing fear and the difficulties that peasants must overcome to reach the offices of urban human rights groups, such practices should be documented as well as possible and this information included in human rights reports. Another situation reported from El Salvador that should be documented is the abuse of persons in refugee camps, particularly in Honduras.

Organizational Structure for the Defense of Human Rights

Any human rights group needs a basic structure to carry out the different functions of assistance to the victim and denunciation of human rights violations. A description of a successful structure for a human rights organization (HRO) follows. This description is based on the structure of the Vicariate of Solidarity, Chile—possibly one of the most sophisticated HROs due to the particular conditions in Chile. It is discussed here to illustrate one way the functions of taking and reporting human rights information can be organized in a HRO oriented to providing services for victims as well as to promoting prevention of abuses.

The policy making body of the organization is composed of demonstrated activists in human rights from the community. An executive committee composed of representatives of the different programs in the organization handles month-to-month operations. Both the policy-makers and the executive committee meet several times a year to evaluate their work and to plan. The majority of people doing the day-to-day work are volunteers who help staff members and make significant contributions to the programs. The use of volunteers may not be ideal but has been necessary for economic reasons and has also added much spirit and dedication to the organization.

An organization that provides victims with services and referrals as well as public education has a variety of functions to fulfill. The Vicariate's organizational chart is shown in Figure 1, and the functions of its units are mentioned below. While many groups will have a less complex organization, they will want to consider the need or possibility for performing these functions either themselves or in coordination with other institutions.

General Services

This includes administration, information, and publications. The administration unit is responsible for all office operations and maintenance including financial procedures of the HRO. The information unit is responsible for meeting the information needs of the different programs in the HRO and of others concerned with human rights monitoring, such as church groups, lawyers, educators, and so forth. The information unit processes information on abuses of human rights coming from different sources, including foreign and domestic press clips, books, and magazines, and it produces summary reports of major publications. The publication unit is responsible for the printing of the HRO's publications.

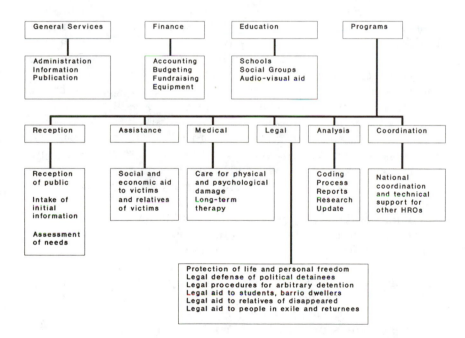

Figure 1. Organizational structure of one human rights organization, the Vicariate of Solidarity (Vicaría de Solidaridad), Chile.

Finances

Included here are accounting, allocation of resources to different programs, fund-raising and equipment acquisition.

Solidarity and Human Rights Education

This area includes developing curricula for schools, universities, and other social institutions to increase knowledge about human rights, organizing workshops for volunteers working in the HRO (internal training), and producing audiovisual material.

Programs: Reception, Social and Legal Assistance, Medical Care, Analysis, and Coordination

Reception involves the initial intake of information, evaluation of the request for help, and referral to the appropriate programs. The social assistance unit provides economic and social aid to political prisoners, relatives of political prisoners and disappeared-detainees, those in internal exile, and those who return from exile. The medical unit consists of a medical team (physician, psychologist, and nurse) that provides medical care to victims in need and documents physical signs of torture on victims, including photographing lesions and other physical sequelae. The Vicariate's work in this area is perhaps the most advanced among human rights groups in the world. The legal unit is responsible for defense in legal proceedings, denunciation of arbitrary detentions, legal and social assistance to relatives of disappeared, legal aid to groups at high risk of repression such as students and shantytown dwellers, and legal aid to exiles and foreigners. An analysis unit maintains individual files on each victim of repression known through the publication unit or other HRO, codifies and files every request for help coming from reception or other program units of this HRO, and develops monthly and yearly reports on violations of human rights. The coordination unit supports and coordinates services to defend and improve human rights in other geographical locations of the country. It coordinates solidarity groups, maintains open communication with them, provides medical and legal expertise when needed, distributes publications, and keeps in contact with people in internal exile.

Relationships with other human rights groups should be maintained carefully. There is a clear need for a flow of accurate information and sharing of material resources. There should be periodic meetings with similar organizations working on behalf of human rights, perhaps under a loose umbrella organization.

Proposed Reporting Guidelines

Definitions

Certain personal human rights are basic since no other rights can conceivably be enjoyed unless these rights are also acknowledged. Thus, for example, while political rights of freedom of association, freedom of speech, and freedom of press are important, "logically preceding them and more fundamentally basic are the [personal] rights to freedom from detention without trial, to freedom from torture, to freedom from extrajudicial execution, and to subsistence. Without these basic rights no other rights are meaningful."[27]

Repressive governments vary their form of repression according to domestic and international pressure. A wave of killing and disappearance may be followed by large numbers of people being arbitrarily detained, tortured, and released or by the appearance of paramilitary forces and death squads. In the climate of violence that prevails in a country where the state allows or perpetrates human rights violations, it is necessary to formulate clear operational definitions for each modality of human rights violation and to continue the process of formulating definitions as states put new forms of violations into practice.

An illustration of this need, and of difficulties in agreeing on common definitions, comes from Chile. In 1983 and 1984, when widespread economic and political problems extending to large sectors of the population led to a rise in protest against the dictatorship and an increase in public demonstrations, the repressive forces shifted their mode of action and became extremely brutal during these demonstrations, without detaining large numbers of people. Government forces, acting in the streets, shantytowns, and open areas and places used for authorized or unauthorized public meetings began to perform routinely the acts detailed in Table 1.[28] Another illustration of the need for making and updating definitions is the case of military operations causing civilian casualties in El Salvador since 1985. These types of actions often have included burning of houses, destruction of crops, harassment of the population, arbitrary detention, collective torture, throat-cutting, violation of women and young girls, air and ground bombardment, and collective intimidation.[29] The detention

TABLE 1. Routine Forms of Physical Abuse by Security Forces Reported in Public Demonstrations in Chile[a]

Beatings with fists, kicks, rifle butts, and chains
Burning of people forced to stand, walk, roll, or lie on open fires
Subjecting people to a mobile unit of electrodes
Pulling the hair of people forced to lie on the ground
Beating of soles of feet or ankles
"Telephone," or clapping the ears while the mouth is kept closed
Forced standing with head bent upwards for long periods of time
Forced running while being beaten or shot at
Beating while running the gauntlet between lines of security forces
Being hit by stones
Being bitten by trained dogs
Being jumped on by security forces while lying on the ground
Hosing of water through mouth and nose
Forced lying on wet ground for long periods of time

[a] Eugenia Rojas, *La definicion de la torture.*

of children in South Africa also represents a special reporting category.

These methods clearly surpass police actions that could be justified as self-defense, and they also violate the basic legal principles of proportionality (police action to be proportionate to its end; that is, not to produce harm greater than if no action were taken) and subsidiarity (police to take the least damaging course of action available). According to the United Nations definition these methods used in this context can be classified as torture or cruel, inhuman, or degrading treatment. The distinction between these terms is subtle. Often the use of the term torture is reserved for a treatment that causes extremely severe pain. A personal human rights abuse surveillance system should allow case definitions that cover a range of place, circumstance, and severity, in this case to document a government's publicly and summarily torturing and abusing citizens who have been neither detained not accused of any crime.

Definitions are also needed for arbitrary detentions. Most detentions of political opponents are arbitrary in that they are not carried out according to international law, even if allowed under government decrees. Article 1 of the United Nations Convention Against Torture specifies that torture "does not include pain or suffering arising only from, inherent in or incidental to lawful sanctions,"[30] but since arbitrary detention is itself illegal, pain or suffering inherent or incidental to this kind of detention is cruel treatment or torture, depending on its severity. It is necessary to document all the circumstances around any arbitrary detention because the detention by itself carries pain and suffering and is an unlawful deprivation of freedom. Arbitrary detentions of individuals or groups can take many forms, during day or night, by unidentified plainclothes or security forces, and so forth. Careful classification of these detentions will allow a rigorous analysis of the human rights situation in a country.

Documentation of torture also needs to go beyond the simplicity of defining physical versus psychological torture. Torture and cruel treatment always have a psychological objective, namely, the control of people's activities directly through pain and indirectly through fear. Regardless of the instrument used for torture—whether electricity or threats to the family—the damage is likely to be both physical and psychological since the human being is a whole and damage to one part results in damage to the remaining parts. Therefore it is necessary to create descriptive categories to document the modalities of torture.

The following definitions follow closely those adopted by the Chilean Commission of Human Rights. These definitions are operational and intended for use in documentation of human rights violations according to international law. They are not based on national legal definitions of similar concepts, which may differ. These definitions are not complete, and are offered as an illustration of and starting point for the work to be done. Development of widely acceptable definitions would require a major collaborative effort by representatives of human rights organizations and by persons with experience in relevant areas such as survey research, human rights international law, and systems analysis.

A necessary approach for producing statistics for analysis is first to establish a definition, such as a definition for murder or political killing, so that one can identify whether a reported death was in fact a killing under that definition. Then for each event, information on characteristics—kind of abuse, circumstances, legal process, method, agent, time, site, physical and social description of the victim, witnesses, and so on—should be obtained. For each of these characteristics a clearly defined set of categories is needed. Here, for example, are suggested guidelines for classifying kinds of "torture or cruel or inhuman treatment" abuses, and their circumstances.

1. Killing. Deprivation of life due to an action executed by government officials or people acting on behalf of the governing regime and carried out with the intention or connotation of political consequences.

- *Summary execution.* Deprivation of life as the consequence of a legal or administrative process, generally brief and disregarding the form and/or spirit of the law.
- *Killing in presumptive armed conflicts.* Deprivation of life explained by public officials as a death in the course of an armed conflict between the opposition and government officials, when the facts have not been adequately proved.
- *Killing by torture.* Deprivation of life as a consequence of torture, applied by public officials or others acting under direct or indirect control of public officials.
- *Killing by abuse of power in a legal process.* Deprivation of life as a consequence of an excessive use of force or violence, without respecting proportionality, by public officials or others acting under their control in an act which is formally legal.
- *Killing in demonstrations by unidentified plainclothes agents.* Deprivation of life of a person by other person(s), who are unidentified and armed in the course of a public demonstration of the opposition.
- *Killing by death squad.* "Gratuitous" killing outside of even the most summary administrative proceeding, by public officials or others acting under their control or with their approbation. This includes a wide range of political assassinations.
- *Genocide.* Systematic killing of a population group by virtue of its general characteristics or location, by public officials or others acting under their control or with their approbation.

2. **Detained-disappeared**. People detained for political or other reasons and whose detention is repeatedly denied by the authorities and whose current location remains unknown in spite of all efforts to find them.

For a detainee to be considered disappeared the following conditions need to be present: (a) habeas corpus report or similar legal procedures to certify the presumptive detention; (b) person is disappeared for a specified minimum number of days (possibly as many as 20 days); (c) the disappeared person needs to be a political dissident or somehow connected to political dissidents or known as an opponent of the government or its agents, or to be part of a category of persons known to be targeted for disappearances; (d) to have exhausted all means to find the disappeared person in hospitals, mortuaries, and so forth, or to have determined that the person has not left the country; (e) the government does not acknowledge the person's detention. However, these conditions are superseded by the presence of witnesses at the time of abduction or detention or any subsequent time, or by other similarly compelling evidence.

3. Arbitrary political detention (arrest, detention, abduction). Arrest, detention, or abduction executed by public officers or people acting under the direct or indirect control of public officers with political intentionality or consequences. In practical terms, deprivation of freedom, for political reasons, when any of the following legal conditions have not been fulfilled: (a) warrant for the arrest; (b) identification of the apprehenders in the presence of witnesses; (c) holding the detainee in public detention centers; (d) providing the detainee an expeditious hearing (which usually means within 24 hours). The arbitrary detention persists until the detainee has a hearing.

- *Individual detention.* Arbitrary detention of an individual political dissident.
- *Massive detention in public demonstrations.* Deprivation of the freedom of one or more persons in the course of a public demonstration, authorized or not authorized by the government.
- *Collective detention.* Deprivation of freedom of a group of persons because of their exercise of their right of association and organization during military occupation of some areas or workplaces. Examples include the military occupation and detention of adult inhabitants of black townships in South Africa or shantytowns in Chile.

4. Political crimes. Political crimes are those for which people are convicted as a result of engaging in activities which are protected as internationally accepted human rights, such as freedom of speech or association. There are two main kinds of political crimes, based on the relationship of the charged offense to international law, or to the charged person's actual activities. First, the protected activity may itself be made illegal. Often, those political activities would not be crimes under a democratic rule, but they are made crimes by the repressive government. These activities include attempts to associate and engage in collective action disapproved of by the government, such as political parties, meetings, unions, or even funerals, as has been the case in South Africa. Second, individuals out of favor with the government may be falsely accused of "ordinary" crimes (like robbery) as a way to eliminate them. Such political prisoners are often indicted and sentenced using sham legal proceedings, confessions taken under harsh interrogation or torture, and false accusations by hired or coerced witnesses. These political prisoners are typically at high risk of continued human rights violations and their condition under imprisonment needs to be followed closely.

5. Exile. Being forced to reside during a specified period of time in places other than the actual residence and other than a place of incarceration.

- *Internal exile.* Being exiled to places within the country other than the actual residence by a judicial or administrative decision.
- *External exile.* Being forced to leave the country due to (a) judicial sentencing, (b) administrative decree, (c) exchange of sentence for expatriation, or (d) "well founded or documented fear of repression or punishment."[31]

6. Torture. According to the 1984 U.N. Convention, torture is "any act by which severe pain or suffering, whether physical or mental, is intentionally inflicted on a person for such purposes as obtaining from him or a third person information or a confession, punishing him for an act he or a third person has committed or is suspected of having committed, or intimidating or coercing him or a third person or for any reason based on discrimination of any kind, when such pain or suffering is inflicted by or at the instigation of or with the consent or acquiescence of a public official or other person acting in an official capacity."[32]

7. Harassment intimidation. Isolated or recurrent acts with the purpose of frightening an individual or a group of people, such as persistent following, verbal threats, anonymous notes, brief kidnappings with or without beating with a political objective, attempted killing.

Intake of Information

Reports of human rights violations may reach a human rights surveillance group through direct sources, such as testimonies by the victim, a next of kin or a witness, or through indirect sources such as the public media. Sources of information should always be noted in HRO records. Each direct complaint of violation of human rights should be carefully documented, starting with an initial testimony. This testimony will be the first step in the defense and rehabilitation of the victim of political repression, in the creation of a national and international awareness of this abuse, and in the promotion of democracy and of internationally accepted human rights principles in that country. A specially trained person should receive either a written testimony or an oral (preferably taped) one, which will be transcribed and signed by the person making the complaint. This testimony will be as complete and detailed as possible. The initial forms will be filled in from information contained in the testimony. A social worker should be able to assess the social, legal, medical, and psychological needs of the victim.

After the priorities for the victims are established, they will be referred to the different service programs within or outside of the human rights organization. The professional staff who will take care of the victims should enter in the protocol all pertinent data on their area of expertise. All information gathered in this process or subsequent actions taken should be filed in a personal folder with an identification number.[33] This is the case management record. Confidentiality policies and procedures should be discussed with the informant, along with possible uses of the data; evidence used for denunciations or legal proceedings will be inherently public, while medical records are confidential. For cases based on indirect reports, such as violations reported by the press, a different set of procedures needs to be followed including detailed accounts of all sources of information and cross-validations carried out.[34]

Forms for recording intake information should be tailored to both the specific information being collected by an HRO and to the particular process of data collection. For this reason, no general model form is presented here. In general, data recording and entry is more efficient and accurate if forms are organized to follow the flow of information intake and are as clear as possible in terms of both the meaning of questions and possible responses. Forms should include places on them for entering codes, and where possible the codes themselves, so that the data can be entered into the computer directly from the original form without an additional coding form being required.

Protocol Information

General information plus details of the abuses that occurred, along with information on physical and psychological symptoms following it, should be gathered to document the above-mentioned human rights violations. Forms should leave room for later addition of data on the health and legal consequences of the abuses.

General information. Name, case number, age, sex, ethnicity (including indigenous status), birth date and place, address, marital status, number of children, level of education, employment status, most recent and most common occupations, and (optional) participation in any volunteer, church, labor, or political groups. Names will be included in case files but may be excluded from any computerized records of abuse cases. In addition, there should be a chronology for each episode involving claims of abuse, including information on these variables:

If killed. Information covering date, place, agents, circumstances, and witnesses, whether executed, death under torture, death in armed conflict, summary execution, killed in demonstration, death while in detention, premeditated killing, other deaths at the hands of agents of the state, or attempted murders. An inquiry and an autopsy procedure should follow any case in which there are reasons to suspect that an arbitrary killing has occurred. A protocol for an adequate autopsy and investigation has been proposed by the Minnesota Lawyers International Human Rights Committee.[35]

If detained. Date, place, and form of detention (kidnapping, arbitrary, legal); branch of police, paramilitary, or military forces involved; kind of detention (individual, collective, massive); length and places of detention and of abuse; names of places and people involved in the detention; names of other detainees seen during detention; information on habeas corpus or other legal procedures (charges, judicial proceedings, sentences, appeals, etc.); date and circumstances of regaining freedom.

If disappeared. Date, place, witnesses, names of people, government forces, other circumstances. Victim characteristics, including physical appearance, weight, height, blood type, hair (color, type, amount, facial hair), fractured bones (place, year), history of bone diseases (e.g., osteomyelitis, spina bifida), scars, congenital malformations, severe lesions, severe illnesses, skull (size, shape), physical proportions of body parts, number of pregnancies, handedness (left or right); names, telephone numbers, and addresses of all physicians, dentists, clinics or hospitals where the disappeared person has ever received medical care (x-rays, medical and dental records should be obtained as soon as possible); dress at time of abduction and any other identifying characteristics of physical appearance, including photographs, especially recent, frontal ones. If dental records are not available, family or others should be asked to supply any identifying dental information such as teeth color, chips, missing teeth, fillings, malocclusion, and so forth.

If in exile. For each episode, place, date, administrative decree. For external exile, whether prohibited reentry, sentence commuted by exile, reentry application filed, authorized reentry (returnee).

If threatened. Form of threats (phone calls, written threats, being followed, verbal abuse, isolated instances of physical violence such as shots and sham accidents, other forms of threats), possible reasons for threats, other people involved.

If tortured. The following information on methods of torture should be gathered:

Beating. With what (slapping, kicking, punching, beating with weapons such as rifle butts, whips, heavy sticks, wet towels), parts of body beaten, specific types of beating such as *teléfono* (clapping on ears while mouth shut) or *phalanga* (beating of soles of feet).

Electricity. Parts of body involved, specific method such as *picaña* or *parrilla* (use of metal bed frame).

Asphyxiation. When done with liquids, called *submarino*. How done, specific method such as *submarino seco* (putting the head in a plastic bag) or *submarino mojado* (immersion in filthy fluid such as water with urine and excrements).

Burns. Burn agent (e.g., cigarettes, boiling water, burning sticks, chemicals), parts of the body burned, mode of use (e.g., used against public demonstrations by throwing people into fires burning in the streets).

Forced postures. (1) Suspension: hanging the victim by the thumbs or arms or legs. A modification is the *pau de arara* (parrot's perch) or hanging the victim from a stick between knees and arms bound tightly together. (2) *Planton* or forced standing, often under the elements, for many hours. (3) Stretching or *potro*: stretching of limbs and trunk. (4) Other forced postures such as isolation with forced sitting or kneeling.

Sexual. Sexual molestation, rape by someone of the other or the same sex, introduction of objects into vagina or rectum.

Nail removal. Extraction of finger or toe nails.

Isolation. Detention in solitary confinement for more than 72 hours.

Physical deprivation. Attempts to induce debility by deprivation of food or water (for more than 48 hours) or sleep (for more than 24 hours).

Other methods of physical torture. Being pulled by the hair, forced jumping or being thrown from heights, other.

Sensorial stress. Bright lights, loud music or noise, blindfolding, cold showers, extreme heat or cold, restriction of movement.

Degradation. Deprivation of personal hygiene, denial of privacy, verbal abuse, overcrowding, infected surroundings, nakedness.

Threat. Sham executions; threats of death, execution, or further torture; threats to family or friends.

Torture by witness. Being made to watch or listen to the torture of others, including family or friends; having family or friends present at one's own torture.

Occasional indulgence. Change of repressor to role of ally in order to disorient the victim.

Hypnosis. Use of hypnosis to control the victim's will.

Pharmacologic manipulation. Use of oral, intramuscular, or intravenous drugs to break the victim's will or harm him/her psychologically or physiologically.

It is important that the *participation of medical personnel in torture* should also be reported in detail, including places, times, and names, activities, and behavior of medical personnel.

In all the above situations, legal procedures may take place, either by the government against the victim (often under national security laws) or by the victim against the government (usually litigations for physical, psychological, social, and financial damages). All circumstances of these litigations should be documented in the victim's file kept by the human rights organization.

If a victim is referred for medical care, the following information will be coded from the physical exam: family history of disease; symptoms before, during, and after detention and torture; review of systems in the medical exam; diagnosis; and follow-up as it occurs. With or without medical referral, however, a standard physical symptoms checklist will be appended for ease of coding and data reporting of physiological sequelae of abuse.

If a victim is referred for psychological care, the following information will be coded from the psychological exam: symptoms before, during, and after the detention and torture occurred; reported changes in personality and behavior immediately after the repressive events; diagnosis; recommendations; and follow-up as it occurs. With or without psychological referral, however, a standard psychological symptoms checklist will be appended for ease of coding and data reporting of psychological sequelae of abuse.

The evolution of legal procedures and of medical and psychological care should be updated in the original file containing the testimony.

Data Protection

Nongovernmental organizations (NGOs) should take all feasible security measures to safeguard the integrity and confidentiality of the data they collect.

There are a number of ways to approach maintaining security on personal computers (PCs). PCs with hard disk drives can be equipped with keys to lock the drive. This limits access to the computer for anyone without a key. While this system can provide some protection against sabotage, it can be circumvented by opening the computer and physically removing the hard disk drive, either on site or after stealing the PC.

Another approach to securing the confidentiality of computer files is to keep sensitive or identifying information in a separate location, access to which is tightly controlled. Records in the data file are only identified by record numbers, which correspond to those in the file(s) of identifying information. Names, places, dates, and other identifying information may all be replaced by such numeric codes in the main data file.

A variant of this approach is to label as many field names in the data file as one wishes with an arbitrary name (i.e., field1, field2, . . .), and to code them with arbitrary code values; the keys to the codes are kept in separate lists or file(s) which can be physically removed from the main data file except when needed to code or decode it. Such decoding or identifying lists can be kept on paper or floppy disks and removed from the main data file each night. This security system can be beaten by physically locating and obtaining both files. It is also a cumbersome approach, since the keys to the codes must be connected to the main program whenever the latter is to be used. This makes use of the file difficult even for those who properly have access to all the files and codes involved. The more uninterpretable the main file is by itself, due to numeric identifiers or arbitrary field names and value codes, the more cumbersome it will be for the operator to use.

A third approach to securing confidential computer data is encryption of files. This involves saving the file in a scrambled state which can only be retrieved and unscrambled by properly entering a password. Access to the files can then be limited to those knowing the password, and passwords can be changed periodically. A number of software programs now readily available allow encryption with password protection at little cost. One example is the program Superkey, which costs about $70 (U.S.). Archiving programs, which save the files in condensed form, may also allow use of a password to prevent unauthorized persons from un-archiving the file into a usable form.

Files should be protected not only from theft or intrusion, but also from unintentional or accidental loss. They should be regularly backed up onto other disks. It is also advisable to send copies of updated files to secure sources out of the country.

Ultimately, such measures may only offer limited protection of information files about human rights abuses from loss or improper access. The security or repressive apparatus of the state can use not only technical resources to obtain or destroy the information, but often legal resources as well. A recent example is the Chilean military's attempts to obtain the case records of the Vicariate in connection with prosecution of charges against some of the organization's medical staff who were accused of providing medical care to someone alleged to be involved in a robbery. The Vicariate refused to turn over the records.

Data Utilization

The first goal of any human rights organization is to help the victims and their families. Once the assistance function of the HRO is asserted, the next priority is prevention of further abuses through publicity and denunciation. The data collection system that we propose here allows production of periodic reports describing the human rights situation in any given country. Since there is a large amount and diversity of violations of personal human rights, statistical and graphical methods are a logical way to organize and summarize the data when the mere enumeration of instances of human rights violations becomes insufficient to demonstrate the magnitude of the problem. This approach has often been used by human rights groups; for example, monthly counts of arbitrary detentions, torture incidents, disappearances, and extrajudicial executions have been published by the Chilean Human Rights Commission and Socorro Juridico. Those counts can be classified by age, sex, occupation, and so forth to provide a profile of the victims.

Methods of analytical epidemiology can also be used to identify high risk groups and to compute human rights indexes, such as incidence of arbitrary detention, torture, disappearance, and extrajudicial execution. This analysis would aim not only at denouncing the human rights violations but at preventing them through forecasting the tendencies of the national repressive apparatus.

Some of these points can be illustrated using data from Chile. Since 1979, the Chilean Commission on Human Rights has been publishing monthly reports with numbers of human rights violations. They classify violations of individuals' rights to protection of life, security, and integrity of the person by increasing severity of the pain and harm inflicted, from harrassment and intimidation through arbitrary political detention, torture, and disappearance and finally to political killing. These data show the magnitude of abuses, their distribution by type of abuse, and time trends overall and for each type of abuse.

To illustrate the insights that can be gained from statistical presentations, data from the Commission's reports are shown in Tables 2–4 and Figures 2–3. Note that these data refer to numbers of known victims, not numbers of incidents. Table 2 and Figure 2 show the number of persons affected annually, between 1979 and 1986, by four kinds of human rights violations. From Figure 2 it is evident that numbers of victims of all four kinds of violations increased dramatically between 1982 and 1983, and remained at a higher level through 1986 than had been recorded prior to 1983. In May of 1983 the political opposition to the government began to organize monthly demonstrations, which became less systematic later. The observed increases in repression reflect the Pinochet regime's reaction to this increased level of public protests.

Table 3 and Figure 3 show additional detail for detentions by category. From 1979 to 1983, most detentions were from individual arrests or from mass arrests made during the occasional public protests. In 1984 the military began occupying poor neighborhoods of the capital, arresting for varying periods all males over age 15. This kind of action, called collective detention by the commission, explains the number of detainees exceeding 30,000 in 1984 and 21,000 in 1986.

Table 4 shows the monthly numbers of individual detentions from 1979 to 1986. For the years 1979 to 1982 there is no clear seasonal pattern, but thereafter peaks occur regularly in September (the anniversary of the 1973 coup) or October and troughs during the summer vacation months of January and February.

Computerized data bases on human rights will increase the speed of access to large amounts of information that may be used as evidence in court. Examples from Argentina are the data base of testimonies of victims of disappearance collected by CELS, and the blood data base established by the Grandmothers of Plaza de Mayo with the purpose of identifying their missing grandchildren through genetic evidence of grandparenthood.[36] In Chile, the Vicariate has long had a computerized data base.

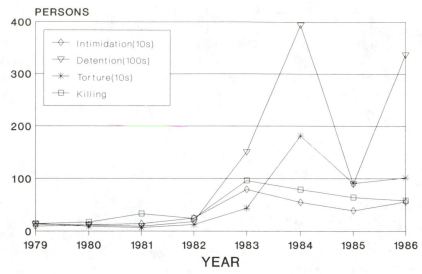

Source: Chilean Human Rights Commission

Figure 2. Persons subjected to human rights violations, Chile, 1979–1986.

TABLE 2. Persons Subjected to Human Rights Violations, Chile, 1979–1986

Type of violation	Year								
	1979	*1980*	*1981*	*1982*	*1983*	*1984*	*1985*	*1986*	*Total*
Intimidation & harassment	92	118	140	245	794	549	390	559	2887
Detention	1325	1129	911	1789	15077	39429	8901	33665	102226
Torture & mistreatment	143	91	68	123	434	1810	907	1013	4589
Killing	14	17	33	24	96	79	64	58	385

Source: Chilean Commission on Human Rights: 1979–1983, Annual report 1983; 1984, Monthly report, December 1984; 1985, Annual report 1985; 1986, Annual report 1986.

Research on physical and mental health effects of political repression could be carried out by analyzing these data on human rights violations. This research could result in a better recognition of the damage caused to the individual victim, to the victim's family, to specific subgroups, and to the general population living in the climate of repression. Therefore, the rehabilitation of the victim both as a member of society, through legal compensation and political recognition, and as a human individual, by the restoration of physical and mental integrity through therapy, will benefit from the analysis of data on human rights violations.[37]

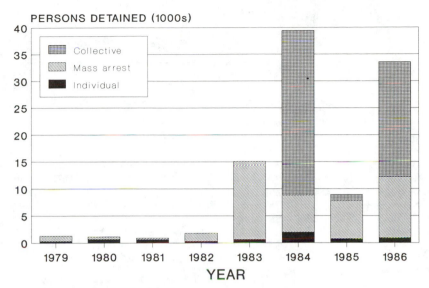

Source: Chilean Human Rights Commission

Figure 3. Persons detained by type and year, Chile, 1979–1986.

TABLE 3. Persons Subjected to Political Detention, Chile, 1979–1986

Type of violation	Year								Total
	1979	1980	1981	1982	1983	1984	1985	1986	
Individual	323	678	648	306	641	1,960	739	921	6,216
Mass arrest	1,002	451	263	1,483	14,436	6,895	7,063	11,304	42,897
Collective						30,574	1,099	21,307	52,980
Disappearance								76	76
Total	1,325	1,129	911	1,789	15,077	39,429	8,901	33,608	102,169
Average/month	110	94	76	149	1,256	3,286	742	2,801	8,514
% of total	1.3	1.1	0.9	1.8	14.8	38.6	8.7	32.9	100.1

Source: Chilean Commission on Human Rights: 1979–1983, Annual report 1983; 1984, Monthly report December 1984; 1985, Annual report 1985; 1986, Annual report 1986.

Conclusion

The human value of procedures that contribute to protecting human beings from being kidnapped, tortured, and murdered should be obvious enough as to not require elaborate comment or justification. Perhaps the value of protecting people's basic personal human rights does need reinforcement, given the human rights records of many governments and the impetus of some others to dismiss or ignore such abuses by shifting the focus from violations of the integrity of

TABLE 4. Individual Detentions by Month and Year: Chile, 1979–1986

Month	1979	1980	1981	1982	Year 1983	1984	1985	1986	Total
January	25	17	61	35	26	25	46	30	265
February	7	5	53	20	20	28	53	49	235
March	29	25	115	44	65	136	53	45	512
April	17	68	61	38	59	173	102	60	578
May	28	126	50	22	42	109	68	59	504
June	28	17	35	31	55	105	31	63	365
July	25	113	46	22	78	229	52	72	637
August	43	56	27	20	56	163	73	70	508
September	45	109	33	31	84	47	129	170	648
October	25	39	31	13	60	530	80	111	889
November	16	78	96	14	62	276	22	126	690
December	35	25	40	16	34	139	30	66	385
Total	323	678	648	306	641	1960	739	921	6216
Average/month	26.9	56.5	54.0	25.5	53.4	163.3	61.6	76.8	51.8
% of total	5.2	10.9	10.4	4.9	10.3	31.5	11.9	14.8	99.9

Source: Chilean Commission on Human Rights: 1979–1983, Annual report 1983; 1984, Monthly report December 1984; 1985, Annual report 1985; 1986, Annual report 1986.

the person to other categories of human rights.[38] Basic human rights are traditionally conceived and understood to start from the most fundamental concept of protection of the individual from physical and psychological violence. However, concepts of civil and political rights are rather more abstract, culturally and politically contingent, and ideologically manipulable, rooted in the idea of particular political forms that may reflect very different kinds of personal, social, economic, and political realities and experiences—which may or may not include protection of persons from harm by the state.[39]

But the question of human rights *is* fundamentally a political one, since their protection or abuse is a function and a practice of governments. The protection of people from systematic violence and abuse is a basic role of the state, and widespread torture is either a practice of states or an indication of their inability to function. Internal attempts to end human rights abuses are properly directed to governments, and those engaged in such attempts often are, or become defined as, part of the political opposition that the abuses are designed to silence. International responses are also directed to both the violator states themselves and to their allies that support them by contributing directly to the terrorist infrastructure or to the general credibility and stability of the abusive government.

Where human rights are a consideration in the behavior of these "terrorist support states," as, for example, is the case according to U.S. statute (and occasionally operationally, via congressional politics), it is important to establish common, accepted definitions of human rights and standards for reporting abuses.[40] Such definitions and standards acceptable to the international scientific and human rights communities should be less amenable to manipulation by particular governments seeking to justify their own internal or foreign policies for their own political agendas than is currently the case with national human rights standards and policies. Ultimately, the pressure to stop human rights abuses must be political pressure, and such pressure, from whatever source and directed toward any object, must benefit from being credible and reliable, less subject to being challenged or dismissed on technical grounds.

In summary, a system of documentation to produce the most valid and reliable reports possible is needed to assess objectively and credibly the systematic violation of basic human rights. Clear operational definitions are needed to measure such violations validly and accurately, that is, to know what we want to measure and that that is what we are actually measuring. Accuracy is closely linked to lack of bias; an accurate method of measurement will produce unbiased estimators. The protocol's maximization of specific verifiable data will guard against overestimation of the abuse problem to the extent possible in a given military-political situation, so that if there is any bias in reports it will be in the direction of underestimation of the problem (literally a conservative bias). Improved validity can also increase verifiability by allowing cross-validation of information coming from different sources, provided they use common definitions. Standardization of data gathering makes it possible to obtain more reliable information, with consequent improvement in precision and reduction in variance of the measures used in human rights reports. And, along with improving validity and reliability, standard measures will increase comparability by allowing comparisons or pooling of reports that have been codified in the same form.

The guidelines suggested here might ultimately be most useful because of their effect on the dissemination of information on human rights abuses. They could improve security both for the data—by making it more easily transferrable to locations beyond the control of national security forces—and for the people involved in the reporting. This is because they can lead to better publicity; heightened visibility raises the potential political costs of verifiable abuses, and, furthermore, reducing the vulnerability of reports to attacks on their credibility increases the likelihood of those reports being publicized widely.

The problem of security for the victims who make the reports to the human rights organization will not be easily solved, but then it is the lack of personal security that is the problem to begin with. There may be increased personal risk in reporting abuses for those making the report, or the perception of increased risk. Therefore, the question of security needs to be discussed with all informants at the time their testimony is taken. CELS has a good policy, offering the alternative of taking testimony in anonymity and requesting the victim's consent before publicly reporting any information that could allow personal identification. The reporting system could be used to support the claims of external refugees to political asylum, based on a "well-founded (and documented) fear of persecution" as individuals and even as members of groups shown to be at high risk of torture or killing in their own countries.

Clearly, one use for comparable and reliable data would be to establish whether there is a "gross and consistent pattern" of abuses by a government. Protocols should be developed to judge this. Such protocols would include standards defining abuses such as we have discussed in this chapter. In addition, they would set out the obligations of states once violations have occurred. Currently the prevalent responses of accused governments are to deny the occurrence of abuses, and for cases they cannot deny to claim that they are isolated incidents not reflecting state policy. The twin protocols for ascertaining abuses and official responses to them could test these claims. They could be the basis for showing the extent to which such abuses exist, and, where they do, establishing the degree to which human rights violations are indeed part and parcel of deliberate policy, or are isolated actions that are aggressively investigated and punished by the government.

Despite repression, HROs have been able to survive and continue their work. Human rights workers and activists, in growing numbers, have begun to meet and exchange information and experiences. These meetings have been useful in identifying common problems and for starting communications networks for using common languages to share information.

The Inter-American Institute for Human Rights in San José, Costa Rica has provided training and advisory services to human rights groups in Central America; the Washington Office for Latin America and Americas Watch have organized seminars to examine methodological issues with non-governmental groups; and a representative of CELS from Argentina recently met with human rights organizations in Peru to share computer software on documentation of human rights. A need persists for meetings of these and other human rights groups to share experiences and methodologies and to develop common standards.

Several international organizations have shown interest in the problems of field reporting of basic human rights violations. The Human Rights Information and Documentation System (HURIDOCS) in Oslo, Norway is a global network whose objective is to optimize the system of exchange of information between groups dedicated to human rights. HURIDOCS has developed standard formats for recording information on human rights violations for documentation and communication on its network. The formats are designed to facilitate information exchange while being flexible enough to adapt to different needs. These formats, which represent a collaborative effort, are described in detail in Chapter 5.

The Commission for the Defense of Human Rights in Central America (CODEHUCA) in San José, Costa Rica defends and promotes human rights in Central America. Since 1986 it has been working to establish an information, documentation, and communication network. CODEHUCA has developed a thesaurus with accompanying protocols and software. They keep a data base of human rights violations by events and actions in defense and data bases of organizations and of bibliographic references.

The Chilean Human Rights Network in Santiago, Chile recently developed a common thesaurus and organized the first Latin American seminar on information and human rights, specifically oriented to the use of computers in HROs.

The Network of Communication and Scientific Documentation in Mental Health and Human Rights was originally organized around mental health workers in the Western hemisphere, but its scope has been expanded to include health in a broader and global perspective. Major goals include the organization of a global network, development of a thesaurus, computerized automation of the centers, and the selection of a telecommunications system.

There have been some efforts towards standardization of procedures of non-governmental human rights organizations. The adoption of a standard reporting protocol suggests as a logical next step the establishment of a central repository for reports of abuses, from which these reports can be analyzed and published regularly. Regular publication of statistics on incidence of torture and related events of state terrorism would allow for the computation of indexes of human rights violations and the tracking of these over time. Such reports could be used to isolate terrorist states and to hold them and governments allied with them accountable for their support of such practices. The information from these protocols, and from reports compiled from them, would be useful to groups and governments everywhere interested in working on behalf of the individuals and populations victimized by the terrorism of their own governments.

The authors wish to acknowledge the help of the following: Dr. Lindsey Thomas and the Minnesota Lawyers International Human Rights Committee; Dr. Diane Sandler, Department of Criminology, University of Cape Town, South Africa; Jeff Budlander; Jeff Ritterman of Southern Africa Medical Aid Fund; Luis Soler Vicent of the Process and Analysis Unit and Ramiro Olivares of the Medical Department of Vicariate of Solidarity; Elisa Cisternas and Pablo Fuenzalidas of the Chilean Human Rights Commission; Fanny Pollarollo, Maria Eugenia Rojas, Elizabeth Lira, and Eugenia Weinstein of FASIC, Santiago; the mental health team at CELS, Buenos Aires, and particularly therapists Matilde Ruderman, Beatriz Veraldi, and Ruben García; data analyst Daniel Frontalini, CELS, Buenos Aires; the Inter-American Institute of Human Rights in Costa Rica, in particular Roberto Cuéllar; Socorro Juridico and the (nongovernmental) Human Rights Commission of El Salvador; and Dr. Cristian Orrego and Dr. Mary-Claire King, School of Public Health, University of California, Berkeley. Special thanks also to Eric Stover, Thomas Jabine, Juan Méndez, and Robert Parke for their thoughtful and critical reviews.

Notes

1. Amnesty International, *Amnesty International Report 1980* (London: Amnesty International Publications, 1980).

2. Amnesty International, *Amnesty International Report 1984* (London: Amnesty International Publications, 1984); Americas Watch and the American Civil Liberties Union, *Report on Human Rights in El Salvador* (New York, Vintage Books, 1982).

3. For Latin America, for example, see António Cavalla Rojas, *Geopolítica y Seguridad Nacional en América*, Lecturas Universitarias #31 (México DF: Universidad Nacional Autónoma de México, 1979). See also Edward S. Herman, *The Real Terror Network: Terrorism in Fact and Propaganda* (Boston: South End Press, 1982).

4. Ibid.

5. Human Rights Watch, *The Persecution of Human Rights Monitors, December 1986 to December 1987: A Worldwide Survey* (New York: Human Rights Watch, 1987).

6. Vicaría de la Solidaridad, *Noveno Año de Labor* (Santiago: Arzobispado de Santiago, 1984).

7. R. Dominguez and Eugenia Weinstein, "Aiding Victims of Political Repression in Chile: A Psychological and Psychotherapeutic Approach," unpublished manuscript, Christian Churches Social Aid Foundation (FASIC), 1985.

8. For explanations of these categories see the section on definitions.

9. Comisión Chilena de Derechos Humanos, *Informe Anual* (Santiago: Comisión Chilena de Derechos Humanos, 1984).

10. Foundation for the Protection of Children Damaged in Periods of Emergency (PIDEE), *Resena de Actividades* (Santiago: PIDEE, 1984).

11. Committee for the Defense of the Rights of the People (CODEPU) International Representation: Kirsten Helin, Case Postale 213, 1211 Geneva 21, Switzerland.

12. Comisión Nacional contra la tortura en Chile, *Acta Constitutiva de la Comisión Nacional contra la Tortura* (Santiago: Comisión Nacional contra la tortura en Chile, 1983).

13. Emilio Fermín Mignone, *Organizaciones de Derechos Humanos en Argentina*, Mimeograph.

14. Physicians for Human Rights, *Record* 1, No. 3 (Spring 1988): 7.

15. Alicia Martín and Julio Daniel Frontalini, *CELS: Programa de documentación, estudios y publicaciones sobre el registro testimonial de la represión* (Buenos Aires: Center for Legal and Social Studies, 1985).

16. *Profiles* magazine for Kaypro users (June 1985).

17. Center for Legal and Social Studies, *Programa de Prevención y Asistencia en Salud Mental para Afectados Directos por la Represión* (Buenos Aires: CELS, 1985).

18. Don Foster and Diane Sandler, *A Study of Detention and Torture in South Africa*, preliminary report (Cape Town: University of Cape Town, Institute of Criminology, 1985). See also D. Foster et al., *Detention and Torture in South Africa: Psychological, Legal and Historical Studies* (New York: St. Martin's Press, 1987).

19. United Nations, "Convention Against Torture and Other Cruel, Inhuman or Degrading Treatment," U.N. Doc. E/CN.4/1984/L.2, Annex (1984), reprinted in E. Stover and E. O. Nightingale, eds., *The Breaking of Bodies and Minds: Torture, Psychiatric Abuse, and the Health Professions* (New York: W. H. Freeman, 1985).

20. Foster and Sandler, *A Study of Detention and Torture in South Africa* (note 18).

21. United Nations, Convention Against Torture (note 19).

22. Amnesty International Mission to El Salvador (July 6–13, 1983).

23. Archbishop Oscar Romero Christian Legal Aid Service, *Report on Human Rights in El Salvador, January to December 1985* (San Salvador: Christian Legal Aid Service, 1986).

24. Holly Burkhalter and Aryeh Neier, *Managing the Facts: How the Administration Deals with Reports of Human Rights Abuses in El Salvador* (New York: Americas Watch Committee, December 1985).

25. Christian Legal Aid Service, *Report on Human Rights in El Salvador* (note 23).

26. Fourth and Fifth National Faculty Delegations to Central America, *Education and Human Rights in Central America: Reports of the Fourth and Fifth Faculty Delegations to Central America* (Berkeley: University of California Faculty for Human Rights in El Salvador and Central America, 1985).

27. Robert Matthews and Cranford Pratt, "Human Rights and Foreign Policy: Principles and Canadian Practice," *Human Rights Quarterly* 7, No. 2 (May 1983): 159–88.

28. E. Rojas, "La definición de la tortura en el contexto de la práctica de

la aplicación de la tortura en Chile, 1983–1984" (Santiago: 1985); Comisión Nacional contra la tortura en Chile, *Biannual Report* (Santiago: Comisión Nacional contra la tortura en Chile, 1984). The use of these forms of repression in Chile were publicized with the widely reported cases of two teenagers who were doused with gasoline and set afire by the military in July 1986; one of the teenagers, from the U.S., died.

29. See notes 24–27 for documentation of these practices.

30. U.N. Convention Against Torture (note 19).

31. This latter is the language in the U.S. code for determining eligibility for political refugee status of exile-immigrants to the U.S. See 8 U.S.C. S.1101(a)(42)(A) (1982).

32. U.N. Convention Against Torture (note 19).

33. A. J. Cienfuegos and C. Monelli, "The Testimony of Repression as a Therapeutic Instrument," *American Journal of Orthopsychiatry* 53 (1983): 43–51. This is also based on forms used for data coding in the Vicariate, FASIC, CCHDH, CELS, and the Institute of Criminology in Cape Town.

34. Martín and Frontalini, *CELS* (note 15); Vicaría de la Solidaridad, *Noveno Año de Labor* (note 6); Domínguez and Weinstein, "Aiding Victims of Political Repression in Chile" (note 7).

35. Minnesota Lawyers International Human Rights Committee, "Protecting the right to be free from arbitrary killing through an adequate autopsy and investigation into the cause of death," unpublished manuscript (Minneapolis, 1985).

36. Martin and Frontalini, *CELS* (note 15); Ana Maria di Lonardo, Pierre Darlu, Max Baur, Cristian Orrego and Mary-Claire King, "Human Genetics and Human Rights: Identifying the Families of Kidnapped Children," *American Journal of Forensic Medicine and Pathology* 5 (1984): 339–47.

37. Elizabeth Lira and Eugenia Weinstein, "Psicoterpia y represión política," *Siglo* XXI (1984); Stover and Nightingale, *The Breaking of Bodies and Minds* (note 19).

38. C. Maechling, "Human Rights Dehumanized," *Foreign Policy* (Fall 1983): 118–35. See also Matthews and Pratt, "Human Rights and Foreign Policy: Principles and Canadian Practice" (note 27).

39. Ibid.

40. Maechling, "Human Rights Dehumanized"; Conclusion of the International Seminar on Torture in Latin America, Buenos Aires, December 1985.

Chapter 5
HURIDOCS Standard Formats as a Tool in the Documentation of Human Rights Violations

Judith Dueck

Human rights organizations in many countries are now actively documenting human rights violations. The basic assumption underlying their painstaking work is that by increasing access to often suppressed or hidden information about inhumanity, those whose humanity is threatened or attacked and those acting on their behalf can be empowered. Information is power. Accurate information about rights, laws, and process, as well as evidence of violations allow individuals, groups, and organizations to take action. This is the premise on which an organization called the Human Rights Information and Documentation System, International (HURIDOCS) was founded in 1982. Martin Ennals, the founding president, explained the rationale for HURIDOCS in these terms:

Information on all aspects of human rights is essential to the universal protection and promotion of human rights. The rapid increase of interest in human rights coincides with the rapid development of information technology. Unless a common and universal system of communication of human rights information is evolved, valuable information will be wasted, existing international machinery will not function, standards and codes agreed between governments and within professional bodies will not become known and their implementation not monitored.

HURIDOCS is a global network of over one hundred human rights organizations. Its aim is to improve access to public information on human rights through more effective and appropriate methods that are compatible with other techniques of information handling. HURIDOCS itself does not collect documents but rather supports and works within a decentralized network of organizations concerned with documentation and information. This chapter describes the efforts of the HURIDOCS Task Force to specify standardized documentation of human rights violations.

One of the purposes of the HURIDOCS network of human rights organizations is to promote the protection of human rights through the wider dissemination of public information on human rights. It aims to facilitate the recording and flow of human rights information through the linking of the participants in the network. A very important component in fulfilling this aim is to bring about the establishment of common or compatible information systems. A high degree of compatibility between information systems can only be achieved if the formats used in the recording and exchange of human rights information are coherent and standardized throughout the network.

The HURIDOCS Standard Formats[1] described in this chapter are intended to assist human rights organizations to record and communicate information related to human rights violations. They were created in response to direct requests from human rights organizations and are based on existing forms, stated requirements, extensive discussion within the Task Force and HURIDOCS network, as well as input from other experts in the field of human rights. It is hoped that the formats will function as a general tool which will facilitate efficient documentation of many types of rights violations. Although the formats can be used to record information concerning many types of violations, a particular emphasis has been placed on torture, arrests and detention, deaths and killings, displacements and destruction of property, disappearances, as well as deportations, external exile, and banishments.

In order to introduce the reader to the HURIDOCS project, this chapter will (1) provide background information about the HURIDOCS Task Force; (2) supply an example of the effective use of standard formats; (3) examine some of the issues that have arisen in the Task Force discussions; and (4) present an overview of the formats as they have been developed to this point.

Background Information

In 1985, HURIDOCS published the *HURIDOCS Standard Formats for the Recording and Exchange of Information on Human Rights*.[2] This book contains forms and guidelines for recording information about published or printed documents on human rights and human rights organizations. These formats are based on international library standards but have been adjusted to meet the needs of human rights organizations engaging in documentation for action. They are being used by a growing number of human rights and related organizations all over the world.

A large number of human rights organizations in developing countries with concrete experience in responding to violations of human rights recommended that forms be developed to facilitate the recording and exchange of information related to the events surrounding human rights violations. The requests for such events-formats to record human rights violations became stronger after the publication of the bibliographic Standard Formats. Those present at the Second General Assembly of HURIDOCS, which took place in April 1986 in Rome, reemphasized the need for such standard formats and a Task Force Leader (this author) was appointed at that time.

A draft paper prepared by the Task Force Leader, based on actual formats used by human rights organizations in their documentation systems, was presented at a meeting of the 19th World Conference of the Society for International Development in New Delhi, India, in March 1988. A HURIDOCS Task force was subsequently appointed and its first meeting was held in Manila in November 1988. (Task Force members are listed in Appendix A.) This Task Force reviewed the document in some depth and made revisions. The formats were then sent to a number of human rights organizations to examine, test, and make suggestions for further revision. In July 1989, a second Task Force meeting was held in Utrecht to continue revisions. At that time, an additional HURIDOCS Conference brought together approximately 25 participants from different intergovernmental and nongovernmental organizations. The meeting assessed the progress made by the Task Force. Conference members strongly encouraged the Task Force and directed it to continue to test and refine the formats. Because the Conference anticipated ongoing input from many groups, it also expressed its conviction that formats should be comprehensive and achieve a broad coverage to serve the variety of needs in the global human rights community.

In 1990 and 1991 the Task Force continued the process of testing, refining, and publishing the standard formats in a preliminary version. A data base computer program[3] has been simultaneously developed although the formats are designed to be used in manual, computerized word processor or data base systems. The formats were translated into Spanish in preparation for a HURIDOCS training session held in Latin America. Hopefully translation into other languages will be possible. A wide variety of organizations and individuals have had input into the project, and for this reason the formats carry commensurate credibility.

The CELS Example

In 1986, the government of President Raúl Ricardo Alfonsín passed the so-called "Ley de punto final" in response to pressure from the Argentine military to put an end to criminal trials of human rights violators, including members of the military Juntas. This law stipulated a time limit of 60 days during which to present any further accusations. After this time—the end point—punitive action against those incriminated would cease, thus eliminating the prospects for investigations of the whereabouts and situations of detainees and disappeared persons.[4] In the face of this development, human rights organizations turned for help to the reporting system developed and used for several years in Buenos Aires by the Center for Legal and Social Studies (CELS).[5] In the CELS formats, perpetrators were identified in terms of the time of the incident reported, place, roles of persons involved, and official posts. The use of formats along with thorough analysis greatly improved the possibilities of pinpointing the personal responsibility of suspected perpetrators. The task was indeed monumental as over 1,000 perpetrators were identified by name. At the end of the 60-day deadline, 450 cases were processed and subsequently reported in a publication that came to be widely used by lawyers throughout Argentina for hundreds of judicial actions.

The same formats continue to be used to produce publications to assist social, political, and local municipal organizations to exert pressure by identifying and coping with the presence in their communities of those rights violators who have evaded the law or otherwise benefited by the laws designed to foreclose accountability of perpetrators.

This example of the use of formats for documentation purposes illustrates their necessity when precise and speedy references were required from a great amount of information or when generalizations were needed based upon attributes found in different files and source documents. There were also many advantages at the recording stage due to the reduction in the amount of information used and the speed with which the operative data could be entered. The careful selection of fields and use of codes made this process possible. Use of CELS standard formats allowed for verification through comparisons and systematic sorting, particularly when faced with apparently contradictory data. Dissemination was enhanced by eliminating ambiguities and contradictions at the source of the information. A cohesive report drawing all the source material together could be sent to a number of organizations. With the use of the standard formats, repetitive work was reduced to a minimum. Joint activities and the effective pooling of information would have been impossible without the use of the CELS standard formats.

The Issues Considered by HURIDOCS

When HURIDOCS accepted the challenge of coping with requests for standard formats, many questions emerged. Where does one begin? What are some of the impediments to constructing useful formats? What are the immediate concerns that face anyone attempting to standardize formats on which to record information about a variety of human rights violations? A great many such issues were discussed in the Task Force meetings, conferences, informal dialogues, and written correspondence. Some of the many interesting and important issues confronted by HURIDOCS are presented here. Many of the issues are not peculiar to the development of human rights formats but were brought into focus as certain definitive, practical decisions had to be made concerning the design of standard formats.

First, human rights organizations emphasize different aspects of documentation. The focus might be on gathering information; on assisting victims; on coding, recording, organizing, and analyzing information; on using the information for research; on actively working toward stopping violations within the local or international setting; or on communicating information about violations. Organizations gathering information may use manual data entry in their work. Organizations analyzing information may find a data base most effective. Organizations communicating information to the international community or the general public may find a word processing format most useful. There must be a recognition of these different aspects of human rights work and an identification of the role of these formats at each stage.

Second, organizations have different orientations: legal, political, humanitarian, and so on. The focus of any given organization could be on a particular group of people such as ethnic, religious, or national minorities, on a particular country, or on the situation internationally. The mandate of an organization has an impact on the type of information required, the type of action to be taken and, obviously, the method of recording information.

Third, some organizations such as the International Labor Organization; the United Nations Educational, Social and Cultural Organization (UNESCO); the Organization of African Unity; or the International Committee of the Red Cross *require* particular information before action is possible.[6] For example, information may be needed regarding the exhaustion of local remedies, or indications may be demanded that the national laws or norms are in contradiction with conventions and treaties ratified at the international level. However, as Eric Sottas (S.O.S. Torture) points out, these requirements, while variable, are sometimes cumbersome as well.[7] A format that includes all the possible questions becomes a very weighty document requiring significant personnel and time to complete. As a consequence, immediate action may become impossible and, in fact, the format may never be completed. In addition, organizations may not have the expertise to report both on the facts of a situation as well as to identify applicable norms, for example relevant articles in international human rights law. Furthermore, other problems of variability also arise.

The types of violations vary. For example, specialized information is required about torture. By contrast, other information is needed when responding to a deportation, disappearance or mass arrest. The formats must reflect the diverse kinds of information needed. In addition, it may be difficult or perhaps impossible to make provisions for recording information about situations where systematic harassment does not directly involve specific well-defined human rights violations.

The types of victims vary. Sometimes the victims are unknown. Or perhaps a relatively simple list of victims is needed. At other times a detailed description of each victim is required. Violations might be against individuals (e.g., restrictions on movement), families (e.g., house demolitions), communities (e.g., mass killings), minority groups (e.g., employment discrimination), arbitrary groupings of people (e.g., group arrests), organizations (e.g., trade unions), or society as a whole (e.g., censorship).

The structure of any given human rights situation varies. One event can involve many victims. One victim can experience many violations. One or many sources of information can contribute to the "event picture." One or many perpetrators can be involved. One event can have many sub-events. Figure 2 below illustrates some ways to configure the formats to document these varying situations.

Some attributes of victims (e.g., sex and age) may be easy to classify and enter, but these attributes are not necessarily the most relevant. Other attributes which may be relevant, especially to establish patterns of group violations, may vary from situation to situation. For example, in Northern Ireland, religion may be most relevant; in the Sudan, it may be religion or tribe membership; in Guatemala or Peru, ethnicity; in South Africa, race. The format must allow the reporter to identify the variables that are most pertinent to the patterns of violation and social divisions in each situation.

The manner in which data are recorded in a format poses particular problems. The question of the use of codes, thesauri, controlled vocabulary, vocabulary lists, or free text for entry of information is a complex issue. There are many difficulties in establishing any kind of controlled vocabulary. Even entering something so seemingly straightforward as a name can be problematic when one considers different cultural conventions, nicknames, transliteration difficulties, and so forth. These issues immediately jump to the fore in creating operational standard formats. Julio Frontalini, who has extensive experience with CELS, addresses these issues in considerable depth.[8]

Formats must facilitate analysis. Frontalini states that controlled entries in standard formats are much preferred to free text entries, which may seem easier and more natural exactly because controlled entries allow users to sort information, compare information, and generate statistics. The formats must facilitate analysis of the situation of the moment, assessment over time, and recognition of changing situations.

Sottas also points to the possible confining nature of standard formats. He gives the example of the abuse of psychiatry for political ends typical before 1990 in certain Eastern European countries and the process by which such abuse came to be included in the now accepted definition of torture. If a rigid standard format had been used, it might have inhibited this process. Forms of repression undergo constant changes, and therefore formats need to be structured in a way that permits documentation of these changes.

Language varies. Defining concepts in a uniform way is difficult even in a single language. Building common definitions over several languages is far more difficult. Even if a common language is used, usage and knowledge vary strongly from place to place. Different geographical locations have different distinctions and terms, and the concepts and terms used may change from situation to situation.

Translation of formats can cause problems. Legal structures, conventions, and procedures vary from country to country. Finding the equivalent terms in different languages, different legal systems, and in different countries at times may be impossible. On the other hand, using translations as a device to test the reliability and eliminate cultural bias may, in fact, be quite useful.

The relationships between rights and violations and the issue of indexing both rights and violations are very complex. This fact immediately becomes evident as soon as one attempts to complete a form indexing an event. The relationship is a "many-to-many" association: one act can violate various rights and on the other hand one right can be violated in many ways. Although the vocabulary related to rights[9] may seem technical and legal, building a controlled vocabulary for violations may not be possible since terminology is not standard. The very definition or understanding of a human right can vary from place to place depending on both national law and adherence to international instruments. Because of the difficulty in developing a global human rights thesaurus, there has been a lack of progress in this area. One solution may be to pool various human rights vocabulary lists such as the *Tesauro Centroamericano*,[10] Human Rights Internet Subject Indexing Terms,[11] the HURIDOCS List of Index-terms,[12] and others to create a human rights vocabulary list rather than attempt to create a structured thesaurus approach.

Each organization develops its own internal way of operating. Some, such as CODEHUCA (Central America), Al-Haq (West Bank), CELS (Argentina) and Task Force Detainees (Philippines) have already developed formats for their own purposes. Adopting international standard formats has to have a significant internal advantage before many organizations will be interested in incorporating them. Some of these organizations may use the formats simply as an output format while others may use them for internal follow-up, administration, and recording.

New organizations require record keeping systems as well as a communications system. Therefore, the formats must include fields of practical interest to individual organizations, even if there is no "communication" value. One must also consider such practical matters as filing methods in designing formats. In other words, the implementation of standard formats can affect the organization to a major degree. Therefore, in designing them, one must think in terms of larger organizational needs rather than of the formats in isolation, even if the larger information handling needs are not addressed in a major way.

User organizations find standard formats helpful to facilitate human rights documentation since information transfer to a variety of organizations can occur simultaneously. Networking among user groups is easier when the transmission of information is fast and cheap by virtue of using standard formats rather than more discursive communications. Organizations are not bogged down with the paperwork of filling out different forms to send to different organizations. The information can be assimilated by a variety of organizations with less internal paperwork. Nevertheless, as between sharing information and compiling it, problems of balance arise. Simplicity is essential, but the formats must be comprehensive enough to meet many requirements adequately. A simplistic approach is unsatisfactory. Yet, the possibility of completing the formats quickly and easily must exist.

Human rights monitoring groups have attained different levels of sophistication in terms of how they organize and manage information. Manual and computerized systems with varying degrees of complexity exist. The forms must be adaptable to varying levels of sophistication between organizations and they must allow for increasing sophistication within organizations. Use of the standard formats will require formulation of a training plan.

The level of expertise varies among human rights organizations. Some employ highly trained lawyers and researchers. Others rely on volunteers who have had no formal training in human rights or related subjects. Some have staff with well-developed communication skills in several languages. Others do not. The formats must be usable by many types of organizations. The instrument must also be effective not only in a variety of organizations but also in a variety of societies with significant differences in development.

Organizations have a variety of confidentiality requirements based on possible repercussions for victims, sources of information, the organization itself, or strategies of operation. The records themselves will be of varying levels of confidentiality as will the fields within the records. The questions of who records what, who has access to what, and who uses the information and for what all center on the confidentiality issue and, in fact, are not strictly a standard formats issue.[13] Yet standard formats bring the issue to the fore, since confidentiality of information must be protected, and this seemingly runs counter to many attempts at international standardization for communication purposes. Clearly there can be a conflict between the need for confidentiality and protection and the need for dissemination and sharing of information.

Since organized information is more accessible than unorganized information, any discussion of standard formats must address the issue of information security. Some years ago, the Uruguayan police broke into one of the most important documentation centers in Latin America.[14] The archives of many movements linked to the Catholic church and lay student organizations over several decades contained lists of names, minutes of meetings, and other material stored in traditional form. It was therefore an enormous task to sift through all the material. Had the material been thoroughly organized on standard formats, it might have been much easier for authorities to obtain what they were looking for. Organized information can be more vulnerable and extra security precautions are necessary, including, for example, encryption of computerized records. On the other hand, reconstruction of a well-organized system is significantly easier. For example, in 1979 CELS was not automated and did not yet have standard formats. On one occasion, the police took its files and returned them only seven or eight years later.[15] Today, the police could take all papers, but CELS would still be able to reconstruct 90 percent of the files on the basis of its computerized records. This assumes, of course, that backup disks are stored securely outside the office where recording functions are centralized.

Technological advances must also be considered with regard to data security. This may relate to good office procedures in handling data, illicit access to data, and deliberate destruction of data.[16] While data security is not a new concept, nor one that applies strictly to standard formats, increased handling of organized data increases the need for data security.

The reliability of information is, of course, crucial when one is expecting action in response to a particular situation. Questions of how one establishes a reliability level, who establishes the reliability level, what are reliability criteria, what is the credibility of the source, what is the probability that the source is reliable—all of these concerns generated considerable discussion both at the Utrecht conference and within the Task Force itself. Although this is not an issue exclusive to standard formats, it is again one that very quickly surfaces when one is dealing with the issue of standardization.

The "truth" of an event is relative and varies depending on whether the source of information is found in police systems, legal systems, mass media, the testimony of victims, witnesses, relatives of the victim, and so on. The task of human rights organizations is to put these "pictures of truth" into one cohesive report that is as objective as possible, reflecting the actual events. The reality of the situation can then be understood in terms of a set of rights involving international instruments, national legislation, and other related literature. The formats must allow for the recording of information from particular sources as well as for the recording and communicating of the composite picture created by the human rights organizations on behalf of the victim.

As stated at the beginning of this section, only some of the many issues confronted within the Task Force have been presented. Even considering only those concerns listed above, many people might see ground for skepticism about the possibilities of developing a standard format, arguing that the variety and complexity of events involving human rights violations could not possibly be covered. However, the need for this type of format has been stated so strongly by nongovernmental organizations that a serious effort is needed to develop them.

The key appears to be adaptability. It is essential to recognize that human rights violations produce many needs and requirements, and that needs and requirements change with changing circumstances and with changing response strategies. Developing standard formats is an ongoing process because the nature of events is ever changing. The consequences of this situation are both clear and complex: the usefulness of the formats employed by human rights groups depends on the extent to which such organizations not only glean what is valuable from the information available to them, but also take the time to evaluate their respective information processing functions and assess how such activities can be improved. For that reason critical comments are not only welcomed; they are required. The results will be invaluable not only for small organizations just beginning to set up but also for expanding organizations as well as for organizations whose quantity of information has reached a stage where sheer mass makes it difficult to retrieve exactly what is needed.

The Formats

It should be stated quite clearly that these formats will not meet all documentation needs of human rights organizations. The formats do not specifically address the issue of information gathering (methods, use of forms such as questionnaires, interview techniques, etc.), internal organization of materials, methods of dissemination, or techniques for analysis. Here, these factors are tangentially considered as they relate directly to recording or communication issues. Clearly, not all the issues described above have been addressed. Rather the approach has been to produce a flexible, adaptable resource tool that has the components to meet the recording and communicating needs of many organizations and can be tailored to meet specific needs. To attempt even the seemingly limited task of creating formats for recording and communicating is highly complex. The value of the formats is, of course, directly related to careful gathering of data, good questioning techniques, accurate recording of information, and subsequent thorough analysis. For organizations wishing to use the formats, serious consideration should be given to arranging for key staff to attend HURIDOCS training sessions.

The HURIDOCS Standard Formats provide an integrated and standardized but adaptable system for the following areas of documentation of information related to human rights violations:

- Event Information
- Victim Information
- Source Information
- Alleged Perpetrator Information
- Intervention Information
- Additional Record Details (for particular events or victims if this is needed).

The basic concept is to define a number of fields in several formats used in an overall structure which can be applied in both computerized and manual systems. Figure 1 illustrates how the individual formats relate to each other. By using a variety of formats that reflect the different types of information needed, one can combine them in a variety of ways to meet the particular documentation requirements of different situations. Thus all the formats or only the pertinent ones can be used in a particular situation or by a particular organization. Figure 2 illustrates some ways to configure the formats to document these varying situations. Event, victim, and other records can be linked through the use of document numbers. In addition, once information is collected concerning a particular perpetrator or victim, for example, the information bank exists if and when additional events occur. Links can then be created by using document numbers.

It is important to determine at the outset the purpose for using the formats. This will vary from organization to organization. For example, an organization may want a detailed summary in English or

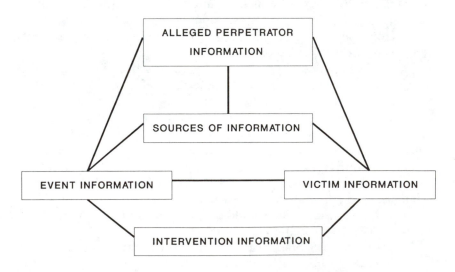

Figure 1. Relationships between HURIDOCS standard formats.

Spanish of information in another language, using the formats as a translation tool and eliminating the need for translation of entire source documents. Alternatively, an organization that has a large number of cases may wish to record only coded information, to be used for statistical analysis and examination of trends. Moreover, an organization may be sending information to receiving agencies with particular information requirements that must be met before action can be taken; thus, the organization adapts the form to meet particular information needs. Finally, an analyst who knows that a particular organization is using the Short Format (discussed below) could possibly use its data base to do certain kinds of statistical analysis helpful to policy makers and social scientists as well as activists.

The formats can be used:

- to describe a single incident based on one source;
- to describe a larger event including a chronology of a number of smaller incidents;
- to summarize an event for internal or communication purposes using a number of sources;
- to interview a witness or victim (to be completed by the interviewer, not the interviewee);
- to update an event record;
- to provide an overview based on documents in another language;
- to assist with analysis and the compiling of statistical data.

Clearly, the formats will be used in different ways by different organizations, depending on their needs, their internal organization and their purpose in using the formats. The formats are not a ready-made system. They are a tool which can be used by groups to develop their own tailor-made systems.

The formats are flexible in that they can be combined in various ways (see Figure 2). They are adaptable in that fields can be added to a short format; alternatively, longer formats can be used, adapting them to specific needs by adding or subtracting fields. Uniformity of language and field format can be achieved on basic information while leaving some flexibility for each organization to choose to communicate or record additional information in fields that suit their own purposes. While it would be helpful to have controlled vocabularies or codes for all the fields, until they are developed free text will have to be used for some fields. As specialized thesauri and controlled vocabulary lists are developed, and as the formats are tested, more definition can be given to some of the free format fields. A number of

(a)

(b)

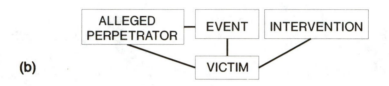

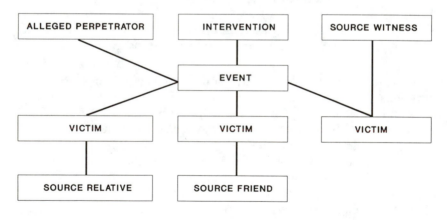

(c)

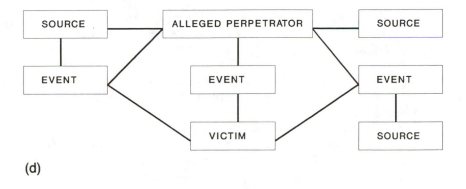

(d)

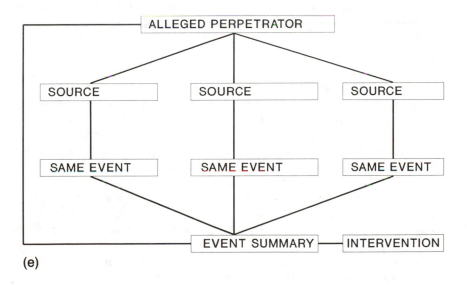

(e)

Figure 2. Sample configurations of the formats. (a) One event, one victim, documented on a short format. (b) One event, one victim, information on the perpetrator. Victim is the information source. Intervention on behalf of the victim. (c) One event, multiple victims, multiple sources. One intervention in response to event. (d) Multiple events, one victim, multiple sources of information. (e) One event, multiple sources.

coded supporting appendices are included in the complete set of formats.[17] The various components of the set of formats are described below.

Short Format. The Short Format serves various purposes. For example, it provides a starting point for the systematic recording of information; it summarizes information for organizations which do not wish or need to complete the full set of formats. Moreover, it records basic essential information for communication. The Short Format is comprised of fields from other formats that are likely to be most commonly used. Most of the fields have been selected from the Event and Victim Formats. Organizations may wish to start with the Short Format and then tailor it specifically to their needs by adding fields from other formats. Many fields in this format are descriptive in nature and use codes as well as free text entries. [The Short Format, in part, with abbreviated scope notes, has been included in Appendix C. Other formats are available in the complete document. It may be obtained from HURIDOCS Advice and Support Unit/Secretariat: Torgare 27, 0183 Oslo 1, Norway.]

Analytical Format. The Analytical Format provides basic coded information that may be particularly useful as a starting point in analyzing and providing statistics about a given situation. All fields in this format except one are restricted to controlled entries and codes. An Analytical Format can be made up by choosing any relevant fields from any format and restricting entries to codes or controlled vocabulary. In this way, one can vary the Analytical Format according to changing parameters in diverse situations. By restricting the entries to controlled entries, it is possible to sort on a variety of parameters such as location, victim characteristics, religion, occupation, dates, type of perpetrator, and so forth. This is a good place to begin for organizations using a data base to input information. Of course, there are some dangers that information may be omitted if this format is used in isolation. However, as a tool of analysis, it is essential and potentially very useful. The Analytical Format is, in fact, a changing and changeable subset of the larger format structure.

Event Information Format. The Event Information Format records the main details of the event which has taken place. A significant number of these fields are included in the Short Format. An event may be a single isolated incident or a grouping of incidents. For example, the event information about an army raid on a refugee camp includes the date of the raid, the name of the camp, identification of the army unit, and so forth. Incidents occurring during the raid (shootings, arrests, restrictions, etc.) could be recorded on separate Event Information Formats but filed or cross-referenced with the larger event. The Event Information Format provides references to other relevant documents held by the organization. The Event Record can be used in conjunction with Victim Records, Source Records, Alleged Perpetrator Records, Lists, and/or other documents. It can also be used alone as long as there is an indication of the type of source material.

Victim Information Event. This format is used to record detailed information about individual victims. If detailed information about individual victims is not required or known, the Event Information Format may be adequate. A number of Event Records can refer to the same Victim Record. A number of Victim Records can refer to the same Event Record.

Source Information Format. Since the first criterion for an information system is the validity of input, it is essential that reporters identify the indicators of reliability of sources. Often the source of information is highly confidential. If this is the case, the confidential information should not be entered into a computerized system or communicated between systems. Codes or direct characterization comments on credibility or reliability might be provided in this case.

Alleged Perpetrator Information Format. This format contains information regarding alleged perpetrators of human rights violations. A number of Event Records or Victim Records might refer to the same Alleged Perpetrator Record. Or a number of perpetrators might be involved in one event or with one particular victim. The term "alleged" is included since initially the form may be completed before it is "proved" that the "alleged" perpetrator is, in fact, the perpetrator.

Intervention Information Format. This format is designed to keep track of actions taken in response to the violation. It also records assistance provided to a victim from relevant sources. Intervention information may be recorded on this separate format or alternatively recorded directly in the Event Information Format or Victim Information Format.

Additional Record Details. Additional details may need to be provided for particular types of events or victims. This information may be required for internal purposes or for use by organizations to whom information is sent. Guidelines for a number of specific types of events have been included in the complete document. Guidelines for other types of events can be developed as individual organizations require them.

To sum up, one might picture a flow of information from "raw data" such as affidavits and questionnaires to appropriate formats where it is recorded and analyzed, or to communication for action and further analysis. Figure 3 outlines this flow of information.

The formats manual includes quite specific directions for users wishing to implement a standard human rights documentation system for recording and communicating information. Certainly poten-

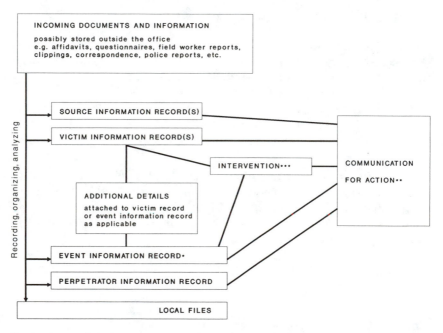

*Contains references to all other documents concerning the case.
**All appropriate records are communicated. These may consist of simply the Short Forms or the communication may include each record listed above with supporting incoming documents depending on the situation.
***An intervention may be on behalf of specific individuals or groups, or in response to a particular situation.

Figure 3. Flow chart, acquisition and use of information on human rights violations.

tial users must be prepared to examine and explore the formats in some depth before applying them. The first step after an initial exploration of the formats is to determine the objectives in utilizing them. As has been stated earlier, the formats can be used in a wide variety of ways. Many decisions must be made before beginning the process of designing a workable system for any given organization. Some of the questions to consider include the following:

Is the format to be used only internally or also for communication?

Will the formats be used principally to design a system to gather, record, organize, analyze or communicate information? Is research or activism an objective?

How is information best organized? by event or case? by victim? by intervention? This will have an impact on filing and numbering systems.

Can some of the recording be done at the information gathering level? In other words, can the information gathering tools be designed to facilitate recording? If, for example, the victim format is used as an interview sheet, the manual level of recording will already be done. Perhaps all that will then be needed is a reference to the gathering document on the event record.

Will the recording be done by hand manually, on a word processor, in a data base or a combination of all three? Some fields lend themselves well to data base activity—such as those on the analytical format—others are better handled on a word processor such as the free text fields. A data base allows for quick retrieval while a word processor allows for a more narrative style of stating the information.

Who will be receiving the information? What are the needs of organizations receiving information?

Once these questions have been considered, organizations can begin the technical steps to design a system to fit their particular needs.

The following directions provide an example of some of the crucial initial activity.

Step 1.   Gather about five to ten cases which reflect the type of documentation your organization is involved in. Gather the original documents (affidavits, letters, interview sheets, questionnaires, recordings, or other forms). Make six photocopies of the Short Format.

Step 2.   Briefly look at the Table of Contents (Appendix B) and the possible configurations in Figure 2. Browse through any other parts of the book that arouse your curiosity. Do not read the manual cover to cover. Rather, use it as a tool.

Step 3.   Complete the Short Format for two of your cases. Expect that the information may not quite fit. DO NOT GET FRUSTRATED YET!!! If you have trouble, or if you are not sure what to include in the field, read the scope notes.

Step 4.   Examine the Short Format in view of its suitability to your organization in terms of space allotment. Examine the formats in Chapters IV, V, VI. They have some optional fields which you may wish to add. DO NOT ADD ANY OTHER FIELDS AT THIS POINT. DO NOT REMOVE ANY FIELDS.

Step 5.   Examine the formats in Chapters VII, VIII and IX (Alleged Perpetrator, Intervention, Additional Record Details). If you think any of these would be useful, set them up for your organization to try out. Use only the fields that you feel are important, but keep the same field names and numbers even if they are not in the same order.

Step 6.   Try out your new set of forms on two more cases. Use all the forms that you have revised or set up as they apply to your type of documentation.

Step 7.   Revise your forms as necessary. Examine the scope notes in some depth. Examine other parts of the manual as necessary. Try using the forms on several more cases. Try using the forms in different ways and in different configurations.

In undertaking these steps, there are several points to remember:

1. Know what you want to do with the information.
2. Know what receiving organizations need in order to act.
3. Know what you need in order to act.
4. Try to keep it as simple and short as possible. At the same time, include all necessary information.
5. Don't decide everything at once. Allow some time to play with the formats and experiment with their use.
6. Develop codes, fields, terminology which you need and send them on to HURIDOCS so that the formats can become increasingly useful to increasingly more organizations.
7. The standard formats are a flexible and adaptable tool. They can assist you with your work most effectively when you have a good grasp of how they work and what you can do with them. As with

any tool, it may take some time to adapt them for your particular needs.

Conclusion

The HURIDOCS Task Force has made significant progress on a difficult and complex project. A number of human rights organizations have demonstrated expertise and skill in developing standard formats for their particular settings. Many of these organizations have generously shared of their experience, time, and resources. Others have indicated the need for formats, are testing the formats, and are making suggestions for revision to ensure that a wide range of needs will be met. This chapter is an attempt to share both the project itself as well as the process with the broader human rights community. It is significant that many people who are concerned about life and death issues in their own countries have taken the time and effort to work on this project in a variety of ways. It is indeed a cooperative effort. Human rights work is also a cooperative effort, and it is certainly a global concern. South, north, east, west—all have a stake in protecting the dignity of humanity. The development of appropriate standard formats provides the human rights community with one more tool needed to build a solid foundation. With a solid foundation of knowledge and information, people and organizations can say with professional certainty and confidence, "specific violations of human rights are occurring and they must stop." If information is indeed power, the effective use of standard formats is one source of strength against oppression.

Appendix A

Task Force Members attending the meetings in Manila (November 1988) and Utrecht (July 1989) were Hubert Chaves, Central American Information and Documentation Network on Human Rights (CODEHUCA), Costa Rica; Ricardo Cifuentes, Information Systems Consultant, Chile; Judith Dueck, Task Force Leader, Canada (previously based in the West Bank); Julio Frontalini, Centre for Legal and Social Studies (CELS), Argentina; Manuel Guzman, Task Force Detainees of the Philippines; Elizabeth Lapham, Justice and Peace Commission, Zimbabwe; Manfred Nowak, Netherlands Institute of Human Rights (SIM); Agneta Pallinder, Amnesty International, United Kingdom; Eric Sottas, OMCT/S.O.S. Torture, Switzerland; Berth Verstappen, HURIDOCS, Norway. Special thanks are due to

Carlos Saldarriaga, Asociacion Pro Derechos Humanos (APRODEH), Peru, who participated in both Task Force meetings and is facilitating the Spanish translation.

Appendix B: Table of Contents of the Complete Document

By providing the Table of Contents for the complete document, "Standard Formats and Human Rights Violations: Toward Compatibility," we hope that the reader will gain an understanding of the specific aspects that are covered in the actual document.

I.   INTRODUCTION
II.   SHORT FORMAT
III.   ANALYTICAL FORMAT
IV.   EVENTS INFORMATION FORMAT
V.   VICTIM INFORMATION FORMAT
VI.   SOURCE INFORMATION FORMAT
VII.   ALLEGED PERPETRATOR INFORMATION FORMAT
VIII.   INTERVENTION INFORMATION FORMAT
IX.   ADDITIONAL RECORD DETAILS
    A. Lists
    B. Legal Information
    C. Deaths and Killings
    D. Displacements and Destruction of Property
    E. Torture
X.   BACKGROUND INFORMATION
XI.   APPENDICES
    A: Guidelines for Recording the Names of Persons
    B: HURIDOCS List of Index-terms
    C: List of Geographical Terms and Codes
    D: List of Language Codes
    E: List of Sample Victim Characteristics
    F: *List of Instruments and their Official Citations*
    G: List of Occupations
    H: "Detection of Torture," *The Minnesota Protocol: Preventing Arbitrary Killing through an Adequate Death Investigation and Autopsy*
    I: Sample Configurations of the Formats
    J: Amnesty International Questionnaire, Part 3, Prison Conditions
    K: Torture Methods

L: Amnesty International Questionnaire on Torture and Ill-treatment

M: Religious Groups

N: Sample Completed Formats

O: Personal Descriptions, Scars, Marks, Tatoos and other Characteristics

P: Ethnic Minorities, Nationalities and Regional Groups

XII. BIBLIOGRAPHY

Appendix C: SHORT FORMAT: Selected Components

Letterhead of sending organization, including the name of the organization, acronym, address, phone, telex, telefax, geographical code and term.

EVENT INFORMATION

*101. Geographical Term
*102. Geographical Code
*103. Document Number *E*
*104. Type of Event
 105. Event Description
 106. Role of Authorities
*108. General Region
*109. Exact Location
 112. Charges or Stated Reason
*113. Remarks
*114. Victim Characteristics
 116. Related Event Record Numbers *E*
 117. Victim Record Numbers *V*
305E. Source Remarks
413E. Alleged Perpetrator Remarks
507E. Intervention Remarks
 121. Date of Entry

Letterhead

VICTIM INFORMATION

 201. Document Number *V*
 202. Name
 203. Age
 204. Date of Birth

205.   Place of Birth
206.   Sex
*207.   Religion
208.   Identification Documents
*209.   Origins
210.   Marital Status
211.   Number of Children/Dependents
212.   Name of Spouse(s)
213.   Health
214.   Background
*215.   Employment
216.   Organizational Affiliation/Activities
217.   Current Status
218.   Remarks
219.   Event Record Numbers *E*
220.   Victim Record Numbers for Family Members *V*
305V. Source Remarks
413V. Alleged Perpetrator Remarks
507V. Intervention Remarks
224.   Date of Entry
227.   Confidentiality

Fields marked with an asterisk(*) are included in the sample Analytical Format with the addition of 107 (Number of Victim), 110 (Initial Date), 111 (Final Date), 132 (Count), 123 (Supporting Documents), 412 (Type of Alleged Perpetrator), 508 (Intervention Request) and 509 (Intervention Status). Analytical Format entries would be restricted to controlled vocabulary or codes.

Short Format: Scope Notes

The forms supplied in the complete document are not intended as master forms to be duplicated as they are. Each documentation center will need to retype them in a size and form which suits the individual application, leaving sufficient space for the different fields which will vary from center to center. The Short Format partly illustrated in this chapter is only a starting point. Fields from other formats in the complete document can be added to tailor the format to exact organizational and communication needs. Considerable experimentation with the forms is advisable. Formats for Sources, Alleged Perpetrators, and Interventions should be used if more specific entries are needed than are provided on the short form. For consistency and field identification purposes, it is important to use the same numbers for the fields as are used in this document even if they do not flow sequentially. *The selected scope notes presented here have been significantly abbreviated.* They are available in the complete document for which the mailing address is given in note 17.

Event Information: Short Format

101/102. Geographical Term/Code. The most appropriate geographical terms and codes describing the area where the event occurred. A table of geographical codes is provided in the complete document.

103. Document Number E. An accession number which identifies this and only this record. Although document numbers have local significance only, they should be included in exchanges for identification purposes.

104. Type of Event. An indication of the broad grouping to which this event belongs. Indicate how broadly the victim characteristics seem to apply in this instance. Use the following letter codes:

P Individual person targeted for a purpose specific to that individual.
G Selected group of people, a group with specific characteristics, e.g., trade union leaders.
R A number of people selected indiscriminately because of their presence in a particular place at a particular time, for example, roundups, demonstrators, etc.

Additional codes may be developed by local organizations. The following list is an example of such codes. Organizations may add to the list as necessary. Use the following sample categories and codes:

801.	Deaths and killings
802.	Torture, cruel and inhuman treatment
803.	Arrest and incarceration
804.	Disappearances, Kidnapping
805.	Deportations, external exile, banishment
806.	Control of Movement
806.1	Curfew
806.2	Internal Exile
807.	Displacements
808.	Destruction of property
809.	Confiscation of land or property
810.	Shooting

811.   Beating
812.   Demonstration and/or crowd control
899.   Other (specify)
Examples:
801/P   Killing of human rights activist.
803/G   Arrest of trade unionists.
810/R   Random shooting of demonstrators by members of armed
        forces.

105. Event Description. A description of the violation or condition
causing concern. Describe what happened. Describe the means used
by the perpetrator. This might be a concrete weapon such as a gun
or it might be a legal tool such as an administrative decree or more
abstract tool such as threats. Do not include information which will
be covered in other fields listed below. Restrict entry to facts. If a
complex event is being recorded or if a larger event is being summarized, number the violations/events/incidents in the order they occurred. A chronology of events with dates is often very helpful.

106. Role of Authorities. A description of the role the authorities played
in the event. Cite evidence of involvement (instigation, toleration,
overlooking, direct involvement, observation, encouragement, attempted prevention, etc.). Include complete identification if available. Provide details as to time of observation, action, and number of
authorities present. Include details of military/armed/security/police
forces with indications of rank, detachment, headquarters, com-
manding officer. Supply particulars concerning government forces,
army, air force, national police, treasury police, civil guard, municipal
police, affiliated organizations, paramilitary, etc. Include description
of uniform, visible weapons, vehicles used, license plate number, or
other identifying factors if relevant. Indicate if personnel was in uniform, plainclothes, or masked in some way. Indicate role in interro-
gations. If a police report was filed, indicate the response to it. If
police were called, indicate how long it took for them to arrive. Indicate evidence of police/government sanction of the event.

If the authorities are in fact the alleged perpetrators and a significant amount of information is known, the information should be entered on the Alleged Perpetrator Information Format instead of
here. General information about military or government presence in
the area may be provided. If additional information about the authorities exists in documents held by the organization, indicate the
document number and the location.

108. General Region. An indication of the district, sub-region or local area where the event occurred. The terms used must be identified by local organizations who will need to compile a hierarchical list of provinces, districts, areas, towns, cities, etc., so entries are consistent. The list should be forwarded to receiving organizations so that they are aware of subregions within districts. Confusion can easily result when a town is referred to in one instance and a region in the next when the same event is being described. Spellings of towns and villages, etc., also need to be consistent.

109. Exact Location. An identification of the exact location where the event occurred. Use as many codes as apply.

01 Home
02 Government/municipal offices
03 Indoor meeting place (e.g., community hall, concert hall, etc.)
04 Place of employment
05 University/postsecondary educational institute
06 School for children/youth
07 Penal institute (prison, jail, detention center, etc.)
08 Hospital/medical institution
09 Open plazas, town square, shopping center
10 Military base
11 Refugee camp
12 Embassy/consulate
13 Religious institution
14 Transport center/carrier (train station, bus, airport, etc.)
15 Service institution (e.g., telephone, hydro-electricity, energy)
16 Financial institution (bank, credit union, etc.)
17 Private business office
18 Media center (newspaper office, TV station, etc.)
19 Union/cooperative office
20 Farm
21 Court
22 Mine/mining site
23 Factory/industrial center
24 Office of political party
25 Office of non-governmental organization (human rights, social services, development, etc.)
26 Police station/post
27 Road, highway, street
28 Monument

29 Bridge
99 Other (specify)

   Indicate the area of displacement, place of disappearance, place where shooting, arrest, questioning, etc. occurred. Include address and phone if relevant. Include penal precinct, name of prison, or legal jurisdiction if relevant.

112. Charges or Stated Reason. An indication if formal charges or stated allegations have been made against the victim. Indicate what the charges or allegations are and who made them. These must not be CONJECTURE on the part of a source. Use caution in completing this field. Note who laid the charges or who stated the reason. Direct quotes of authorities or perpetrators may be entered.

113. Remarks. Additional comments from the source identified in field 305. This field may be used to report additional pertinent information. Guidelines or codes may be created by individual organizations if particular information is desired. Details such as number of people directly affected (e.g., family members) and how they are affected could be included.

   Any details particular to the event not covered above can be entered here. This field could also contain particulars that transpired *before* the event occurred but may have been influential in causing the event to occur. It could also contain particulars about individuals who were involved *before* the event occurred. Include full identification if possible, and restrict comments to facts rather than conjecture. What and who influenced the beginning of the event? The information might or might not be causal either directly or indirectly. Note mass gatherings or assemblies, demonstrations, strikes, etc. This material is descriptive and includes material which may or may not be significant. EXTREME CAUTION SHOULD BE EXERCISED IN THE MANNER IN WHICH MATERIAL FROM THIS FIELD IS RECORDED AND COMMUNICATED.

   Note. Unless the format is being used as a summary document, fields 104–113 are based on information supplied by the source identified in field 305E. If material from other sources is used in this record, indicate the record number or other identification in brackets at the end of the specific entry.

114. Victim Characteristics. An indication of the characteristics of the victim which may have caused his/her victimization or which may provide him/her special protection under the law, that is, because they were at a particular place at a particular time, or because they were trade union leaders, students, activists, members in particular organizations or groups, employed in particular professions, adherents to a particular religion, AIDS patients, members of a particular tribe, caste, race or minority, etc. Also note characteristics which provide special protection under the law. A list of victim characteristics is provided in the complete document.

Use caution in entering information which will endanger specific victims, for example, membership in an illegal organization linked to a specific person's name. This type of information might be held by the organization. Caution must be used if it is communicated, since such information could have disastrous effects on the victim.

116. Related Event Record Numbers. An indication of where information can be found about events related to this event.

117. Victim Record Numbers. An indication of where more information can be found about the victims of this event.

305E. Source Remarks. An indication about the source of information for fields 104 to 113 on this record. This may be information concerning the primary source (e.g., witnesses) or the secondary source (e.g., organizations).

Due to space limitations for this publication, the scope notes for the SHORT FORMAT–VICTIM INFORMATION are not included here.

Bibliography of Support Materials Which May Be Useful

Jean Aitchison, *International Thesaurus of Refugee Terminology*, published under the auspices of the International Refugee Documentation Network (Dordrecht: Martinus Nijhoff Publishers, 1989), 476 p. Multilingual thesaurus in English, French, and Spanish.

Laurence Boisson de Chazournes, Adama Dieng, Fernando Mejía, Pierre de Senarclens, Eric Sottas, and François de Vargas, *Practical Guide to the International Procedures Relative to Complaint and Appeals Against Acts of Torture, Disappearances and Other Inhuman or Degrading Treatment* (Geneva: S.O.S. Torture/World Organization Against Torture, 1988), 92 p.

Ian Brownlie, ed., *Basic Documents on Human Rights*, 2nd edition (Oxford: Oxford University Press, 1987), 505 p.

Gabriela Carbonetto and Ricardo Cifuentes, *Tesauro Centroamericano sobre Derechos Humanos* (San José: Programa de Defensa de la Autonomía y Solidaridad con las Universidades Centroamericanas, Confederación

Universitaria Centroamericana-CSUCA, 1987). This thesaurus is bilingual (Spanish-English) .

DEVSIS: Manual for the preparation of records in development-information systems: recommended methods for development-information systems (Ottawa: International Development Research Center, 1982).

Marcella Fierro, "New Hope for Identifying the Unidentified," *American Journal of Forensic Medicine and Pathology* 5(4) (December 1984).

Human Rights Internet, "Subject Indexing Terms," in *Master List*, volume 12 (Fall 1987), (Cambridge, MA: Human Rights Internet, 1987), pp. 70–100.

International Labor Office, *Revised International Standard Classification of Occupations (ISC-88) with references to ISCO-68* (Geneva: International Labor Office—Bureau of Statistics, January 1988), 37 p. (In English, Spanish, and French.)

List of Organizations, Serial Numbers and Acronyms: revised version (Utrecht: HURIDOCS, 1985).

Minnesota International Human Rights Committee, *The Minnesota Protocol: Preventing Arbitrary Killing Through an Adequate Death Investigation and Autopsy* (draft May 1989).

Randy B. Reiter, M. V. Zunzunegui, and José Quiroga, "Guidelines for Field Reporting of Basic Human Rights Violations," *Human Rights Quarterly* 8, No. 4 (November 1986): 628–653; see Reiter et al., this volume, Chap. 4.

Paul Seighart, *The International Law of Human Rights* (Oxford: Oxford University Press, 1983).

Bjorn Stormorken, *HURIDOCS Standard Formats for the Recording and Exchange of Information on Human Rights* (Dordrecht: Martinus Nijhoff Publishers on behalf of HURIDOCS, 1985), 175 p.

Bjorn Stormorken and Leo Zwaak, *Human Rights Terminology in International Law: A Thesaurus* (Dordrecht: Martinus Nijhoff Publishers; Human Rights Documentation Center-Council of Europe, 1988), 234 p.

United Nations Center for Human Rights, ed., *Human Rights: A Compilation of International Instruments* (New York: United Nations, 1988), 416 p. United Nations sales number E.88.XIV.1, UN doc. ST/HR/1/REV.3, ISBN 92 1 154066 6.

Gert Westerveen, ed., and UNESCO, *International Instruments of Human Rights (20 years covenants)* (Paris: UNESCO, 1986, French edition, 1988).

Notes

1. The term "format" refers to the empty form on which information can be recorded. The term "record" refers to a completed format. The term "standard format" as used in this chapter refers to a set of fields in a prescribed order with prescribed scope notes. Standard does not imply that all organizations will use all formats and all fields for all situations. It does mean that this structure and listing of fields with prescribed scope notes can be used as an instrument in the process of developing global standardized methods in the area of human rights.

2. Bjorn Stormorken, *HURIDOCS Standard Formats for the Recording and Exchange of Information on Human Rights* (Dordrecht: Martinus Nijhoff Publishers on behalf of HURIDOCS, 1985).

3. The computer program is being developed by Ricardo Cifuentes, a hu-

man rights consultant based in Chile. The program was demonstrated at the HURIDOCS Conference in July 1989.

4. This example is drawn from "Advantages in the Use of Standard Formats" by Julio Daniel Frontalini, presented at the HURIDOCS Conference in July 1989 and published by HURIDOCS and the Netherlands Institute of Human Rights (SIM) in *HURIDOCS News*, Special Issue, "Human Rights Violations and Standard Formats: Towards Compatibility in Recording and Transferring Information" (February 1990): 13–14.

5. For analysis of the *Navy Mechanics School Case* initiated by the Center for Legal and Social Studies, Argentina, see George C. Rogers, "Argentina's Obligation to Prosecute Military Officials for Torture," *Columbia Human Rights Law Review* 20 (1989): 259.

6. See, for example, the procedures outlined in Laurence Boisson de Chazournes, Adama Dieng, Fernando Mejía, Pierre de Senarclens, Eric Sottas, and François de Vargas, *Practical Guide to the International Procedures Relative to Complaint and Appeals Against Acts of Torture, Disappearances and other Inhuman or Degrading Treatment* (Geneva: S.O.S. Torture/World Organization Against Torture, 1988).

7. Eric Sottas, "The Dangers Posed by Standard Formats for the Transmission of Cases of Serious Human Rights Violations," paper presented at the HURIDOCS Conference in July 1989, *HURIDOCS News* (February 1990): 26–30.

8. Frontalini, "Advantages in the Use of Standard Formats" (note 4).

9. An example of a "rights" classification system is Bjorn Stormorken and Leo Zwaak, *Human Rights Terminology in International Law: A Thesaurus* (Dordrecht: Martinus Nijhoff Publishers; Human Rights Documentation Center-Council of Europe, 1988).

10. Gabriela Carbonetto and Ricardo Cifuentes, *Tesauro Centroamericano sobre Derechos Humanos* (San José: Programa de Defensa de la Autonomía y Solidaridad con las Universidades Centroamericanas, Confederación Universitaria Centroamericana-CSUCA, 1987). This thesaurus is bilingual (Spanish-English).

11. Human Rights Internet, "Subject Indexing Terms," in *Master List*, volume 12 (Fall 1987) (Cambridge, MA: Human Rights Internet, 1987), pp. 70–100.

12. This list is included in the complete formats document available from the HURIDOCS Secretariat.

13. This issue is addressed by Hubert Chaves in "Confidentiality of Information," paper presented at the HURIDOCS Conference in July 1989.

14. This example is quoted by Eric Sottas in "The Dangers Posed by Standard Formats for the Transmission of Cases of Serious Human Rights Violations" (note 7).

15. This example was provided by Julio Frontalini in the discussions at the HURIDOCS Conference in July 1989.

16. Agneta Pallinder, "Data Security," paper presented at the HURIDOCS Conference in July 1989, *HURIDOCS News* (February 1990): 30–35.

17. A table of contents of the complete document is provided in Appendix B to give the reader an idea of the scope of the complete document.

Further information concerning these formats can be obtained from HURIDOCS Advice and Support Unit/Secretariat:

Torggate 27, 0183 Oslo 1, Norway
Telephone: 47–2–200247
Telefax: 33–42–75012347   (quote   on   first   line   "BOX:GEO2:
HURIDOCS").
Telex: 918023 geonet g (quote on first line "BOX:GEO2:HURIDOCS").
Electronic mail: GEONET:GEO2:HURIDOCS

Criticism, comments, results of testing, suggestions for improvements, in-
dications of problem areas and possible solutions, and additions to this chap-
ter are desired. Send responses to:
Judith Dueck, Task Force Leader
828 Ash Street, Winnipeg, Manitoba, Canada R3N OR8
Telephone: 204–488–7538 (home); 204–589–4374 (work)
Telefax: 1–204–943–2597 c/o MEDA
Telex: (021) 07–587700 FOODGRAINS c/o MEDA

Chapter 6
The Rights of Collectivities: Principles and Procedures in Measuring the Human Rights Status of Communal and Political Groups

Ted Robert Gurr and Barbara Harff

Virtually all the quantitative data used in comparative cross-national research on human rights is concerned either with the status and victimization of individuals, or the policies and properties of governments. These are commonly characterized as the micro and macro, or individual and national, levels of analysis. The neglected middle ground concerns the political status and rights of political and communal groups. The authors of this chapter have pursued two separate lines of research in developing comparative data at the group level of analysis. This chapter explains the circumstances that led us into quantitative research in this largely uncharted terrain and the procedures we have developed for mapping it.[1]

Three Levels of Analysis in Assessing Human Rights

Our rationale for studying human rights at the group level can be clarified by contrasting it to quantitative research at the more familiar micro and macro levels.

Micro Data on Violations of Civil and Political Rights

In this approach, observation and measurement focus on events that in Helen Fein's phrase "violate the life integrity" of individuals. The prevailing strategy is to count and analyze actions targeted at individuals, such as imprisonment and execution without due process, torture, and "disappearances."[2] Such events are rather widely reported by journalists and human rights monitoring groups, for example by Amnesty International and Americas Watch, and can be counted and categorized with some precision.

The most common criticism of this approach is that reporting is incomplete and inconsistent.[3] The unreliability of the basic data is an ever-present threat to the validity of generalizations based on their analysis. The approach also can be criticized for its narrow scope: it concentrates on severe violations of civil and political rights and is not applicable to violations of cultural or economic rights.

Macro Data on Civil and Political Rights

Three different strategies are used for assessing the status of civil and political rights at the societal or national level. First, some comparative analyses employ indicators constructed by aggregating data of the kinds described above about the victimization of individuals. These indicators permit aggregate comparisons over time within countries, as well as synchronous comparisons among countries. The strategy is less than optimal because it is based on incomplete and inconsistently reported information, as noted above.

A second macro research strategy centers on specific coercive acts or sanctions employed by regimes. The relevant phenomena include some acts directed at individuals, but conflate them with events such as declarations of states of emergency, acts of censorship, and so on, which in the aggregate can be used as indicators of the extent to which governments violate civil and political rights. The 1972 and 1983 editions of the *World Handbook of Political and Social Indicators* report such data, which have been used in a number of comparative studies (see Chapter 14, by David L. Banks).

Neither of these two strategies can be used to assess positive efforts to protect civil and political rights. They are based on acts of violation, not protection. Analyses based on data on acts of coercive sanctions also are open to the criticism that they do not take full account of the institutionalized, hence more subtle, patterns of coercive control and denial of civil and political rights that characterize durable authoritarian regimes. The widespread practice of surveillance and threat can severely restrain civil and political rights even if few overt sanctions are used.[4] Furthermore, none of the methods discussed above are reliable means for assessing the extent to which economic, cultural, or other nonpolitical rights are either restricted or enhanced. Ideally, they can and should be complemented by indices of the extent to which societies provide for the social and economic rights of their citizens (see R. J. Goldstein's discussion in Chapter 2 of this volume).

A third macro research strategy compensates for some of these disadvantages by relying on summary ratings of degrees of restriction or protection of broad categories of rights. This has been called a "standards-based" approach. The best known global ratings are the Freedom House annual assessments of countries' civil liberties and political rights. The objectivity of such ratings and the knowledgeability of those who make them have been impugned by critics. In fact, most practitioners of this kind of data-making are specific about the guidelines they use, and some have employed panels of experts to make or review the ratings.[5] From a measurement point of view, indicators based on carefully specified rating scales have considerable face validity. Moreover, the use of panels of judges to make ratings should enhance reliability by increasing the level of agreement among coders, and improve validity by compensating for biases and limited information of individual coders.

Data on the Status and Victimization of Groups

We have been pursuing two different projects that focus on the status and victimization of collectivities rather than individuals. In the Minorities at Risk project, the relevant collectivities are communal minorities, i.e., groups within larger, politically organized societies, whose members share a distinctive collective identity based on cultural and ascriptive traits that are recognized by them and by the larger society. This study is not concerned with the legal question of whether communal groups have rights as such.[6] The question is whether the economic or political rights of members of a group are abridged or denied by state and society because of the group's defining traits, its social status, or the claims made on the group's behalf. The most significant economic right for some minorities is protection of their traditional means of livelihood; for others it is the opportunity to participate on an equal footing in the mainstream economy. The most important political rights are group members' physical security and their freedom to protect and promote their communal interests. Our key indicator of whether a communal group is at risk of violations of these rights is the existence of systematic differential treatment of group members vis-à-vis the larger society. In an ongoing project, described below in greater detail, about 260 such groups have been identified in the 126 larger countries of the world. Basic information is being gathered on the size, status, characteristics, and actions of each such group.[7]

In the Genocides and Politicides project, the focus is on gross violations of human rights perpetrated by regimes against communal and political groups since 1945. Forty-four such episodes have been identified thus far in a global survey, which have victimized about 30 separate political and class groups and 35 communal groups.[8] For each episode, information has been gathered and coded on the identity and number of victims, the underlying circumstances and means of their victimization, and the character and objectives of the regimes that carried out the atrocities. This study differs in several respects from the Minorities at Risk project. It is more restrictive in the sense that it analyzes only the groups that have been severely victimized; it is more comprehensive in the sense that it takes account of politically defined victim groups as well as of communal ones.[9]

Origins of the Studies

While these two studies are of considerable relevance to the empirical study of human rights violations, they were undertaken for rather different purposes.

Minorities at Risk

The first author's interest in communal minorities dates from his comparative research in the late 1960s on the correlates of political violence. This research was designed to test a generalized version of relative deprivation theory.[10] It was postulated that discrimination against subordinate communal groups was a pervasive source of deprivation and motivation to rebellion by the affected group.[11] A similar argument was made about deprivation and political violence among regional groups that sought greater political autonomy. To test the arguments, a list was compiled from a variety of regional and country studies of groups that were subject to discrimination, had separatist aims, or both, in the world's 119 larger countries and colonies. At first the only data gathered on the groups were population estimates for around 1960. These were used to calculate an indicator of their proportional size. Later, four-category ordinal scales were used to rate the intensity of discrimination and of separatist potential in each group. In the late 1970s a more intensive follow-up survey was made of group discrimination and separatism in 86 countries as of 1975.[12] A series of empirical studies showed that indicators constructed from the coded data were consistently correlated with countries' magnitudes of political violence in the 1960s.[13]

Time and events change one's perspectives. In the early 1980s the first author wrote several essays that posed some general answers to the question of "why states coerce." This interest was provoked in part by old criticisms of the "one-sided" approach to conflict taken in T. R. Gurr's *Why Men Rebel,* and in part by reading some of the second author's early case studies of genocide. The exigencies of maintaining power in the face of long-standing intercommunal hostilities figured prominently in the theoretical explanation of state coercion.[14] This line of reasoning raised a different kind of question: not, why do minorities rebel? but rather, what are the historical origins and contemporary political dynamics of conflict and repression between dominant groups and communal minorities? In the fall of 1986, a new round of empirical work began when the first author was invited by James R. Scarritt, a senior Africanist, to coauthor a paper on minority rights issues for the Second World Congress of Human Rights. Building on the earlier data on group discrimination and separatism, we began a systematic inventory of communal groups that were at risk of future rights violations because of their past or present economic and political status. Some operational specifics of the project are sketched below. One point needs to be highlighted here: the human rights aspects of the Minorities at Risk study are only one facet of a larger concern with the origins, dynamics, and outcomes of intercommunal conflict.

Genocides and Politicides Since World War II

The second author's interest in the prevention of genocide, which began in the 1970s, culminated in a monograph in which a jurisprudential argument was developed that prescribed intervention as the ultimate sanction in cases of massive human rights violations.[15] During the course of research it became evident that most scholarly research on the topic could be roughly divided into two distinct strands. Genocide studies consisted either of historical studies concentrating on the Holocaust as a unique event, or international legal treatises lamenting the horror of genocides, while simultaneously insisting on the sancity of sovereign states.[16] Comparative research on the causes of genocide had just begun, exemplified by the scholarly works of Dadrian, Fein, Horowitz, and Kuper.[17] During the 1980s the topic became more "fashionable," and a body of scholarly research has begun to accumulate. What remains notably lacking is systematic quantitative research. To our knowledge Rudolph Rummel and the second author have to date generated the only two cross-national data sets that systematically identify episodes of mass political murder by governments.[18]

At first the most puzzling questions, for the second author, were how civilized nations and/or individuals could turn savagely against noncombatants, and why people elsewhere tolerated such atrocities. In an attempt to understand the psychological underpinnings of mass murder, a survey technique was applied in two countries to determine the extent to which emotional arousal, prompted by the depictions of atrocities, translated into empathy for victims and support for remedial political action. The results clearly show that certain governmental acts are readily recognized as human rights violations, at least in Western societies.[19] By extension, most of those who perpetrate mass murder presumably are aware that their acts are criminal in the eyes of the larger community and in international law. These findings pointed toward another question: why individuals empowered by their governments to kill others may do so without succumbing to excessive guilt. The situation is not so different from the systematic training of combat soldiers, who kill in battle without hesitation yet function as normal citizens during peacetime.

The most troubling aspect of the capacity of many "normal" people to kill without moral compunctions is the role of the state, which provides the arena, incentives, training, and justification for its soldiers, police, and death squads to kill noncombatants. The Genocide and Politicide project in its present form began with the accumulation of a set of case studies of states that had committed genocides and political mass murders since World War II. The emphasis soon expanded to systematic compilation of information on all episodes during the post-Holocaust era: the purpose was to define and identify the entire universe of episodes and state perpetrators. The study includes ongoing episodes because, by observing their processes, it may be possible to design strategies of intervention that will deter leaders from further killings.

Definition and Recognition

From the above sketches, it should be evident that our concerns with the victimization of groups raise methodological and substantive issues that are quite distinct from the micro and macro approaches to human rights analysis. Some of the differences are a result of our special interests in conflict between dominant and subordinate groups. Others follow directly from the fact that the relevant dimensions of groups' rights and their victimization by the state are different, at least in part, from the dimensions measured in micro and macro studies. First we will comment on the ways in which we have dealt with the problems of operational definition: How do we determine, with a minimum of ambiguity, that a group is at risk, or that a geno/politicide has occurred?

Minorities at Risk

This project focuses on communal groups that are differentially treated as a matter of social practice and/or public policy. This definition poses two operational problems: determining what is a "communal group" and what constitutes "differential treatment." Communal groups, which we also refer to as identity groups, have three defining properties: (1) Most or all of their members share a collective identity; (2) this identity is based on distinctive cultural, historical, and/or ascriptive traits; and (3) these traits are recognized as socially important by other groups within a larger, politically organized society. The key to identifying communal groups thus is not the presence of a particular trait such as language, ethnicity, separate historical experience, or religious belief, but rather the shared perception that these traits differentiate the group from others in significant ways. It follows from this conception that groups which are distinct at one time are in other times and places indistinguishable from the larger society. Differential treatment often is both a cause and a consequence of strong feelings of group identity. Moreover the dominant group may treat a multiplicity of identity groups as an undifferentiated minority, and by doing so unintentionally encourage those groups to develop a sense of common cause and identity.[20]

There are vastly different estimates of the numbers of communal or identity groups in the contemporary world. Nietschmann thinks there are 5,000,[21] Nielsson and Jones identify 575 ethnic groups (as they call them) that are actual or potential nations.[22] The differences among estimates are due mainly to levels of aggregation used by the analyst—does one count all tribal Indians in the Americas as one identity group, or count each tribe separately? In the Minorities at Risk study, groups ordinarily are identified at the highest level consistent with social practice and perceptions. In each country in the Americas, our unit of analysis ordinarily is "tribal Indians" because of their common treatment by the dominant societies, and because many of them have come to share a sense of identity that extends beyond specific tribes (see note 20). Where there are significant differences in treatment and status, for example between forest-dwelling and agricultural Indians in parts of Latin America, our data make such a distinction.

Two related indicators are used to determine whether a communal group is at risk of human rights violations, or more broadly of involvement in open conflict. One is the existence of malign differential treatment by the larger society; the other is the policy or pursuit of more favorable differential treatment that aims at promoting group interests. Malign differential treatment may occur through widespread social practice or deliberate government policy, or both. Some policies of differential treatment are regarded virtually everywhere as rights violations, for example when black South Africans are denied basic political rights that are enjoyed by South Africans of European descent. Other kinds of differential treatment reflect imposed solutions to intergroup conflicts. National minorities in the U.S.S.R., for example, are allowed to preserve their own languages and culture, but many of them continue to demand greater political autonomy on grounds that cultural autonomy is not enough. Some policies of differential treatment are remedial, designed to compensate for old wrongs, such as Affirmative Action programs for African Americans. In virtually all instances, policies of benign and remedial differential treatment reflect historical legacies of special treatment that were anything but benign: conquest, enslavement, persecution, social exclusion. Moreover social patterns of malign discrimination against minorities often coexist with remedial public policies, as is evident in the treatment of some communal groups in both the U.S. and the U.S.S.R. And legacies of discriminatory treatment and persecution that supposedly are dormant can reemerge in altered political circumstances. It is not too many years since Lebanon was described as the "Switzerland of the Middle East" because of the amity of relations between its Christian and Muslim communities. There are also those special cases, exemplified by Maronites in Lebanon, in which dominant minorities have maintained their position and privileges by differential treatment of subordinate majorities. The potential for open conflict is inherent in such situations, and the dominant group is invariably at risk of future persecution.

In summary, any identity group that has recently been the focus of differential social treatment, or the source of demands for better treatment, is regarded as at risk of future violations of members' human rights. The study is limited to groups for which differential treatment has been an issue at some time since 1960, on the assumption that such risks are low if the issue has not been manifest in the last generation. Operationally, the study includes four types of groups that fall within these general guidelines:

(1) *Groups subject to political discrimination.* These are communal groups that now or recently (since 1960) have been systematically limited in their enjoyment of political rights, or access to political positions, by comparison with other groups in their society. This use of

an internal standard of comparison, rather than some universal standard, sharply distinguishes our approach from that taken in standards-based ratings of human rights.

(2) *Groups subject to economic discrimination.* These groups now or recently have been systematically excluded from access to desirable economic goods, conditions, or positions that are open to other groups in their society. Thus far we have identified 68 groups that are actively subject to political or economic discrimination, or both, while another 117 groups live with the consequences of past discrimination.

(3) *Separatist groups and regions.* All regional groups that now or in the recent past have actively sought greater autonomy belong on a roster of minorities at risk. Such groups generally define their differences from dominant groups using the same kinds of markers used by other communal groups: they claim separate histories, distinct cultures and languages, sometimes different ethnicities and religious beliefs. The fact that they claim special political status because of such differences is *prima facie* evidence that they harbor aspirations that are not satisfied by present political arrangements. Such claims often arise from, or are intensified by, discriminatory treatment of the group. And such claims all too often lead to escalating cycles of unequal conflict in which the state perpetrates gross violations of human rights, as has happened to the Iraqi Kurds and the people of East Timor. We have identified 37 groups that actively support separatist movements and 35 others that have done so at some time since 1945, or that have actively supported separatist kindred in adjoining countries.

(4) *Advantaged minorities.* These groups, paradoxically, are at risk because of their advantages rather than their disadvantages. We have identified 28 groups that currently exercise disproportionate political power and/or material advantage vis-à-vis restricted majorities. South Africa is an example of a society where cleavages are polarized: a dominant minority enjoys both political and material advantage. Malaysia and Indonesia are examples of societies with balanced disparities, in which the material advantages of Chinese minorities are balanced by the power advantages of dominant groups. The ruling elites of many post-colonial African countries are dominated by minority tribes that have established more or less temporary ascendancy over others. Inherent in all such arrangements are potentials for intensified conflict and rights violations, though to varying degrees.

Our survey has been limited to the 126 countries whose populations in the mid-1980s exceeded one million. The 261 minorities thus far identified include only those which meet one of these size thresholds: they number at least 10,000, or at least 0.1 percent of the country's population. The groups are widely distributed across all world regions, with somewhat greater concentrations in Africa south of the Sahara, Eastern Europe, and Asia.

The reliability with which we have identified the four different kinds of minorities at risk is to some degree problematic. All tallies cited above refer to the list published in the *Human Rights Quarterly* article cited in note 1. As more information is obtained on particular countries and groups, additional groups continue to be added and a few others deleted because they do not meet the operational criteria identified above. The explicitness of the criteria narrows the terms of discussion and makes it relatively easy for people with more special-ized knowledge to second-guess decisions about inclusions and exclu-sions. The more general issue is whether it is valid to regard all the groups identified as being at risk. Our basic supposition is that the degree of risk varies, and that the more detailed information being coded on each group (below) will make it possible to assess degrees of risk. Within the parameters of the distinctions made above, the short-term risks of serious rights violations are highest for active sep-aratists and for groups already subject to active discrimination. The approach thus far has been to err on the side of inclusiveness.

Genocides and Politicides

Genocide and politicide are both forms of extreme state repression designed to destroy actual and perceived opposition groups. In epi-sodes of genocide, people are defined primarily by their membership in a particular ethnic, religious, national, or racial group, whereas in politicide the victims are defined primarily in terms of their political position, that is, in terms of their class, political beliefs, or organized opposition to the state and dominant group.

The essential element in the conceptual definition of genocide and politicide is a coherent policy by a single ruling group which results in the deaths of many members of the targeted groups, however sus-tained the episode and however diverse the victims. (More than a third of the 44 episodes thus far identified include multiple victim groups.) The definition parallels that of the Genocide Convention, but differs by excluding acts "causing serious bodily or mental harm to members of groups." The "mental harm" clause would extend the definition to innumerable groups which have lost their cohesion and identity but not at the cost of many lives. On the other hand, the Convention says nothing about groups of victims defined and tar-geted because of their political views and actions, which we do in-clude. Of the 44 episodes, only five are identified as "pure" genocides, whereas twenty are "pure" politicides. In seven other episodes the victims were targeted primarily because of their communal traits, and in twelve episodes they were victimized primarily because they were identified as members of the political opposition. Overall politicides are more numerous and just as deadly as genocides.

Communal victims share distinctive traits, such as language, race, an enduring culture, or on the psychological level a "we" feeling by which they see themselves as being different from other social groups. In many cases such differences are irrelevant to the governing functions of heterogeneous nation-states. In other instances the sense of different identity is strengthened because of differential treatment by governments, and intercommunal conflict may occur. The birth of a sense of nationhood is often a result of differential treatment by governing authorities. Depending on the strength, political cohesion, and outside supporters of the group, oppositional activity may increase to the point of open rebellion, at which time governing authorities may choose to use any type of coercive strategies, including mass murders, to either quell or eliminate opposition.

The scenario of a politicide typically is different. In some instances political groups have no shared communal traits but rather are members of a political party, ideological movement, or class. Repression typically occurs as a result of their political activity or status, not because members are bound by ethnicity, religion, or race. This is the crux of the difference between a genocide and a politicide. In genocides victims are targeted because they are members of a group with distinctive communal traits, sometimes but not always engaged in some form of oppositional activity. In politicides, victims are members of groups defined by their political affiliations. The two kinds of victimization may occur simultaneously, of course—at least 6 of the 44 episodes include multiple victim groups, some of them political and some communal. An example is the case of Kampuchea, in which the Muslim Chams were victimized primarily because of their communal traits and all others because of their political status or perceived political opposition to the Khmer Rouge.

Given these definitions and distinctions, more detailed operational criteria were used in determining what constitutes an "episode." The 44 instances identified thus far include only those in which (a) many noncombatants were deliberately killed; (b) the death toll was high (in the thousands or more); and (c) the campaign was a protracted one. The "noncombatant" guideline helps distinguish between warfare and geno/politicides. Civil and revolutionary wars are always the occasion for military action against rebels, but not necessarily for reprisals against unarmed civilians. Twenty-three of the 44 episodes of geno/politicides occurred during or immediately after civil and revolutionary wars when the challenged regime set out to destroy groups of unarmed civilians on the suspicion that they supported or sympathized with the rebels.

With regard to the second guideline, "body counts" per se do not enter the definition of episodes because attempts at eliminating small groups are just as much geno/politicides as are attempts to destroy much larger groups. In practice the attempted destruction of small groups often goes without notice, especially when it occurs in the context of larger episodes of massive state repression. Some small-scale episodes thus remain to be identified in further research. The Ache Indians of Paraguay are the smallest victimized group identified thus far, with fewer than one thousand victims.

The third guideline concerns the length of episodes. The killings in the events included here all lasted for at least six months. Long duration is not intrinsic to the definition of geno/politicides, but it usually is the case that the physical destruction of a group, all or in part, requires substantial time and effort. This guideline rules out single, isolated massacres such as the massacre of Palestinians in Beirut's Chatilla and Sabra refugee camps in September 1982. The 44 episodes do include some discontinuous series of massive reprisals against a target group, such as those directed against Guatemalan leftists and Indians, and against Iraqi Kurds. These series of incidents are defined as single episodes because each was decided and executed by a single ruling group using similar tactics. The threshold between one or two massacres and an episode remains inherently indeterminate.

One other operational problem arose repeatedly when categorizing episodes. While the conceptual distinction between genocide and politicide is clear enough, operationally there are a substantial number of mixed episodes in which some members of communal groups are organized politically and are victimized because of their political activity. The Kurds in Iraq are a case in point. Rural Kurds who actively support separatist movements have been attacked with all the military means at the government's disposal, including chemical weapons. The Kurds in Mosul and elsewhere who participate in government-sanctioned political and economic activities are not at risk of repression so long as they do not support the separatists. Technically, therefore, the mass murder of Kurdish separatists is categorized as politicide, not genocide.

Information about the coverage of the two studies is summarized in Tables 1 and 2, which list the countries covered, the time spans, the numbers of episodes and groups, and breakdowns by major type

TABLE 1. Overview of Minorities at Risk Study

Units of analysis:	Communal minorities (identity groups) subject to differential social treatment, n = 261
Time periods for inclusion:	Groups subject to discrimination at any time since 1960; groups seeking greater autonomy at any time since 1945; Advantaged minorities in the 1980s
Countries included:	126 independent countries with populations greater than 1 million in the mid-1980s
Period coded:	Status of groups in 1980s; group involvement in open conflict in 5-year intervals from 1945–49 to 1985–89

Types of groups and their regional distribution:[a]

	Groups subject to discrimination	Groups seeking more autonomy	Advantaged minorities
Western and Eastern Europe			
Latent (pre-1980s)	24	7	—
Active (1980s)	16	4	0
Asia and Oceania			
Latent	29	4	—
Active	13	20	6
North Africa and the Middle East			
Latent	13	6	—
Active	16	6	3
Africa south of the Sahara			
Latent	25	16	—
Active	17	7	19
Americas			
Latent	26	2	—
Active	6	0	0

[a] Totals add to more than 261 because some groups both are subject to discrimination and seek greater autonomy.

and geographic region. As might be expected, there is some overlap between the groups identified in the two studies. The geno/politicide project identifies 35 victimized communal groups, all but four of which are included in the minorities project. Three of the exceptions are groups that have since gained independence from the authorities that victimized them: the Malagasy, the Bengali of Bangladesh, and the Kongo of Angola. The fourth are the Bubi of Equatorial Guinea, a country too small to be included in the minorities project. In another study, from which these observations are drawn, we have compared the two data sets more closely. Specifically, we assess the

TABLE 2. Overview of Genocides and Politicides Study

Units of analysis:	Episodes of mass murder against communal and political groups, n = 44
Time period for inclusion:	Episodes occurring between 1945 and 1987, including three that began during WWII and continued afterwards
Countries included:	All independent countries and dependencies
Period coded:	The duration of each episode, varying from less than one to more than ten years

Types of episodes and their regional distribution:[a]

	Genocides	Repressive, hegemonial politicides	Revolutionary, retributive politicides
Europe	2	2	0
Asia	2	6	5
Islamic	0	6	3
Africa (except Egypt and the Maghreb)	1	7	5
Americas	1	3	1

[a] Episodes are dated by the period in which they began. Episodes whose victims were politically active members of communal groups are classified as politicides. Mixed episodes—those with separate communal and political victim groups, or with both repressive and revolutionary objectives—are categorized according to their primary victims or objectives.

prospects that the targets of previous geno/politicides will be victimized in the future and offer similar risk assessments for other minorities that are now actively separatist or subject to active discrimination.[23]

Coding Groups and Events

The next task is to develop measures or indicators of the theoretically relevant features of the groups and events with which we are concerned. Stohl et al. identify three discrete procedures that are involved in any such project: specifying relevant dimensions, operationally defining each, and measuring (coding) the groups and events on each dimension.[24] Implementing these steps is logically discrete from the prior step of defining groups and episodes, but in practice the decisions taken at each stage interact with, and often require rethinking of, other decisions. For example, in the process of working out operational definitions of the measurement dimensions and coding particular cases, it sometimes was necessary to respecify some of the original concepts. Thus the distinction between genocides and politicides has been reformulated several times. In both projects we have had to second-guess the coding and categorization of groups and episodes as work proceeded. As a result, readers of successive working papers and publications from both projects will find some variation in the number of cases included and in how they are categorized.

The coding systems currently in use are complex, and data collection and coding is in progress. What follows are illustrations of aspects of the coding and discussions of some issues and procedures, not complete accounts.

Coding Minorities at Risk

Listed below are the dimensions on which the groups are being coded, within the constraints of data availability.[25]

I. GENERAL PROPERTIES OF THE GROUP

1. Ethnocultural and religious traits that distinguish the group from other groups in the society
2. Distinctive economic roles, if any
3. The group's population, its geographical dispersion, and distinguishing demographic traits
4. Cohesiveness of the group
5. Manifestations of open conflict with other communal groups

II. GROUP STATUS

1. Why the group is at risk: codings for patterns of discrimination, separatism, and special advantage
2. Extent of cultural, political, and economic differentials between the minority and the dominant social group
3. Legal and political status within the state structure
4. The group's demands and grievances in the 1980s

III. POLITICAL CHARACTERISTICS OF THE GROUP

1. Authority structures, by decade, 1940s–1980s (if any)
2. Modern political associations or movements, by decade (if any)
3. Political/ideological orientations of group leaders, 1980s

IV. ANTI-REGIME POLITICAL ACTION (if any)

1. Domestic manifestations of political action, by decade
2. External anti-regime political and military action, by decade

3. Insurgency campaigns

V. PROCESSES AND OUTCOMES OF PROTRACTED CONFLICT (if any)

1. External military and other interventions for group or regime
2. International attempts at mediation and their consequences
3. Group losses and gains that resulted from protracted conflict

VI. ADVANTAGED MINORITIES

1. Type(s) of advantage
2. Origins of the group and its advantages
3. How advantages are perpetuated
4. Challenges to group's advantages

Several general observations are in order about the coding system. Its choice of dimensions reflects a series of compromises between what we ideally would like to measure about the status and actions of minorities and the kinds of information available in the scholarly and journalistic sources that are available. The coders have alternated repeatedly between specifying dimensions and categories and trial coding of typical groups. At each round, the questions are (1) Are the categories, as defined, suitable for unambiguous coding of the traits of the groups in the trial run? (2) Are there other important properties of the groups that should also be coded? These trial runs have led to three major revisions of the coding system. New dimensions and categories have been added at each revision and operational definitions have been sharpened.

Second, there was no a priori decision to restrict measurement to interval-level data such as tallies of numbers of victims or indicators of income inequality. The variables and coding categories were designed to maximize the information included in the data set rather than to maximize statistical precision. A few of the variables are directly measured using interval data, such as a group's population and the reported size of fighting units. As discussed in the next section, the reliability of such data are often suspect. Other variables are dichotomous. For example, each ethnocultural group is coded using di- or trichotomies on five different traits that may distinguish it from other groups in the larger society. The coding decision is whether and how the group differs from the dominant group in language, social customs, religious belief, physical appearance, and region of residence. At a later stage, these codings could be used to construct an interval scale of minority distinctiveness based on the number of differentiating traits.

Many other variables are operationalized as ordinal scales, such as the scales for rating patterns of discrimination, reproduced in Figure 1. These scales operationalize two of the general criteria used when deciding whether a group is to be counted as a minority at risk. The categories are used to record basic distinctions among the types of

---

WHY IS THE GROUP AT RISK IN THE 1980s?

U127 / / Political discrimination. Of what pattern (code most severe)?

1 = Substantial underrepresentation in political office and/or participation due to historical neglect or restrictions. Explicit public policies are designed to protect or improve the group's political status.

2 = Substantial underrepresentation due to historical neglect or restrictions. No social practice of deliberate exclusion. No formal exclusion. No evidence of protective or remedial public policies.

3 = Substantial underrepresentation due to prevailing social practice by dominant groups. Formal public policies toward the group are neutral or, if positive, inadequate to offset discriminatory practices.

4 = Public policies (formal exclusion and/or recurring repression) substantially restrict the group's political participation by comparison with other groups. (**Note:** Discount repression during group rebellions. What is decisive is patterned repression when the group is not openly resisting state authority.)

U128 / / Economic discrimination. Of what pattern (code most severe)?

1 = Substantial poverty and underrepresentation in desirable occupations due to historical marginality, neglect or restrictions. Public policies are designed to improve the group's material well-being.

2 = Substantial poverty and underrepresentation due to historical marginality, neglect or restrictions. No social practice of deliberate exclusion. No formal exclusion from economic opportunities. No public policies aimed at improving the group's material well-being.

3 = Substantial poverty and underrepresentation due to prevailing social practice by dominant groups. Formal public policies toward the group are neutral or, if positive, inadequate to offset active and widespread discrimination.

4 = Public policies (formal exclusion and/or recurring repression) substantially restrict the group's economic opportunities by contrast with other groups. (**Note:** This category makes no assumption about the group's relative economic status. Public restrictions on the opportunities of economically advantaged groups are coded here.)

Figure 1. Minorities at Risk study, coding for the question, "Why is the group at risk in the 1980s?"

discrimination to be observed in the universe of analysis—whether it is historical or contemporary, and whether it is reinforced by explicit public policy or repressive actions. The four categories of each dimension of discrimination are designed for analysis as ordinal scales of the severity of discrimination.

Another ordinally scaled variable that is central to the assessment of group rights and status is the extent of differentials between a minority and the dominant group. A full and precise assessment of this dimension would require an enormous amount of information, most of it unavailable, on such variables as income distribution across groups, (in)equality of representation in political positions, and differences in beliefs and customs. Our alternative was to devise three summary scales to provide crude profiles of cultural, economic, and political differentials. The five-category scales and coding guidelines are reproduced in Figure 2. The examples are drawn from trial codings. Note that coding decisions about the extent of differentials are

---

How great are intergroup differentials?

Use this five-category scale to rate the differentials on each of three dimensions. Check each category on which there is a significant intergroup difference. The category counts are guides to judgment, not firm rules. If the sources do not permit an informed judgment, code 9.

0 = no socially significant differences. A "socially significant" difference is one that is widely seen, within the minority, and/or the dominant group, as an important distinguishing trait of the group.

1 = slight differentials. **Guideline:** There are socially significant discrepancies between the minority and the dominant group on one or two of the specified qualities.

2 = substantial differentials. **Guideline:** There are socially significant discrepancies with respect to three specified qualities.

3 = major differentials. **Guideline:** There are socially significant discrepancies with respect to four specified qualities.

4 = extreme differentials. **Guideline:** There are socially significant discrepancies with respect to five or more specified qualities.

9 = no basis for judging.

U136 / / Cultural differentials. Judge by reference to similarities or differences with respect to ( ) ethnicity or nationality, ( ) language, ( ) historical origin, ( ) religion, ( ) social customs, and ( ) urban/rural residence.

Examples of 1: Catholic v. Protestant Dutch, Scottish v. English.
Examples of 2: French v. Anglo Canadians, Brazilian Blacks v. Euro-Brazilians.

built up from a series of dichotomous judgments about specific differences. These codings are adequate for comparative analysis across large numbers of groups. The basic framework could be elaborated and refined in greater detail for case studies of particular groups.

Coding Genocides and Politicides

Existing case studies provided the rough information to generate the first coding scheme. In the process of actually coding information, using the materials on each episode accumulated over time, the cod-

---

Examples of 3: Arab v. Jewish Israelis, Philippine Muslims.
Examples of 4: Aborigines v. white Australians, Brazilian Indians v. Euro-Brazilians.

U137 / / Political differentials. Judge by reference to ( ) access to positions of political power (national or regional), ( ) access to civil service positions, ( ) recruitment to military and police service, ( ) voting rights, ( ) effective right to organized political activity on behalf of group interests, and ( ) effective right to equal legal protection.

Examples of 0: French and Anglo Canadians, Sunni and Shi'ite sects in Iraq, Albanians in Yugoslavia.

Examples of 2: Overseas Chinese in Indonesia, Kurds in Iraq, Southern Sudanese, Mestizos in most of Latin America, Melanesians in West Irian.

Examples of 4: Rural blacks in South Africa v. white South Africans, Baha'is in Iran.

U138 / / Economic differentials. Judge by reference to inequalities in ( ) income, ( ) land and other property, ( ) access to higher or technical education, ( ) presence in commercial activities, ( ) presence in professions, and ( ) presence in official positions. The scale is extended to -2 to permit coding of economically advantaged minorities who are excluded from political power.

Examples of -2: Chinese in Malaysia, Jews in Morocco.
Examples of 0: Spanish Basques, Sikhs in India.
Examples of 2: Blacks and Hispanics in the U.S., Palestinians on the West Bank, Albanians in Yugoslavia.
Examples of 3: Amerindians in North America, Melanesians in West Irian.
Examples of 4: Rural blacks in South Africa, Indios in most of Latin America.

Figure 2. Minorities at Risk study, coding for the question, "How great are inter-group differentials?"

ing scheme was extended and the dimensions sharpened, and we began to differentiate between different types of genocides and politicides. Previous chapters and articles explored theoretically the question of why states kill.[26] With the accumulation of data and the sharpening of the dimensions of the phenomena came our realization that geno/politicides are complex and multifaceted phenomena and possibly a series of distinct events having fewer elements in common than we had previously thought. The following are properties common to many but not all episodes: (1) institutionalized procedures that enable states to target unwanted groups of people within their domain; (2) leaders' will to use the means available; and (3) the availability of groups serving as scapegoats for whatever intra-elite or external conflict challenges the power of the ruling elite. The term *scapegoating* is used here to characterize a process in which the victims in any objective sense are innocent of wrongdoings but are perceived, correctly or not, as a threat to the political and social hegemony of the ruling elite. We know little about what triggers these deadly events, or why some governments settle disputes peacefully whereas others react with deadly force. The dimensions of the coding scheme, summarized below, reflect the most recent theoretical arguments, in which geno/politicides are regarded as multidimensional phenomena.[27]

We begin with the identity of the victims and categorize the relative importance of ethnicity, religion, region of residence, regional location, class/occupation, and political role as factors leading to the group's victimization. In addition, estimates are recorded of the numbers of victims in any given episode and the numbers of refugees outside the country at the end of an episode.

Second, the coding scheme categorizes the theoretically significant characteristics of the state and ruling elite. The categories include types of regimes and the ethnic, religious, and class character of the ruling elite.

Third, the circumstances of the mass murder are categorized. Different patterns of historical conflict between the state and victim groups are classified. The circumstances directly leading to the onset of murder and the direct involvement of the highest authorities are assessed. Other coding dimensions differentiate the kinds of units involved in the killings (military units, internal security forces, vigilantes, etc.) and the tactics used. The final categories are concerned with the status of the group at the end of an episode, and the regime's general policy toward the group, ranging from reconciliation to continuing repression.

A summary typology follows the coding scheme, differentiating between hegemonial and xenophobic genocides and between retributive, repressive, and revolutionary politicides, followed by one category for mixed or ambiguous cases.

Each dimension of the coding scheme reflects underlying theoretical concerns. The following is an example of the coding of the circumstances surrounding a geno/politicide. The question is whether and to what extent the highest authorities were involved. Did they give explicit orders? Or were there general directives that gave operational latitude to subordinates? Or did authorities simply tolerate or tacitly encourage mass actions by subordinates? These questions concern the question of intent. The Genocide Convention defines genocide as a specific act with the intent to destroy a national, racial, or religious group. In the strict legal sense, acts in which the government in question denies complicity or intent cannot be considered genocides. And in most contemporary episodes, few have followed the Nazi example, which was to announce publicly their intent to dispose of all Jews.

The culpability of the highest authorities for mass murder could be coded in 38 of the episodes. In 24 of them, the information of our case studies indicated that authorities explicitly ordered actions that demonstrated their intent to dispose of targeted groups. Three of these 24 episodes were worst-case scenarios, in which governments gave both specific orders and operational latitude to subordinates and also tolerated murderous acts by vigilantes or death squads. In nine episodes the evidence suggests that elites relied only on general directives that gave operational latitude to the subordinates who actually made the decisions to carry out the killings. In another five episodes the killings were tolerated but not inspired by governing elites, that is, they were executed mainly by groups such as vigilantes and death squads.[28]

Surprisingly, intent was not as difficult to judge as it appeared at the onset of the research. Most often researchers see intent as a purely psychological disposition or as a condition that does not take any specific form but exists in some latent way, for example in the minds of the potential perpetrators. In its manifest form, intent expresses itself in particular actions whose content leads observers to judge whether or not the target groups are designated as expendable or merely in need of sanctions. Thus, for example, the isolated killing or incarceration of a group leader is more often an act of intimidation than evidence of an intent to eliminate the group. The treatment of Palestinian Arabs by Israeli security forces is evidence of the intent to intimidate. If Israeli authorities were to impose the kind of measures advocated by extremists such as the Kach movement, it would move much closer to the scenario that leads to a geno/politi-cide.

Some may argue that if we could probe the minds of those who make policy, we would be closer to predicting whether a geno/politi-cide is in the making. To this we answer, based on the coded studies, that the processes and policies that lead toward the elimination or decimation of groups are long term ones. We do not need psycholog-ical evidence to recognize that potentially genocidal processes are un-derway. Geno/politicides are not unpremeditated policy decisions taken in response to sudden emergencies.

Validity and Reliability of Group Data

The fact that groups are victimized is difficult to conceal, especially if they are treated severely. This is equally true of systematic discrimi-nation and of mass murder. Authorities in the states responsible for such conditions seldom deny that they occur. Instead they are likely to offer justifications for their policies of differential treatment; they label the victims of mass murder as rebels or enemies of the state, and they minimize the suffering and death caused by state policies. Thus an analyst who is concerned with the human rights of groups and who knows a country well can ordinarily make valid inferences about which minorities are at risk and which groups are actively vic-timized. The more challenging task is to make reliable assessments of the extent of risk and the severity of victimization. This is especially difficult in authoritarian states that deny access to observers and ex-ercise close censorship over the flow of political information.

We offer several suggestions for researchers who are interested in extending and improving the precision of the kinds of research out-lined in this chapter. The suggestions should also be of value to those who are interested in monitoring and evaluating the changes in poli-cies and in group status that foreshadow gross violations of human rights.

(1) Complement global surveys with in-depth analysis by regional and country experts, using multiple sources. It is inevitable that global and historical surveys of the kinds we have done must rely mainly on secondary sources. We have used a variety of scholarly studies, journalistic accounts, and reports from activist groups, but their coverage and reliability vary greatly. According to the Minori-ties at Risk study, the quantity and quality of information on a group are best in open, Western societies: a great deal more is known about the status of, say, African Americans or immigrant workers in Ger-many than is known about threats to the well-being of forest-dwelling

Amazonian Indians or the non-Muslim southerners of Chad. In the Genocide and Politicide study there is far more information on episodes that captured global attention, like Kampuchea under the Khmer Rouge and the Argentine military's "dirty war" against the left, than on half-concealed cases like the Soviet treatment of Ukrainian nationalists in 1947–48 and the Pakistan government's campaigns against restive Baluchi tribesmen in the 1960s and 1970s.

There is a great need for researchers with specialized information and access to amplify the documentation and coding we have done. One step is to research as thoroughly as possible the scholarly and journalistic materials available in research libraries. Scholars and observers in the Third World may lack such library resources, but they have other invaluable assets: they often can interview indigenous people and obtain local sources, especially those written in vernacular languages, that are not available elsewhere. They also are in a position to monitor current developments (statements, actions) on a week-to-week or month-to-month basis in a way that more distant scholars cannot do.

(2) When evaluating and reporting statistical data, seek multiple estimates and report ranges rather than the false precision of single estimates. Three kinds of data about victimized groups are often reported with what appears to be precision: (a) the population of communal groups; (b) the number of victims of rebellions, politicides, and genocides; and (c) the number of refugees from such conflicts. In conflict situations all three kinds of data are politically sensitive and subject to manipulation by all parties to the conflict, including outside observers. Numbers of external refugees ordinarily are known with the greatest precision because of the presence of observers from the U.N. High Commission for Refugees. Numbers of internal refugees are much more difficult to ascertain.[29]

(a) Census data pose well-known problems of precision, even when the census-takers use internationally codified census techniques. Population data on communal groups pose far greater problems of reliability because there are no universal standards for determining group membership. Even if census-takers ask direct questions the responses are problematic, especially for people who may not want to acknowledge the stigma of belonging to a marginal group. Some states do not report any census data on minorities because of the sensitivity of the issue. In most of independent Africa, for example, "tribal" identifications are thought to be vestiges of the past and a threat to emerging national identities. Therefore few current official estimates are ever reported (Kenya and Nigeria are significant exceptions), and the analyst must guess the current population of the

Baganda, Bemba, Hutus, and dozens of other highly politicized groups by projecting the results of the last colonial census (if there was one) onto current estimates of total population. Other states deny the very existence of the minority. It is official policy that no Kurds live in Turkey, only "mountain Turks"; and that no Turks live in Bulgaria, only "Islamicized Bulgars." And even if there are seemingly hard data on the size of communal minorities, group spokespersons almost invariably claim that they are underenumerated by large margins.

(b) In most cases of genocide and politicide in the Third and Fourth Worlds there are not and cannot be precise estimates of numbers of victims because no one, neither the authorities nor the targeted groups, has reliable information on the death toll in the pacification campaigns, massacres, and executions; or on deaths from deportation, hunger, and disease that make up these episodes. The same is true of all but most localized rebellions and civil wars involving communal groups. Governments almost always downplay the human costs of their policies, while it is in the interest of group spokesmen and those who empathize with their victimization—including advocacy organizations and most journalists—to use high estimates as a way of calling international attention to their plight. Unfortunately, some scholars who see the world through a particular ideological prism are guilty of the same careless treatment of estimates.

The result is that multiple estimates abound. In the Geno/Politicides study the published lists of episodes specify the ranges of the estimates given in our sources without attempting to evaluate their accuracy. High estimates are usually two to five times greater than the low estimates, occasionally ten times greater. The "true" figures presumably fall within these ranges. In the Minorities at Risk study, a modified geometric scale has been devised to record estimates of numbers of deaths and refugees from protracted social conflicts. Procedurally, the median or most reliable estimate is determined from the sources, and the category within which the estimate falls is coded. In previous research on conflict events, the first author has standardized such geometrically scaled data (for purposes of aggregation and regression analysis) by assigning each event the midpoint value of the code intervals.[30]

1–2000	16–30,000	250–500,000
2–4000	30–60,000	500–1,000,000
4–8000	60–120,000	1–2 million
8–16,000	120–250,000	2–4 million

(3) Use increasingly refined judgmental scales to quantify narrative information. Most of the data generated in the studies reviewed here have been "made," not collected, by coding information from scholarly and journalistic sources using nominal and ordinal scales. The methodologies for doing so are well-established.[31] What we have done in the Minorities and Geno/Politicides studies, as outlined above, is to specify the theoretically relevant dimensions; then to devise and revise scales which capture the observed variation among our cases on those dimensions. In both studies we are reasonably confident of the reliability of the codings that make use of broad categories. More discriminating coding, for example about particular types of government policies toward minorities, has proved difficult to do with reliability. As more information becomes available, coding decisions tend to change.

There are two specific ways to improve the reliability and validity of codings on groups and by extension to improve the adequacy of coded data on human rights and their violation. Reliability can be improved by asking several coders to code the same bodies of information, then to compare notes. We have done so, selectively, in both studies as part of the process of refining the coding categories and training coders. Formal tests of intercoder reliability have yet to be done. The validity of codings should be enhanced by submitting coded information on specific events or groups to country experts for review and critique. The judges also may be asked to supply additional information that justifies their (re)coding.[32] We hope to do this on a trial basis at a later stage in the Minorities at Risk project.

We have placed on record the rationale and procedures being used in the studies of minorities and of geno/politicides as a guide to others who may be encouraged to do this kind of comparative research. The analysis of the human rights status of groups is "underdeveloped," but it need not remain so. It should complement ongoing efforts to improve the measurement of individual violations and to code broad national patterns of support for and abridgement of rights.

Notes

1. This chapter incorporates elements of four published and forthcoming papers, but includes a more extended discussion of rationales and procedures than they provide: Barbara Harff and T. R. Gurr, "Research Note. Toward Empirical Theory of Genocides and Politicides: Identification and Measurement of Cases since 1945," *International Studies Quarterly* 32 (September 1988): 359–371; T. R. Gurr and James R. Scarritt, "Minorities Rights at Risk: A Global Survey," *Human Rights Quarterly* 11 No. 3 (August 1989):

375–405; Barbara Harff and T. R. Gurr, "Victims of the State: Genocide, Politicides and Group Repression since 1945," *International Review of Victimology* 1, No. 1 (1989): 23–41, and Barbara Harff, "State Perpetrators of Political Mass Murder since 1945," paper presented to the Conference on State Organized Terror: The Case of Violent Internal Repression, Michigan State University, 2–5 November 1988. We wish to thank Thomas B. Jabine, Michael Hartman, and David P. Forsythe for their comments on a draft of this chapter.

2. This methodological approach is referred to as an events-based approach by Michael Stohl et al. (Chapter 8, this volume) and by the editors of this volume (Chapter 1). Events may be conceptualized and measured at different levels of analysis. Counting political executions is micro-level event analysis; identifying episodes of politicide or protracted social conflict is macro-level event analysis.

3. See Lopez and Stohl (Chapter 8) and Goldstein (Chapter 2) in this volume.

4. See Goldstein's critique in Chapter 2, this volume, and Raymond D. Duvall and Michael Stohl, "Governance by Terror," in *The Politics of Terrorism*, ed. Michael Stohl (New York: Marcel Dekker, 1983).

5. For a review of criticisms of Gastil's Comparative Survey of Freedom, and his response to them, see Raymond D. Gastil, *Freedom in the World: Political Rights and Civil Liberties, 1986–87* (Westport, CT: Greenwood Press, 1987), pp. 79–98. For studies that rely on judges to rate human rights conditions in Latin America see, for example, Russell H. Fitzgibbon, "Measuring Democratic Change in Latin America," *Journal of Politics* 29 (February 1967): 129–166; and Lars Schoultz, "U.S. Foreign Policy and Human Rights Violations in Latin America: A Comparative Analysis of Foreign Aid Distributions," *Comparative Politics* 13, No. 2 (January 1981): 149–170. For similar studies of Africa see Fred R. von der Mehden and Kim Quaile Hill, "Area Experts' Images of African Nations," *Comparative Political Studies* 12 (January 1980): 497–510 and James S. Scarritt, "Changes in the Rights to Participate in Politics and Their Relation to Development: Zambia 1973–1985," in *Human Rights: The African Context*, ed. George W. Shepard, Jr. and Mark Anikpo (Westport, CT: Greenwood Press, 1989).

6. For a recent analysis of the status of minority groups in international law see Hurst Hannum, "The Limits of Sovereignty and Majority Rule: Minorities, Indigenous Peoples, and the Right to Autonomy," in *New Directions in Human Rights*, ed. Ellen L. Lutz, Hurst Hannum, and Kathryn J. Burke (Philadelphia: University of Pennsylvania Press, 1989), pp. 3–24.

7. The project has received institutional support from the Center for Comparative Politics at the University of Colorado, Boulder, where it was initiated, and from the Center for International Development and Conflict Management at the University of Maryland, where it is now headquartered. Support for coding groups' involvement in conflict has been provided by the U.S. Department of Defense's Academic Research Support Program. In 1988–89 the project was the topic of the first author's research as Jennings Randolph Peace Fellow of the U.S. Institute of Peace. The project's principal research assistant is Monty Marshall, with other assistance provided by Michael Hartman at the U.S. Institute of Peace and Martha Gibson, Kook Shin Kim, Keith Jaggers, and Jeffrey Ringer at the Center for Comparative Politics.

8. The communal/political distinction is somewhat problematic. Many episodes have multiple targets, some political, others communal. Most victimized communal groups also were politically active. These distinctions form the basis for the typology used in Harff and Gurr, "Toward Empirical Theory" (note 1).

9. This study was begun by Barbara Harff with institutional support from the Center for Comparative Politics. Since 1986 it has been centered at the U.S. Naval Academy and supported by a series of summer grants from the Naval Academy Research Committee. Students and research assistants who have contributed to the case studies of geno/politicides are Rachel Frick, Kirpal Singh Khalsa, Scott Larson, Monty Marshall, Doug Robnett, and Donna Stolar.

10. T. R. Gurr, *Why Men Rebel* (Princeton, NJ: Princeton University Press, 1970).

11. "Minorities" is used in this chapter as a shorthand term for communal groups that are subordinate to the dominant social and political group. A few "minorities" are in fact numerical majorities, for example, blacks in South Africa, the Hutu in Burundi, and Indians in Bolivia and Guatemala.

12. Operational definitions, measurement scales, and list of the groups are reported in T. R. Gurr, *New Error-Compensated Measures for Comparing Nations: Some Correlates of Civil Violence* (Princeton, NJ: Princeton University, Center for International Studies, Research Monograph No. 25, 1966), pp. 79–90; and in T. R. Gurr and Erika B. K. Gurr, "Group Discrimination and Potential Separatism in 1960 and 1975," in *World Handbook of Political and Social Indicators III*, 3rd ed., ed. Charles Lewis Taylor and David Jodice (New Haven, CT: Yale University Press, 1983), vol. 1: 50–57, 66–75.

13. T. R. Gurr, "A Causal Model of Civil Strife: A Comparative Analysis Using New Indices," *American Political Science Review* 62 (December 1968): 1104–1124; T. R. Gurr and Raymond Duvall, "Civil Conflict in the 1960s: A Reciprocal Theoretical System with Parameter Estimates," *Comparative Political Studies* 6 (July 1973): 135–170; Douglas A. Hibbs, Jr., *Mass Political Violence: A Cross-National Causal Analysis* (New York: Wiley, 1973); T. R. Gurr and Mark Irving Lichbach, "A Forecasting Model for Political Conflict within Nations," in *To Auger Well: Early Warning Indicators in World Politics*, ed. J. David Singer and Michael D. Wallace (Beverly Hills, CA: Sage Publications), 153–193.

14. T. R. Gurr, "The Political Origins of State Violence and Terror," in *Government Violence and Repression: An Agenda for Research*, ed. Michael Stohl and George A. Lopez (Westport, CT: Greenwood Press, 1986), 45–71; and "Persisting Patterns of Repression and Rebellion: Foundations for a General Theory of Political Coercion," in *Persistent Patterns and Emergent Structures in a Waning Century*, ed. Margaret P. Karns (New York: Praeger for the International Studies Association, 1986), pp. 149–168.

15. Barbara Harff, *Genocide and Human Rights: International Legal and Political Issues* (Denver: University of Denver, Graduate School of International Studies, Monograph Series in World Affairs, 1984).

16. Barbara Harff, "Humanitarian Intervention: An Annotated Bibliography," in Israel Charny, ed. (New York: Facts on File, forthcoming).

17. Vahakn N. Dadrian, "A Typology of Genocide," *International Review of Sociology* 2 (1975); Helen Fein, "A Formula for Genocide: Comparison of the Turkish Genocide (1915) and the German Holocaust (1939–1945),"

Comparative Studies in Sociology 1 (1978); Irving Louis Horowitz, *Taking Lives: Genocide and State Power* (New Brunswick, NJ: Transaction Books, 1980); Leo Kuper, *Genocide: Its Political Use in the Twentieth Century* (New Haven, CT: Yale University Press, 1981).

18. R. J. Rummel, "Libertarianism and International Violence," *Journal of Conflict Resolution* 27 (March 1983): 27–71; "Deadlier than War," *IPA Review* (Australia) 41, No. 2 (1987): 24–30.

19. Barbara Harff, "Empathy for Victims of Massive Human Rights Violations and Support for Government Intervention: A Comparative Study of American and Australian Attitudes," *Political Psychology* 8, No. 1 (1987): 1–20.

20 Europeans in Latin America have customarily used the disparaging term *Indio* to characterize all indigenous peoples who follow traditional lifeways, irrespective of linguistic and tribal divisions among them. Public policy and social practice have seldom recognized the distinctions the indigenous peoples make among themselves. As a result there are diverse and competing bases for group identification and political action among Latin American Indians, some of whom defend traditional tribal interests, others of whom act on wider identities. An incisive analysis of these issues and their political consequences appears in Richard Chase Smith, "A Search for Unity Within Diversity: Peasant Unions, Ethnic Federations, and Indianist Movements in the Andean Republics," in *Native Peoples and Economic Development: Six Case Studies from Latin America*, ed. Theodore Macdonald, Jr. (Cambridge, MA: Cultural Survival, January 1985), pp. 5–38.

21. Bernard Nietschmann, "The Third World War," *Cultural Survival Quarterly* 11, No. 3 (1987): 2–16.

22. Gunnar Nielsson and Ralph Jones, "From Ethnic Category to Nation: Patterns of Political Modernization," paper presented to the International Studies Association, 1988 annual meeting, St. Louis, MO.

23. Harff and Gurr, "Victims of the State" (note 1).

24. Lopez and Stohl, Chapter 8, this volume.

25. As of this writing (June 1989) trial coding has been done on all variables for about 20 groups and the first-round coding of the others is about half completed. The first-round coding is limited to variables listed in I, II, and VI, plus IV.1. Copies of the coding system currently in use can be obtained by writing the first author at the Center for International Development and Conflict Management, Mill Building, University of Maryland, College Park, MD 20742.

26. Barbara Harff, "Genocide as State Terrorism," in Stohl and Lopez, *Government Violence and Repression* (note 14), pp. 165–187; "The Etiology of Genocide," in *Genocide and the Modern Age: Etiology and Other Case Studies of Mass Deaths*, ed. I. Walliman and M. Dobkowski (Westport, CT: Greenwood Press, 1987), pp. 41–59; and "The State as Mass Murderer: A Theory of Genocides and Politicides," unpublished paper.

27. Copies of the coding sheet used are available from the second author at the Department of Political Science, U.S. Naval Academy, Annapolis, MD 21402.

28. These findings are drawn from the analysis of the coded data reported in Harff, "State Perpetrators" (note 1).

29. A detailed global analysis of the patterns of conflict that generate refugee flows, with extensive data on external and internal refugees, can be

found in Aristide R. Zolberg, Astri Suhrke, and Sergio Aguayo, *Escape from Violence: The Refugee Crisis in the Developing World* (London and New York: Oxford University Press, forthcoming).

30. The procedure was used to construct indicators of the extent of participation in, and deaths from, civil conflict for the causal modeling studies cited in note 13.

31. The phrase "data-making" has been used by J. David Singer to characterize his Correlates of War project and is exemplified in his data sets on international and civil war: see Melvin Small and J. David Singer, *Resort to Arms: International and Civil Wars, 1816–1980* (Beverly Hills, CA: Sage Publications, 1982). For an overview of coding procedures used in macroquantitative research see T. R. Gurr, *Politimetrics: An Introduction to Quantitative Macropolitics* (Englewood Cliffs, NJ: Prentice Hall, 1972), chaps. 3–5. The *World Handbook of Political and Social Indicators* (note 12) includes descriptions and data for many coded indicators of properties of political systems as well as of civil conflict events.

32. On the use of coding of human rights conditions by expert judges see the references in note 5, especially Scarritt, "Changes in the Right to Participate in Politics."

STANDARDS-BASED DATA

Chapter 7
Political Rights and Political Liberties in Nations: An Evaluation of Human Rights Measures, 1950 to 1984

Kenneth A. Bollen

Human rights come in many forms. But most internationally recognized rights fall into one of the three categories: (1) political rights and liberties; (2) rights to protect the integrity of a person; (3) social and economic rights. Each warrants attention in its own right. I focus on the first category. In part, the importance of political rights and liberties follows because of their influence on other rights. For instance, torture, arbitrary arrest, detention, exile, and "disappearances" are examples of violations of personal integrity rights. These violations are most likely to occur when political rights and liberties are weak. The influence of political rights and liberties on social and economic rights is more ambiguous,[1] but when the former rights are strong there is the *potential* to bring about greater social and economic rights.

Political rights and liberties also are relevant to contemporary world events. The return to more democratic political systems in Argentina, Brazil, Portugal, Spain, Poland, and the Philippines are cases in point. So are the repressive regimes of South Africa, Afghanistan, and other countries that show declines in or low levels of these rights.

Monitoring these political rights and liberties requires measures. Without them our assessment of rights must be based on rough impressions that probibit comparisons between countries and analyses of the shifts within a country. With empirical indicators we can begin to track such differences.

Despite the advantages of measuring political rights and liberties, we should not close our eyes to the problems with such indicators. One is a practical difficulty. The availability of annual, worldwide data on political rights and political liberties is limited. A second problem is the possibility of measurement error, both random and systematic. Random error is expected since it is typical in social science measures. Systematic error can arise from the subjective nature of ratings and the information on which ratings are based. Indeed some authors argue that assessments of "human rights" based on U.S. State Department reports or on data from Freedom House have conservative biases in favor of countries with pro-U.S. positions.[2] Others argue that Amnesty International has a left-wing bias.[3] The evidence in support of these charges is largely anecdotal but is nonetheless sufficient to demand more general empirical analyses.

The purposes of this chapter are threefold. First, I seek to indentify data sources that provide measures of national political rights and political liberties. I deal mostly with measures that are available for more than one year and for both developing and developed countries. Second, I discuss the measurement properties of these indicators. I pay particular attention to their reliability, validity, and methodology of construction. Third, I suggest directions for future research. Specifically, I highlight ways to assess validity and reliability and to improve measurement procedures.

Definitions

Human rights is such an emotionally charged topic that a consensus on what it entails is nearly impossible. However, working definitions for political rights and political liberties are required to guide the selection of measures. My working definitions are as follows:

Political rights exist to the extent that the national government is accountable to the general population and each individual is entitled to participate in the government directly or through representatives.

Political liberties exist to the extent that the people of a country have the freedom to express any political opinions in any media and the freedom to form or to participate in any political group.

I emphasize that my focus is on national or countrywide indicators. Regional variations in rights and liberties are not treated except to the extent that they affect national levels.

When political rights are present, the government derives its authority from the population. The dominant mechanism for implementing these rights has been elections. Thus, evaluating political rights requires studying electoral characteristics. For instance, are elections held within a reasonable period of time? Is there any evidence of rigged elections? Are there restrictions on who can hold public office or vote? By answering questions such as these, we can gauge the degree of political rights.

The second concept is political liberties. Political liberties concern the existence of restrictions on political activities. Are any political parties banned? To what extent are the printed and broadcast media free from government interference? Can members of the population protest government policies without fear of repression?

Because of the general nature of these concepts, many potential indicators could be developed. For instance, ratings of the fairness of elections or the extent to which the political elite come to power via open elections are measures of political rights. Scores for the freedom of the press (or other media) or the freedom to assemble or organize into political parties are examples of indicators for political liberties. Though the pool of potential measures is large, it is important to choose only those that follow from the working definitions discussed above.

Are Political Democracy Indexes Appropriate Measures?

In this section I discuss the soundness of using indexes of political democracy to measure political rights and political liberties. This is an important topic since far more research has been directed toward scaling democracy than toward scaling rights and liberties. It may be desirable to build upon this research rather than start from scratch. I briefly treat the abstract, ideal relations between the concepts of political democracy, political rights, and liberties. Then I review in more detail the democracy indexes in practice.

In an earlier work, I defined political democracy as the extent to which the political power of the elite is minimized and that of the nonelite is maximized.[4] Conceptually, political democracy is closely related to political rights and liberties. Strong political liberties and strong political rights indicate substantial political power for the nonelites. That is, a high degree of political democracy manifests itself in a high degree of government accountability and freedom of expression. When political democracy is low, we expect both political rights and liberties to be low. This suggests that political liberties and rights should have a strong positive association. Bollen and Grandjean find evidence that these two variables are perfectly correlated once the influence of measurement error is removed.[5]

These links are important because they suggest that some indicators of political rights and liberties may be discovered in indexes of political democracy. Hazards exist in relying on cross-national measures of political democracy, however. The primary difficulty is that researchers have tended to confound democracy with other related concepts. For instance, several indexes of political democracy combine measures of stability and democracy. The pioneering work of Lipset provides an example. European democracies are operationalized as those countries that have had an "uninterrupted continuation of political democracy since World War I."[6] Cutright's widely used index scores countries for a two-decade period from 1940 to 1960, while many other democracy indexes also contain a stability component.[7]

Stability can have little to do with political rights and political liberties, however.[8] Spain had a stable political system under Franco but clearly the political rights and political liberties were few. Similarly, political stability in Nepal has not translated into political rights and political liberties. At the other extreme, Argentina now stands relatively high on these factors but it has not had stability. I do not mean to imply that stability is unimportant; the fact that the change to democracy is recent and therefore fragile in Argentina, Spain, Portugal, and elsewhere is a source of concern. Those advocating political rights and liberties would certainly hope to see democracy have some permanence in these societies, but this does not negate the argument that stability does not equal democracy. Another problem with measures that include stability is that they characterize a period of years and do not allow the monitoring of yearly changes. Such indexes are not useful for our purposes.

Voter participation is another indicator sometimes employed in political democracy indexes.[9] Although a low turnout at the polls raises doubts as to whether political rights are enjoyed equally, the extent of participation is conceptually distinct from the ability or potential to participate. Low turnout may arise from voter apathy; or, as Lipset suggests, voters' satisfaction with the government may reduce their motivation to participate.[10] Moreover, the legal obligation to vote, the accessibility of polls, and voter registration policies also affect turnout. Thus, for several reasons, voter participation should be treated separately from rights and liberties.[11] In fact many of the countries that have a poor record on political rights and liberties have very high voter turnout figures.[12]

A third questionable component that is included in several measures of political democracy is whether a country has a multiparty or "competitive" political system. Vanhanen, for instance, defines the competition component of his democracy measures as "the smaller parties' share of the votes cast in parliamentary or presidential elections or both, . . . calculated by subtracting the percentage of the votes won by the largest party from 100."[13] Other researchers use different weighting schemes or measures but employ the same strategy of penalizing a country to the extent that one party dominates.[14]

An advantage of such indicators is that if accurate voting percentages are available, this can be a relatively objective measure. Even assuming that the voting figures are perfect, however, there are reasons to question whether this is a valid measure of political rights or liberties. First, there is an inherent ethnocentrism, in that the multiparty system that characterizes most Western nations is de facto the most democratic. Second, differences on a competition scale need not correspond to differences in political democracy. If one country's smallest political party receives 35 percent of the vote and another's receives 45 percent, the latter is treated as ten percentage points greater in competition (or democracy) than the former. Yet such differences may not be meaningful. Finally, is it true that a democratic system must result in votes being closely split between competing parties? Surely not: citizens with full political rights and liberties may share a consensus on which party should rule. I, like many researchers, wonder about political rights and liberties in societies where victories are lopsided and one party dominates. I also agree that the *banning* of opposition parties to force a one-party state represents a restriction on political liberties. But this is not the same as automatically scoring the degrees of democracy based on the percentages of votes or legislative seats. The meaning of the percentage of votes for different parties is ambiguous because this quantity is affected by many factors that are distinct from the degree of democracy.

Clearly, democracy indexes need "pruning" before they are suitable to measure political rights and political liberties. The next section presents measures that survive this pruning. Even for these ratings the problem of bias remains. Most measures are developed by Western scholars in general and often only by those from the United States. This means there is a potential for rights and liberties ratings being influenced by the relation of the country to the West and the "visibility" of the country in the Western media. I will return to this point later in the chapter.

Data Sources

This section presents indicators that correspond to the definitions of political rights and liberties stated above. In most cases the match between the measure and concept is apparent, and I list the indicators without comment. For some, the validity of the measures is less clear, and I explain the complications in their use. I select variables based on several criteria. First, I do not include indicators of voter turnout or party composition,[15] or indicators that are aggregated over periods of five or more years, for the reasons presented in the previous section. I also concentrate on measures that are available for more than one year, since my focus is on time-series data for the post-World War II period of 1950 to 1984. Finally, the measure should be available for fifteen or more nations since I seek indicators that can monitor a number of countries over the same time period.

Most of the indicators are rating systems in which one or more judges transforms relevant information into scale scores. The major exception is the count of government sanctions variable which I review below. Other indicators such as the number of political prisoners, "disappearances," and tortures are not included for several reasons. First, it is unclear whether these indicators are best considered as violations of political rights and liberties or as violations of the rights to protect the integrity of a person. I believe that they fall more within the latter category. The second reason is a more practical consideration of data availability. I do not know of any time-series data for a large number of countries that measure these characteristics.

The following sources and indicators met the above criteria.[16]

(1) *Cross-National Time-Series Data Archive* by Arthur S. Banks.[17] Banks's data file contains numerous social, economic, and political indicators for many nations over most of the 1950 to 1984 period. The most relevant political rights measures are:[18] openness of the nominating process (segment 19 field 4), selection process for effective executive (segment 21 field 6), selection process for legislative body (segment 22 field 5), and the effectiveness of the legislative body (segment 22 field 4). One measure of political liberties reflects the freedom of group opposition (segment 19 field 6). Each is rated on a three or four point scale.

(2) *Annual Survey of Freedom in the World* by Raymond Gastil.[19] Gastil's ratings of political rights and civil liberties for most countries and dependencies of the world have appeared in the periodical *Freedom*

at Issue since 1973 and in a bound serial *Freedom in the World* since 1978. A recent volume of *Freedom in the World* contains a complete listing of his rankings through 1984. The first indicator appears to track political rights as defined above. The civil liberties variable measures political and other related liberties (e.g., freedom of religion, freedom of emigration) and thus is somewhat broader than the political liberties definition given above. The rankings are available annually (semiannually for some of the early years). Each scale has seven categories.

(3) *The Dimensionality of Nations Project* by Rudolph J. Rummel.[20] This early cross-national project contains some potentially useful variables. Indicators of political rights include the openness of the electoral system and whether the political leadership is elitist. For political liberties a censorship score and freedom of opposition scale appear. One variable, constitutional status, distinguishes authoritarian or totalitarian from constitutional regimes, but it is unclear whether this is a measure of rights, liberties, or neither. All of these measures are available for 1950, 1955, 1960, 1963, and 1965 and all have three point scales. Country coverage ranges from about seventy to over 100 nations, with the best coverage for the more recent years.

(4) *World Handbook of Political and Social Indicators II and III.*[21] *World Handbook II* contains one measure of political rights, electoral irregularity, which ranks into three categories the fairness of elections at four time points (1950, 1955, 1960, and 1965) for a number of countries (N = 82, 90, 101, and 97, respectively). As a note of caution, Taylor and Hudson suggest that the judges for this variable may have unduly penalized single-party systems.[22] A second variable, government sanctions, has excellent coverage (each year from 1948 to 1967 for 136 countries). At first glance it seems to be a measure of political liberties. It counts "the actions taken by the authorities to neutralize, suppress, or eliminate a perceived threat to the security of the government, the regime, or the state itself."[23] The three types of actions included are (1) censorship (e.g., banning articles or books); (2) restrictions on political participation (e.g., declaring martial law, mobilizing troops for domestic security); and (3) sanctions against (e.g., arrests or detainment for spying). There are some difficulties with this measure, however. First, it is likely that some regimes fabricate espionage charges as a means to suppress legitimate opposition, but these are confounded with all spying cases. Second, there is a built-in bias against countries with high political liberties to begin with: the greater the freedom, the more negative sanctions the government can impose. In contrast, a country low in political liberties has fewer potential restrictions to impose, because many of these negative sanc-

tions are already in effect.[24] Sanctions are more likely when a regime feels internally or externally threatened. In addition, reports of new sanctions are less likely to be known when a high level of information control already exists. Thus, this government sanction variable has a complex relation to political liberties and should not be used without some adjustments.

World Handbook of Political and Social Indicators III updates to 1977 the government sanction variable, reproduces selected years of Gastil's political rights and civil liberties measures, and provides measures of political discrimination circa 1960 and 1975. The latter show the percentage of the population experiencing discrimination in the political system and a separate four-point scale of severity of discrimination. Discrimination against ethnic, linguistic, regional, or religious groups is the focus. The relation of these variables to political rights and liberties is likely to be complex. Imagine a society totally ruled by one person. Since everyone else is equal in having no rights or liberties, the political discrimination would be low. Rather than measuring levels of political rights, these variables establish differences in the application of a given level of rights across groups.

(5) *Freedom in National Press Systems* by Raymond B. Nixon (1965, 1960).[25] Nixon reports expert rankings of press freedom for eighty-five countries in 1960 and 117 countries in 1965.[26] Each measure has nine categories. No measures of political rights are reported.

(6) *World Press Freedom* by Ralph L. Lowenstein.[27] With the aid of the Freedom of Information Center at the University of Missouri (Columbia), Lowenstein prepared a survey of expert native and non-native judges of "press independence and critical ability." Summary measures are available for 1966 and 1967 for 94 and 84 countries respectively. The values range from a low of -4.0 to a high of 4.0.

(7) *Violence and Repression in Latin America* by Ernest A. Duff and John F. McCamant.[28] Duff and McCamant define repression as "the use of governmental coercion to control or eliminate actual or potential political opposition." This definition corresponds to the lack of political liberties. Thus, their measures of repression detect low levels of political liberties. Duff and McCamant's four measures are: suspension of constitutional guarantees; arrests, exiles, and executions (of political opponents);[29] restrictions on the organization of political parties; and censorship of media. Each measure ranges from zero to four. The coverage over time is excellent, including twenty Latin American countries for each year from 1950 to 1970.

(8) R. H. Fitzgibbon and K. F. Johnson's revised index of political democracy in Latin America.[30] Fitzgibbon and Johnson have collected fifteen indicators on twenty Latin American countries, several

of which are appropriate in the present context. A measure of the freeness or fairness of elections falls under political rights. Indicators of political liberties include freedom of speech and free party organization. Other variables such as independent judiciary and civilian supremacy are likely to influence rights and liberties, but they are not direct measures of these concepts. All of Fitzgibbon and Johnson's variables have been measured at five-year intervals since 1945 and all of them are averages across a number of judges. The major coverage limitation is the restriction to Latin American countries.

(9) Other measures. As mentioned in the previous section of this chapter, several political democracy indexes contain measures of political rights and liberties though most use combinations of the above cited indicators. My 1950, 1955, 1960, and 1965 indexes of political democracy draw on data from Banks, Nixon, and Taylor and Hudson.[31] Arat uses some of the same measures to construct her democracy index but adds a "competition" component and modifies the government sanction variable.[32] Her index is annual from 1948 to 1977. Perry creates indicators of "political contestation" for 1960, 1963, 1967, and 1970.[33] Some of the measures tap political rights and liberties as defined above but many measure concepts quite distinct from these (e.g., "fettered capitalism," "government control of banking and trade"). Humana's *World Human Rights Guide* has several indicators of political rights and political liberties for the period up to April 1983.[34] It is not clear whether these ratings are only for 1983 or cover more than one year.

Summary

Table 1 provides a summary of the major data sources for political rights and political liberties measures reviewed above. It lists the authors, years covered, countries covered, and number of indicators for each concept. As is clear from this table, the three sources with the best combination of temporal and geographical coverage are Banks, Gastil, and the *World Handbooks II and III*.[35] For the remaining data sources, those with good geographical coverage are typically not good for temporal coverage and vice versa.

Measurement Properties

I divide this section into two parts. The first concerns the methodology of data collection and the errors that enter this process. The sec-

TABLE 1. Summary of Data Sources for Political Rights and Political Liberties
    Measures, 1950–1984

Author(s)	Time coverage	Country coverage	Number of Indicators of:[a]	
			Political rights	Political liberties
1) Banks (1971, 1979)	annual[b] 1950–1984	worldwide	4	1
2) Gastil (1985)	annual 1973–1984	worldwide	1	1
3) Rummel (1976)	1950, 1955, 1960, 1963, 1965	worldwide	2	2
4) Taylor and Hudson (1972); Taylor and Jodice (1983)	1950, 1955, 1960, 1965 (fairness of elections)	worldwide	1	0
	ca. 1960, ca. 1975 (political discrimination)	worldwide	1	0
	annual** 1950–1977 (government sanctions)	worldwide	0	1
5) Nixon (1965, 1960)	ca. 1960, ca. 1965	worldwide	0	1
6) Lowenstein (1967)	1966, 1967	worldwide	0	1
7) Duff and McCamant (1976)	annual 1950–1970	Latin America	0	4
8) Fitzgibbon and Johnson (1976, 1982)	1950,** 1955, 1960, 1965, 1970, 1975, 1980	Latin America	1	2

[a] See text for description of indicators.
[b] Series begins pre-1950, before the time period of this writing.

ond part reviews the limited evidence on the reliability and validity of
political rights and liberties measures.

Methodology for Data Collection

I begin this section by describing an ideal situation for measuring
political rights and liberties. Like all ideals it is not attainable. Rather
it serves as a target at which to aim and a standard by which to
evaluate the measures presented in the last section. In the ideal situation a country's record on rights and liberties would be complete,
up-to-date, and readily available. Incidences of ballot alterations,

restrictions on the franchise, restrictions of eligible candidates, the frequency of elections, electoral bribes or corruption, falsely registered voters, weighted votes, or other political rights violations would be identified and registered. Similarly, the complete scope of the freedom of the media, the liberty of groups to oppose the government, the freedom of speech, the ability to organize or meet, and the breadth of other political liberties would be known. Moreover, judges would be objective in translating this perfect information into rights and liberties ratings. This would include the use of an explicit and complete checklist where the information could be evaluated, and an explicit set of rules for combining the checklist information into measures.

The actual situation deviates from the ideal in a number of respects. The information available is incomplete and the judges are subject to biasing influences. Consider first the information component. Figure 1 helps to illustrate some of the constraints. The figure shows six rectangles with the smaller ones subsets of the larger ones. The largest rectangle represents the ideal situation (described above) of knowing all characteristics, recorded and unrecorded, relevant to

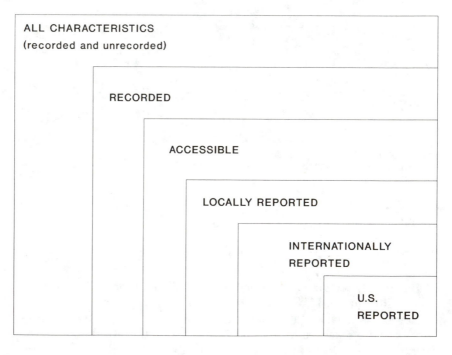

Figure 1. Political rights and political liberties characteristics.

the political rights and political liberties in a country. The second rectangle is a subset of the first and contains recorded characteristics. Some of these are military, police, or government records that are restricted in circulation. These records could document the arrests of political prisoners or list those who are political targets for the military or paramilitary groups. Alternatively, less sensitive but relevant information (e.g., denials of protest permits) could be archived. Only a subset of these documents would be accessible to reporters, researchers, or others in the general public.

The accessible characteristics make up the third box in Figure 1. An even smaller segment of the accessible information is locally reported, as represented in the fourth box. I define "locally reported" broadly. It includes information discovered by domestic reporters and reported domestically as well as reports of foreign correspondents which originate locally but are publicized only outside of the country. Thus this category encompasses all information reported to the public whether the "public" is domestic, foreign, or both. The reasons that not all accessible information is reported vary: government censorship, personal taste of media editors or research scholars, and limited publication space all play a role. The subset of locally reported information that travels beyond the country's borders is internationally reported information and is shown as the fifth rectangle. Finally, the smallest subset, the sixth box, is the internationally reported information that reaches the United States. As mentioned earlier, most political rights and liberties measures are formed by U.S. scholars who extensively employ information from U.S. or Western publications. Thus, we should know particularly the relation of the last two subsets to the universe of total characteristics.

Movement from the larger to the smaller rectangles of Figure 1 resembles a filtering process where some information passes through and some does not. If the filters act to create an essentially random sample at each stage, then not much distortion should result with any of the subsets of information. But if the filters are more selective, bias is probable.

Unfortunately, it is the latter situation which is more likely. Only particular characteristics have the chance to pass from one box to the next (see Figure 1). One factor that acts as a filter at each transition is the information technology of a nation. Recording of characteristics requires a minimal level of literacy and technological development sufficient to catalog such information. These requisites are strongest in the industrialized societes. In poorer societies they are less common. Thus, other things being equal, the more industrialized a country, the more complete are its records.

Socioeconomic development is not the only filter.[36] The passage of information from the recorded characteristics in the second box to the accessible ones in the third box can be affected by the openness of a nation. Since political rights and liberties generally are recognized as desirable, authoritarian regimes are unlikely to report restrictions placed on their citizens. The information is politically sensitive. If foreign and domestic reporters and researchers also are forbidden from examining government documents, then very little information makes it to any of the later boxes. Restrictions on the movements of reporters and on the number of foreign reporters impose further constraints on the observations of political rights and liberties. Government censorship of the local news media forces limitation on reports of even accessible information. To the extent that the internationally reported records depend on censored local ones, international knowledge about rights and liberties in a country is inhibited. Ironically, it is possible that a nation which is relatively open may appear lower in rights and liberties simply because violations are more likely to be reported to the outside world.[37]

Other information filters also play a role. One such factor that affects the comprehensiveness of international reports is the general media coverage a country typically receives. Its size, power, strategic significance, and the number of foreign correspondents stationed there affect its coverage. For example, during the Vietnam War, South Vietnam's electoral practices received considerable attention in the Western media. Similarly, because of the strategic interests of the United States, the Philippines January 1986 election had wide U.S. exposure. Also, international media differ in their coverage of world regions. Many U.S. newspapers and periodicals (e.g., the *New York Times*) have less coverage of Africa than do European publications. Another factor with consequences for international and U.S. coverage is the amount of communication between a country and other major nations. Communication can be measured directly by the volume of mail and phone calls or more indirectly by the presence of significant immigrant groups who can relay information from relatives abroad. For instance, communication between Mexico and the United States is enhanced not only by geographical proximity but by the Mexican immigrants in the United States. Cuban refugees provide greater contact with Cuba.

Another filter that affects the information reported internationally and in the United States is the degree to which current practices deviate from past ones. In a nation with a history of repression, new incidents of repression are less likely to be reported in the international media. In contrast, in a country with a strong democratic tradition, the presence of fraud in an election will excite general interest.

Finally, some mention should be made of the growing phenomenon of international election observers. These groups visit a country during the electoral process to assess whether the elections are "fair" and "free." The observations typically are short-term and based on one trip. The advantage of these observation teams is that they can bypass the normal, often biased sources of electoral information. A disadvantage is that they still may not have complete access to the relevant information, yet they may provide a false sense of objectivity. For example, the government hosts may avoid situations or places which portray a negative image of the elections. Some critics have charged that many observer missions sent by the United States are a means to legitimate the elections of leaders who are friendly to the United States.[38] Though we need to keep in mind these criticisms, election observers have the potential to reveal more direct information on political rights and liberties than is otherwise possible.

In sum, many factors act to filter knowledge of the characteristics of a country that appear in the different categories of information represented in Figure 1. Some filters can contribute to an overly optimistic perspective on rights and liberties while others can underestimate them. It is hard to predict the net effect of these factors but it seems likely that locally, internationally, and U.S. reported information contain biases that in turn can distort ratings of political rights and liberties.

The organization, processing, and interpretation of this information is the task of judges and a number of influences may affect their assignments. Figure 2 represents the major factors. Some effects are explicit while others are implicit. An explicit influence is the danger to a judge who participates. For instance, Johnson describes his experiences with a Latin American survey of democracy, "As I write these lines from Buenos Aires in November, 1976, I would not think of asking my panel of experts from last year to repeat their survey participation—four of them have been threatened by right-wing death squads, and two are in hiding after having received threats from the left."[39] Under such conditions, a judge who continues to participate would have difficulty in maintaining an objective perspective.

Other influences can be subtle, unknown to the judges or not consciously expressed by them. As an example, the political orientation of judges can bias ratings. Right-wing judges may rate right-wing governments more favorably while left-wing judges may do the same for left-wing governments. Judges who consult for the governments

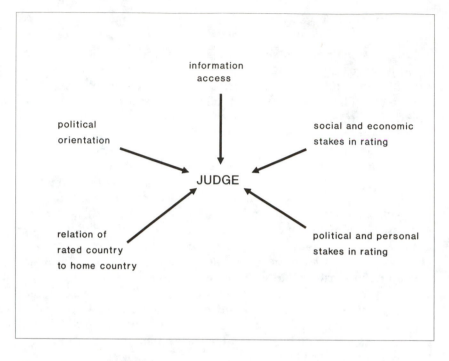

Figure 2. Factors influencing judges' ratings of political rights and political liberties.

being rated, or who are funded by organizations with a stake in the ratings, may have economic interests that affect their evaluations. The relation of judges' home countries to the rated country can subconsciously slant judges' ratings. The importance of these influences on judges in practice remains unknown.

In sum, the type of information and the judges who interpret this information affect political rights and liberties ratings. The information biases and the judges' biases can combine to create a common systematic error in all indicators that originate from the same publication or organization.

I turn now to the effects that the types of information and judges may have on the measures reviewed in the last section. I emphasize two publications with good temporal and geographical coverage—those by Banks and Gastil.[40] I begin with Banks's *Cross-National Time-Series Data Archive*. The variables I identified from this source in the previous section are only a small part of the *Archive*. According to Banks the sources consulted in forming these ratings number in the hundreds. Given this quantity, Banks did not list the specific sources for each country and for each year. However, he does provide a list of sources for the complete *Data Archive* which includes books, periodicals, encyclopedias, almanacs, and newspapers.[41] For instance, the *New York Times Index*, the *London Times*, *Facts on File*, *Encyclopaedia Britannica Yearbook*, and *Africa Report* are a few of the references listed. In addition, since 1974 Banks has been the editor of the *Political Handbook of the World*, which brings him in contact with other publications. Judging from the list, the bulk of the information seems to come from U.S. and European publications. Referring back to Figure 1, this would probably place the type of information mostly in the rectangles of "international" and "U.S. reported" with some locally reported information. Banks is the primary interpreter of this information, and is responsible for assigning derivative ratings.

Gastil describes his information base as follows:

The basic references for the undertaking are the annual editions of the *Political Handbook of the World* edited by Arthur Banks for the State University of New York and the Council on Foreign Relations, and the *Worldmark Encyclopedia of Nations*. Unlike most books and scholarly articles on nations, these references offer directly comparable information on the topics of most interest to the Survey. This information is modified by general background and reading, including wherever possible monographs on particular countries or comparative works. Events relevant to freedom are followed in the press, especially in the *New York Times*, the *Christian Science Monitor*, *Keesing's Contemporary Archives*, the *African Research Bulletin*, and *Latin America*. In addition, other journals are regularly consulted, such as the *Swiss Review of World Affairs*, *Foreign Affairs*, the *Middle East Journal*, *Asian Survey*, or the *Far Eastern Economic Review*. . . . Initially important for the comparison of press freedom were the reports of the Freedom of Information Center; more recently we rely on the reports of the International Press Institute, and the Freedom of Press Committee of the InterAmerican Press Association. The reports of Amnesty International and other human rights groups are carefully considered, as are the opinions of those professionally concerned with particular countries. The U.S. State Department is another valuable source . . . [and] an Advisory Panel has been established to provide informed critiques of both ratings and theory; other experts are consulted when needed.[42]

In terms of the information consulted, Gastil's work seems similar to that of Banks. Many references are checked but most are published in the United States or Europe. The suggestion, however, is that experts who have first-hand experience in some of the countries also inform the process. Thus, Gastil's information largely falls within the internationally reported and U.S. reported boxes of Figure 1 with some local reports.

Based on this description of references, Banks's and Gastil's information is largely confined to the last two boxes of Figure 1. As such they are forced to rely on information that has been filtered through the other boxes and that is subject to the potentially biasing influences reviewed above.

It is also noteworthy that Gastil cites Banks's *Political Handbook of the World* as a reference for his ratings. This raises the possibility that any errors in Banks's information may influence Gastil's measures. Another similarity of the two measures is the use of a single judge. Gastil is primarily responsible for interpretations of the assembled information, though a panel advises him on these ratings.

What about the judgment process? How do Banks and Gastil move from the information available to the ratings? Banks provides a brief description of the categories for each of his variables. Based on these descriptions and the information he draws upon, a country is placed into one of the ranked positions. There does not appear to be an explicit "checklist" or set of rules that are followed.

Gastil provides a fairly detailed description of each category of his political rights and civil liberties measures, giving examples to illustrate factors that affect a country's rating.[43] Unfortunately, he appears to confound his political rights and civil liberties ratings with other concepts. For instance, his rating of political rights is partially affected by whether there is a "one-party, no party, or competitive party system" and by the percentages of votes that go to the majority party in multiparty systems. In addition, foreign control and literacy also seem to enter ratings.[44] The relative weights of these factors in the final ratings are unclear, so the magnitude of this contamination is unknown. In fact, the details of the procedure by which the information from the above sources is employed to lead to the ratings are not documented. Gastil states: "For both political and civil rights there is an informal checklist of questions to be considered when making judgments. . . . It is necessary to look at patterns of answers, and ask whether, in terms of democracy, country A belongs with countries with similar ratings, or belongs above or below that level."[45] McCamant and Scoble and Wiseberg question whether it would be possible for an independent judge to replicate Gastil's ratings.[46]

In short, Banks's and Gastil's measurement efforts rely mostly on U.S. and European information supplemented by local experts where possible. Each is the final judge for their measures of rights and liberties. For each, there is ambiguity in the exact criteria or checklists that are employed to move from the raw information to the measures.

Given the ambiguity it is natural to ask which of the factors of Figure 2 that can influence judges might affect the ratings of Banks and Gastil. This is a difficult question to answer. Critics have suggested that a conservative bias may enter Gastil's judgments, based on his survey's sponsorship by Freedom House.[47] Some critics describe Freedom House as a "conservative American think tank" or more extremely as a "right-wing propaganda agency."[48] Several researchers claim that this conservative slant has led to incorrect rights and liberties ratings for some countries. For instance, Nagle states that Gastil's 1975 classification of Sweden in the next to the highest political rights category reflects a conservative bias against progressive welfare states. Scoble and Wiseberg note a bias in the ratings in favor of Third World allies of the United States and against neutralist or hostile countries. Herman and Brodhead also argue that Freedom House exhibits this trait. On the other hand, McCamant notes several cases that he believes are misclassified but says "the scoring does not have any obvious geographical or ideological bias, except perhaps for a strong distaste for Cuba."[49]

Considered together, these criticisms suggest that some nations may have been incorrectly rated on Gastil's measures. However, none of the criticisms of which I am aware have demonstrated a systematic bias in all the ratings. Most of the evidence consists of anecdotal evidence of relatively few cases. Whether there is a systematic or sporadic slant in Gastil's ratings is an open question.

Banks's measures have not received the same attention as Gastil's. Given the similarity in information sources and the similar use of one judge, Banks's indicators also should be examined for systematic measurement error.

Regardless of the direction of distortions, it is highly likely that every set of indicators formed by a single author or organization contains systematic measurement error. The origin of this error lies in the common methodology of forming measures. Selectivity of information and various traits of the judges fuse into a distinct form of bias that is likely to characterize all indicators from a common publication. This does not mean that the bias is large or that the measures cannot be used. It does mean that the variance in measures can be explained by at least two components, the actual level of rights or liberties and a bias effect. The relative contribution of these components is not known. Bollen and Bollen and Grandjean provide limited evidence for the existence of source bias in a confirmatory factor analysis of political rights and political liberties indicators.[50] Their studies find that the errors of measurement for several indicators from Banks are correlated due to their common origins. However, far more work is needed to determine both whether these results can be replicated and the saliency of these biases.

The other data sources described in the last section differ from Banks and Gastil in their measurement procedures. For example, Nixon, Taylor and Hudson, Duff and McCamant, Lowenstein, and Fitzgibbon and Johnson have panels of judges.[51] The sizes of the panels vary from two to nearly 600. The composition of the panels also differs, with most including non-U.S. members or area specialists. As an example, in 1970 Johnson had approximately equal numbers of Latin American and U.S. scholars and journalists as judges. Nixon had five international journalist experts on his panel: two European, two American, and a rotating fifth expert on the country or area being assessed. An advantage of panels of judges is that they provide more complete information than single judges. For instance, locally reported information (see Figure 1) is more available to many of these panels of judges. Also, a group of judges is less likely to reflect the idiosyncratic influences that can affect one judge's decisions (see Figure 2). It would be a mistake, however, not to allow for biases in these measures as well. Every distinct method of collecting and processing data can lead to such components of error.

Another dimension on which these publications differ is the detail provided about the coding rules for forming variables. Lowenstein provides considerable detail, listing the twenty-three items that were judged by his panel for each country, and he discusses ambiguities in coding.[52] Other sources are less clear.

The main disadvantage of these alternative publications is that they are not available annually or are restricted in regional coverage. But they can supplement Banks's and Gastil's measures. This would mean that the count and composition of indicators would vary for different years. For example, in 1966 Lowenstein's measure of press freedom could be added to Banks's set of measures. Rummel's measures can be added to Banks's for 1950, 1955, 1960, 1963, and 1965.

Furthermore, some measures can play a useful role in evaluating the reliability and validity of other indicators. Many of the measures that are restricted in coverage are formed by panels of specialists in particular political liberties (e.g., freedom of the press) or for particular regions. We would expect these judges to have greater access to information than those doing the more general ratings. Also, the presence of many judges should reduce the biasing influences that are likely for a single judge. For instance, Fitzgibbon and Johnson's political rights and liberties measures for Latin America could be compared to Banks's and Gastil's measures. Consistency in ratings would increase our confidence in Banks's and Gastil's measures. Systematic deviations, if present, could help isolate potential biases in ratings.[53]

Reliability and Validity of Measures

Measurement reliability refers to the consistency of measures. That is, to what degree do two measures of the same trait give the same results? Validity concerns whether one is really measuring a concept. Reliability differs from validity. One can get very consistent (i.e., reliable) measurements that are not valid; therefore the properties should be considered separately.[54] Researchers have varied ways of estimating reliability and validity, not all of which lead to the same results. Readers should ensure that similar procedures were used before comparing reliability or validity estimates from different studies.

Ideally, information on reliability for all the political rights and political liberties variables would be reported by the data sources. Unfortunately this is more the exception than the rule. The two most important sources, Banks and Gastil, do not report estimates of reliability for their political rights and political liberties measures. Results from Bollen can be used to form reliability estimates for Banks's measures.[55] In a circa 1960 confirmatory factor analysis, the reliabilities of the freedom of group opposition, executive selection, and the combined effectiveness/legislative selection variables are about .70, .46, and .71 respectively.[56] Arat uses the corrected correlations of items to the sum of all items as an estimate of reliability for some of Banks's measures. The corrected item to total correlations for freedom of group opposition (party legitimacy), executive selection, legislative selection, legislative effectiveness, and openness of nomination process are .90, .67, .49, .94, and .87 respectively.[57] David Banks finds high rank-order correlations (about .9) between Gastil's measures and Humana's, which suggest substantial reliability. Overall the available estimates show moderate to high degrees of reliability. But reliability should not be confused with validity.

Empirical studies of the validity of Banks's and Gastil's indicators are rare. For the issue at hand, the question is whether their measures really reflect political rights and political liberties as defined above. Bollen and Arat report correlations of some of Banks's measures with their own and with other indicators, but far more analysis is needed. Some sources of invalidity were discussed above. Specifically, the information available for making the ratings (see Figure 1) and the judges themselves (see Figure 2) can lead to invalidity.

There is a scattering of evidence on the measurement properties of other political rights and liberties measures besides Banks's and Gastil's. Lowenstein reports the discrepancies between native and nonnative judges of press freedom.[58] Johnson reports a high degree of consistency of assessments over time for the Latin American countries. Nixon reports a .96 tetrachoric correlation[59] between an alternative press control measure and his 1960 index. As an indicator of political democracy, Bollen finds Nixon's 1960 measure to have a reliability of .85. Bollen's composite democracy index has a reliability coefficient of about .9 for 1960 and 1965. Arat's corrected item-total correlation for her adjusted government sanction measure is very small ($-.14$). Her overall index has a Cronbach's alpha reliability of .94.[60] Bollen, Perry, and Arat report moderate-to-high correlations of their "democracy" indexes with other indexes as tests of validity.[61] Hill and Hurley find a high correlation of Nixon's press freedom measures with Fitzgibbon and Johnson's press freedom for Latin American countries.[62] Taylor and Hudson and Taylor and Jodice have very good appendices that describe the methodology and reliability of their event data, including the government sanction variable.[63]

Suggestions for Future Research

My suggestions for future research fall under two categories: better analyses of existing measures and the construction of new ones. In general much more information on the measurement properties of current indicators is needed. One way to do this is for the data sources to provide more complete information on the data collection methodology. Specific details on the characteristics considered for each indicator, the checklists employed, and the methods of interpreting and resolving contradictions that may be present in reference material would be helpful. Furthermore, studies of reliability need to be undertaken. If the coding rules are sufficiently clear this could be done by independent researchers whose ratings could be compared to Banks's and Gastil's ratings. Standard psychometric procedures for assessing reliability could be applied.

Also, more analyses of validity are needed. We need to ensure that measures of political rights and liberties conform to the conceptual definitions. In addition, we need to look for systematic biases in these measures. This latter issue has received hardly any empirical study. Yet if such biases are serious enough they can undermine the usefulness of the measures.

Structural equation techniques[64] including confirmatory factor analysis could prove useful in analyzing many of these problems. Bollen and Bollen and Grandjean provide examples of confirmatory factor analyses applied to rights and liberties data.[65] Models can be built that allow for random and nonrandom measurement error. Separate latent variables representing political rights and political liberties as well as biases can be explicitly incorporated into such models. Reliability estimates can be obtained as the variance explained in a measure by all latent variables in the model. The contributions of measurement biases versus the valid components can be compared. Furthermore the empirical association of political rights and political liberties can be estimated.

Improved analyses of old measures are not enough. Construction of new measures also should be encouraged. It may be possible to quantify largely qualitative reports such as those produced by Amnesty International and the U.S. State Department. Cingranelli and Pasquarello and Carleton and Stohl are engaged in such projects for measuring human rights.[66] It is important that any such efforts clearly and explicitly describe the coding rules.

Also, we should encourage the use of panels of judges to form ratings. A panel of judges is likely to have wider expertise than an individual. Furthermore, diversity in the nationalities of the judges could improve the validity of the measures. The more local information that is employed in rating countries, the better the quality of the ratings is likely to be.

Lastly, scaling procedures that lead to variables that are closer to the interval level of measurement should be encouraged. For instance, magnitude scaling estimation techniques[67] might be suitable. The judges could be given a standard that indicates a moderate degree of a particular political liberty or right and this standard assigned a value (e.g., 100). Judges then would compare each country to this standard by giving the proportion or multiple of the presence of the liberty in the real country versus the hypothetical. For instance, suppose the hypothetical country has several legal political parties while banning two or three "extremist" parties. Also, suppose that there are mild to moderate restrictions placed on some party activities, though it is possible to run an electoral campaign successfully. The degree of party liberties would be given a score of 100 for this hypothetical country. The judges would assess whether the liberties of political parties in a real country is greater or less than this and by what multiple. A real country judged to have party liberties a fifth of the standard would receive a score of twenty while one eighteen times greater would have 1,800 as a value. Such measures may produce more accurate and sensitive indicators.

Conclusions

Is an annual time series of political rights and political liberties for a large sample of countries available? The answer to this question is yes. When multiple sources are used, such a time series can be constructed for most of the post-World War II period. However, our knowledge about the measurement properties of these variables is limited. There have been few studies of reliablility and validity. The potential for measurement bias is even less explored.

Such neglect is not due to lack of importance. Without taking account of measurement error, we may incorrectly assess trends in national political rights and liberties. We also cannot accurately compare countries on these characteristics, nor can we be confident that we have correctly assessed any country's standing. The implications for research and policy decisions are great. For example, we cannot know whether a country's rights record affects its likelihood of receiving U.S. foreign aid if the human rights measures favor U.S. allies. Similarly, we cannot be confident about measures that show improvements or declines in rights or liberties if our proxies for these concepts are biased.

Future work requires a dual strategy. The first is to provide better documentation and better analyses of the existing measures. The second is the development of new measures. Without such attempts, the scientific study, policy analysis, and promotion of public awareness of human rights will make little headway.

I wish to thank Richard Claude, Barbara Entwistle, T. B. Jabine, Robert Jackman, and Ronald W. Wilson for comments on an earlier draft of this paper and Diana McDuffee for assistance in the computer literature search. The support of the Human Rights and Statistics project of the American Association for the Advancement of Science is gratefully acknowledged.

Notes

1. See, e.g., Kenneth A. Bollen and Robert Jackman, "Political Democracy and the Size Distribution of Income," *American Sociological Review* 50 (August 1985): 438–457.

2. See Harry M. Scoble and Laurie S. Wiseberg, "Problems of Comparative Research on Human Rights," in *Global Human Rights: Public Policies, Comparative Measures, and NGO Strategies*, ed. Ved P. Nanda, James R. Scarritt, and George W. Shepherd, Jr. (Boulder, CO: Westview Press, 1981), pp. 147–171; and Edward S. Herman and Frank Brodhead, *Demonstration Elections* (Boston: South End Press, 1984).

3. See Raymond D. Gastil, ed., *Freedom in the World: Political Rights and Civil Liberties, 1978* (Boston: G. K. Hall, Freedom House Books, 1978), pp. 28–30.

4. Kenneth A. Bollen, "Issues in the Comparative Measurement of Political Democracy," *American Sociological Review* 45 (June 1980): 370–390.

5. Kenneth A. Bollen and Burke D. Grandjean, "The Dimension(s) of Democracy: Further Issues in the Measurement and Effects of Political Democracy," *American Sociological Review* 46 (October 1981): 651–659.

6. Seymour Martin Lipset, "Some Social Requisites of Democracy: Economic Development and Political Legitimacy," *American Political Science Review* 53 (March 1959): 69, 73.

7. See Phillips Cutright, "National Political Development: Measurement and Analysis," *American Sociological Review* 28 (April 1963): 253–264; Phillips Cutright and James A. Wiley, "Modernization and Political Representation: 1927–1966," *Studies in Comparative International Development* 5 (1969–1970): 23–41; Arthur K. Smith, "Socio-Economic Development and Political Democracy: A Causal Analysis," *Midwest Journal of Political Science* 13 (February 1969): 95; Irma Adelman and Cynthia Taft Morris, "A Conceptualisation and Analysis of Political Participation in Underdeveloped Countries" (Mimeographed, 1971); Philip Coulter, *Social Mobilization and Liberal Democracy* (Lexington, MA: Lexington Books, 1975); Christopher Hewitt, "The Effect of Political Democracy and Social Democracy on Equality in Industrial Societies: A Cross-National Comparison," *American Sociological Review* 42 (June 1977): 450–464; Tatu Vanhanen, *Power and the Means of Power* (Ann Arbor, MI: University Microfilms International, 1979); Tatu Vanhanen, *The Emergence of Democracy* (Helsinki: Commentationes Scientiarum Socialium, 1984).

8. Ernest A. Duff and John F. McCamant, *Violence and Repression in Latin America: A Quantitative and Historical Analysis* (New York: Free Press, 1976), pp. 17–18.

9. Measures of political democracy that include voter turnout are those by Smith, "Socio-economic Development" (note 7); Robert A. Dahl, *Polyarchy: Participation and Opposition* (New Haven, CT: Yale University Press, 1971); Robert Jackman, "On the Relation of Economic Development to Democratic Performance," *American Journal of Political Science* 17 (August 1973): 611–621; Coulter, *Social Mobilization* (note 7); Steven Stack, "The Effects of Political Participation and Socialist Party Strength on the Degree of Income Inequality," *American Sociological Review* 44 (February 1979): 168–171; and Vanhanen, *Power* (note 7).

10. Seymour Martin Lipset, *Political Man: The Social Basis of Politics* (Baltimore: Johns Hopkins University Press, 1981; orig. Garden City, NY: Anchor Books, 1963).

11. See also Samuel P. Huntington and Joan M. Nelson, *No Easy Choice: Political Participation in Developing Countries* (Cambridge, MA: Harvard University Press, 1976).

12. Bollen, "Issues in the Comparative Measurement" (note 4), p. 373 n. 3.

13. Vanhanen, *Power* (note 7), p. 28.

14. See Cutright, "National Political Development"; Cutright and Wiley, "Modernization"; Smith, "Socio-Economic Development"; Coulter, *Social Mobilization* (note 7); Charles S. Perry, "Political Contestation in Nations: 1960, 1963, 1967, and 1970," *Journal of Political and Military Sociology* 8 (Fall 1980): 161–174; Zehra Fatua Arat, "The Viability of Political Democracy in

Developing Countries" (Ph.D. dissertation, State University of New York at Binghamton, 1985).

15. Although I have avoided direct measures of party composition, it is possible that this characteristic affects the judgments of other variables (e.g., freedom of group opposition). I suspect that any such effects would be far less than those that occur when party composition indicators are employed, but this is a question that should be empirically investigated.

16. In preparing for this review of measures, I supplemented my knowledge of indicators in several ways. First, I wrote to a number of scholars who are active in this area. Second, I did a computer assisted literature search. I searched U.S. Political Science Documents Data Base, Sociological Abstracts, and Social Science Citation Index. Some of the key terms I used for the search included political democracy, political liberties, political rights, civil liberties, human rights, international, cross-national, comparative, and various combinations of these categories. For the search of the Social Science Citation Index I looked for citations of authors of papers that have presented political rights or liberty measures. I should note that some references of which I was aware did not emerge in the computer search. I point this out to alert the reader to other possible omissions.

17. Arthur S. Banks, *Cross-Polity Time-Series Data* (Cambridge, MA: MIT Press, 1971); and *Cross-National Time-Series Data Archive User's Manual* (Binghamton: State University of New York at Binghamton, 1979).

18. Some researchers may be tempted to include additional scales from Banks as measures of political rights and political liberties. For instance, there is a variable for whether the regime is civilian, military-civilian, military, or other. Although most civilian regimes allow greater political rights and liberties than military regimes, both groups are heterogeneous. In addition, the correspondence of this measure to the theoretical definitions of rights and liberties in the previous section of this chapter is loose at best.

19. Gastil, *Freedom in the World* (note 3).

20. Rudolph J. Rummel, *The Dimensionality of Nations Project* (Ann Arbor, MI: ICPSR Codebooks, 1976).

21. Charles Lewis Taylor and Michael C. Hudson, *World Handbook of Political and Social Indicators II* (Ann Arbor, MI: Inter-University Consortium for Political Research, 1971); Charles Lewis Taylor and Michael C. Hudson, *World Handbook of Political and Social Indicators*, 2nd ed. (New Haven, CT: Yale University Press, 1972); Charles Lewis Taylor and David Jodice, *World Handbook of Political and Social Indicators III*, 3rd ed. (New Haven, CT: Yale University Press, 1983).

22. Taylor and Hudson, *World Handbook II*, pp. 24–25.

23. Ibid., p. 69.

24. Bollen, "Issues in Comparative Measurement" (note 4), p. 367 n. 7.

25. Raymond B. Nixon, "Factors Related to Freedom in National Press Systems," *Journalism Quarterly* 37 (Winter 1960): 13–28; and Raymond B. Nixon, "Freedom in the World's Press: A Fresh Appraisal with New Data," *Journalism Quarterly* 42 (Winter 1965): 3–5, 118–119.

26. Nixon's 1960 measure refers to 1 January 1960. He also mentions his reliance on reports prior to this date. Thus, the measure is probably best thought of as referring to 1959 rather than 1960. Similar comments are relevant to the 1965 measure.

27. Ralph L. Lowenstein, "Measuring World Press Freedom as a Political

Indicator" (Ph.D. dissertation, University of Missouri, 1967); *World Press Freedom, 1967; Freedom of Information Center Report No. 201* (Columbia, MO: School of Journalism, University of Missouri at Columbia, 1968); Ralph L. Lowenstein, "Press Freedom as a Barometer of Political Democracy," in *International and Intercultural Communication*, ed. Heinz-Dietrich Fischer and John Calhoun Merrill (New York: Hastings House, 1976).

28. Duff and McCamant, *Violence and Repression* (note 8).

29. A good case could be made that this is more a measure of violations to the integrity of a person than of political rights or liberties. Because of this, some may wish to exclude this indicator.

30. Russell H. Fitzgibbon, "Measurement of Latin-American Political Phenomena: A Statistical Experiment," *American Political Science Review* 45 (June 1951): 517–523; Kenneth F. Johnson, "Measuring the Scholarly Image of Latin American Democracy, 1945–1970," in *Statistical Abstract of Latin America*, ed. James A. Wilkie (Los Angeles: University of California, 1976), 17: 347–365; Kenneth F. Johnson, "The 1980 Image-Index Survey of Latin American Political Democracy," *Latin American Research Review* 17, No. 3 (1982): 193–201.

31. Bollen, "Issues in Comparative Measurement" (note 4); Banks, *Cross-National Manual* (note 17); Nixon, "Factors Related to Freedom" (note 25); and Taylor and Hudson, *World Handbook* (note 21).

32. Arat, "Viability of Political Democracy" (note 14).

33. Perry, "Political Contestation" (note 14).

34. Charles I. Humana, *World Human Rights Guide* (London: Hutchinson 1983).

35. Given the complex relation of the *World Handbooks'* government sanction variable to political liberties, it should not be employed until this link is fully studied. I believe that my earlier adjustment to this variable, Bollen, "Issues in Comparative Measurement" (note 4), and that of Arat, "Viability of Political Democracy" (note 14), are not adequate.

36. See Stanley J. Heginbotham and Vita Bite, "Issues in Interpretation and Evaluation of Country Studies," in *Human Rights Conditions in Selected Countries and the U.S. Response*, U.S. Congress, House Committee on International Relations (Washington, DC: U.S. Government Printing Office, 1978), pp. 341–357, for an excellent discussion of the factors that affect the adequacy of human rights data. Most of the factors they include are treated here.

37. It would be tempting to adjust ratings for the lack of access to relevant information. The obstacle to doing so is that there is no empirical work that shows the extent of such bias (if any). Without an estimate of bias, adjustments are difficult to justify.

38. Herman and Brodhead, *Demonstration Elections* (note 2).

39. Johnson, "Measuring the Scholarly Image" (note 30), p. 90.

40. Banks, *Cross-National Manual* (note 17); and Gastil, *Freedom in the World* (note 3).

41. Banks, *Cross-Polity Data* (note 17), app. 2; and Banks, *Cross-National Manual* (note 17), app. 1.

42. Gastil, *Freedom in the World* (note 3), pp. 8–9.

43. Ibid.

44. Ibid., pp. 9, 13, 18.

45. Ibid., p. 5.

46. John F. McCamant, "A Critique of Present Measures of 'Human Rights Development' and an Alternative," in Nanda et al., *Global Human Rights* (note 2), pp. 123–146; and Scoble and Wiseberg, "Problems of Comparative Research" (note 2), pp. 152–163.

47. Scoble and Wiseberg, pp. 160–163.

48. John D. Nagle, *Introduction to Comparative Politics* (Chicago: Nelson-Hall, 1985), p. 95; and Herman and Brodhead, *Demonstration Elections* (note 2), p. 7.

49. Scoble and Wiseberg, "Problems of Comparative Research" (note 2), pp. 160–163; Herman and Brodhead, *Demonstration Elections* (note 2). See also McCamant, "Critique of Present Measures" (note 46), p. 132.

50. Bollen, "Issues in Comparative Measurement" (note 4); Bollen and Grandjean, "Dimensions of Democracy" (note 5).

51. Nixon, "Factors Related to Freedom"; Taylor and Hudson, *World Handbook II* (note 21); Duff and McCamant, *Violence and Repression* (note 8); Lowenstein, "Measuring Press Freedom" (note 27); and Johnson, "Measuring the Scholarly Image" (note 30).

52. Lowenstein, "Measuring Press Freedom" (note 27). For a broader concept of human rights in Latin America, see Lars Schoultz, *Human Rights and United States Foreign Policy Toward Latin America* (Princeton, NJ: Princeton University Press, 1981).

53. David L. Banks, "Patterns of Oppression: A Statistical Analysis of Human Rights," *Proceedings of the Social Statistics Section of the American Statistical Association* (1985), provides some evidence of biases by comparing Gastil's and Humana's measures.

54. See Jum C. Nunnally, *Psychometric Theory* (New York: McGraw-Hill, 1978).

55. Note that I modify the Banks measures. See Bollen, "Issues in Comparative Measurement" (note 4).

56. The reliabilities estimate the squared correlation between each measure and the latent variable, political democracy. Reliabilities range between zero and one and they can be interpreted as the proportion of variance in the indicators explained by the latent variable.

57. These are the correlations of each indicator with the sum of all measures in an index with a correlation for the fact that the indicator is a component of the index. The reliability estimates are based on a sample that included all countries for all years that Arat analyzes. The figures may be misleading since the observations are not independent and would tend to inflate the association between some variables.

58. Taylor and Hudson, *World Handbook*, 2nd ed. (note 21), pp. 51–53.

59. The tetrachoric correlation is an estimate of the correlation between two continuous variables that underlie two categorized measures. It is based on the assumption that the latent variables have a bivariate normal distribution.

60. Arat, "Viability of Political Democracy" (note 14). Cronbach's alpha estimates the reliability of a composite of indicators. One can interpret it as the squared correlation of the latent variable and the simple sum of indicators.

61. Bollen, "Issues in Comparative Measurement" (note 4), p. 380; and Perry, "Political Contestation" (note 14).

62. Kim Quaile Hill and Patricia A. Hurley, "Convergent and Discrimi-

nant Validity Tests for Fitzgibbon-Johnson Political Scales," *Quality and Quantity* 15 (1981): 433–443.

63. Taylor and Hudson, *World Handbook II* (note 21); Taylor and Jodice, *World Handbook III* (note 21).

64. Karl G. Joreskog and Dag Sorbom, *Lisrel VI User's Guide* (Mooresville, IN: Scientific Software, 1984); and Peter M. Bentler, *Theory and Implementation of EQS: A Structural Equations Program* (Los Angeles: BMDP Statistical Software, 1985).

65. Bollen, "Issues in Comparative Measurement"; and Bollen and Grandjean, "Dimensions of Democracy" (note 5).

66. David L. Cingranelli and Thomas N. Pasquarello, "Human Rights Practices and the Distribution of U.S. Foreign Aid to Latin American Countries," *American Journal of Political Science* 29, No. 3 (August 1985): 539–563; and David Carleton and Michael Stohl, "The Foreign Policy of Human Rights: Rhetoric and Reality from Jimmy Carter to Ronald Reagan," *Human Rights Quarterly* 7, No. 2 (May 1985): 205–229. See also Steven C. Poe, "Human Rights and U.S. Foreign Aid: A Review of Quantitative Studies and Suggestions for Future Research," *Human Rights Quarterly* 12, No. 4 (November 1990): 499–512.

67. Milton Lodge, *Magnitude Scaling: Quantitative Measurement of Opinions*, Quantitative Applications in the Social Sciences, no. 07-025 (Beverly Hills, CA: Sage Publications, 1981).

Chapter 8
Problems of Concept and Measurement in the Study of Human Rights

George A. Lopez and Michael Stohl

Over the past fifteen years human rights have received a great deal of scholarly attention. A careful examination of this literature reveals four distinct approaches to the consideration of human rights. The first argues that human rights is a legitimate, if not critical, social science concept for inquiry in comparative and international affairs. Beginning with the work of Dworkin[1] and more recently manifest in Forsythe,[2] Donnelly,[3] and Vincent,[4] this approach to human rights ranges from philosophical treatments of rights[5] to comparative studies that illustrate the regional and cultural character of rights across the globe.[6]

The second approach, rooted in the scholarly and judicial traditions of international law, examines the legal and institutional dimensions of human rights. A particular focus of this approach is the development of effective human rights strategies and organizational machinery at the international level for holding governments accountable for violations of human rights.[7]

The third approach emerged in the early and mid-1970s as a result of U.S. congressional advocacy of human rights and the subsequent adoption of those themes by the Carter administration. Social scientists interested in evaluating the impact of these executive and legislative initiatives on the foreign assistance and foreign policy decisions of the U.S. government have been primarily responsible for the emergence of this growing literature.[8]

The fourth and newest area of scholarly inquiry is an extension of the third approach and informs much of this article. It examines methods of collecting information on human rights violations, and it aims to improve monitoring techniques and to increase the method-ological and statistical sophistication of data analysis of violations. As most human rights researchers and policy makers know, part of what also has developed under this rubric has been a major industry, of sorts, in think-tank-like assessments. These assessments have gener-ated considerable discussion in scholarly and policy circles, much of it controversial. Although our own work will be much different from these, we note this work as part of developments in the field.[9]

In light of this plethora of research, it is embarrassing but neces-sary to admit that relatively little concrete progress has been made in either improving cross-national and cross-ideological discussions of human rights, or in positing the relationships among human rights and particular social, economic, and political structures and pro-cesses. Further, both scholarly and policy debates are mired in argu-ments about the motive, context, and accuracy of strategies for human rights data collection and its interpretation. In short, *it is still impossible for diverse scholars and policy makers to agree on the quality of a particular government's human rights performance, or to state with any as-surance which variables lead to improvements or retrogressions in that govern-ment's human rights behavior, or to predict when such changes will occur.*

In this chapter we argue that in order to resolve these critical issues in human rights scholarship and advocacy we must improve the sen-sitivity of our monitoring and the sophistication of our measurement of human rights and their violation. Such advances will require more nuanced information collection and the use of a multidimensional approach to assessing the meaning of that information—with each activity informed by political judgement. Below we discuss the issues of information collection and multidimensional measurement explic-itly, with a recognition of the importance of political analysis inter-spersed throughout. In the process, we also demonstrate why some existing attempts to measure human rights, even when they reflect some of these intentions, fall short in operation.

Problems of Observation—or—Can We Recognize a Human Rights Violation When We See It?

Existing human rights information sources suffer from a number of well-known inadequacies, most notably that the quantity and quality of this information is often inconsistent across nations, over time, and vis-à-vis different rights. This poses a special dilemma to social scientists interested in moving beyond the recording of violations (however essential that function is to human rights advocacy) to an analysis of their fluctuation, causation, or related questions.

Remedies for such problems are not likely to emerge from the action of the major monitoring agencies themselves, as might be inferred from the following Amnesty International statement:

Amnesty International is often asked to compare and contrast the human rights record of different countries or of successive governments. It does not and cannot do this. Government secrecy and intimidation obstruct the flow of information from many countries and can impede efforts to corroborate allegations; this fact alone makes it impossible to establish a reliable and consistent basis for comparison. Furthermore, prisoners are subjected to widely differing forms of harassment, ill-treatment and punishment, taking place in diverse contexts and affecting the victims and their families in different ways; this fact would render any statistical or other generalized comparison meaningless as a real measure of the impact of human rights abuses.[10]

Amnesty's position complicates matters for those interested in creating adequate measurement schemes for human rights. Beyond these practical concerns, however, there are a number of conceptual and political issues that further obstruct the compilation of data on human rights violations.

We isolate four of these for discussion because they illustrate the centrality of conceptualization and judgement in any measurement of human rights. The burden of avoiding the pitfalls these issues pose must obviously accrue to the judgment of individual scholars and other observers. This is necessary if we are to be able effectively to account for diverse political contexts. In short, informed judgments by experts with a detailed knowledge of a particular situation over time are necessary to ensure the validity of any particular measure. It is meaningless to adhere dutifully to strict counting or coding criteria of specific violations if this simply produces invalid measures. As we shall discuss shortly, this is evident in the data presented in the *World Handbook of Political and Social Indicators.*

First, as Duvall and Stohl make clear, the absence of actual behavioral indicators at a given point in time may not be a reliable indicator of the absence of human rights violations.[11] Within a state which has an efficient apparatus for suppressing human rights, repression often radiates a pervasive and lingering "afterlife," which affects the behavior of people long after the observable use of coercion by state agents has ended. Because a general learning process has taken place and people are cowed into submission, the threat of further repression remains implicit as well as real. In essence, the behavioral terror process has become part of the political structure, if not of the political expectations of those living within that structure. As such it is no longer observable as a discrete behavioral event across time.

This basic fact, if not a bitter irony, of the reality of gross violations of human rights very much complicates the collection of essential information on such violations that would permit their serious study. Simply stated: an effective strategy for abusing human rights at one point in time results in a relative absence of behavioral events (i.e. other observable abuses) at various later points in time.

A second major problem arises (in the area of motivations and goals) when judging the activities of a regime by issuing a score for its violations of human rights. In both stable and unstable regimes, different parts of "the state" may have conflicting objectives in implementing (or not implementing) a rights violating policy. Only some of these may involve the intention to repress or terrorize.

This problem might arise, for instance, when human rights abuses become extended over long time periods, so that the agents carrying out this activity develop objectives of their own. These often involve their own survival, power aggrandizement, revenge, and so forth. These objectives can diverge from those of their superiors in the state apparatus, even if those people originally decided upon the course of abusive action the agents enforce. Such situations were routinely reported in various African nations regarding the actions of local military units in the 1970s. They have often been taken to the extreme by paramilitary and military units in Guatemala and El Salvador since the mid-1970s. The measurement question thus becomes: Whose intentions are important for determining whether certain actions constitute state violations of human rights, or are these acts solely "excesses" of local persons and groups?

One clue to unraveling this type of problem might be found in analyzing the attempts of superiors to regain control of their policies in the face of rights violating actions that were not ordered. The longer such violations are allowed to continue, the less willing we should be to believe that the state is opposed to such acts undertaken by its agents. It will obviously be difficult to make an absolute determination in such cases, but the important point is that the longer the abuses occur without the regime at least attempting corrective actions, the more confident we may be in attributing the abuses to the regime itself.[12]

Death squad activity in El Salvador after 1979 constitutes a case in point. Little doubt existed, at least until the latter half of 1984, that the death squads were serving the wishes of the Salvadoran "state." The lack of progress made by the judicial and executive systems in curbing these excesses was related to the belief of those comprising the Salvadoran state that their interests were being served. After the election of President Duarte in 1984, it became obvious to most observers that Duarte himself did not direct the death squads and that they did not act in his name. Yet the facts indicate that the death squads continued to operate with the connivance of other senior state officials. Various members of the Salvadoran population had their rights violated in the name of "the state," and by the action of state agents, even though some of the more important members of that state, particularly the new president, were opposed to such activities.

A third problem is illustrated by societies which are experiencing internal wars. In such situations, the question is whether we measure the lack of human rights protection as a failure of the government, or, rather, as an indicator of the state of political instability in the country. If insurgents make the society a dangerous place in which to live, do we give the nation as a whole a low score, or do we count only those abuses which are attibutable to government forces above and beyond the "handling" of the insurgent threat?[13]

Related to these issues are the changes in the character and quantity of violations which appear or are deliberately undertaken by a government during armed forces operations and self-defense actions against an insurgency in civil war. The traditional international law of war has always expressed concern about abuses against noncombatants, but this issue acquires an added dimension when the increase in noncombatant deaths occurs in a country with a poor prior human rights record.

For example, a regime may have drawn harsh criticism for the numbers of dissidents it had unlawfully jailed or for its responsibility for disappearances of opposition leaders. In order to improve its human rights appearance, the regime may very well halt these activities undertaken by police and clandestine groups. It may opt instead for the political murder of large numbers of suspected dissidents or opposition leaders in rural areas as a routine strategy in the conduct of a counterinsurgency campaign by the armed forces.[14]

Finally, the issue of arbitrariness or illegality often complicates the collection and measurement of human rights information. Many writers argue that the essential quality of human rights violations is that they are either arbitrary, in the sense that they do not conform to the due process of the law, or illegal, in that they are carried out in the face of clear prohibitions against such measures within the local legal system itself.[15] The latter case is particularly frequent when the state is using surrogate agents to carry through a campaign of human rights abuses.

It may well be that in many instances of human rights abuse, state agents frequently break or ignore their own laws, so that the security organs of the state can be said to be acting illegally. There are, however, so many ways in which state policies involving violations can be made to conform to the country's legal code (and vice versa), as well as so many variations in legal codes across countries, that any definition of human rights abuse that includes the attribute of "illegality" will probably create more problems than it solves. The frame of reference for this, of course, is Nazi Germany after the 1935 Nuremberg laws. Many of the practices in which Hitler engaged against German Jews were clearly within the legal framework of the German state of the time. Yet there is no argument that they should be included as clear instances of human rights abuses—even by standards of the 1930s.

The complications involved in using the legal/illegal or arbitrary/nonarbitrary criteria for distinguishing "human rights violations" from the "legitimate use of the state's coercive sanctions" thus seem considerable. The advantages for including these criteria appear uncertain at best. Hence, we would argue that it would be a mistake to use such characteristics to distinguish the state as human rights violator from the state as something else.

Problems with Existing Data Sources

To date the major efforts at measuring human rights violations have either ignored the various conceptual issues we have raised, or they have dealt with them inadequately. As somewhat pioneering efforts, many studies have, for understandable reasons, focused on the practical or physical problems associated with collecting human rights information, including the problem raised in the Amnesty International quote cited earlier. But such difficulties are encountered, in one degree or another, in the measurement of every social concept. While we should not underemphasize the magnitude of such problems, we also need to consider the types of conceptual and political issues we have briefly outlined here. A failure to do so is likely to result in unclear and/or in invalid measurement. This is true of the data available in two prominent social science volumes used for operationalizing human rights violations, *The World Handbook for Political and Social Indicators*,[16] and the measures constructed by Freedom House.

The *World Handbook* is an attempt to provide a comprehensive data set for a wide variety of political and social indicators. One subset of these indicators, which includes both "governmental sanctions" and "political executions," comprises what the *Handbook* editors refer to as the category "State Coercive Behavior." The former involves three types of governmental sanctions: censorship, arrest, and restrictions on political behavior (which includes everything from imposing curfews, banning a political party and harassing its members, to the imposition of martial law). Executions are defined as "event(s) in which a person or group is put to death under order of the national authorities while in their custody."

The data collected for these indicators represent counts of these types of events, compiled in the expectation "that the relations between these twitches of government activity and the pattern of protest will prove interesting for comparative analysis."[18] In other words, these data were collected because of an underlying theoretical premise regarding the nature of anti-regime violence. They were not collected for theoretical concerns connected solely or directly to the violence of the state, or human rights abuses.

Beyond this, as a compilation of events-based data the *Handbook* provides no means for accounting for those situations in which the very effectiveness of past abuses minimizes the need for many manifest events. To illustrate, the *Handbook* indicates that the Soviet Union for the years 1948 and 1950 had four and twelve cases of governmental sanctions. The United States had twelve and nineteen for these same two years. If governmental sanctions were the measure of repression, as the *Handbook* suggests, the United States would appear to be a more repressive society than the Soviet Union in those years.[18] In addition, the *Handbook* data (or actually, its compilers) never address the issues raised by governments' mixed motives and general political instability.

It should also be clear that much of what is counted in the *Handbook* are legal actions by the state, such as the imposition of censorship and curfews and the banning of political parties. Indeed, even the political execution variable focuses almost exclusively on those individuals who are executed after having been sent through the legal system, however fraudulently, and are admittedly in custody. In most abusive societies, however, executions are "extrajudicial" and thus not officially recognized or claimed by the state.[19] In data compilations such as the *Handbook*, then, they simply are not counted. The implications for human rights monitoring and comparative assessments of national performance are critical.

In the case of Guatemala, a nation that has experienced thousands of government murders in the past thirty years, the *Handbook* reports only thirty-five political executions from 1948 to 1977 (El Salvador is reported as having none). Further, Guatemala is listed as a state which imposed only five sanctions in the period of 1970 to 1977. By contrast the *Handbook* records the imposition of such sanctions 195 times during the same time period for the United States.

These and similar problems are clearly due to the emphasis on legal distinctions, in conjunction with the unevenness of available events information. Taken together, these problems greatly undermine the utility of the *World Handbook* data set for human rights based research.

Every year since 1973, Freedom House, under the direction of Raymond Gastil, has ranked each country in the world on a political and a civil rights scale.[20] The Freedom House data, presented in the annual volume *Freedom in the World*, illustrate the use of standards-based data collection efforts. These scales exhibit a number of problems, but at least they implicitly take into account some of the political issues we have discussed. If one reads through the descriptions of the scale ranking employed by Freedom House, it becomes clear that at various stages the issues surrounding the lack of manifest events, illegality, instability, and the mixed motives of government are considered.

Unfortunately, as others also have demonstrated before, these and other dimensions incorporated into the scales are never specified for their individuality, that is, the discrete units which comprise the scale. Nor is a scale ever disaggregated. The various dimensions evident in the Freedom House scales are simply presented as one summative assessment. The implicit range of each dimension and the weighting system (if any) employed in comparing countries and the decisional (mathematical) rule used to bring together units as a single ranking are never discussed.[21] In short, the operationalizations of the scale ranks, while comprehensive, are quite vague. In John McCamant's words:

To test the adequacy of these criteria, I removed the rankings, scrambled the order, and asked five students to rank the criteria according to the seriousness of the violation of civil rights. No one came close to the order given by Gastil. . . . If it is impossible to even know which criteria represent more serious violations, it is certainly impossible to use them for evaluating information on different countries.[22]

Thus, while the Freedom House scales implicitly tend in the proper direction, that is, in moving beyond overly simple events data, they nevertheless fall well short of adequate measures. Somehow Gastil and his colleagues have incorporated into the scales a wide variety of dimensions of the human rights concept. The Freedom House scales, therefore, highlight the need for an explicitly multidimensional approach to human rights measurement.

The fundamental problem with the *World Handbook*, *Freedom in the World*, and similar efforts is their failure or inability to account for the diverse political factors which affect the interpretation of human rights behavior.[23] Similar abuses may manifest themselves differently in different political contexts. And thus, in short, the statistical analysis of human rights must always be informed by political analysis. While we acknowledge that this is no small task as a requirement for the measurement of any concept, it is foolish to simply ignore it.

If we are to capture the complexity of the concept adequately, as well as avoid the charge of simplistic "number crunching," we must bring political knowledge to bear in shaping our collection of information and measurement schemes. And such collection and judgement must openly discuss the discrete indicators and decision rules which inform it. Such approaches may well lack statistical elegance, but they are absolutely necessary to ensure that quantitative data retain validity and interpretable meaning.

A Multidimensional Approach to Measuring Human Rights

At its best, social science measurement proceeds in five general steps: (1) an important social concept is delineated, in this case human rights; (2) the relevant dimensions of the concept are specified and disaggregated; (3) each of these dimensions is operationally defined and calibrated; (4) each dimension is measured with the data available; and, (5) if appropriate and desired, the constituent dimensions are reaggregated into a composite measure.

Human rights scholars have expended a great deal of energy on the first step, the delineation and definition of the concept. The few existing efforts at measurement, however, have usually bypassed the second step altogether. Human rights has instead been treated as a unidimensional concept, or, as in the case of the Freedom House scales, as an unspecified amalgamation of diverse dimensions.

Virtually all measurement efforts to date have concentrated exclusively on the quantity of human rights violations; that is, how many or how frequently are various rights violated? But human rights is a complex social concept. We should suggest that here exist three dimensions of general relevance to human rights measurements: severity, frequency, and range.[24] This is not to deny that many other possible dimensions exist and may well prove essential to particular research projects. But we believe that these three dimensions encompass the variation in which human rights scholars are usually interested and may be open to immediate use with existing data on violations from publicly available sources. We will discuss each in turn.

Severity

The "severity" of human rights violations indicates the level of state violations by focusing on the harm done to the victims. Defined in this manner, the severity of a violation addresses (or begs a judgement on) the quality of the human rights abuse. The lowest level of abuse may involve the infliction of some symbolic humiliation upon a victim or a deprivation of livelihood. The greatest could involve deliberate physical injury or loss of life. Arbitrary arrest and torture would lie somewhere between the two on this severity scale.

We recognize that establishing gradation measures for activities all of which are atrocious and despicable runs counter to both philosophical treatments of rights and the recording practice of many of the major advocacy and monitoring groups. However, as social scientists we find such an approach attractive. Not the least of the reasons for this attraction is that it appears consistent with a number of conceptual and measurement trends in the study of victimology.[25]

Many measurement efforts identify different types of violations, but these efforts tend to treat severity as only a qualitative, or nominal level, variable. There is no scaling along the dimension. Rather, different types of violations are simply treated as categorical differences. Humana's recent work is illustrative.[26] He examines dozens of different types of abuses, some minor, some extremely harsh. Yet, applied against any similar number of individuals, each distinct abuse is scored equally.

Severity should properly be treated, however, as a quantitative variable. It should be possible to rank types of abuse from low to high, from the least abusive to the most abusive. A regime which "disappears" citizens should be viewed as a worse human rights violator than one which "only" imprisons opponents, and so on.[27]

Frequency

The "frequency" of human rights violations refers to the number of occurrences of each of the various types of state violations during a given time period. Arbitrary imprisonment without trial would comprise a different frequency level depending upon whether it was an isolated occurrence, affecting only a few people each year, or a regular feature of the activities of the state security forces. The frequency of human rights violations addresses the issue of quantity in that it refers to how often particular activities are utilized.

Most efforts at measuring human rights have concentrated on measuring the frequency of violations as we have defined it. By examining frequency singly, however, rather than in combination with severity (and with range, below), these analyses may well be misleading. It might be that, in one instance, the severity of human rights violations is limited to activities stopping short of deliberate physical injury, but that they take place after affecting large numbers of victims. This might be contrasted with another case where assassinations are carried out, but infrequently.

Regimes often alter their strategies, varying the levels of both the frequency and severity of their violations. In such instances, an approach which examines only frequency may lead to an inappropriate conclusion that the human rights situation is improving. An example is provided by Berman and Clark, who report:

A decline in reported instances of torture in the Philippines in 1977 was explained by opponents of the Marcos regime as representing a trend on the part of officials to move away from detaining prisoners who could provoke criticism of the government towards the practice of arranging the disappearances of opponents.[28]

Thus what may have appeared on the surface as an improvement in human rights behavior actually may have involved only a shift in emphasis: the frequency of torture was decreased but the severity of the violations, from torture to disappearance, was increased. The point, of course, is that at any given level of frequency an increase in severity should be recognized as a deterioration of the human rights situation. In Humana's scheme, again only an illustration, a regime which denies the right of peaceful assembly to a "moderate" number of citizens is ranked a 2 and a regime which tortures a moderate number of citizens is also ranked as a 2. But is the latter not in fact a worse human rights violator than the former? An accurate assessment of human rights requires us to measure both dimensions, severity and frequency, and to examine the interaction of the two.

Range

The third dimension we will discuss is range. The range of human rights refers to the size and character of the population targeted for human rights abuses. In any society we obviously want to know how widespread the repression is in raw numbers. But we also want to know against which segment of a society are the state's agents acting—a particular professional group, an entire socioeconomic class, the rank and file members of some mass organization, or the members of a religious or linguistic community?

This concept of a different range for violations is quite distinct from the other dimensions discussed above.[29] It comes nearest to dealing with the question of whose rights are being threatened and, by implication, how deeply this cuts into the society. Range helps us recognize the differences between two regimes that utilize a similar severity and frequency of violations, but in which one threatens vast segments of society, and the other only a small minority. The latter remains reprehensible, of course, but we may nevertheless wish to recognize it as less abusive than the former. In short, it makes a difference whether the state is violating the rights of a small elite or a total community. None of the existing efforts to measure human rights explicitly addresses this concern.[30]

In sum, it seems clear that these three dimensions encompass the kinds of variation in which most analysts are usually interested. By explicitly measuring each, moreover, it should be easier to chart variations in human rights abuses, as well as the different tactics regimes employ. Further, by disaggregating the concept in this manner, we provide clearer opportunities for introducing needed judgements regarding the political peculiarities of individual cases and thus better ensuring valid measurement.

Toward Improved Operationalization

What practical steps can we take to improve upon existing measurement efforts and to begin to employ conceptually driven schemes like that outlined above? It should be clear that there exists no single "correct" manner in which to measure human rights. And, thus, rather than present a single example here, we will instead outline a number of steps which are likely to help improve all measurement efforts.

First, we need to return to the issue of raw information. As noted, and as is obvious to the casual observer, the state of existing information is quite poor. Because of the lack of scholarly interest and/or resources to date, in conjunction with the considerable difficulties associated with collecting such information—governments rarely extend themselves to advertise abuses—the quality of available information is very uneven. Many events are simply never brought to the public attention, and others come to light only long after the fact. Systematic sources detailing abuses for a single case are rare, and those with broader coverage are virtually nonexistent.[31]

It seems, at present, that we have little choice but to rely on journalistic accounts, the annual reports of the U.S. State Department, and the reports of Amnesty International and other relevant government and nongovernmental organizations (the Organization of American States, Americas Watch, Helsinki Watch, the International

Commission of Jurists, and so on). Each of these sources exhibits shortcomings. The unevenness of international news reporting is well established;[32] the State Department reports have been accused, rightfully in many instances, of political bias;[33] and the information provided by other organizations tends to be spotty and, consciously or unconsciously, presented in a manner which makes comparative analysis difficult.[34]

In light of this situation, we can make only two, albeit unsatisfactory, suggestions. First, pressure can be generated to encourage governmental and nongovernmental organizations alike to improve and regularize reporting practices. Concerned scholars need to press for improvement in at least these types of information sources.

Perhaps more promising, however, is the potential for improving the collection of journalistic information. Given the current availability of a variety of new services, with broad coverage of both the developed and developing countries, in machine-readable format, it should be relatively easy to improve the availability of journalistic human rights information. Very few resources have been expended in recent years on cross-national data collection, but this appears to be an area in which a modest investment would produce significant returns.

For the foreseeable future, unfortunately, such steps seem unlikely; as a result, our second suggestion is that we necessarily make do with existing information sources. "Making do" involves several steps. First, wherever possible, multiple sources of information should be employed. Given the current situation, no single source can possibly be adequate by itself. The data on government coercion available in the *World Handbook of Social and Political Indicators* suffer, among other reasons, because of their sole reliance on the *New York Times* for events information.[35] Two or more (preferably more) sources should always be used when relying on events data.

Second, care should be given to explaining what sources of information are used and what strengths and weaknesses these sources have. It is unclear, for instance, what sources of information are employed in the construction of the Freedom House scales. So far as anyone knows, Freedom House does not collect its own information, yet no reference is made to sources in its publications. Such omissions can only undermine the reliability and replicability of measurement efforts.

Third, we must adjust our measurement schemes to the level of precision actually evident in the information we employ. Our measurement procedures should neither demand nor imply greater precision than actually exists. Such "false precision" is evident in several existing measurements and efforts. Schoultz, for instance, had scholarly experts rank countries on a four-point scale and then averaged the judges' scores. In this manner, Ecuador was coded 2.05 and El Salvador 2.35.[36] The difficulty is that, in fact, we have no real idea what the difference between 2.05 and 2.35 means; it has no interpretable meaning. By virtue of the averaging process, a simple ordinal scale was transformed into an interval level scale. While unquestionably inadvertent, an impression is given of far greater precision than actually exists. In short, if available information allows us to make only nominal or ordinal level assessments, we only do ourselves and others disservice by forcing such information into measurement schemes designed to produce interval or ratio level measures.

Fourth, the use of a multidimensional approach, as we have outlined conceptually, will greatly increase the clarity of measurement procedures, in addition to capturing the complexity of the concept more adequately than existing measures can. The use of such an approach should improve measurement at all levels of information quality.

Finally, as has been a major part of our argument, measurement must be influenced by political analysis and judgment. We must utilize scholarly judgment to make informed political judgments in scoring human rights behavior. For instance, we earlier discussed the need to make inferences regarding the motives of various segments of governments. Such inferences lack ideal "objectivity," of course, but are nevertheless inevitable in all statistical work in the social sciences.[37] Moreover, by dealing with them explicitly we will both increase the validity of our measures and at least minimize the contaminating influence on reliability. Addressing the issue squarely, in other words, will strengthen rather than weaken our measurement.

Conclusion

On the basis of the foregoing discussion, it might be argued that efforts to improve human rights information and to treat human rights violations as a multidimensional phenomenon are overly complex and hence doomed to failure. It might be further argued that we should simply muddle along with the few existing measurement efforts. But that would miss, we believe, the major thrust of the preceding discussion.

It was not our intention to argue that measurement needs to be overly complex. Rather, we are interested in ensuring that the simplification that is necessary and inherent in all measurement, particularly in the early stages of the research endeavor, not be at the expense of either theroretical content or the distinguishing features of human rights abuse as a political process. For whatever information used, we require some simple indicators of differing aspects or dimensions of human rights violations. At this stage, we can only hope that such categorizations are of a more/less structure, and reflect, roughly, the level achieved by a government in a given time period.

Given our present ability to collect and classify such information, it should be apparent that events-based data collections will be difficult to establish and justify without enormous investments of resources, at both the collection and measurement stages. Standards-based assessments of violations are thus more likely to be useful, at least in the short run. Ultimately, however, an events-based data set should be developed because the phenomenon of human rights violations requires knowledge of the state of human rights violations, the structures of violation, and the impact of particular events on those structures and the rest of the political system.

The sole use of standards-based assessments and, in effect, second-hand events data sets seems inadequate to this task. While at the same time, the development of an events-based dataset will necessarily require a large scale collection effort, focusing specifically on those factors of theoretical importance to human rights—even if after the fact of those rights abuses. In the meantime, however, we believe the suggestions we have made can be used to make significant improvements in our measurement of human rights behavior.

An earlier version of this paper was published as Michael Stohl, David Carleton, George Lopez, and Stephen Samuels, "State Violation of Human Rights: Issues and Problems of Measurement," *Human Rights Quarterly* 8, No. 4 (November, 1986): 592–606. We are grateful to our two colleagues for their insights and contributions in that article. We are also indebted to Rhoda Howard and Jack Donnelly for their helpful suggestions on section IV of this paper.

Notes

1. Ronald Dworkin, *Taking Rights Seriously* (Cambridge, MA: Harvard University Press, 1977).
2. David P. Forsythe, *Human Rights and World Politics* (Lincoln: University of Nebraska Press, 1983).
3. Jack Donnelly, *The Concept of Human Rights* (New York: St. Martin's

Press, 1985), and *Universal Human Rights in Theory and Practice* (Ithaca, NY: Cornell University Press, 1989).

4. R. J. Vincent, *Human Rights and International Relations*, 2nd ed. (London: Cambridge University Press, 1988).

5. Henry Shue, *Basic Rights: Subsistence, Affluence, and U.S. Foreign Policy* (Princeton, NJ: Princeton University Press, 1980).

6. Vera M. Green and Jack L. Nelson, eds., *International Human Rights: Contemporary Issues* (Standfordville, NY: Human Rights Publishing Group, 1980); F. M. Burlatsky et al., *The Rights of the Individual in Socialist Society* (Moscow: Progress Publishers, 1982); Lars Schoultz, *Human Rights and United States Policy Toward Latin America* (Princeton, NJ: Princeton University Press, 1981); Claude E. Welch, Jr. and Ronald I. Meltzer, eds.. *Human Rights and Development in Africa* (Albany: State University Press of New York, 1984); and Rhoda Howard, *Human Rights in Commonwealth Africa* (Totowa, NJ: Rowman and Littlefield, 1986).

7. Examples abound, but most helpful are Richard B. Lillich and Frank C. Newman, *International Human Rights: Problems of Law and Policy* (Boston: Little, Brown & Co., 1979); Jorge I. Dominguez et al., eds., *Enhancing Global Human Rights* (New York: McGraw-Hill, 1979); Ved P. Nanda, James R. Scarritt, and George W. Shepherd, Jr., eds., *Global Human Rights: Public Policies, Comparative Measures, and NGO Strategies* (Boulder, CO: Westview Press, 1981); David P. Forsythe, "The United Nations and Human Rights, 1945–1985," *Political Science Quarterly* (Summer 1985); and Jack Donnelly, "Human Rights at the United Nations, 1955–85: The Question of Bias," *International Studies Quarterly* 32, No. 3 (September 1988): 275–304.

8. Issues of the policy journals *Foreign Affairs* and *Foreign Policy* have debated the various dimensions of this development over the past decade. Other helpful analyses include Shue, *Basic Rights* (note 6); Schoultz, *Human Rights* (note 7); Peter G. Brown and Douglas MacLean, eds., *Human Rights and U.S. Foreign Policy* (Lexington, MA: D.C. Heath & Co., Lexington Books, 1979); and Donald P. Kommers and Gilburt D. Loescher, eds., *Human Rights and American Foreign Policy* (Notre Dame, IN: University of Notre Dame Press, 1979). Further controversy has arisen as a result of assessments by empirical social science literature investigating the issue—see Lars Schoultz, "U.S. Foreign Policy and Human Rights Violations in Latin America: A Comparative Analysis of Foreign Aid Distributions," *Comparative Politics* 13, No. 2 (January 1981): 149–170; Michael Stohl, David Carleton, and Steven E. Johnson, "Human Rights and U.S. Foreign Assistance from Nixon to Carter," *Journal of Peace Research* 21, No. 3 (1984): 215; David Carleton and Michael Stohl, "The Foreign Policy of Human Rights: Rhetoric and Reality from Jimmy Carter to Ronald Reagan," *Human Rights Quarterly* 7, No. 2 (May 1985): 205–229; David L. Cingranelli and Thomas N. Pasquarello, "Human Rights Practices and the Distribution of U.S. Foreign Aid to Latin American Countries," *American Journal of Political Science* 29, No. 3 (August 1985): 539–563; and James M. McCormick and Neil J. Mitchell, "Is US Aid Really Linked to Human Rights in Latin America?" *American Journal of Political Science* 32 (February 1988): 231–239.

9. The controversies revolve around data sources like those we discuss in this chapter. The most important literature that reflects the issues of measurement and so forth includes Kenneth A. Bollen, "Political Rights and Political Liberties in Nations: An Evaluation of Human Rights Measures,"

Human Rights Quarterly 8, No. 4 (November 1986): 567–592; Rhoda E. Howard and Jack Donnelly, "Human Dignity, Human Rights and Political Regimes," *American Political Science Review* 80 (September 1986): 801–817; Jack Donnelly and Rhoda E. Howard, "Assessing National Human Rights Performance: A Theoretical Framework," *Human Rights Quarterly* 10, No. 2 (May 1988): 214–248; Barbara Harff and Ted Robert Gurr, "Research Note Toward an Empirical Theory of Genocides and Politicides: Identification and Measurement of Cases Since 1945," *International Studies Quarterly* 32, No. 3 (September 1988): 359–371; and Neil J. Mitchell and James M. McCormick, "Economic and Political Explanations of Human Rights Violations," *World Politics* 40 (July 1988): 476–498.

10. Amnesty International, *Amnesty International Report 1984* (London: Amnesty International Publications, 1984), p. 4.

11. Raymond D. Duvall and Michael Stohl, "Governance by Terror," in *The Politics of Terrorism*, ed. Michael Stohl (New York: Marcel Dekker, 1983), pp. 179–219.

12. The best discussion of this can be seen in the Americas Watch Report, *Draining the Sea . . . Sixth Supplement to the Report on Human Rights in El Salvador* (New York: Americas Watch, March 1985).

13. See, for example, Americas Watch Report, *Human Rights in Nicaragua 1985–1986* (New York: Americas Watch, March 1986), which discusses the impact of the war in Nicaragua on the situation of human rights in that country.

14. Such an approach, as used in El Salvador, is discussed by the groups Americas Watch and the Lawyers Committee for International Human Rights, *Free Fire: A Report on Human Rights in El Salvador* (New York: Americas Watch, 1984).

15. See, for example, the arguments by Dominguez and Rodley in Jorge I. Dominquez et al., *Enhancing Global Rights* (note 7), pp. 21–154.

16. Charles Lewis Taylor and David Jodice, *World Handbook of Political and Social Indicators III: Political Protest and Governmental Change*, vol. 2 (New Haven, CT: Yale University Press, 1983).

17. Ibid., p. 76.

18. Ibid., p. 116.

19. For a detailed discussion of this phenomenon see Edy Kaufman and Patricia Weiss Fagen, "Extrajudicial Executions: an Insight into the Global Dimensions of a Human Rights Violation," *Human Rights Quarterly* 3, No. 1 (February 1981): 81–100.

20. Raymond D. Gastil, ed. *Freedom in the World: Political Rights and Civil Liberties, 1980* (Boston: G. K. Hall, Freedom House Books, 1980). The volumes for 1981–1985 are published by Greenwood Press, Westport, Connecticut.

21. See Harry M. Scoble and Laurie S. Wiseberg, "Problems of Comparative Research on Human Rights," pp. 147–171; and John F. McCamant, "A Critique of Present Measures of 'Human Rights Development' and an Alternative," pp. 123–146; both in Nanda et al., *Global Human Rights* (note 7).

22. McCamant, "Critique," p. 132.

23. Two new sources, the DataBase Project on Palestinian Human Rights, with offices in Jerusalem and Chicago, and Jack Donnelly and Rhoda E. Howard, eds., *The International Handbook of Human Rights* (Westport, CT: Greenwood Press, 1988) represent an informed events-data collection and a

qualitative, sociopolitical country assessment respectively; in some ways each meets a few aspects of the criteria we have articulated here. In light of this, each source warrants a detailed investigation in its own right. Unfortunately such an analysis lies beyond the current scope of this chapter.

24. An early version of these concepts under different descriptions may be found in Christopher Mitchell, Michael Stohl, David Carleton, and George A. Lopez, "State Terrorism: Issues of Concept and Measurement," in *Government Violence and Repression: An Agenda for Research,* ed. Michael Stohl and George A. Lopez (Westport, CT: Greenwood Press, 1986), pp. 1–25, and in Stohl et al., "State Violations of Human Rights" (note 1).

25. See, for example, Robert Elias, "Transcending Our Social Reality of Victimization: Toward a New Victimology of Human Rights." *Victimology* 10 (1985): 6–12.

26. Charles Humana, *World Human Rights Guide* (New York: PICA Press, 1984, 1986). See especially the remarks on pages 7–8 of the 1984 edition.

27. To illustrate the need to address severity, we consider a paper by David Banks which compares two sets of human rights ratings, those of Freedom House and Humana. Humana's scales in the first volume cover "the period of 1983" and were updated in a new volume in 1986. The ratings are the work of one well-meaning researcher who reveals in his introductory remarks a singular lack of the methodological knowledge required for such a task. The data that he has produced should thus be approached with great care, if not genuine suspicion as to their reliability and validity.

Banks compares the two sets of human rights ratings and concludes that they are quite consistent. He then uses cluster analysis methods on the Humana scores to group sixty-three of the seventy-four countries rated into seven clusters which, it is argued, are "plausible agglomerations." Finally, he explores methods of variable reduction, seeking small subsets of Humana's forty variables that can recapitulate the seven clusters previously obtained. Discriminate analyses and the quite new Classification and Regression Trees methodology suggest about half a dozen variables which are nearly as effective as all forty.

Banks's paper includes all of the raw data used in this analyses. This makes it quite easy to second guess him by trying alternative analyses. For example, we can sum the three Humana variables most directly related to Articles 4, 5, and 9 of the Universal Declaration of Human Rights. If we do so, the rank correlation between these and the Gastil Civil Rights Scale drops from the .89 correlation that Banks obtained to .77 with a corresponding increase in the number of discrepancies. See David L. Banks, "Patterns of Oppression: A Statistical Analysis of Human Rights," *Proceedings of the Social Statistics Section of the American Statistical Association* 62 (1985): 154–162.

28. Maureen R. Berman and Roger S. Clark, "State Terrorism: Disappearances," *Rutgers Law Journal* (Spring 1982): 531, n. 16.

29. Some consideration of what we discuss as range is evident, however, in the Freedom House scales. But, again, since these scales incorporate so many different dimensions, none of which is individually specified, it is unclear exactly what role our description of range plays in their final product.

30. We have, however, read a provocative data-based essay which employs this threefold scheme with some success. See Gordon Bowen, "Dark Light in the Guatemalan Dawn: Measuring Human Rights Improvements amid Systematic State Terror," in *Testing Theories of State Violence and State Terror,* ed.

George A. Lopez, Michael Stohl and David Carleton (Boulder, CO: Westview Press, 1990).

31. Again here, this may be changing as the transnational collection and disseminations of the DataBase Project on Palestinian Human Rights may illustrate.

32. See the discussions in Ted Robert Gurr, *Politimetrics* (Englewood Cliffs, NJ: Prentice-Hall, 1972); Michael Stohl, *War and Domestic Political Violence: The American Capacity for Repression and Reaction*, vol. 30 of Sage Library of Social Research (Beverly Hills, CA: Sage Publications, 1970); and Edward S. Herman, *The Real Terror Network: Terrorism in Fact and Propaganda* (Boston: South End Press, 1982).

33. For the most recent in a series of such analyses, see The Americas Watch, Helsinki Watch, and Lawyers Committee for International Human Rights, *Critique: Review of the Department of State's Country Reports on Human Rights Practices for 1984* (New York, May 1985).

34. Recent discussions also reflect debate about data gathering approaches, and the use of different monitoring and assessment strategies may itself be volatile. See Ken Anderson and Richard Anderson, "Limitations on the Liberal-Legal Model of International Human Rights: Six Lessons from El Salvador," *TELOS* 66 (winter 1985/86): 91–104. For further arguments, see Nigel S. Rodley, "Monitoring Human Rights Violations in the 1980s," in Dominguez et al., *Enhancing Global Human Rights* (note 7), pp. 117–151. For a discussion with a focus on legal extensions of human rights claims in the form of public documents and pronouncements of international organizations, see Philip Alston, "Conjuring Up New Human Rights: A Proposal for Quality Control," *American Journal of International Law* 78 (July 1984): 607.

35. Taylor and Jodice, *World Handbook* (note 16).

36. For this critique see Schoultz, "U.S. Foreign Policy and Human Rights Violations in Latin America" (note 8), p. 152, table 1.

37. See Hubert Blalock, *Casual Inference in Non-Experimental Research* (Chapel Hill: University of North Carolina Press, 1964); Neil Smelser, *Comparative Methods in the Social Sciences* (Englewood Cliffs, NJ: Prentice-Hall, 1976); and Robert Jackman, "Cross-National Statistical Research and the Study of Comparative Politics," *American Journal of Political Science* 29, No. 1 (1985): 161–182.

THE ROLE OF GOVERNMENT ORGANIZATIONS

Chapter 9
Human Rights Reporting as a Policy Tool: An Examination of the State Department *Country Reports*

Judith Eleanor Innes

Since their inception in 1976, the annual *Country Reports on Human Rights Practice*[1] have come to be widely known and respected. This compendium, now more than 1,000 pages long, presenting statistics and analyses of human rights in virtually all nations has gained wide attention from the public and policy makers. Many in Congress view it as the most authoritative and complete statement on human rights conditions available today, and they make regular use of the findings in debates and public statements. The document itself is a best-seller in the Government Printing Office. Human rights organizations and governments around the world each year await the publication of the *Reports* and take considerable trouble to respond to them. While there are serious criticisms of chapters on particular countries, even most critics who scrutinize these closely agree that on the whole the volume reflects a professional effort to report accurately and fairly.

This situation is remarkable because the *Reports* have been produced by administrations whose initial appointees were openly antagonistic to applying human rights criteria in foreign policy and whose later pursuit of human rights policy could at most be described as reluctant. Many were opposed to embarrassing friendly nations with public critiques. Some disagreed with the basic premise that human rights violations in communist and noncommunist nations should be viewed as comparable. Despite these difficulties, the *Reports* have actually improved in coverage and consistency during the Reagan years.

It is my argument that this improvement has occurred because the reporting requirement itself has altered practices and norms within the Department of State and created an arena for public evaluation of the information. Accurate and unbiased human rights reporting has become an intrinsically important goal for many key actors within the State Department. Public debate over the information among experts and human rights organizations has helped increase consistency in definition, accuracy in measurement, and comprehensiveness of coverage. The *Reports*, as a consequence, have come to be, to some important degree, independent of the administration's political stance.

I also argue that the *Reports* have become influential through the process of preparing, presenting, and publicly debating the findings. It is typically assumed that the influence of reports of this type is to be measured by the degree to which policy makers use the end product—the information and statistics—as criteria to formulate their policies. At this early stage of human rights data and policy, however, the process effects of reporting are the most significant.

This chapter has two purposes. It is, first and foremost, about the *Country Reports* themselves. It looks at their origin and at how the data are produced and used within the Department of State; it focuses on key events in the *Reports'* history and evolution; and it explores the attitudes and perceptions of some of the important users. On the other hand, it is a case study addressed to the more general question of how statistics can shape policy. It asks under what conditions statistics may become influential and how that influence works. As a case, it has parallels in other policy arenas where statistics have become prominent in decision processes. These parallels begin to point the way toward a theory of information use in policy—a theory of how and when statistics make a difference.

The arguments in this chapter are grounded in three types of work. First, the author's experience in 1980 as a consultant to the State Department, developing indicators and methods for the economic and social section of the *Reports*, gave insight into the procedures and debates in their preparation.[2] Second, reviews of Congressional Hearings and other documents on human rights provided much of the context of the public debate. Third, an understanding of current practices and attitudes was gained from follow-up interviews conducted in 1985 with three groups: current and former staff of the Bureau of Human Rights; Congressional staff from both parties who have over the years been key actors mobilizing

Congressional action on human rights; and some staff of nongovernmental human rights organizations (NGOs). For this volume a few
additional telephone interviews were conducted in 1988, which
showed that the contentions of a 1986 version of this chapter remain
basically valid.

History and Evolution of the *Country Reports*

Origins

The *Country Reports* have their origins in struggles between Congress
and the executive branch over foreign policy. Congress has been the
initiator of legislation denying assistance and loans to governments
with poor human rights records, while the executive branch, even
when advocating for human rights policies, has resisted such limitations on its freedom of action. In its effort to assure its objectives are
implemented, Congress has routinely required the administration
formally to report various types of information, while the latter has
often dragged its feet or at times openly resisted this obligation. Some
in Congress have advocated standards linking particular levels of
abuses to policy, but even the Carter administration resisted pressure
to do this.

The first Congressional initiatives, in 1973 and 1974, were modest,
"sense of Congress" resolutions suggesting that the president curtail
assistance to governments seriously violating human rights. These
were responses to the realization that U.S. security assistance and
weapons might have been used for repression in the client nations.
The Nixon administration's response to Congress was a report that
argued that because human rights violations were widespread (and
presumably unrecorded), there was no objective way to make distinctions among nations. Further (the report continued), neither U.S. interests nor the human rights cause would be served by "public
obloquy and impaired relations with . . . recipient countries."[3] Such
an analysis of human rights conditions as the State Department's was
kept classified.

At this point Congress began to put in place the major components
for implementing the use of human rights criteria in foreign policy.
The first of what would be a long series of requirements, which set
the pattern for later legislation, was the Harkin amendment to the
Foreign Assistance Act. It specifically prohibited U.S. development
assistance to "any government which engages in a consistent pattern
of gross violations of internationally recognized human rights."[4]

Subsequently, Congress declared that "a principal goal of the foreign policy of the United States shall be to promote the increased observance of internationally recognized human rights by all countries."[5] In doing so, Congress went beyond the idea simply of limiting assistance and established a general principle for all foreign policy.

Then in 1976, Congress, to implement this policy better, established in the Department of State the position of Coordinator for Human Rights and Humanitarian Affairs, which it later upgraded to Assistant Secretary. This congressionally initiated legislation also established the first *Country Reports*, requiring, for each country proposed for security assistance, that an annual report on human rights practices be submitted to Congress.[6] This mandate expanded soon after to include all U.N. member nations. Finally, Congress established human rights oversight systems in the Commission on Security and Cooperation in Europe and the Subcommittee on Human Rights and International Organizations in the House Foreign Affairs Committee. Both have held hearings over the years and given attention to human rights abuses in particular countries and human rights practices more broadly.[7] The Subcommittee on Human Rights has responsibility for legislation and gives close attention to U.S. policies. In the years that followed its inception, it was to be actively involved in building the growing list of legislation limiting foreign assistance and other activities for nations where human rights abuses are significant.[8]

The Early Stages of Human Rights Policy, 1977–1978

At the outset, a major obstacle to the implementation of human rights policies was the question of how to apply them in practice. Historically, the United States has provided foreign aid to counter communism, support development, and protect its strategic and economic interests. Even the human rights legislation permits assistance to be given to violating nations if, for example, they are strategically important or if the aid is deemed key to a long term development program. Moreover, many political officials and some foreign service officers originally resisted the idea of human rights policy, even within the Carter administration. Some feared it would reduce the flexibility of foreign policy, and some opposed in principle limiting foreign assistance for human rights reasons, arguing it would interfere with coherence of policy toward a country.

But even when there was agreement to apply human rights criteria, significant problems remained in operationally defining these criteria and in choosing appropriate responses to types and levels of abuses.

No one could agree on how to characterize a "consistent pattern of gross violations." There were no guidelines to what could be expected and no systematic way to compare human rights situations in different countries. Violations of integrity of the person, such as political killing or torture, came in practice to have priority. Other violations, particularly of civil or political rights, were seen as more ambiguous. Some argued that marginal improvements should be rewarded, while others contended the absolute levels were crucial. The Carter strategy of pressuring countries where the United States had influence caused concern that we were ignoring worse records of other, less friendly nations. Even the high level interagency group appointed to resolve conflicts was not able to establish clear policy principles. Doubts about the basic advisability of human rights policies were fed by skepticism that such policies could ever be applied consistently or fairly.[9]

By 1978 two *Reports* had been produced, the first by the outgoing Ford administration and the second by the Carter administration, but the reporting effort was not well enough developed to alleviate the problems. A Library of Congress study at that time found that within

these broad areas of uncertainty [ambiguous or conflicting policy criteria] initiatives seem often to be shaped by information flows, chance and bureaucratic politics. In the absence of an information collecting system that provides equitable coverage of problems in different countries, some countries are subject to careful scrutiny because they are the focus of extensive journalistic and private institutional reporting, as well as the concern of sizable expatriate populations in the U.S. For other countries, reporting on human rights conditions is very limited.[10]

A relatively complete reporting system could have helped to reduce the uncertainty over the facts of human rights and allowed the debate to decide how to apply policy goals. The unevenness of the information meant it was difficult to establish policy criteria or use human rights principles to counterbalance other concerns.

The arrangement for reporting, observers and participants argued, created tensions among the reporting obligation, the mission to maintain diplomatic relations with nations, and other foreign policy objectives. Gathering of information for the *Reports* began in the diplomatic missions, which used guidelines from the State Department Bureau of Human Rights and Humanitarian Affairs (HA) outlining content, format, and style. Foreign service officers in these missions and embassies were assigned the responsibilities of gathering information and preparing the draft reports were understandably reluctant at first to pose sensitive questions to local officials. The geographic desks in the Department of State reviewed the drafts with their own policy concerns in mind and their own knowledge of the region. By the time the *Reports* went to Congress, they had clearance from every State Department office concerned with the *Reports*, and complaints came back from some embassies that the obligation to report violations created stress with the host country. The preparation of the document occasioned time-consuming and contentious negotiation within the Department. Typically, the desks sought to make the analysis compatible with the policies they were pursuing, while HA sought to eliminate language or arguments they saw as politically biased and to reduce what they labeled "clientism"—a tendency to paint an overly positive picture of a host country. Even within HA, clientism was to some degree a problem in the early years.

Because these conditions suggested it would be difficult for HA to produce unbiased reports, the Library of Congress study in 1978 suggested that Congress consider finding or creating another type of organization to produce reports. The authors did not, however, offer any particular suggestion, noting rather the difficulty of producing a report equal or superior in scope and objectivity. They raised the issue of whether it should be an international or U.S. effort but offered little insight on that question either.[12]

The Carter Administration and the *Reports,* 1978–1980

In-house production of the *Country Reports* was to continue, however, and it was to become the prime reason for their influence. The arrangement was to contribute to the accuracy, completeness, and credibility of the document. It was also to force changes within the organizational and policy making system of the State Department. With personnel in virtually every country, the Department could produce a document based on first-hand information and cover a full range of human rights. No other organization had a comparable capacity. In the process, changes were to occur in attitudes within the Department of State and in the nature of internal policy discussion.

Improvement in *Reports* of this period was primarily a result of the efforts of Carter's assistant secretary, Patricia Derian, and her staff. In the early years they found that topics covered for one country were likely to be neglected for others. Conditions might be vaguely described as "serious," or "improving," or emotionally described as "disgraceful." Some reports seemed to be making excuses for a government's actions, while others made harsher assessments for similar actions. To deal with these problems, HA developed an increasingly standardized reporting format. For each country the report was organized into several main topics, dealing with (1) integrity of the person (torture, killing, etc.); (2) civil rights; (3) political rights; and (4) economic and social rights or vital needs. Each of these was subdivided into more specific topics, for example, freedom of assembly or freedom of religion. Embassies were told to discuss both the laws and the actual practices for each topic and pressured to provide illustrative examples and, where possible, quantitative estimates of violations to incorporate into the text. A brief introduction to each country gave an overview of recent political events, wars, or natural disasters to provide a context.

The Bureau of Human Rights and Humanitarian Affairs sent guidelines to the embassies describing the purpose of each section and each year added clearer and more complete definitions and criteria for categorizing violations. These focused on particular topics each year to incrementally improve reporting. For example, the 1979 guidelines ask that reports note whether torture was authorized and whether disciplinary action was taken. They ask that particular attention be paid to disappearances, refugee policies, and the status of women. In addition they require information bearing on the credibility of data—the reliability of sources and details on the frequency, methods, and places of abuses.

Under Derian's direction, HA put particular effort into making the sections on economic and social rights more objective. These sections, which dealt with issues like the rights to education, employment, and an adequate standard of living, had been given less attention than others, and they tended to be vague and frequently to reflect clientism. The Bureau decided to incorporate economic and social indicators, so key statistics for each country on basic issues such as literacy and health were selected from those published by the World Bank.[13] These were sent to the respective embassies, which were directed to weave them into their reports. The reports were to account for particularly high or low figures and note what a government's relevant policies were. This strategy reflected HA's philosophy about the proper role of statistics. One or two in the Bureau had argued that these sections should be reduced entirely to statistics, in the name of objectivity. A few resisted using statistics at all, believing they were not meaningful. For most, however, the idea of using statistics with interpretations and context information was an improvement on earlier practice. It made reports more comparable while still permitting foreign service officers to use their qualitative knowledge of the situation to make sense of numbers that had different meanings and reliability for each nation.

A second major factor in the improvement of *Reports* during the

Carter administration was public scrutiny and prodding from Congress and the NGOs. The House Subcommittee held hearings on the submission of the *Reports* and on the implementation of human rights policies, inviting administration officials and representatives of NGOs to testify. The former had to explain their findings, while the latter offered critiques, along with alternative statistics and interpretations. In the course of these hearings, congressmen became insightful critics, asking penetrating questions. Some NGOs began to publish and distribute detailed critiques of the *Reports*. The Bureau in turn sent the critiques to embassies for use in the following year. The process provided incentives to all participants to work to improve the quality of the data.

Challenges to Human Rights Policy, 1981

With the advent of the Reagan administration, human rights policy and the *Country Reports* were put to the test. The fact that both outlasted the challenges—albeit with alterations—is testimony to the degree to which they both had become institutionalized.

The first challenge was Reagan's nomination for assistant secretary of Ernest Lefever, a man who was widely perceived as opposed to human rights policies, at least in the form in which Congress and the Carter administration had defined them. It was something of a surprise to observers when the Republican-dominated Senate Foreign Relations Committee voted against his appointment. It is rare for such nominations to be turned down, even when there are disagreements over policy. Committee members apparently did not believe the nominee was committed to implementing human rights policy regardless of the political alignment of a government. Their action was another clear message from Congress to the administration and an indicator of the degree to which human rights had become an accepted objective for U.S. foreign policy.

The Reagan administration did not, however, accept the message immediately. During the spring and summer of 1981 the administration seriously considered discontinuing the *Reports* or giving the responsibility to the Department's geographic bureaus where the primary concern would no longer be human rights. The president made no further nomination for assistant secretary, and within the State Department high level policy discussions often excluded HA staff. Moreover, administration policies created other difficulties. Differentiation of "totalitarian" and "authoritarian" nations complicated efforts to assess human rights practices evenhandedly. The focus on terrorism seemed to drain attention from human rights, and it introduced complications into interpretation and measurement of violations. Powerful people in the administration were once again arguing that human rights inappropriately limited options. Not surprisingly, HA staff and many observers saw the Bureau and its functions as seriously threatened.

The annual *Country Reports*, however, did have to be prepared. Congress required them, and in hearings in the spring of 1981, strong support for the *Reports* had been expressed from across the political spectrum.[14] Indeed an amendment to the foreign aid bill was passed expanding the reports to include all U.N. members. Moreover, within the State Department, much of the original skepticism and resistance had dissipated. Administration critics of the reporting process were surprised when a quietly conducted survey of foreign posts revealed that most respondents believed in human rights reporting. Several added that human rights objectives were prime reasons for their being in the foreign service.

Finally, in the fall, Reagan nominated Elliott Abrams for assistant secretary and, in doing so, made the commitment to continue the reporting process, but with a Reagan administration stamp. The administration was to retain the format and style established under Derian, along with the same basic production and review procedures. It was also to add introductions explaining administration policy and to alter limited aspects of the *Reports* to mesh with its policies. It appeared that little might remain, however, of executive implementation of human rights policy other than the *Reports*.

Evolution of the *Reports* in the Reagan Administration, 1982–1988

Despite this shaky start in the new administration, the *Reports* continued to increase in consistency, detail, and public acceptance. With experience and previous reports as models, improvements at the margin were getting easier. The continuing critiques of the NGOs were beginning to show their effects on the product. Embassies' knowledge bases had improved as they developed local networks and learned to differentiate reliable from unreliable sources. The Bureau's guidelines accumulated each year, adding to the topics getting detailed and systematic attention. In 1984, for example, guidelines requested discussion of religious traditions affecting women's rights, of the role of elites and the military in the political system, and of the effects of the security apparatus. Then in the 1985 *Reports* a glossary was added defining the concepts applied in measuring abuses such as torture, disappearance, and political killings.[15] This reflected the results of years of internal debate over the ambiguity in many of these concepts, which had led to inconsistent reporting and misunderstanding of the reports.

The professionals who prepare the *Reports* appear to have been largely responsible for their increasing credibility and objectivity during this period. The Bureau's staff are career Foreign Service Officers (FSOs), not political appointees, nor ordinary bureaucrats. They are somewhat independent of the particular politics of an administration, not only because of their career status, but also because they have professional expertise and values. The *Country Reports* team is increasingly willing and able to resist pressures to slant the *Reports* for political purposes. The group has been made up of FSOs with decades of field experience; some have had ambassadorial rank. When they debate an issue with a desk officer or embassy, their knowledge gives them the ability to detect clientism and the credibility to win arguments. As one ambassador said to an HA staff member on learning of his background, "I guess I can't pull the wool over *your* eyes." Team members seem clearer on their mission today than they were in 1980, saying it is to accurately describe human rights practices. The time for other policy considerations, they contend, is *after* the *Reports* are published.

The Reagan administration has used the introductions to the *Reports* as its primary vehicle for policy statements. The first year, for example, the introduction said the administration would use traditional "quiet" diplomacy to deal with nations abusing human rights. Introductions have discussed the differences between totalitarian and authoritarian governments, the priority the administration gives to political rights, and the pragmatic justification for pursuing human rights policy.

Substantive changes in the body of the *Reports* were more limited than observers had originally expected, though there were some. The first was to include acts of terrorism and thus to look at both government and opposition actions. A second change was a result of legislation in 1985. Thereafter, worker rights such as collective bargaining, occupational safety, and acceptable wages and hours were discussed.[16]

The most controversial substantive change in the *Reports* has been on the question of economic and social rights. At first, the administration eliminated discussion of government's policies on economic and social rights, arguing they were difficult to interpret and detracted from the "vital core" of human rights.[17] They retitled this section of the *Reports* "Economic, Social and Cultural Situation," keeping it as background information and continuing to incorporate broad social and economic indicators. While Reagan officials had proposed to eliminate the section altogether, this was a compromise. But the administration remained uncomfortable with even this, partly on ideological grounds in view of its own domestically conservative stance on such issues. Moreover, Communist nations tended to give higher priority to these issues and to have better showings on them than many allies. This practical reality clashed with the belief that political freedom precedes economic development. The introduction to the 1986 *Reports* states:

Experience demonstrates that it is individual freedom that sets the stage for economic and social development; it is repression that stifles it. Those who try to justify subordinating political and civil rights on the ground they are concentrating on economic aspirations invariably deliver on neither. This report eliminated altogether the section on the Economic and Social Situation, along with its statistics. In its place it provides a discussion of issues of discrimination against ethnic minorities, women and other groups.[18]

The changes reflected Reagan policies and were controversial at the outset, stimulating protest within the Department. Critics were concerned the inclusion of terrorist acts was not in the spirit of the *Reports*, which dealt with government abuses, and they feared that discussing terrorist acts would appear to excuse government repression. This change, however, seems to have been accepted by now. Some felt that economic and social rights should continue to be covered despite the difficulty of setting policy because they were among the internationally recognized human rights (by the United States as well) and because they did not detract from consideration of other rights. Indeed some took the opposite view from the administration, contending that meaningful political participation was contingent on some degree of literacy and health. Most of the human rights NGOs focus, however, on physical abuses and political and civil rights. Accordingly there was relatively little public outcry when the economic and social issues were eliminated. An uneasy truce seems to have been reached.

Assessment of the *Reports*

Opinions in 1985

Among those interviewed for this study, regardless of their political party or role, there was a virtual consensus on three major points. On the one hand they believed that the *Reports* for most countries represented a basically fair effort to display an accurate picture. On the other, they contended that the chapters for a subset of countries—the largest number mentioned was 15 to 20—were so politically biased or inaccurate as to be meaningless. Chapters most often criticized were on El Salvador, Nicaragua, South Korea, and other countries for which the administration was pursuing controversial policies. Nonetheless, all regarded the *Reports* as valuable tools in human rights policy making.

Further questioning revealed that respondents' views were far from simplistic. They believed that the *Country Reports* were within an acceptable range of accuracy, given the difficulties of gathering and reporting such inherently elusive information on a worldwide basis. Many actually, however, relied on other sources of data that they thought were more complete and up to date. Respondents felt the data were accurate enough to aid the overall debate, accurate enough for most of the *Reports* users, who (unlike themselves) were only peripherally involved in human rights. They assumed that the responsibility for any deliberate manipulation of the facts lay in the high levels of the Reagan administration. They went out of their way to affirm their confidence in the professionalism of HA staff, even while criticizing the *Reports*. Moreover, all respondents denied thinking there was any deliberate falsification of the statistics. Rather, they argued, biases were introduced through language, omissions, interpretations, and explanations.[19]

A published critique of the *Reports* for 1984 by a group of NGOs captures the flavor of what respondents said in interviews. This critique says on the one hand:

In general, the State Department's annual report on human rights worldwide is an ever-more useful compendium of information. The Department deserves credit for the increasing professionalization of human rights monitoring that is reflected in most of the reports we examined.

On the other hand it notes:

Regrettably, as in the past, there are important exceptions to the generally high standard of reporting. The most striking are the reports . . . [on] El Salvador, Guatemala, Honduras and Nicaragua. In the case of the first three, the reports seem to make every effort to minimize abuses; in the case of Nicaragua, the report goes in the opposite direction, grossly exaggerating abuses. The effect is to paint an unrealistically rosy portrait of human rights . . . in the region supported by the United States and an unrealistically grim portrait . . . in the country opposed by the United States.[20]

This critique examined 31 reports, focusing on countries where human rights were of particular concern, including both "friendly" and "unfriendly" nations. Their overall assessment was that four other reports were "poor," but that in the other 23 reports "a careful reader can obtain a generally accurate picture of the human rights situation."

The critiques of selected individual reports, which these organizations compile for each year of the State Department document, largely accept the statistics. Their criticism focuses instead on inconsistencies of terminology and presentation and on what they believe are ways of discussing the problems designed to "soften reports of violations by perceived allies." The introduction to the critiques of the 1987 report cites the following "techniques" that it contends are used in the reports for this purpose: "mentioning violations without describing them fully"; "providing justifications or excuses for human rights violations"; "focusing on improvements in the human rights situation rather than abuses that persist"; "emphasizing unfulfilled governmental promises to implement reforms"; "repeating allegations made by others rather than reporting the violations directly"; "attributing allegations of human rights violations to sources that are suspect"; and "omitting the political context of violations in a way that obscures their significance."[21] The introduction offers specific examples of each technique and the volume as a whole focuses on these concerns.

The ideas these criticisms imply for reducing bias are really no different from those one would apply in the presentation of any kind of research. Moreover, they are specific enough so that HA can apply them in future reports. Indeed the 1986 instructions to FSOs in the field on preparing the reports reflect such criticisms from earlier years by offering, topic by topic, a series of questions that should be asked to ensure the report is not misleading. For example under freedom of the press, FSOs are directed not only to give the government's official stance, but to distinguish theory from practice. In addition they are asked whether criticism of government is tolerated, whether academic freedom is respected, and whether there is surveillance of public meetings; and they are asked for precision in describing "self censorship" by the media.[22]

Effects of the *Country Reports* on the Department of State: Changes in Organizational Attention and Policy Making

In the Department of State, the requirement to produce and publish a human rights report has set in motion a series of changes. A recent article in *Common Cause Magazine* contends that "What's surprising is the extent to which the annual human rights reports have not only managed to survive but thrive, gradually evolving from an idea into an institution."[23] The *Reports* have become a force in themselves within the government.

A primary consequence of the reporting process has been to increase the level of expertise and the base of knowledge about human rights in Washington and the embassies. A secondary result has been to encourage the growth of a cadre of human rights proponents within the State Department. To some extent, such a cadre would be expected to form simply because people are assigned to HA or named human rights officers in embassies: self-selection of volunteers who care about the issues combines with a natural tendency for people to internalize the goals of their job. The research and analysis involved in reporting, moreover, reinforce these values as staff discover, document, and report abuses. As Richard Schifter, Assistant Secretary for Human Rights, said, "Through this process, as you can readily see, the entire bureaucracy is sensitized to the human rights issues, sensitized to the point that it almost instinctively seeks to respond."[24]

In addition, the requirement for the Department to produce the *Reports* has systematically forced not only the people gathering data but the organization as a whole to give attention to human rights. It has increased the understanding of the significance of human rights issues throughout the Department as many staff review the draft reports and their interpretations. According to HA staff, many in the Department have come to appreciate that human rights issues involve more than a limited number of people in prisons, but are linked to a country's political, security, and military situation. They believe also that others increasingly share their view that human rights concerns are pragmatic as well as idealistic elements of foreign policy.

Some long term State Department officials contend that the preparation of the *Reports* actually stimulates policy making on human rights. The analysis and review process forces questions to be asked internally that would not otherwise be addressed. The decision on what a report on a given country should say can be tantamount to making a policy toward its government, particularly as the Department is required to certify governments as eligible for aid on the basis of the *Reports'* findings. The various bureaus in the State Department and in the White House have to negotiate an interpretation of the data and an attitude toward governments whose abuses it documents. The administration must be prepared with policies which correspond with its interpretations of events. Because of public scrutiny and the competing data-gathering groups, there are real constraints on how

much leeway policy officials have in shaping facts or offering interpretations in the reports. Inevitably, policy has to make some accom-
modation to the findings.

Finally, the reporting effort helps to empower human rights proponents within the State Department. The data that are gathered
provide evidence and arguments for their positions and give them an
aura of expertise. At least to the extent that the writing of the *Reports*
is a policy making exercise, a spokesman for a human rights perspective is involved in policy. Staff of the HA are also increasingly involved in preparations for the daily press briefing, which, some in the
Department contend, is the occasion for the detailed formulation of
much policy.

Effects of the *Reports* on Congress and NGOs: Empowerment and Education

In Congress the *Reports* have effects also. They are published as congressional documents and are widely used. Staff depend on them to
prepare briefing papers for a variety of foreign policy purposes, not
limited to human rights. Their economic and social statistics were
cited by respondents in 1985 as prime reasons for the *Reports'* usefulness as a reference. The *Reports* are compact and complete, and both
congressmen and their staffs tend to regard them as the most up-to-
date source of facts. Their publication and the hearings which focused on them have called congressional attention to human rights.
Discussion of the numbers and their interpretation educates members of Congress about the nature and causes of human rights
abuses.

The *Reports* have also affected the relative power of Congress and
the administration. Because they are official public documents, their
findings represent the position of the United States on whether certain abuses are occurring. In practice, congressional users take the
findings to be a minimum estimate of abuses because they see the
State Department as conservative in what it counts. If abuses are in
the *Reports*, the fact that they occurred is generally accepted. Thus
the findings offer leverage over the administration. Congressmen use
the data to direct specific questions to administration witnesses and
to criticize policy. Statistics become "talking points," as one staffer labeled them—concrete ways to begin a substantive discussion of
whether the administration response to the abuses is appropriate.

The hearings help also to empower the NGOs by providing a legitimate way for them to participate in the public debate. Since much of
what these organizations do is to gather information, several even

preparing their own full-scale reports, they can present data and interpretations which have considerable credibility. They can analyze the *Reports* in great detail to pinpoint bias or error. They can also use the administration's own data as a basis for criticizing policy, noting when public statements or actions are inconsistent with findings. In relying on official data, NGO's arguments have persuasiveness that their own unofficial figures cannot provide. Congressmen take seriously the NGO's testimony and their reports—particularly when the NGO is viewed as politically neutral. It is not surprising that NGOs support the idea of the *Reports* even when they disagree with some findings.

Effects of the *Reports* on the Public and Foreign Governments: Some Thoughts

Experienced State Department observers contend that the official publication of the *Reports* has become a symbol of U.S. commitment to human rights. The size and detail of the document, almost regardless of its findings, suggest to the public and to other governments that human rights is an issue of importance in the United States. One can of course reasonably respond that symbols can be empty of content. An administration could publish the *Reports* without a commitment to act. Symbols, however, do tend to reinforce public values and to create expectations. The publication of the *Reports* helps to legitimize the idea that human rights are and should be a significant concern of U.S. policy.

While the research for this chapter did not try to assess the degree to which foreign governments alter their policies in response to the *Reports*, it did indicate that these governments are acutely aware of the document. When the *Reports* is first released, quite a few delegations and phone calls come from foreign embassies to Congress and the State Department to protest, explain, or try to set the record straight. At least two nations have circulated newsletters with their own accounts of human rights conditions. The official U.S. view of a government's human rights record matters because of the threat that it will withhold aid, but even governments that are not aid recipients do not relish having human rights abuses publicized.

The *Reports* are increasingly circulated and read in the United States and abroad. Though no one interviewed could provide more than anecdotal evidence, respondents contended that users of the *Reports* in the United States now include researchers and teachers, ambassadors as well as junior FSOs assigned to new posts, and people doing business abroad. There is evidence, they say, that other nations make use of this document to assist them in setting foreign policy.[25] The individual report for some countries has been officially or unofficially translated and locally circulated, though the practice is far from universal.

Other European nations and the European community have considered or are now producing their own human rights reports, relying to a great extent on the U.S. document as a model. These do reflect different policy emphases. Indeed a prime reason for not simply relying on the U.S. version has been policy disagreements and concerns about bias in relation to certain issues or countries. Yet as Pritchard has noted in her careful comparison of the U.S. and Norwegian reports, the "differences appear to be due, for the most part to different definitions of human rights and different national priorities."[26] She cannot identify one as more objective than the other.

Statistics as a Policy Tool

The roles of statistics—the actual numbers provided within the reports—need highlighting, as they have thus far been only indirectly discussed. The main consequences of requiring quantitative information in the *Reports* are of three kinds: first, it has influenced organizational behavior in the Department of State; second, it has helped to alter the political process surrounding policy making; and third, it has helped increase the impact and credibility of the *Reports*. All of these effects work in the direction of strengthening human rights as an operating objective of the U.S. government.

First, the requirement has altered standard operating procedures, organizational norms and goals, and the relative power of interests within the Department of State. The fact that reporting includes an effort to quantify violations has reinforced these effects. The reporting has in general directed organizational attention to human rights. The effort to quantify has required the building of expertise and has meant that, over time, many FSOs have learned in direct, empirical ways about human rights. The data have helped create internal advocates for human rights by changing the perceptions of the data gatherers, and, in turn, the data lend credibility to these advocates in internal policy debates and help mobilize public support for their efforts. The whole reporting activity has helped within the Department of State to legitimize human rights issues as foreign policy concerns.

Moreover, the measurement effort itself requires that the organization make policy decisions which they could otherwise avoid. The process of defining rights violations represents the place where, for the first time, discussion moves from vague generalities to operational policies. The process of deciding how to categorize abuses and how to present the information has become a negotiation among the bureaus in the State Department, including HA.[27] One result is that violations in some countries that might never be formally examined are brought to the attention of policymakers. Another is that policies may be made about issues that might otherwise be ignored.

The incorporation of statistics in the *Reports* has helped to alter the politics of human rights outside the Department by giving human rights proponents opportunities to be heard and resources to be effective. The discussion of the statistics has helped to place human rights in the public eye and on the political agenda. Moreover, the numbers provide leverage to NGOs and congressional supporters of human rights to question administration policies.[28]

The inclusion of statistics has been crucial also to the ultimate impact of the *Reports* themselves. Their credibility is linked to the statistics, which give an aura of objectivity to their interpretive aspects. Statistics have made the *Reports* more widely used as a reference, more likely to be cited in speeches, and easier for academics to analyze. In addition, they make the individual reports more comparable over time and between nations and, in turn, permit the establishment of clearer policy criteria. Because of statistics it is now possible to discuss policies which respond to improvements or declines in human rights conditions. The statistics not only help to make the interpretive part of the *Reports appear* more objective, but actually to *become* more objective. They anchor the interpretations and make them more likely to be consistent from country to country. They force the development of common criteria.[29]

What is striking, however, is that although the inclusion of statistics in the *Reports* appears to affect policy, it is not crucial what precise level of violations the statistics show. No one interviewed could point to cases where the data changed minds or were pivotal to specific decisions. Most contended that congressmen used the data selectively to support positions already arrived at. Though some do get new understanding from the *Reports*' data, they provide background "enlightenment" rather than decision criteria.[30] Moreover, leading decision makers have access to other, more detailed and up-to-date information than could possibly be supplied by an annual summary report such as this.[31] They are well aware of the limited reliability of such statistics and know that their meaning is contingent on many variables in each nation. Finally, for better or worse, human rights criteria are only one set among several that policy makers apply. Though they may even accept the numbers as approximations to truth, the statistics alone are unlikely to change a particular decision. Efforts to develop more precise numbers are not likely to be worthwhile in terms of policy.

It is not surprising that Carleton and Stohl[32] found little correlation between statistical indexes of human rights violations and foreign assistance under either Carter or Reagan. In the late seventies, human rights goals had not been incorporated into standard operating procedures of the Department of State, which had other agendas and criteria internalized into its practices. It is also not surprising that the authors found a slightly higher correlation in the Reagan administration than in the Carter period. Dealing with human rights had become both more salient and more routine.

This brings us to the question of whether and under what conditions human rights statistics could become intrinsically influential because of what they reveal—under what circumstances policies might be genuinely and substantively linked to statistics. To answer this question one may trace parallels to the small handful of quantitative indicators that have come to shape public perceptions of problems and to define the goals and standards for policy implementation. Two of the most prominent examples, the unemployment rate and the Consumer Price Index, became influential only after decades of debate over policy and definitions. The official statistics at first were frequently challenged by interest groups until their methods were publicly established as reliable and unbiased. Thirty to forty years after the first efforts at measurement, it became possible to alter policy in direct response to increases or decreases in the statistics.

The human rights policy and reporting system has a number of parallels, which could mean that in time human rights data could have impacts similar to these national indicators. There is a congressionally established policy commitment to human rights similar to that for the economy in the Employment Act of 1946, and a congressionally mandated reporting requirement paralleling the Economic Report of the President and the monthly surveys of unemployment and prices. The Bureau has mounted a relatively professional effort to gather, interpret, and report the data in a manner not unlike the Bureau of Labor Statistics (BLS), though HA's work is more subject to political control. However, HA has had only ten years, while the BLS has had a century to establish its autonomy. A system of congressional oversight gives publicity to human rights and creates congressional expertise, as the Joint Economic Committee does for economic issues.[33]

Though the similarities are compelling, important differences remain. Most notably the U.S. government will never have the control of the international human rights data gathering process that it does for data on such issues as its own employment and inflation levels. Moreover, the character of much human rights information means that it is not necessarily public and it may be deliberately hidden or misrepresented. Data collection will never be done by statistically trained personnel with the single purpose of recording information in an unbiased, reliable way. Data gatherers will be those who have other tasks and other missions but who are qualified to understand what they are recording.

In any case, human rights policy is young as yet and there are many unresolved issues over what it should be and how it should be applied. If these cases and those from other policy arenas are any model, we should expect many years of debate over policy while we continue to refine measurement, before the two can be closely and substantively linked. If the other cases can be used as a guide, only when the policy principles are clear will the measurement be accepted, and then only if the important parties to policy making agree on the concepts and methods of measurement.

Recommendations

To improve human rights reporting and tighten its links to policy, the foregoing analysis suggests a number of strategies.

Among current activities, several are important to maintain. First, the production of the *Reports* in the Department of State should be continued, as it is responsible for many important effects. Second, congressional hearings should continue to highlight and critique the *Reports*, as the effort improves their quality and visibility. The ongoing effort to clarify and get public acceptance of the definitions of rights violations is also crucial at this stage. Academic analyses are helpful in framing these definitions, but if the statistics are to be used, their definition and methods must continue to be achieved through a negotiated process involving the important policy actors, along with academics.

There are some things, not now being done, which experience in other policy fields suggests would be useful. In particular the participation of NGOs and academic experts in evaluating and improving the methods of gathering and analyzing the data should be formalized and regularized through task forces, advisory groups, or user groups. These techniques, used by the Bureaus of the Census and Labor Statistics, contribute to improvement and credibility of their data and assure the participation of key groups in the negotiation over definitions and methods. A second useful strategy would be to train FSOs not only in the nature of human rights violations, but also in research methods. To be nearly as credible as the statisticians in the BLS, they need to be professional in gathering evidence, assessing its bias, and reporting objectively.

Some ideas have been suggested to improve the reporting effort that I do not recommend. For one thing, it is not worthwhile to put substantial effort into getting significantly greater detail in the data at this time. Nor is it useful to try to develop summary indices. The numbers are neither sufficiently reliable nor intrinsically important enough to policy making to justify either of these efforts. The suggestion, moreover, that quantitative standards be established for automatic implementation of human rights policy seems to me particularly inappropriate. Leaving aside the issue of whether it is legitimate or even desirable to bypass the political process and its methods of weighing countervailing values, the effort is undesirable on other grounds. While quantitative standards can be helpful as rough guidelines, the judgment of experienced analysts is essential to interpreting the numbers in particular contexts. Repression shows up statistically in very different ways in different cultures. Moreover, policy makers, who in any case use statistics mainly impressionistically, are unwilling to apply a simple statistical standard to their decisions.

My final recommendation is to recognize that it will take time for results to be visible. We are talking about changing long-standing norms and practices in foreign policy. The task is to change how people think and what they expect and value and to try to change how institutions behave. Such work cannot be done overnight.

Notes

1. These are submitted by the Department of State to the House Committee on Foreign Affairs and the Senate Committee on Foreign Relations. They are published as Joint Committee Prints in approximately February of each year.

2. This work is outlined in Judith Innes de Neufville, "Social Indicators of Basic Needs: Quantitative Data for Human Rights Policy," *Social Indicators Research* 11 (1982): 383–403.

3. "Report to Congress on the Human Rights Situation in Countries Receiving U.S. Security Assistance," submitted to Senate Foreign Relations and House International Relations Committees Nov. 14, 1975.

4. The International Development and Food Assistance Act of 1974, which became section 116 of the Foreign Assistance Act, PL 94–161. This act made exceptions for assistance that could be demonstrated to benefit the needy.

5. Section 502 (B) (a) (1) of the Foreign Assistance Act.

6. International Security and Arms Export Control Act. PL 94–329, June 30, 1976.

7. Margaret E. Galey, in "Congress, Foreign Policy and Human Rights Ten Years After Helsinki," *Human Rights Quarterly* No. 3 (1985): 334–372, outlines in some detail the congressional oversight system.

8. For a listing of this legislation to 1983 see Vita Bite, "Current U.S. Legislation Relating Human Rights to U.S. Foreign Policy," unpublished, Congressional Research Service, The Library of Congress (June 1983).

9. This analysis draws on the report prepared by the Library of Congress, U.S. Senate Committee on Foreign Relations, "Human Rights and U.S. Foreign Assistance: Experience and Issues in Policy Implementation (1977–78)" 96th Congress, 1st Session (Washington, DC: U.S. Government Printing Office, 1979).

10. Ibid., p. 5.

11. A description of the process of preparing the *Reports* as it was in 1980 by the then Acting Assistant Secretary Stephen Palmer, Jr. is published in U.S. Congress, House Committee on Foreign Affairs, Subcommittee on Human Rights and International Organizations, "Foreign Assistance Legislation for Fiscal Year 1982 (Part 6)," Hearings and Markup, 97th Congress, 1st Session (Washington, DC: U.S. Government Printing Office, 1981), pp. 232–241.

12. Library of Congress, "Human Rights" (note 9), p. 21.

13. The choice and purpose of these indicators is discussed in de Neufville, "Social Indicators" (note 2), as is the rationale for combining the statistics with the qualitative discussion.

14. U.S. Congress, House Committee on Foreign Affairs, *Foreign Assistance Legislation for Fiscal Year 1982*, in Hearings "Review of State Department Country Reports," pp. 1–52 (note 17).

15. U.S. Congress, House Committee on Foreign Affairs and Senate Committee on Foreign Relations, *Country Reports on Human Rights Practices for 1985*, app. A (Washington, DC: U.S. Government Printing Office, 1986): 1427–1429.

16. Section 502 (a) of the Generalized System of Preferences Renewal Act of 1984.

17. U.S. Congress, House Committee on Foreign Affairs "Review of State Department *Country Reports* on Human Rights Practices for 1981," Hearing before the Subcommittee on Human Rights and International Organizations. April 28, 1982. 97th Congress, 2nd Session (Washington, DC: U.S. Government Printing Office, 1982). Statement of Elliott Abrams, pp. 3–19.

18. U.S. Congress, House Committee on Foreign Affairs and Senate Committee on Foreign Relations, *Country Reports on Human Rights Practices for 1986* (Washington, DC: U.S. Government Printing Office, 1987).

19. For broader public discussion of the quality of the *Reports* see U.S. Congress, House Committee on Foreign Affairs, Subcommittee on Human Rights and International Organizations, *Review of U.S. Human Rights Policy*, Hearings, 98th Congress, 1st Session (Washington, DC: U.S. Government Printing Office, 1984).

20. Americas Watch, Helsinki Watch, and Lawyers Committee for International Human Rights, *Critique: Review of the Department of State's Country Reports on Human Rights Practices for 1984* (New York: Americas Watch, 1985), p. 1.

21. Americas Watch, Helsinki Watch, and Lawyers Committee for International Human Rights, *Critique: Review of the Department of State's Country Reports on Human Rights Practices for 1987* (New York: Americas Watch, 1988).

22. U.S. Department of State, "1986 *Country Reports* on Human Rights Practices: Instructions," State Dept. #282859, 9 September 1986.

23. Peter Montgomery, "Keeping Score," *Common Cause Magazine*, May/June 1988, pp. 30–32.

24. Richard Schifter, "Human Rights and U.S. Foreign Policy" U.S. Department of State, Bureau of Public Affairs *Current Policy* No. 962 (Washington, DC, June 1987). A speech given before the Institute for International Affairs, Stockholm, Sweden, 18 May 1987.

25. See also statement by Jeri Laber, of Helsinki Watch, in U.S. Congress, *Review of Human Rights Policy* (note 19) p. 69.

26. Kathleen Pritchard, "Human Rights Reporting: A Comparison of the United States and Norway," paper prepared for presentation at the Western Political Science Association Meeting, 10–12 March 1988, San Francisco, California.

27. Public negotiation over methods has been an important factor in the policy use of unemployment and population statistics. See Judith Innes de Neufville, "Knowledge and Action: Making the Link," *Journal of Planning Education and Research* 6, No. 2 (1987): 86–92.

28. Several studies show that the preparation and presentation of quantitative information has effects comparable to those in other organizations and public decision making processes. See for example, William H. Dutton and Kenneth L. Kraemer, *Modeling as Negotiating: The Political Dynamics of Computer Models in the Policy Process* (Norwood, NJ: Ablex Publishing Co., 1985); Judith Innes, "The Power of Data Requirements," *Journal of American Planning Association* 54 (1988): 275–278; and Janet A. Weiss and Judith E. Gruber, "Deterring Discrimination with Data," *Policy Sciences* 17 (1984): 49–66.

29. Thomas E. Pasquarello, "Human Rights and U.S. Foreign Policy: The Case for Quantification," paper prepared for the annual meeting of the Western Political Science Association, San Francisco, California, 10–12 March 1988.

30. See Carol H. Weiss, *Social Science Research and Decision-Making* (New York: Columbia University Press, 1980), chap. 1 for a review of literature on research utilization and the argument that research is most useful as background "enlightenment."

31. A comparable finding is made by Nathan Caplan and Eugenia Barton, who studied the uses of the national social indicators report by policy-makers. See "The Potential of Social Indicators: Minimum Conditions for Impact at the National Level as Suggested by a Study of the Use of Social Indicators 1973," *Social Indicators Research* 5 (1978): 427–456.

32. David Carleton and Michael Stohl, "The Foreign Policy of Human Rights: Rhetoric and Reality from Jimmy Carter to Ronald Reagan," *Human Rights Quarterly* 7, No. 2 (May 1985): 205–229.

33. This story is told in more detail in de Neufville, *Social Indicators and Public Policy: Interactive Processes of Design and Application* (Amsterdam: Elsevier, 1975).

Chapter 10
Human Rights Reporting in Two Nations: A Comparison of the United States and Norway

Kathleen Pritchard

In attempts to assess the status of human rights, an underlying philosophical debate remains regarding the essential nature of human rights. From one perspective rights are essentially qualitative phenomena not susceptible to measurement. This position, it is countered, has resulted in value-laden and biased assessments of human rights conditions leading now to a call for quantifiable, and presumably more objective, measures of human rights practices. This call is made not only by academics and advocates, but also by governments where policies, at least rhetorically, relate foreign assistance to human rights practices in recipient nations. References to the human rights/foreign assistance connection, though by no means common, have been identified in the policy documents of Canada, Denmark, the Netherlands, Norway, the United States and West Germany.[1] To various degrees, these governments acknowledge the need for reliable human rights information if these policy statements are to be implemented. Of course, recognizing the need for reliable data on human rights practices is only a step in the direction of obtaining or using such information.

The governments of both the United States and Norway stand in the forefront of attempts to produce standardized assessments of international human rights. In response to calls from their respective legislative bodies, both governments publish annual reports on human rights practices in other nations. The U.S. *Country Reports*, first published in 1976, are well-known and frequently cited sources of data concerning human rights practices.[2] By contrast, the Norwegian reports[3] are a relatively new but potentially valuable source of human rights data. The second issue, printed in 1986, was the first to be translated into English, making it more widely available to the international community.

Although neither country pretends to offer sophisticated statistical analysis, reports of this sort are increasingly coming to be seen as sources of raw information from which to produce quantitative data for scholars and others concerned with human rights practices.[4] This chapter presents a systematic comparison of the 1986 human rights reports of the United States and Norway. The section below compares the general purposes, design, and methodology used by these two countries. The following section provides specific examples of the reporting on particular rights in particular nations. The comparison uncovers some interesting examples of the differences in the definitions of human rights and the data selected to assess their practice. The final section addresses the impact of these reports and the question of "objective" reporting.

General Goals and Design of the Two Reports

The Norwegian *Yearbook*, in addition to having a briefer history than the U.S. report, is more limited in its scope. Unlike the 167 countries covered in the U.S. report, it includes assessments of only ten countries (Botswana, Kenya, Mozambique, Tanzania, Zambia, Bangladesh, India, Pakistan, Sri Lanka and Nicaragua), all recipients of Norwegian development aid. This research is thus limited to a systematic comparison of the U.S. and Norway's assessments of human rights practices in these ten countries. The extent to which conclusions may be generalized beyond these countries is also limited, since it is possible that the ten countries included in the Norwegian report are not representative of the reporting found in the U.S. report as a whole. Still, there is geographic variation (five countries in Africa, four in Asia and one Latin American country), and only one of the ten (Nicaragua) is a country for which the U.S. assessment is frequently identified as being politically biased.[5] The additional caveat that these are all developing nations should also be noted, given that human rights data for Third World nations are generally more suspect than data on developed countries.[6]

Although the report from Norway covers fewer countries, the coverage given to those countries is more extensive than in the U.S. report. The Norwegian reports range from 11 to 42 pages, averaging 24 pages per country. The U.S. reports (on the countries compared) range from 6 to 17 pages, with an average of 10 pages per country.

This is slightly misleading, however, given the variance in the two reports in the number of words per page. An idea of the difference in the extent of coverage might better be portrayed by comparing the number of words per country report. In the case of Botswana for example, the U.S. report is 3,360 words long while the report from Norway is approximately 11,150 word in length. Still the essential weakness of page counts or word counts as indicators of adequacy of coverage should be stressed. More is learned from a review of the different aspects or dimensions of human rights that are included or excluded from these reports.

Scope of Rights Considered

One could reasonably presume that the luxury of having a smaller number of countries to cover would automatically permit Norway to concentrate on a wider scope of human rights. And in fact, the list of human rights on which Norway reports is far more extensive than the rights on which the United States reports. In both cases, however, the scope of rights included in the report reflects a conscious decision on the part of the respective countries. The U.S. *Country Reports* for 1986 focus exclusively on civil and political rights in both the definition and use of human rights statistics. The justification of this more limited definition of human rights is interesting.

We have found that the concept of economic, social and cultural rights is often confused, sometimes willfully, by repressive governments, claiming that in order to promote these "rights" they may deny their citizens the right to integrity of the persons as well as political and civil rights. . . . [W]e consider it imperative to focus urgent attention on violations of basic political and civil human rights.[7]

The 1986 format of the U.S. report replaced the discussion of the "Economic, Social and Cultural Situation" found in some previous editions with sections entitled "Discrimination Based on Race, Sex, Religion, Language or Social Status" and "Conditions of Labor." According to a note in the Appendix,

[t]his change was made to better focus the reports on the right to non-discriminatory treatment in all facets of life . . . in lieu of a necessarily general and superficial survey of the broad economic, social and cultural situation in each country.[8]

By contrast, the authors of the Norwegian report chose a different route. In addition to assessing civil and political rights, the report from Norway includes economic and social rights as well. Justifying this approach, the authors note that "it is not acceptable to rank human rights in 'essential' and 'less important' rights," adding that civil and political rights "are far from the only ones of relevance to Norwegian development aid policy with its traditional emphasis on the basic needs of the poorest sections of the population."[9]

Thus, the selection of rights to be reviewed in both countries reflects government priorities and underlying philosophical differences. As de Neufville notes in discussing the preparation of the U.S. reports, "deciding how to categorize abuses and how to present information was in itself the product of negotiation."[10] It might also be argued that the different approaches reflect differences in the original impetus of the two reports.

In both the United States and Norway, the impetus for the reports came from an attempt on the part of the respective legislative bodies to link foreign assistance to human rights practices in recipient nations. In this sense, the reports raise the important policy question of the appropriate link between aid and human rights practices. Interestingly, however, the two countries focus on different aspects of this linkage.

In the United States, original congressional initiatives in this area came in response to charges that U.S. security assistance and weapons were associated with human rights abuses and violations.[11] Although the recent plethora of U.S. legislation, which attempts to relate foreign assistance to human rights practices, includes concerns of development aid (e.g., the Harkin amendment), the reports themselves are required specifically for countries proposed as recipients of security assistance. The U.S. document cites Section 502(B)(b) of the Foreign Assistance Act of 1961, as amended, which requires a report on the observance of, and respect for, internationally recognized human rights in each country proposed as a recipient of *security assistance*.[12] The primary concern with security assistance helps to explain the focus on civil and political rights.

By contrast, the emphasis in the link between foreign assistance and human rights for Norway is clearly placed on development aid and not security assistance. The impetus for the Norwegian *Yearbook* stems from a 1984 to 1985 government report to the Storting, the Norwegian National Assembly. Stortingsmelding No. 36 seeks to connect Norwegian development assistance to human rights conditions in recipient countries.[13] The *Yearbook* series, then, is intended to provide information that will aid in decision making regarding *development assistance*, and serious attention is paid to socioeconomic rights conditions.

In the *Country Reports*, the United States provides data on bilateral assistance broken down by economic and military aid. Norway also provides data on the amount of Norwegian bilateral assistance going to the host country, as well as a breakdown by type of assistance. For comparison purposes, these figures are summarized in Table 2 and discussed later in the chapter. While the different purposes of the two reports surely influence the scope of rights considered, these practical reports also reflect other theoretical issues involved in defining the scope of human rights.

Obviously important to the user of any statistical measure is the source from which the information is drawn. In the field of human rights, this is an issue of even greater than usual concern. The literature contains frequent calls that, in the interests of objectivity, evaluations of human rights practices be conducted by nongovernmental organizations.[14] In contrast to the U.S. *Reports*, which are written and submitted by the State Department, the Norwegian *Yearbook*, funded by the Ministry of Development Aid, is prepared by the Christian Michelsen Institute, an independent contractor. If in fact independent assessments are more objective than those prepared by government personnel, one would expect some interesting differences in the selection, use, and interpretation of human rights data. This is an issue to which I return later in the chapter.

Although neither country documents the use of data to the extent that might be required by scholarly standards, a comparison here also suggests some interesting differences. The report from Norway provides an index with a listing of all general sources (including the U.S. *Country Reports*), as well as the specific sources cited for each country. The authors visited three of the ten countries.[15] The U.S. report is much less specific in citing sources and notes that the document is "prepared by a cast of hundreds" and is "based on all information available to the U.S. government," explaining that "[f]or obvious reasons, much of our information cannot be attributed to specific sources."[16] While the need to protect sources might be understandable in this situation, it raises important questions about the validity and reliability of the data.

Reporting Period

Although both countries title their reports as 1986 volumes and cover roughly the same time period, the U.S. report came out in February 1987 and includes most of 1986, while the Norwegian volume was initially published in June 1986 and refers primarily to 1985 and only to the early months of 1986. Thus, in some instances, discrepancies between the two reports reflect this time difference. With few exceptions however, overall human rights conditions do not vary significantly over such a short period of time. Still, in the ten nations under investigation here, it is potentially significant in at least Mozambique and Bangladesh where major political events occurred during this time period.[17] Due to the different times of publication of the 1986 reports, these events are not covered in the Norwegian reports. To assure comparability in these cases the 1985 U.S. *Country Reports* were consulted as well.

Conceptual Differences in Reporting Categories

Table 1 reflects the categories used by the two countries to report on rights. These categories display several interesting differences. Some reflect the difficulty of classifying a right as purely civil/political or socioeconomic.[18] For example, in the U.S. report, freedom of association is clearly considered a civil right. In the Norwegian report, however, freedom of association, along with the right to strike, is considered and reported as an economic and social right. In the U.S. report, the right to strike is considered under the separate category "Conditions of Labor." The categories themselves are thus a bit deceptive and are clearly inadequate guides for obtaining comparable information. The problem of forced labor in Tanzania provides a concrete example of the confusion that results from trying to categorize abuses. According to the Norwegian report on Tanzania, forced labor is an abuse of the right to "freedom of movement."[19] The United States also has a category entitled "freedom of movement" where one finds passing reference to the Tanzanian problem[20] although it is addressed in the U.S. report under "Arbitrary Arrest, Detention and Exile."[21]

Other differences in categories and the information included under them are interesting and provide insights on national priorities in human rights. For example, the United States deals specifically with freedom of religion as a right, while Norway reports on this under the rubric of "Ethnic, Cultural, and Religious Minorities." Roughly comparable are Norway's "Freedom of Expression" and the U.S. "Freedom of Speech and Press," although here the *Country Reports* include academic freedom, a topic seldom mentioned in the Norwegian *Yearbook*. Also of interest is the fact that a nation's use of capital punishment, a distinct category for Norway, is not mentioned in the U.S. reports. In this way, the reports reveal almost as much about the reporting countries themselves as they do about the nations on which they report.[22]

While political rights in the U.S. *Reports* are described as "the right

TABLE 1. Reporting Categories

NORWAY	U.S.
I. Civil and Political Rights	*I. Integrity of Person Freedom from:*

A. Political Killings & Disappearance	A. Political Killing
B. Torture, Cruel Inhumane Treatment, Punishment	B. Disappearance
C. Arbitrary Arrest, Detention, Position of Judiciary	C. Torture, Cruel Inhumane Treatment, Punishment
D. Capital Punishment	D. Arbitrary arrest, Detention
E. Freedom of Expression	E. Denial of fair public trial
F. Freedom of Movement	F. Arbitrary interference with privacy
G. Political Participation	

II. Economic and Social Rights	*II. Civil Liberties*
A. Right to Food and Health	A. Freedom of Speech and Press
B. Right to Work	B. Peaceful Assembly and Association
C. Freedom of Association, Right to Strike	C. Freedom of Religion
D. Right to Education	D. Freedom of Movement

III. Ethnic Cultural and Religious Minorities	*III. Political Rights*
	A. Right to Change Government

	IV. Government Attitude Regarding Human Rights Investigations
	V. Discrimination Based on Race, Sex, Religion, Language or Social Status
	VI. Conditions of Labor

of citizens to change their government," the right to political participation is more broadly defined in the Norwegian *Yearbook* which, under this category, describes "opportunities for wielding political influence through different channels of participation—not solely the electoral process, but through participation within the parties in single party systems and at the local as well as national levels."[23] Under "Political Rights" the U.S. reports on women's roles in the political system. Generally, the overall situation of women is fairly consistently addressed under the U.S. category "Discrimination Based on Race, Sex, Religion or Social Status." Interestingly, it is here, and only with respect to women, that social and economic rights are discussed, and in several cases supported with statistics on literacy, health, education, and employment. Norway, with no specific category on the rights of women, discusses women's roles more consistently and extensively under the categories "Right to Food and Health," "Right to Education," and "Right to Work" where their position in the labor force is discussed. Under "Conditions of Labor" in the U.S. report, women are seldom mentioned.

Comparison of Selected Items In the 1986 Reports

While the previous examples highlight the difficulty of utilizing neatly comparable categories of human rights, it is also obvious that what is truly important is the information presented and not the category under which it falls. And indeed, there are occasions when a comparison of the information contained in the two reports, regardless of reporting category, is hearteningly similar. So close are the assessments of human rights in some instances that the frequent caution to use multiple sources of information[24] seems alarmist. The similarity of wording in the two reports on Zambia is particularly striking. Consider these examples where the same observation is repeated (although under different categories) almost verbatim—one is simply a paraphrase of the other.

NORWAY	*U.S.*
Freedom of Association and the Right to Strike	*Freedom of Peaceful Assembly and Association*
In historical terms trade unions in Zambia have been rather strong ever since the establishment of the large copper mines in the 1930's. Today, the countrywide Zambian Congress of Trade Unions (ZCTU) represents about 300,000 employees organized in 18 national labor unions.[25]	Zambia has a history of strong labor union organization dating from the establishment of large copper mines during the 1930's. Zambia's 18 national labor unions, which are organized by industry or profession, are all members of Zambian Congress of Trade Unions (ZCTU).[26]
Ethnic Cultural and Religious Minorities	*Freedom of Religion*
Freedom of Religion is guaranteed in the Constitution and it is adhered to. Zambia has no state religion, and there is no discrimination on religious grounds.[27]	Freedom of Religion is constitutionally guaranteed and has been publicly supported by President Kaunda. Zambia has no state religion and adherence to a particular faith does not confer either advantage or disadvantage.[28]

NORWAY	U.S.
Arbitrary Arrest and Detention	*Denial of Fair Public Trial*
Criticisms have been made of the strong presidential influence on the selection of judges who may be harmful to the independence of the judiciary. Still there are no reports of particular cases in which the selection of judges has been exploited by the President in this manner.[29]	Independent observation confirms the independence of the Zambian judiciary from executive branch influence. The President's power to appoint and transfer judges has sometimes been cited as proof that judiciary independence can be compromised. However there is no evidence that such power has swayed court decisions.[30]

One might now be lulled into thinking that, despite different conceptual categories of rights, basic assessments of human rights practices by the United States and Norway are the same. Careful reading of the two reports, however, also reveals some very subtle differences in almost identical passages resulting in different impressions. For example, see the following reports on trade unions in India.

NORWAY	U.S.
Freedom of Association and Right to Strike	*Freedom of Peaceful Assembly and Association*
During recent years Indian trade unions have complained several times to the International Labor Organization charging the authorities with having violated ILO conventions and recommendations. According to the ILO, Indian authorities, on their side, have cooperated in the investigations made by the ILO Committee on Freedom of Association.[31]	In recent years Indian unions have complained several times to the International Labor Organization Committee on Freedom of Association charging violations of ILO conventions and recommendations. *Such complaints are usually presented by the Marxist unions.* The government has cooperated in the committee's investigation.[32]

In almost identical passages, the U.S. version seems to imply that because the complaints of human rights abuse stem from Marxist unions (a fact unmentioned by Norway) they are somehow less serious. Similarly, in the report on Tanzania, the U.S. portrays "10 family cells" as oppressive political units while Norway presents them as educating and conflict-solving mechanisms.

NORWAY *Political Participation*	*U.S.* *Arbitrary Interference with Privacy*
The party has wielded relatively extensive control at the local level for instance through neighborhood units, the so-called "ten-house cells." These cells consist in principle of ten households organized under the leadership of a party member. The cells supervise the rationing system, which may constitute a powerful means of political control. The cells also have responsibility for political education and for helping to solve whatever conflicts may arise between members.[33]	The party attempts to control activity at all levels of society through its system of 10 family cells. . . . Although party membership is voluntary, the government uses the party structure to intervene in the private lives of its citizens. The Chama Cha Mapinduzi has party cadres covering the smallest units of society. Individual cells vary in size from single family homes to large apartment buildings and may contain from 10 to several hundred individuals. Unpaid "10 cell" leaders are the party officials responsible for resolving problems at the grassroots level and reporting any suspicious behavior or event within their neighborhoods to authorities.[34]

Not all discrepancies are a matter of subtle impressions however. There are several cases of minor differences in the data that are offered. Some again appear in otherwise strikingly similar paragraphs. Consider this description of the most recent election in Zambia.

NORWAY *Political Participation*	*U.S.* *Respect for Political Rights*
In 1983, *766* candidates ran for the 125 seats. More than 25% of all incumbents were defeated, including seven ministers of state.[35]	In the latest parliamentary elections in 1983, *760* candidates contested 125 seats, 40 incumbents were defeated, including 7 ministers of state.[36]

While a difference of only six candidates in a 1983 election might be considered trivial, it is indicative of the caution one ought to exercise in applying the data, particularly since the number of candidates running in an election is not a statistic open to much debate. It is also the kind of statistic one sees used to estimate the amount of political freedom in a country.[37] Unfortunately, not all such statistical differences are so minor. Compare these reports of union membership in Tanzania.

NORWAY *Freedom of Association*	U.S. *Freedom of Peaceful Assembly*
In the early 1980s JUWATA represented a total of about 350,000 employees, that is, *65%* of the workers in the modern, industrial and public sectors.[38]	JUWATA represents about *60%* of the workers in the industrial and government sectors.[39]

While a difference of 5 percent might not be considered a major discrepancy, trade union membership is relatively easy to verify, and it is a difference that might result in different findings when applied. Admittedly, the number of refugees in a country is less easy to document, but in the following two cases, the two reports differ by 30,000 and 107,000 in their estimates of the number of refugees in Tanzania and Zambia respectively.

NORWAY *Freedom of Movement*	U.S. *Freedom of Movement*
An estimated *100,000* people have taken refuge in [Zambia], most of them from Angola, but also from many of the other neighboring countries.[40]	The United Nations High Commissioner for Refugees estimates that there are approximately *130,000* refugees in Zambia.[41]
There are approximately *100,000* refugees in Tanzania. Most of them come from Burundi.[42]	As of January 1986 there were about *207,000* refugees and displaced persons in Tanzania of whom 82% were from Burundi, with most of the rest from Rwanda and Zaire.[43]

Similarly disturbing is the discrepancy of 60,000 found in the two reports in their estimates of the number of Asians in Tanzania.

NORWAY *Ethnic, Cultural and Religious* *Minorities*	U.S. *Discrimination Based on Race, Sex,* *Religion, Language or Social Status*
There are some *100,000* persons of Arab background, approximately the same number of *Asians* and about 15,000 whites.[44]	The *Asian* community, estimated at about *40,000*, is both culturally and economically exclusive.[45]

One assumes that such a difference would have an impact on any human rights study that employed, as many do, ethnic diversity as a variable.[46]

If the reader is left with any doubt about the need to consult multiple sources in gathering human rights data, or more generally, the need to apply extreme caution in utilizing these widely varying estimates, the following passages on the extent of the problem of debt bondage in India should be considered.

NORWAY *The Right to Work*	U.S. *Conditions of Labor*
The leader of the Bonded Liberation Front in New Delhi [had established for a U.N. subcommission] that an estimated *6 million people* in India were living under slavery-like conditions which conflict with the Indian labour laws. . . . The Indian authorities have admitted that debt bondage still exists in the country, but claim that less than 1 million people are affected by the problem.[47]	Bonded labor, illegal since 1976, continues. Most commonly bondage arises from debt incurred at usurious rates and continued through a lifetime. Bonded laborers are most commonly employed in agriculture and construction. . . . Estimates of the number of bonded laborers range from *500,000 to 2,000,000*.[48]

Here we have estimates of violations of the same human right in the same country during the same time period ranging from half a million to twelve times that amount!

These examples point out some rather serious differences in the statistics reported by the United States and those reported by Norway for the same cases during the same time period. While most users of either report are expected to be generally aware of the difficulty of applying these figures in any exacting manner, it is interesting to point out that reviewers of the U.S. *Country Reports* find them to be basically fair and accurate and "all denied believing there was any deliberate falsification of statistics."[49] One might, of course, argue that the differences are slight and to be expected given the general lack of availability and reliability of statistics on developing nations. Still, it is appropriate to wonder how the results of some studies that use this report as the source of data might vary if the statistics found in the other report were used instead.

Conflicting Information

Perhaps more disturbing than conflicting statistics are those cases in which the two reports provide directly contradictory information on the same country. In both respects, an attempt is made to distinguish between the legal promise of a right and the reality of its actual practice. While one might expect some discrepancies in the interpretation of actual practice, one also finds differences in the accounts of legal guarantees. Consider these cases of assessment of the legal status of the rights of freedom from torture in India, or the right to strike in Tanzania.

NORWAY	U.S.
Torture and Cruel, Inhumane or Degrading Treatment	*Torture and Cruel, Inhumane or Degrading Treatment*
The laws of India do not explicitly prohibit torture.[50]	Torture and cruel treatment are prohibited by law in India.[51]
Freedom of Association and the Right to Strike	*Freedom of Peaceful Assembly and Association*
Strikes are prohibited by law [in Tanzania].[52]	Strikes are not prohibited by law [in Tanzania].[53]

Of course, not all the differences are so direct. Some are the result of subtle language or omissions. Interpretations on freedom of the press in India provide a good example.

NORWAY	U.S.
Freedom of Expression	*Freedom of Speech and Press*
The federal laws do not authorize censorship, but state laws are used against journalists and local media. Index on Censorship reports that journalists have been victims of different kinds of pressure. Journalists and photographers have allegedly been murdered. . . . According to PUCL [People's Union for Civil Liberties] the media of India frequently suffer from different kinds of indirect pressure through withholding of state advertisements. The state also buys up critical newspapers and some critical reports are censored.[54]	There are no restrictions on criticism of the government in the lively and free Indian press.[55]

The Norwegian version goes on to cite reports of a journalist being placed under house arrest after being charged with "creating hatred against the government," of newspaper offices being burned down, and journalists being beaten by police. It is difficult to believe that this is the same "free Indian press" that the United States describes. Another striking difference is seen in the case of India where Norway and the United States provide different interpretations of the government's role in the Sikh community.

NORWAY	*U.S.*
Political Killings and "Disappearances"	*Discrimination Based on Race, Sex, Religion, Language or Social Status*
Newly available information supports the allegations that the killings and ill-treatment of the Sikhs was planned and carried out with the tacit approval of the police. A report published in 1984 by two Indian human rights organizations (People's Union for Civil Liberties and People's Union for Democratic Rights) concludes that the *government was not only passive, but also directly involved in the violations.*[56]	[Terrorist violence in India has] increased tension and distrust between Hindu and Sikh communities leading to spontaneous outbreaks that have resulted in damage to property, injuries and death. The police forces have had difficulty containing some outbreaks but there is *no evidence to support the charge of government involvement in this violence.*[57]

The Case of Nicaragua

As previously noted, the report on Nicaragua is one for which the United States had consistently been cited for political bias during the period of the "Sandinista Regime." The statistics contained in the Norwegian and U.S. reports in this case are difficult to compare since much of the Norwegian data is based on an on-site visit that occurred in January 1986, and the presentation tends to include background material beginning with the first phases of the war. Both the U.S. and Norwegian reports on Nicaragua are disproportionately long. In fact, the Norwegian report includes Nicaragua not as a recipient of development assistance (as all the others are), but rather as a nation in which Norway has a particular interest.

One recent review of the U.S. report on Nicaragua notes a "curious omission": "The 500 word introduction . . . neglects to mention that a war is underway to overthrow the government."[58] Norway, by contrast, *introduces* its report on Nicaragua by calling it "a country at war,"[59] and much of the human rights situation is explained in terms of the costs of war. Similarly, the U.S. report offers no hint of U.S. involvement in the conflict,[60] while the Norwegian report notes early on that the "USA pursues a conscious policy of destabilization against the Nicaraguan government," and that the "contra forces have been partly financed and organized by the USA."[61]

In the case of Nicaragua, the United States *is* accused of falsifying statistics. The Lawyers Committee reports that the "Department of State exaggerates so much in attempts to demonize the Sandinistas,"[62] and the Norwegian report asserts that the *Country Reports* contain "examples of *systematic* exaggeration of the number of political killings and 'disappearances' in Nicaragua."[63]

And again, the focus on civil and political rights and the exclusion of socioeconomic rights in the U.S. report leads to a different overall impression. An examination, based on a broader definition of human rights in Nicaragua, leads Norway to conclude that "[S]ince . . . 1979, Nicaragua has enjoyed pronounced improvements in most areas of human rights, but there are severe constraints on several political and civil rights. Progress has been most visible in the social and economic fields."[64] In assessing these rights, Norway finds that "a combination of public priorities and popular mobilizations have turned Nicaragua into a model country as regards the development of health services and public contributions to ensuring basic needs. In certain fields, the improvements are dramatic."[65] The report goes on to cite statistics which demonstrate achievements in the fields of nutrition, health care, and literacy.

Summary and Conclusions

As in the case of Nicaragua in particular, the most obvious distinction between the two reports in general is a result of the choice of rights on which the two countries report. Further comparison of the two reports uncovers some interesting examples which serve to emphasize the point that different definitions of human rights, and the statistics selected to assess their practice, can lead to different conclusions about human rights conditions in the same country. For example, in the case of Botswana, problems cited by Norway and documented by statistics include growing social and economic inequality and severe levels of malnutrition, particularly among children. These go unmentioned in the U.S. report. "The main human rights problem in Botswana," according to the report from Norway, is the situation of the San (bushmen) population.[66] Interestingly, the main problem by Norwegian standards is mentioned only in passing in the

U.S. report, where we learn that the "government does not repress or deny" the rights of this population.[67]

Similarly, the U.S. report provides information that is neglected or omitted in the Norwegian report. In addition to providing more information on the status of women and academic freedom, the U.S. *Reports* include statements on the status of private enterprise and free trade. For example, we learn from the U.S. report on human rights practices in Kenya that the nation "has a well-developed private sector" and that "the government has begun to display an awareness of the need to promote even greater privatization in most areas of the economy."[68] These facts go unmentioned in the Norwegian assessment of Kenya, where instead we are informed that one-third of the population is below the poverty level, one-half the population is illiterate, and there is an extremely unequal distribution of land. Conditions among the Nomad population, where 80 percent fall below the poverty level, are cited as a major problem. The conditions of the Nomads (12 percent of Kenya's population) are unaddressed in the U.S. report.

In the introductory section on each country, the U.S. *Reports* provide an "economic background statement." Not surprisingly, here the focus is on the development of the private sector. For example, in the case of Bangladesh, the development of the private sector is reported to be a key element in the government's program of economic development.[69] This policy is not mentioned in the Norwegian assessment of Bangladesh. Far greater emphasis, however, is placed on the outcome of economic policies in the Norwegian *Yearbook*. While the U.S. *Reports* acknowledge that Bangladesh remains one of the poorest and most densely populated countries in the world, the Norwegian assessment describes in detail the extent of the problems and the effect of policies aimed at addressing the problems. After warning that the statistics should be interpreted with caution, data are presented on food consumption patterns, undernourishment, landholdings, infant mortality, and distribution patterns. While privatization is a presumed good in the U.S. report, Norway tells us that privatization, in some instances, has led to less than favorable results.[70] Similarly, in the case of Tanzania, the U.S. presents the "good news" that "the government accelerated the process of economic reform which stimulated a 2.5 percent growth rate in 1984 and 1985. In 1986 the government strengthened the reform program. . . ."[71] While Norway acknowledges that the reforms have probably caused growth in production, their report also notes that "these measures have reduced the standard of living of parts of the population."[72]

It should be recalled that with the 1986 *Country Reports* the U.S.

replaced the 1985 category "Economic, Social and Cultural Situation" with two new sections entitled "Discrimination Based on Race, Sex, Religion, Language or Social Status" and "Conditions of Labor." The stated rationale was to "better focus on the right to nondiscriminatory treatment . . . in lieu of a necessarily general and superficial survey of the broad economic, social, and cultural situation in each country."[73] When one actually examines the reporting in this new category, however, it would be difficult to conclude that much progress was made in focusing the report or avoiding general and superficial statements. What is omitted is also misleading. In the U.S. report on Zambia, for example, we learn that "[E]conomic and social needs and cultural aspirations are met on a generally nondiscriminatory basis in Zambia."[74] Contrast this with the picture presented by Norway where we learn that "income inequalities in Zambia are among the most severe in Africa and have increased substantially,"[75] and that there are major disparities on age, sex, and geographic location in the enjoyment of the rights to education, health, and work.

These examples highlight the different impressions that may be left depending on the chosen range and scope of rights to be reported on, and the different presentation and interpretation of statistical data and other information. The general conclusion that might be drawn from this assessment is that much work remains in the development of comparable human rights reporting, and that sole reliance on such reports for reliable statistical data is premature at best. While the governments of the United States and Norway are to be lauded for their embryonic efforts, imprudent scholars who take these reports for more than this are to be cautioned.

Similar Impact

In assessing the general impact of the two reports, one finds similar results. In both cases, the reporting on human rights conditions undertaken by, or on behalf of, the governments of the United States and Norway has been credited with strengthening the information base on human rights, promoting increased awareness, and providing policy input for decision makers.[76] The reports also have brought increased attention to, and review of, government foreign policy and the human rights connection by scholars and private and professional organizations. It is less certain whether they have had the intended effect of actually tying foreign aid to human rights conditions.

In neither case is the connection between foreign assistance and human rights performance explicitly addressed in detail in the reports, nor is it seen as an absolute. In discussing U.S. human rights policy, the *Country Reports* never purport to establish a direct link.[77] While the reports are required for each country proposed as a recipient of security assistance, no discussion of the actual connection is offered. In fact, the statistical sheets for each country, which provide data on economic and military assistance, and which *could* be used to draw some connection, are misleading. No distinction is made between categories under which countries received "no assistance" and categories for which the information is "unavailable." Both are coded as "0" and it is only in the appendix where one learns that some of the categories coded as such represent data that were not available at the time of the report.[78]

Assuming the data were accurate and complete, there remains the theoretical question of how such quantitative information on human rights might best be used to determine aid policies. While one might challenge the wisdom of the U.S. approach, the intent of the

TABLE 2. 1985 Bilateral Assistance[a] to the Countries Compared
    (US $, millions)

	NORWAY[b]		U.S.[c] $	
		(%)		(%)
Botswana	12.6	(06)	23.7	(02)
Kenya	24.0	(11)	76.9	(08)
Mozambique	24.1	(11)	38.8	(04)
Tanzania	51.5	(24)	9.4	(01)
Zambia	18.9	(09)	52.4	(05)
Bangladesh	25.4	(12)	205.3	(20)
India	26.5	(13)	190.9	(19)
Pakistan	11.1	(05)	339.2	(34)
Sri Lanka	11.6	(06)	67.4	(07)
Nicaragua	5.7	(03)	0	(00)
TOTAL	211.4		1004.0	

Source: Data are derived from the U.S. Department of State, *Country Reports on Human Rights Practices for 1986* (Washington, DC: U.S. Government Printing Office, 1987) and Tor Skalnes and Jan Egeland, eds., *Human Rights in Developing Countries 1986, A Yearbook on Countries Receiving Norwegian Aid*, Christian Michelsen Institute (Oslo: Norwegian University Press, 1986).
[a] On a per capita basis, bilateral assistance to the ten countries compared amounts to $50.76 from each Norwegian compared to $4.17 from each American. Population data from the *Statistical Abstract of the U.S.*, 1987, Table 1437.
[b] Norwegian data were originally reported in krone. Conversion to U.S. dollars was based on figures from the *Federal Reserve Bulletin* (1987) which gives 7.58 krone as the average 1985 foreign exchange rate per U.S. dollar.
[c] Figures for U.S. military assistance are also provided in the *Country Reports* as well as some data on 1986 bilateral economic assistance. 1985 economic data were selected here for comparison purposes. It should be noted that the U.S. amount includes loans which are not generally considered assistance.

legislation which requires such reporting is to reduce aid to nations that exhibit patterns of human rights abuse. Other things being equal, according to this policy we would expect those nations receiving the most damaging human rights reports to be receiving the least amount of aid. But in fact, among the countries under review, Pakistan and Bangladesh are granted the greatest amount of aid despite their relatively poor records on civil and political rights, while Botswana receives a reasonably good report and receives the least.

The Norwegian report does attempt to grapple with the issue of the connection between assistance and human rights practice. The position put forth in the report is interesting and follows the spirit of U.S. legislation, which makes exceptions for prohibitions against assistance if it can be demonstrated that the aid benefits the needy.

> If it is established beyond reasonable doubt that a government is accountable for serious human rights violations, a pertinent approach would be to limit the more general transfers of financial and commodity aid . . . [providing assistance] increasingly targeted and earmarked for specific projects among the poor and persecuted parts of the population, reducing transfers to the regimes' own programs and budgets proportionately.[79]

The Norwegian policy, however, with its focus on development assistance and the commitment to aid the neediest, would lead to a different expectation regarding the human rights/aid connection. Here, we might expect that those nations exhibiting the greatest need according to the socioeconomic indicators (e.g., high rates of infant mortality and illiteracy) would receive the greatest aid. But in fact Pakistan, which demonstrates almost the greatest need by both these measures, receives only five percent of the Norwegian aid reported here. Conversely, Tanzania demonstrates considerably less need and receives almost a quarter of the total aid.

Since all things are seldom equal, however, a serious effort to establish the connection between human rights conditions and aid policy would require a consideration of other factors. Such a review would, for example, have to include a look at longer term trends in both aid and human rights performance, as well as data adjusted for population base. Further, particularly in reviewing the U.S. connection, it would be wise to recall the admonition that punitive measures do not always encourage positive human rights performance and to consider the fact that measures short of aid cuts may be used to back up human rights policy. Nevertheless, this assessment seems to reinforce the argument that human rights reporting provides background "enlightenment," but not actual decision making criteria for funding.[80]

If this is the case, and if the reports themselves provide inadequate information for conversion to reliable statistics for use by serious scholars, is human rights reporting of this sort worth the attention it has received? Yes, but its value seems to lie clearly with the increased attention paid to the topic as a result of these reports. This point is indirectly related to the final question to be raised here: the question of whether human rights reporting is best undertaken by governmental or nongovernmental bodies.

More Objective?

It has come to be an article of faith that the antidote to politically biased assessments of human rights practices is reporting by nongovernmental organizations (NGOs). This simple prescription, however, ignores the fact that NGOs, too, can be politically biased. Anyone familiar with the Freedom House rankings, for example, is well aware of the charges of political bias in these reports.

The comparison of the human rights reports of Norway and the United States would seem to provide an example from which one could draw some conclusion on this issue. Frankly, I find it difficult to conclude that the Norwegian reports, prepared and submitted by an independent contractor, are more objective than the reports prepared by the U.S. government personnel. Clearly, there are different perceptions of the human rights situations found by the two reporting bodies, but there is no evidence that these differences are related to the reports being prepared independently. The differences appear to be due, for the most part, to different definitions of human rights and different national priorities.

This is not to say that the two reports are of equal value. Each has its respective strengths and weaknesses. On the one hand, the number of countries in the more extensive U.S. report is an advantage. But, on the other hand, this obviously prohibits the depth of coverage that the Norwegian report provides. It should also be noted that the extensive number of countries covered by the U.S. report represents a policy choice by the State Department since it *exceeds* the coverage required by the legislation. Similarly, the decision to interpret "internationally recognized human rights" as being limited to civil and political rights reflects a State Department decision and results in a much less complete picture of human rights conditions than the Norwegian report. This may be a reflection of political bias, but not one necessarily due to the report being prepared by the government as opposed to an NGO.

The Norwegian reports, by choosing a broader definition of human rights, do provide a more comprehensive view of human rights, though in a more limited number of countries. Additionally, these reports generally provide a comparative perspective, and frequent reference is made to the human rights situation in relation to other nations in that region or other recipients of development aid, for example. Another point on which the Norwegian contributors are to be complimented is their nation by nation fact sheet, which provides comparable statistics for each country. But again, these differences do not appear to be due to independent reporting as opposed to governmental reporting.

In contrast to the standard call for independent assessments, this analysis uncovers some rather compelling arguments for the extent of government involvement in the preparation of the U.S. reports. Perhaps most convincing is the development of expertise and interest in human rights issues among government officials. While the reports are intended to provide the respective legislative bodies with better information on specific countries, the unintended but important consequence, in the case of the U.S., has been the development of heightened awareness in the State Department and the creation of "human rights officers" in the U.S. embassies in each nation who must specialize in the human rights situation in that country in order to prepare the report. In some cases, this has become a full-time position serving a liaison role between local individuals and groups lodging or investigating complaints of human rights abuses, and the State Department in Washington.[81] In Washington, departmental officers too have become increasingly sensitized to human rights issues as a result of the reporting requirement.[82] The reporting requirement thus generates a degree of expertise and interest not previously obvious in the government itself. Granted, the Norwegian reports, produced by an independent contractor, may also result in increased knowledge and awareness, but it is uncertain whether they have the same spill-over effect on government personnel. And perhaps this is not so necessary or important in the case of Norway, given the size of the country and the relatively short distance between NGOs and government officials.

What seems to be most important in guarding against political bias in human rights reporting is the opportunity the reports provide for governmental and NGO interaction and feedback in assessing human rights practices. And there is evidence in both Norway and the United States that both the government and the NGOs take the opportunity to review and critique these reports. The analysis of these reports also adds insight to the ongoing debate raised at the onset about the nature of human rights as qualitative or quantitative phenomena. While both reports provide ample evidence that human rights conditions can be gauged by objective measures or indicators, the goal of "objective" coverage of such phenomena is chimerical.[83]

Notes

1. See the report by the Dutch Human Rights and Foreign Policy Advisory Committee, *Development Cooperation and Human Rights* (The Hague, July 14, 1987), pp. 55–58. Interestingly, this Advisory Committee recently recommended that the Netherlands adopt the "Norwegian Model" (annual, public reports, prepared by an independent body, on human rights in nations that are recipients of foreign aid). The Minister of Foreign Affairs rejected the recommendation however, on the grounds that such reports would be a mere "reformulation" of existing information, and for their potential to result in occasions in which the government would be forced to comment publicly on "delicate" situations. See pp. 60, 69–70 of the Report.

2. The reports assessed here are the U.S. Department of State, *Country Reports on Human Rights Practices for 1986*, submitted to the U.S. Congress, House Committee on Foreign Affairs and Senate Committee on Foreign Relations (Washington, D.C.: U.S. Government Printing Office, 1987).

3. Tor Skalnes and Jan Egeland, eds., *Human Rights in Developing Countries 1986: A Yearbook on Countries Receiving Norwegian Aid*, Christian Michelsen Institute (Oslo: Norwegian University Press, 1986).

4. For examples of those who have used the *Country Reports* to produce quantitative data sets see David Carleton and Michael Stohl, "The Role of Human Rights in U.S. Foreign Assistance Policy: A Critique and Reappraisal," *American Journal of Political Science* 31 (November 1987): 1002–1015; David L. Cingranelli and Thomas N. Pasquarello, "Human Rights Practices and the Distribution of U.S. Foreign Aid to Latin American Countries," *American Journal of Political Science*, 29, No. 3 (August 1985): 539–563. Even critics suggest that the reports can be used (if cautiously) as a source of valuable information. See Robert Justin Goldstein, "The Limitations of Using Quantitative Data in Studying Human Rights Abuses," *Human Rights Quarterly* 8, No. 4 (November 1986): 607–627.

5. See Judith Innes de Neufville, "Human Rights Reporting as a Policy Tool: An Examination of the State Department *Country Reports*," *Human Rights Quarterly* 8, No. 4 (November 1986): 681–699; Americas Watch, Helsinki Watch, and Lawyers Committee for International Human Rights, *Critique: Review of the Department of State's Country Reports on Human Rights Practices for 1985* (New York: Americas Watch, 1986).

6. For basic generalizations on the availability and reliability of human rights data, see Goldstein, "Limitations" (note 4), p. 613.

7. U.S. Department of State, *Country Reports, 1986* (note 2), p. 3.

8. Ibid., p. 1344.

9. Skalnes and Egeland, *Human Rights in Developing Countries 1986* (note 3), pp. 17–18.

10. de Neufville, "Human Rights Reporting" (note 5), p. 695.

11. See generally, David Forsythe, "Congress and Human Rights in U.S. Foreign Policy: The Fate of General Legislation," *Human Rights Quarterly* 9 No. 3 (August 1987): 382–444; and de Neufville, "Human Rights Reporting" (note 5), pp. 683–684.

12. U.S. Department of State, *Country Reports 1986* (note 2), pp. 1–2.

13. Skalnes, and Egeland, *Human Rights in Developing Countries 1986* (note 3), pp. 15–16.

14. See Richard Claude and Thomas Jabine, "Editor's Introduction," *Human Rights Quarterly* 8, No. 4 (November 1986): 555.

15. The Norwegian Reporting team visited Nicaragua, Sri Lanka, and Zambia. Requests to visit India were turned down. See Skalnes and Egeland, *Human Rights in Developing Countries 1986* (note 3), p. 12.

16. U.S. Department of State, *Country Reports 1986* (note 2), p. 1343. For a general description of the reporting process see de Neufville, "Human Rights Reporting" (note 5), pp. 685–686.

17. For example, the death of President Machel in an airplane crash in October 1986 was followed by the first elections since 1980 in Mozambique. Bangladesh underwent a transition from martial law to civilian rule in November 1986 and also experienced the return of parliamentary elections and the lifting of most restrictions on political activity.

18. See generally Henry Shue, *Basic Rights: Subsistence, Affluence, and U.S. Foreign Policy* (Princeton, N.J.: Princeton University Press, 1980).

19. Skalnes and Egeland, *Human Rights in Developing Countries 1986* (note 3), p. 97.

20. U.S. Department of State, *Country Reports 1986* (note 2), p. 331.

21. Ibid., p. 328.

22. This observation was made by George Lopez in a review of an earlier draft of this paper.

23. Skalnes and Egeland, *Human Rights in Developing Countries 1986* (note 3), p. 12.

24. The call for multiple sources of human rights information is common. For examples, see Michael Stohl, David Carleton, George Lopez, and Stephen Samuels, "State Violation of Human Rights: Issues and Problems of Measurement," *Human Rights Quarterly* 8, No. 4 (November 1986): 604; Carleton and Stohl, "Role of Human Rights" (note 4).

25. Skalnes and Egeland, *Human Rights in Developing Countries 1986* (note 3), p. 133.

26. U.S. Department of State, *Country Reports 1986* (note 2), p. 367.

27. Skalnes and Egeland, p. 136.

28. U.S. Department of State, *Country Reports 1986*, p. 367.

29. Skalnes and Egeland, p. 120.

30. U.S. Department of State, *Country Reports 1986*, p. 366.

31. Skalnes and Egeland, p. 191.

32. U.S. Department of State, *Country Reports 1986*, p. 1151 (emphasis added).

33. Skalnes and Egeland, p. 98.

34. U.S. Department of State, *Country Reports 1986*, pp. 326, 329.

35. Skalnes and Egeland, p. 124 (emphasis added).

36. U.S. Department of State, *Country Reports 1986*, p. 368 (emphasis added).

37. See, for example, Raymond D. Gastil, ed. *Freedom in the World: Political and Civil Liberties, 1983–84* (Westport, CT: Greenwood Press, Freedom House, 1984).

38. Skalnes and Egeland, p. 109 (emphasis added).

39. U.S. Department of State, *Country Reports 1986*, p. 330 (emphasis added).

40. Skalnes and Egeland, p. 121 (emphasis added).

41. U.S. Department of State, *Country Reports 1986*, p. 368 (emphasis added).

42. Skalnes and Egeland, p. 97 (emphasis added).

43. U.S. Department of State, *Country Reports 1986*, p. 332 (emphasis added).

44. Skalnes and Egeland, p. 111 (emphasis added).

45. U.S. Department of State, *Country Reports 1986*, p. 334 (emphasis added).

46. For one example of a study employing ethnic diversity as a correlate of human rights practices see Han S. Park "Correlates of Human Rights: Global Tendencies," *Human Rights Quarterly* 9, No. 3 (August 1987): 405–513.

47. Skalnes and Egeland, p. 189 (emphasis added).

48. U.S. Department of State, *Country Reports 1986*, p. 1154 (emphasis added).

49. de Neufville, "Human Rights Reporting" (note 5), p. 691.

50. Skalnes and Egeland, p. 172.

51. U.S. Department of State, *Country Reports 1986*, p. 1148.

52. Skalnes and Egeland, p. 109.

53. U.S. Department of State, *Country Reports 1986*, p. 330.

54. Skalnes and Egeland, pp. 175–176.

55. U.S. Department of State, *Country Reports 1986*, p. 1150.

56. Skalnes and Egeland, p. 170 (emphasis added).

57. U.S. Department of State, *Country Reports 1986*, pp. 1153–54 (emphasis added).

58. Americas Watch, *Critique* (note 5), p. 87.

59. Skalnes and Egeland, p. 262.

60. Americas Watch, *Critique*, p. 87.

61. Skalnes and Egeland, see especially pp. 262, 285.

62. Americas Watch, *Critique* (note 5), p. 103.

63. Skalnes and Egeland, p. 265 (emphasis added).

64. Ibid., p. 262.

65. Ibid., p. 284.

66. Ibid., pp. 42–43.

67. U.S. Department of State, *Country Reports 1986*, p. 22.

68. Ibid., p. 146.

69. Ibid., p. 114.

70. Skalnes and Egeland, p. 154.

71. U.S. Department of State, *Country Reports 1986*, p. 326.

72. Skalnes and Egeland, p. 106.

73. U.S. Department of State, *Country Reports 1986*, p. 1344.

74. Ibid., p. 368.

75. Skalnes and Egeland, p. 132.

76. For general assessments of the impact of the reports see de Neufville, "Human Rights Reporting," (note 5) and Bard-Anders Andreassen and Hugo Stokke, "Human Rights Monitoring in View of the Principles of Foreign Aid Policy—Or How to Dress-up Cinderella," Outline of a Paper delivered at the International Political Science Association's Research Committee on Human Rights Meeting, The Hague, June 1987.

77. U.S. Department of State, *Country Reports 1986*, pp. 3–4.

78. Ibid., p. 1355.

79. Skalnes and Egeland, pp. 16–17.

80. de Neufville, "Human Rights Reporting" (note 5), p. 697.

81. Richard Schifter, "Human Rights and U.S. Foreign Policy," U.S. Department of State, Bureau of Public Affairs, *Current Policy* No. 962 (Washington, DC, June 1987).

82. See generally, de Neufville, "Human Rights Reporting" (note 5).

83. This point was best made by an anonymous reviewer of an earlier draft of this work.

Part III
Analyzing Human Rights Data

INTRODUCTION

The development and analysis of human rights data are not completely distinct processes. The choice of procedures for collecting and processing data must be informed by a reasonably clear view of how the data will be used. The analyst or other user, if not involved in the development of the data set that he or she plans to use, would be ill-advised to proceed without first reviewing the concepts, definitions, and procedures used to produce the data set.

Nevertheless, in reviewing the papers accepted for inclusion in this volume, we found that most of them could be clearly identified as focusing on one or the other of the two areas: data development or analysis. Part III contains the chapters that focus on how different kinds of human rights data are used and the specific analytical techniques that are employed. Chapters 11, 12, and 13 are about analyses of events-based data for three different countries—the United States, the Netherlands, and Argentina—and Chapter 14 illustrates the use of several techniques to analyze standards-based data for international comparative analysis. The final chapter provides a listing, in standard format, of 29 data bases that contain quantitative information on human rights and related topics.

Methods of Statistical Analysis

For the most part, human rights statistics fall within the broad category called social statistics. Most of the wide array of analysis techniques used in social statistics can be applied to human rights data, possibly excluding the statistical analysis of controlled experiments—a method which is widely used in the physical sciences but much less often and with considerable difficulty in the social sciences.

The techniques that are available vary in complexity from simple descriptive statistics, involving the calculation of means, medians, standard deviations, and other summary measures, to sophisticated analytical techniques, based on elaborate models and formal assumptions about the structure of the data, which seek to understand causal relationships and to provide a basis for explanation and prediction. Many kinds of analysis require large amounts of calculation and thus have only been introduced or used widely since the beginning of the computer age.

John Tukey divides analytical techniques into two categories: exploratory and confirmatory. The techniques of exploratory data analysis, which owe much to Tukey and his colleagues,[1] are used to summarize and display data in ways that make the structure of the data more evident. This process often leads to the development of hypotheses and formal models, which are then used for confirmatory analysis. Statistical graphics is an important tool of exploratory data analysis.

Formal techniques for confirmatory analysis include hypothesis or significance testing, regression analysis, causal modeling, time series analysis and many others. A systematic enumeration of the techniques that are used in the social sciences is far beyond the scope of this introduction. Some useful summaries of the current state of the art are provided by Land and Clogg in a special *Proceedings* volume issued for the sesquicentennial celebration of the American Statistical Association in 1989.[2]

Choosing Appropriate Techniques for Analysis

Of the first four chapters in Part III, only that by Nowak and Von Hebel relies entirely on the methods of exploratory data analysis. The other three use a variety of confirmatory analytical techniques. How did the authors decide which methods to use?

Obviously, the choice of analytical techniques depends on what one is trying to accomplish. Consider three types of goals: advocacy, policy guidance, and scholarly research. *Advocacy* requires the presentation of analytical results to the general public or to other, more select audiences that one wishes to influence. To be effective, the findings must be easily understood by people who may have had, at most, a course in elementary statistics. Simple descriptive statistics, with substantial use of statistical graphics, are likely to be the most effective method of conveying information to such audiences.

Data for *policy guidance* have as their audience policy makers for a variety of organizations: international bodies, national governments, and nongovernmental human rights groups, all of whom need information to help them monitor the results of existing policies and programs and to evaluate the desirability of proposed changes in policy and reallocation of their resources. For such uses, more formal and sophisticated kinds of statistical analysis are often needed, but those who do the analyses must still remember that most policymakers have neither the time nor the necessary statistical background to develop a detailed understanding of complex models and other analytical tools that may have been used. The need to explain the results in a convincing fashion to non-statisticians should be considered in the choice of analytical techniques: a simple model may be preferable to one that tries to include every variable that could conceivably affect outcomes. (Some statistical modelers argue that simple models are better for other reasons, as well.)

For *scholarly research*, the main audience may be more receptive to the use of the best available analytical techniques, regardless of their complexity, to pursue efforts to understand, explain, and predict human rights related phenomena. However, researchers should be cautioned that easy-to-use statistical packages cannot be a substitute for (rather than a supplement to) a proper knowledge of statistical methodology.[3] Here is where the interdisciplinary approach that we emphasize in this volume comes most into play. Good research requires both subject-matter experts, to pose the problems and help to evaluate and interpret analytical results, and statisticians, who understand what the analytical techniques and their associated software packages do and are able and willing to choose those that are best suited to the research, rather than the ones with which they are most familiar.

Papers Included In Part III

The first two chapters in Part III are about statistics and the law. Both involve statistical analysis of data for a defined set of court cases, but from this common beginning they take different paths. Glenn Dickinson and William B. Fairley in "Statistical Evidence of Racial Disparities in Death Sentencing" (Chapter 11) describe the use of such data as evidence in a specific U.S. case, whereas Nowak and von Hebel use the data to analyze trends, for the period 1980 to 1986, in decisions of the Netherlands Supreme Court in cases involving appeals to international human rights treaties.

Dickinson and Fairley describe the use of statistical evidence in an attempt to overturn a Georgia man's death sentence on the grounds that the state's capital sentencing system was racially biased against blacks. The use of statistical evidence in U.S. court proceedings has increased substantially in recent decades, perhaps most notably in cases brought under anti-discrimination statutes. Both plaintiffs and defendants use expert witnesses, who, as might be expected, present interpretations of the data that are favorable to their clients, leaving judges in the difficult position of having to resolve conflicting technical claims.[4] Statistical evidence was a major factor in *McCleskey v. Kemp*, which went all the way to the U.S. Supreme Court. The procedures used to extract from court records the data that were presented as evidence of discrimination and the choice of methods to analyze and interpret those data were intensively debated by the opposing parties in the case.

Whereas the statistical arguments in *McCleskey v. Kemp* involved sophisticated methods of confirmatory analysis, the treatment of the data by Manfred Nowak and Herman von Hebel in Chapter 12 falls in the category of exploratory data analysis. They reviewed all of the 18,551 decisions handed down by the Netherlands Supreme Court's three chambers, on civil, criminal, and tax law, between 1980 and 1986. From these, they identified 325 cases that included one or more references to an international or regional human rights treaty. For these cases, the data set they analyzed contained a limited number of variables, including the chamber, the year of the decision, the treaties and articles referred to, and the outcome, that is, whether or not a violation of any of the treaty provisions referred to was found.

Their straightforward analysis of this simple data base provides some clear evidence of trends, during the period of study, in the relative frequency of references to human rights treaties in Supreme Court cases. It identifies the treaties and treaty provisions that were most often referred to and the relative frequency with which the Supreme Court found violations of these provisions. As should be the case with applications of exploratory data analysis, the data suggest hypotheses that might be tested and other kinds of confirmatory analysis that could be performed if more detailed information were compiled and analyzed for the decisions that were studied. We believe that further statistical analyses of court proceedings, in a variety of settings, can prove to be a valuable tool in the study of human rights law.

The data analyzed by Clyde Collins Snow and Maria Julia Bilhurriet in Chapter 13 shed light on one of the blacker chapters in the recent history of human rights violations, the so-called "Dirty War" in Argentina between 1976 and 1983. Their data base came from a survey of cemeteries in the Province of Buenos Aires. The survey, initiated in 1985 by the Secretary of Human Rights under the Alfonsín government, collected information on the number and characteristics of "no name" burials, or burials of unidentified persons, in these cemeteries during the period from 1970 to 1984.

Through careful use of hypothesis testing and other formal methods of statistical analysis, Snow and Bihurriet show conclusively that a substantial proportion of the unidentified bodies in the cemeteries included in the study must have been bodies of the *desaparecidos*, those who were seized by the government or paramilitary forces during the period of the "Dirty War" and subsequently tortured and executed. A key feature of their analysis was the inclusion of data for periods immediately before and after the Dirty War as a control. The differences in the numbers and characteristics of "no name" burials for the "Dirty War" and the periods before and after it leave little doubt about the validity of their conclusions.

What Snow and Bihurriet have done is much more than an after-the-fact exercise in the "epidemiology of homicide." Their findings can help to build a strong and objective body of evidence, useful to the courts in proceedings against the perpetrators of human rights abuses during Argentina's "Dirty War" and to families of the disappeared seeking to trace the remains of their relatives.

In Chapter 14 the analytical focus shifts from events data to standards-based data on human rights performance by country. David Banks, the author, has pioneered the application of state-of-the-art techniques of exploratory data analysis to country scores and rankings on human rights variables available from sources such as Freedom House and Charles Humana.[5]

The data bases used by Banks have been criticized for conceptual and technical deficiencies and even for displaying political biases of their compilers.[6] Few would deny that improvements are possible; nevertheless, it would be a mistake to assert that these data, with all of their imperfections, have no value for analysis. Banks, recognizing the limitations of the data, has sought to use analytical techniques that are robust, that is, not unduly sensitive to misspecified models and errors in the data. He also favors analytical techniques that have intuitive simplicity so that results can be understood by policy makers and the general public. In this chapter, Banks updates and expands his earlier analyses, using techniques such as cluster analysis, classification and regression tree analysis, stepwise discriminant analysis, and factor analysis.

These four chapters can only begin to illustrate the interest and potential benefits of greater exploitation of available and newly developed sources of human rights data. They will have served their purpose if some of our readers are inspired by these examples to apply statistical techniques to analyze data that are relevant to their own interests in the broad field of human rights. Such quantitative research does not necessarily require the creation of entirely new data bases. Many existing data sets that have been developed and maintained at considerable effort and expense have been under-utilized and are available on request at little or no cost. Researchers have the options of relying entirely on secondary analysis of existing data bases or of combining information from such data bases with new information that they have collected from primary sources.

To facilitate the use of existing data bases, Chapter 15, the final chapter in Part III, provides a listing of 29 human rights data bases, using a standard format to describe their content and other attributes and to identify the sponsoring organization and a contact person who can provide additional information about the characteristics of the data base and how it can be accessed.

Notes

1. John W. Tukey, *Exploratory Data Analysis* (Reading, MA: Addison-Wesley, 1977).

2. Kenneth C. Land, "Measurement Issues in Social Statistics," pp. 201–213; and Clifford C. Clogg, "Modelling Social Statistics," pp. 214–225 in *Proceedings of the American Statistical Association, Sesquicentennial Invited Paper Sessions* (Washington DC: American Statistical Association, 1989).

3. Shayle R. Searle, "Statistical Computing Packages: Some Words of Caution," *American Statistician* 43 (1989): 189–190.

4. For a recent examination of issues associated with the use of statistical evidence in the courts, see Stephen Fienberg, ed., *The Evolving Role of Statistical Assessments as Evidence in the Courts* (New York: Springer-Verlag, 1989). The same issues are summarized by Fienberg in "Political Pressure and Statistical Quality: An American Perspective on Producing Relevant National Data," *Journal of Official Statistics* 5 (1989): 207–222.

5. For some of his earlier results, see David L. Banks, "Patterns of Oppression: A Statistical Analysis of Human Rights," *Proceedings of the Social Statistics Section of the American Statistical Association* (1985): 154–162; and "The Analysis of Human Rights Data over Time," *Human Rights Quarterly* 8, No. 5 (November 1986): 654–680.

6. See, for example, Bollen (Chapter 7) and Goldstein (Chapter 5) in this volume.

EVENTS-BASED DATA

Chapter 11
Statistical Evidence of Racial Disparities in Death Sentencing: A Critical Analysis of *McCleskey v. Kemp*

Glenn Dickinson and William B. Fairley

The Supreme Court of the United States has considered forms of statistical evidence in discrimination cases for more than one hundred years.[1] If a general statement can be made about the Court's treatment of statistical evidence, it is that the justices give considerable credence to such evidence—sometimes. When the statistics show a particularly stark racial disparity in, for example, the granting of licenses or qualification of voters, the Court has found a violation of constitutionally protected rights.[2] But the mere presence of a disparate impact is not proof of unlawful discrimination.[3]

Lawyers for Warren McCleskey, a black man who was convicted of murdering a white Georgia police officer, presented sophisticated statistical studies showing that Georgia defendants convicted of killing whites were much more likely to receive death sentences than defendants convicted of killing blacks.[4] The studies purported to show that McCleskey's sentence was influenced by an arbitrary difference in sentences handed out to defendants whose victims were white rather than black and thus violated his constitutional rights. The Supreme Court accepted the studies as "valid,"[5] but the justices sharply disagreed over what the studies showed. The five-justice majority concluded that the racial disparity in sentencing was not significant enough to support the conclusion that McCleskey's constitutional rights had been violated. The four dissenting justices, looking at the same studies, found "powerful evidence" of discrimination.[6]

To make sense of this apparent contradiction, it is necessary to examine the statistical evidence presented in *McCleskey*, the criticisms leveled by the state, and the treatment the evidence received at different levels of the federal courts. The evidence itself is complicated, and experts who testified for each side held sharply opposing views on the effectiveness of the statistical methods used and the validity of the conclusions reached. Majority and dissenting opinions in the federal courts were likewise divided.

A bare majority in the Supreme Court eventually upheld Mc-Cleskey's sentence in a strongly worded opinion which has met with even stronger criticism; the *Harvard Law Review* termed the ruling "logically unsound, morally reprehensible and legally unsupportable,"[7] and some legal scholars compared it to such signal injustices as *Dred Scott v. Sanford, Plessy v. Ferguson* and *Korematsu v. United States*.[8] A bill was introduced in the U.S. Senate that would prohibit any death sentence under state or federal law if the sentence furthered a racially discriminatory pattern.[9] The General Accounting Office also reviewed 28 statistical studies of discrimination in capital sentencing, including the studies used in *McCleskey*, and found "a pattern of evidence indicating racial disparities in charging, sentencing, and imposition of the death penalty."[10] Not everyone was displeased with the decision, of course; the head of a Washington, D.C.-based advocacy group that supports the death penalty reportedly welcomed the decision, saying that had the court ruled otherwise, "sociologists and statisticians would have become more important than judges and juries."[11]

The Road to Death Row

Warren McCleskey and three other armed men entered the Dixie Furniture Store in Marietta, Georgia, on the morning of 13 May 1978. McCleskey entered through the front door, drew a pistol, and made the customers and staff lie on the floor. The other three men entered through a loading dock in the rear, rounded up the employees, and began tying them up with tape. At that point, Officer Frank Schlatt, responding to a silent alarm, pulled up in front of the building, entered, and started down the store's center aisle. As he approached the middle of the store, two shots rang out. Schlatt collapsed, hit in the head and the chest, and died. The robbers fled with the store receipts and the manager's watch.

McCleskey was arrested several weeks later on an unrelated charge and confessed that he had been involved in the furniture store robbery. He was tried in Superior Court of Fulton County, Georgia, and convicted 12 October 1978 of two counts of armed robbery and one count of murder. A separate hearing was held to consider whether McCleskey should be sentenced to die.

McCleskey entered the capital sentencing system at a time when the United States was putting to death relatively few prisoners by comparison to other periods. The number of executions declined fairly steadily between 1930 and 1967,[12] when executions were suspended pending the outcome of several legal challenges. The high for this period occurred in 1935, when 199 people were put to death. In 1967, the year the moratorium went into effect, only two death sentences were carried out.

Yet during this entire period, capital-sentencing statutes remained on the books, and courts continued to impose death sentences. While only two people were executed in 1967, 85 were sentenced to die. The number of prisoners on death row increased—from 219 at the end of 1960 to 608 at the end of 1970.[13] Many of those sentenced to die had their sentences commuted to prison terms; others were granted new trials; some had convictions overturned. A few died of suicide or natural causes. The rest waited.

Death-penalty opponents had long pointed out that capital punishment had been imposed more often on blacks than on whites; of the 3,859 people put to death in the United States between 1930 and 1968, 2,066 were black.[14] In the South, the disparity was more striking. Between 1924 and 1964, Georgia executed 82 whites and 340 blacks.[15] While statistics showed the crime rate among blacks was several times higher than among whites,[16] many death-penalty opponents argued that this did not entirely account for the difference in sentencing rates; racism, too, was said to play a part.[17]

In 1972, the Supreme Court handed down its decision in *Furman v. Georgia*,[18] a group of cases challenging the death penalty on the grounds that it violated the Eighth Amendment prohibition of cruel and unusual punishment, as applied to the states by the Fourteenth Amendment. The court ruled 5–4 that the sentences were unconstitutional. The plurality held that there were no rational criteria that distinguished the few cases in which the death penalty had been imposed from the many in which it had not, and therefore the death penalty was being administered in an arbitrary and capricious fashion.

The *Furman* decision stood against the wide discretion allowed judges and juries under most state capital-sentencing procedures, and its effect was to render these statutes unconstitutional. The states responded swiftly; within the next four years, at least 35 states enacted new death-penalty laws to conform with the *Furman* constraints.[19] Georgia amended its statute to include a list of 10 aggravating circumstances, at least one of which must be found before the death penalty may be considered.[20] When a death sentence was imposed, the Georgia Supreme Court was required to review the case and sentence.

The amended Georgia statute faced its first Supreme Court challenge in 1976, in *Gregg v. Georgia*. Troy Gregg was convicted of robbing and murdering two men who had picked him up hitchhiking. He was sentenced to die in the Georgia electric chair, and the state supreme court upheld the conviction and sentence on review. The U.S. Supreme Court examined Georgia's sentencing procedures and ruled that the requirements introduced "on their face satisfy the concerns of *Furman*"[21] by providing some guidelines for deciding who lives and who dies. The sentence was affirmed.

In Warren McCleskey's case, the jury applied the amended Georgia sentencing statute and found two aggravating circumstances: the murder had been committed in the course of an armed robbery, and the murder had been committed upon a peace officer engaged in the performance of his duties. McCleskey offered no mitigating evidence, and the jury recommended the death penalty, which the judge subsequently imposed. The state supreme court reviewed the sentence as required and affirmed the sentencing jury's decision.

Statistical Evidence of Racial Disparities

McCleskey's case was taken up by the NAACP Legal Defense and Education Fund. Attorneys for the LDF, the name by which it is commonly known, were serving as counsel in approximately ten Georgia death-penalty cases in addition to McCleskey's, as well as cases in other states,[22] and were considering how to develop a constitutional challenge based on the argument that the states still were imposing capital punishment in a racially discriminatory manner.

In *Gregg*, the Supreme Court had held that the Georgia statute fit within the constraints laid down in *Furman*—that the law channeled the discretion exercised by judges and juries, providing guidelines that protected against arbitrary decisions to put certain people to death while letting others live. But the Court had held that the statute was constitutional *on its face*; this left open the possibility that it might be unconstitutional *in application*. If death sentences were handed down in a racially discriminatory fashion, the capital sentencing system would still be subject to attack on the grounds that it operated in an arbitrary and capricious fashion.

Discriminatory sentencing would also be a violation of the Equal Protection Clause of the Fourteenth Amendment, which provides that no state shall "deny to any person within its jurisdiction the equal protection of the laws." If death sentences were influenced by racial prejudice, then those defendants who were condemned for racially biased reasons would not receive the same treatment as defendants whose sentences were not influenced by such biases. However, the Supreme Court in *Washington v. Davis* had held that a plaintiff asserting an Equal Protection challenge must show the defendant had an intent to discriminate.[23] This intent could be inferred in some situations, such as jury venire and employment, by showing a disparate impact along racial lines.[24] However, the disparity had to be particularly stark.[25]

The difficulty for McCleskey's attorneys would be showing a racial disparity that could not be explained by the myriad of legitimate factors that influenced criminal sentencing. Recent studies, such as one undertaken by University of Iowa law professor David C. Baldus and several colleagues, indicated that statistical techniques could be used to balance out the effect of these legitimate factors to see if race did play a part. The Court might be persuaded to rule a state's capital-sentencing system unconstitutional if statistics could be used to show that the system was still producing racially biased outcomes, although it complied with *Gregg* and was therefore constitutional on its face. John Boger, the attorney who argued McCleskey's case before the Supreme Court, put it thus: "*Gregg* was premised on the assumption that things will work if you have this sort of system. Baldus tested that assumption."[26]

Baldus had been involved in several previous projects using statistics to analyze legal issues. In one of these, the effect of race of the victim and race of the defendant on death sentencing in Georgia had been examined by Baldus; Dr. George Woodworth, an associate professor of statistics at the University of Iowa; and Charles A. Pulaski Jr., an Arizona State University law professor specializing in criminal procedure. This study, the Procedural Reform Study, used multiple regression analysis, a standard statistical technique for estimating how a single factor—in this case, whether a death sentence is handed down following a capital conviction—is affected by other factors identified by the statistician.

The researchers examined the cases of about 600 offenders who were sentenced to death or life imprisonment after conviction for murder, or who were sentenced to death after pleading guilty to murder charges. Preliminary analysis suggested that, while the race of the defendant may have had no effect on sentencing outcome, the race of the victim did; killers of whites seemed to receive the death penalty slightly more often than killers of blacks. The LDF funded a second, more detailed study of the question.

In both the Procedural Reform Study and the subsequent Charging and Sentencing Study, Baldus and his colleagues drew up a questionnaire to be filled out for each case. The questions concerned the crime, subsequent legal proceedings, and information about the defendant and the victim. The information was obtained from state parole board files. The researchers set out to list the factors that would have a substantial influence on the sentencing decision in a murder trial. They then used several statistical techniques designed to determine whether race of the victim or race of the defendant had an impact on the decision to return a death sentence.

The two studies differed in several regards.[27] In the Charging and Sentencing Study, the researchers expanded the universe of cases to comprise all Georgia offenders convicted of murder or voluntary manslaughter whose crimes occurred after 28 March 1973, and who were arrested before 21 December 1978—about 2,500 cases. The Procedural Reform Study focused on two stages in the post-conviction process: the prosecutor's decision whether to seek the death penalty, and the sentencing jury's decision whether to impose the death penalty. The second study was more "longitudinal," testing for racial disparities at all stages from indictment to sentencing. Baldus and his colleagues expanded their questionnaire for the second study to include factors not covered earlier. More questions were asked regarding aggravating and mitigating circumstances and the prior record of the defendant, and a section was added to allow the researchers to include strength of the evidence in their analysis.

Table 1 gives the unadjusted data for death sentence cases classified by race of defendant and by race of victim. The unadjusted data showed that murder cases ended in death sentences eight times more often when the victim was white than when the victim was black ($11.0/1.3 = 8.5$). However, white defendants were sentenced to death at a rate of 1.8 times that of black defendants ($7.4/4.1 = 1.8$).

Like other numbers that had been cited to support or to reject the claim that capital sentencing was racially biased, these figures do not take into account the factors that influence a sentencing decision. Capital crimes differ not only in severity but also in, among other things, the strength of the evidence presented, behavior of the defendant while in custody and at trial, role played by co-perpetrators, other charges brought, and personal characteristics of the defen-

Table 1. Unadjusted Racial Disparities in Death Sentencing

Race of victim	*Death-sentencing rate*[a]	
White	108/981	(11.0%)
Black	20/1503	(1.3%)
Race of defendant		
White	60/808	(7.4%)
Black	68/1676	(4.1%)
Composite of defendant & victim		
Black defendant/white victim	50/233	(21.5%)
White defendant/white victim	58/748	(7.7%)
Black defendant/black victim	18/1443	(1.2%)
White defendant/black victim	2/60	(3.0%)
All cases	128/2484	(5.1%)

Source: David C. Baldus, George G. Woodworth, and Charles A. Pulaski, Jr., *Equal Justice and the Death Penalty: A Legal and Empirical Analysis*, p. 315. Copyright © 1990 by David C. Baldus, George G. Woodworth, and Charles A. Pulaski, Jr. Reprinted by permission of Northeastern University Press.
[a] Number of death sentences/total number of murder and manslaughter convictions.

dant—all of which are legitimate factors relevant to charging and sentencing. It was possible that these factors alone accounted for the difference in sentencing rates, and, for example, that the racial difference in death-sentencing rate depending on the race of the victim resulted from a tendency of white-victim crimes to be more serious in criminal justice terms.

The task facing Baldus and his colleagues was to identify legitimate factors, or variables, that might have an impact on the decisions to seek and impose a death sentence, and to control for these, while comparing death-sentence rates between black- and white-victim crimes and between black and white defendants. Potential effects of omitted variables, mismeasured variables, and missing data would also need to be tested.

The researchers applied several statistical techniques to see whether there was a relationship between racial factors and the sentence in each case, while controlling for other factors. First, they made a series of cross-tabulations controlling for selected aggravating factors included in the Georgia statute. Taking all the cases in which the defendant committed murder in the course of another felony (McCleskey's fell in this group), they found that 38 percent (60 of 160 cases) of the blacks who killed whites received the death penalty, while 14 percent (15 of 104) of the blacks who killed blacks were sentenced to die. In those cases, again including McCleskey's, where the contemporaneous felony was armed robbery, the death sentencing rates were 34 percent (42 of 123) for blacks who killed whites and 5 percent (3 of 57) for blacks who killed blacks.

These cross-tabulations alone were not convincing, however, since they controlled only for a single variable, albeit an important one. The researchers checked their findings with a multiple regression analysis (primarily logistic regression) by which they sought to take into account simultaneously the effect of many other factors that influenced the decision.

The goal of a multiple regression analysis is to develop a model, in the form of a mathematical equation, that accurately represents effects of a number of factors on a given factor of interest—here, the effects of a number of factors on the decision to return a capital sentence. In a multiple regression model, the factors that have been identified are represented in the equation as a sum of independent variables, multiplied by effects per unit ("coefficients"), and the outcome is represented by a predicted numerical value for a dependent variable. Since chance also plays a part in the outcome, the equation includes a residual term which is intended to stand for all other effects not included in the equation that influence the outcome. The statistician seeks to keep the value of this term as small as possible.

Broadly speaking, the regression analyses found that crude differences in rates of sentencing by race of victim overstated by a factor of about two the average percentage difference in death-sentencing rate between black and white victim murders. Nevertheless, the analyses indicated a racial difference unaccounted for either by the usual model for chance variation in the data of the sample or by the nonracial variables explicitly controlled for in the analyses.

The researchers identified a model using 39 variables as their best statistical representation of the impact of race of the victim on the outcome of the trial. This analysis showed that, these 39 factors being equal, the odds that someone who killed a white person will be sentenced to death are 4.3 times greater than the odds faced by someone who killed a black person.

Judicial Treatment of the Evidence

Armed with these findings, McCleskey's attorneys petitioned the federal district court for a writ of habeas corpus, claiming 18 grounds, including that they had statistical studies demonstrating racial discrimination in Georgia's capital sentencing system. The court granted a hearing, set for 8 August 1983, to evaluate the evidence.

At the hearing, the attorneys argued that Georgia's capital-sentencing system, although constitutional on its face, was not constitutional in operation. The statistical studies showed racial disparities that were arbitrary and capricious in violation of the Eighth Amendment and that also demonstrated a pattern of purposeful discrimination contrary to the Fourteenth Amendment.[28] The district court hearing involved extensive testimony on the statistical surveys—how the data were collected, how the numbers were computed, what the studies showed. Baldus and Woodworth both testified.

The state also relied on expert witnesses, who testified that they had found serious flaws in the studies, sufficient to make their conclusions unreliable. The testimony at the hearing was highly technical, covering in detail the various findings. It became something of a "battle of the experts," with each side buttressing its own position and probing for weak points in the other side's—and the level of the discussion becoming increasingly complicated and difficult for any but the experts to follow.

Baldus pointed out certain important limits of the statistical methods used. Asked by Judge J. Owen Forrester whether statistics could be used to quantify the effect that race played in McCleskey's case, Baldus responded flatly, "No. I can give an opinion based upon an analysis of the data, but I can't say a particular factor constituted fifteen or twenty percent of the force."[29] He went on to explain that the studies showed only that, taking all the cases in the aggregate and controlling for legitimate factors, defendants who killed whites received the death penalty at a higher rate than defendants who killed blacks.

He also stressed that the analysis could not conclusively prove that racial discrimination caused the sentencing disparities. But the studies did show that the disparities did not result from any of the legitimate factors identified, and as a result one could infer that discrimination was present, given the state's history and the dearth of alternative explanations following this detailed statistical analysis.

To someone skeptical about the value of statistics, this sort of caution can sound like hedging and render the argument singularly unconvincing. McCleskey's attorneys already faced a significant hurdle in presenting their complex evidence. The studies' results were not obvious or easily grasped. This is no reflection on the researchers; there simply is no such thing as a simple multiple regression analysis of sentencing. The concern felt by McCleskey's attorneys on this point is demonstrated by the fact that they spent some time in the early stages of the hearing going through sample regression equations in order to demonstrate the technique.[30] It could be said that they gave the court a short course in statistics—a prerequisite to an understanding of the material that followed.

The state's expert witnesses attacked McCleskey's statistics on two fronts. Roger L. Burford, a professor of quantitative business analysis at Louisiana State University, gave general testimony on the value of the methods used by Baldus and his colleagues. Burford expressed a certain agnosticism toward statistics, saying, "In general, I don't believe that it is possible to prove in a strict sense anything either pro or con by the use of statistics."[31]

Dr. Joseph Katz, an assistant professor in the quantitative methods department at Georgia State University, examined the methods and the data used by Baldus and his colleagues. Katz pointed out that for some of the factors listed on the questionnaire—such as whether a plea bargain was offered—it could not be determined in a large number of cases whether the factor had been present or absent.[32] This was accepted by the court as evidence that the data base used had certain gaps. Katz also testified that the usual method of dealing with such unknowns is to omit them from the analysis, while Baldus and his colleagues had treated them as though the factor definitely was absent.[33]

Katz also argued that since white-victim murders tended to be more aggravated and less mitigated than black-victim murders (a fact noted by Baldus and his colleagues), a higher death-penalty rate for white-victim murders was to be expected. Katz did not produce any regression analysis, however, to support the contention that the tendency of white-victim murders to be more aggravated accounted for all of the racial disparity revealed by the unadjusted data.[34]

Testimony in support of the statistical evidence was offered by Dr. Richard Berk, a professor of sociology from the University of California at Santa Barbara, who had worked on an analysis of sentencing for the National Academy of Sciences. Berk gave the studies high praise: "[T]here's no doubt that at this moment, this is far and away the most complete and thorough analysis of sentencing that's been done. I mean there's nothing even close."[35]

The hearing continued for two weeks in August and one day in October before adjourning while Judge Forrester considered his decision. On 15 December 1983, while McCleskey waited for the district court's ruling, 44-year-old John E. Smith became the first person to die in Georgia's electric chair under the new capital-sentencing statute.

Judge Forrester returned his decision in February 1984, issuing a stinging rejection of the evidence, identifying some forty flaws[36] in the techniques used to collect, codify, and analyze the data and concluding that the results "are not the product of good statistical methodology."[37] An examination of a few of the salient points of the critique will be sufficient to illustrate how unimpressed he was with the statistical evidence.

He began with a charge leveled by the state that the information used to code the questionnaires was incomplete: it was assembled from files that were only a summary, not intended to give an encyclopedic account of each case. This was evidenced by the substantial number of factors coded "unknown" on the questionnaires. The questionnaires themselves were found to be inadequate since they "could not capture every nuance of every case "[38] and hence did not take into account every factor that might influence sentencing.

The opinion criticized the researchers for their handling of the factors coded "unknown." In the regression analysis, these items had been treated the same as factors that were definitely absent, on the theory that if the file contained no mention of the particular item, the prosecutor and the jurors probably didn't know about it either; thus it would have had no effect on sentencing. While the state's expert had said factors with a large number of "unknown" codes should have been excluded from the analysis, Judge Forrester asserted that it would have been more rational to code the "unknowns" as having been present.

In his holding, Judge Forrester selected one model employing all the approximately 230 variables as producing the most reliable results, despite Baldus's testimony that the 39-variable model was preferable. The judge's rationale for this choice was that a regression equation including all the factors that might influence sentencing outcome would provide more reliable results than one including only the major factors.[39] This theory seems in accord with common sense, but it is at odds with the generally accepted view among statisticians that in regression analysis, bigger is not always better.

In raising his objections, the judge discounted or ignored testimony offered in an attempt to answer these challenges. McCleskey's attorneys had put on the stand a witness from the state parole office who testified as to the completeness and accuracy of the records.[40] In response to the purported miscoding of the "unknown" factors, the researchers recoded those factors as present and ran the regressions again, obtaining almost identical results for the effect of race of the victim on sentencing. They then excluded the factors entirely, as the state's expert had suggested; the race of the victim effect increased.[41] It had also been suggested that the number of factors coded "unknown" indicated that the data used was incomplete; the researchers recoded the "unknowns" in such a way as to support the legitimacy of the sentence (e.g., in death penalty cases, aggravating factors listed as "unknown" were recoded as present, while mitigating factors listed as "unknown" were coded as absent), and the race of the victim effect decreased but still persisted.[42]

The court was unconvinced by these results, and instead accepted the state's argument that the tendency of white-victim murders to be more aggravated accounted for the disparity in sentencing rates.[43] Since all the aggravating factors identified by the state in this analysis were taken from among the variables included in the studies,[44] the researchers attempted to control for them in the regression equations. That white-victim murders tend to be more aggravated and black-victim murders tend to be more mitigated had not been disputed by Baldus and his colleagues. Their effort had been designed to determine whether the tendency of white-victim crimes to be more aggravated accounted for *all* of the sentencing disparity. They concluded that it did not. They had not argued that race was the *only* factor that influenced sentencing, but that it had a significant enough impact to be called a de facto aggravating circumstance, which clearly would be unconstitutional. The district court did not find the argument persuasive.[45]

McCleskey's attorneys filed an appeal in the U.S. Court of Appeals, asking it to overturn the district court's ruling.[46] The appeals court took a different approach to the evidence, assuming *arguendo* that the studies employed valid statistical methodologies—a legal tactic designed to facilitate disposition of the case by relieving the judges of the need to review the district court's lengthy criticism. But the majority was unmoved by the statistical analysis; the court ruled 9–3 that the results were inadequate to support McCleskey's discrimination claim, since the sentencing disparities revealed were "marginal," occurring in only "a small percentage of the cases."[47]

In arriving at this assessment, the court focused on one part of the researchers' findings, in which Baldus and his colleagues had set up regression equations controlling for different groups of variables and then compared the results of these regressions to determine the difference in death-sentencing rates between white-victim murders and black-victim murders. For example, including 230 variables in the regression, the researchers had found that the average death-penalty rate was six percentage points higher in white-victim crimes.[48]

Baldus and his colleagues explored this result further by dividing the cases up according to their overall level of aggravation, using the 39-variable model.[49] They noted that in crimes with a low level of aggravation, a death sentence was rarely returned, regardless of race of the victim, while in cases with a high level of aggravation, the death penalty was quite likely—again, regardless of racial factors. They then reasoned that if race was having an effect on sentencing, it

would most likely occur in the cases in the middle levels of aggravation, where the sentencing decision was not so easily made as in the
extreme cases, and the jurors were allowed to exercise more discretion. Analyzing only this midrange of cases, the researchers found
that the disparity in sentencing rates rose to 20 percentage points.[50]

But when the appeals court described these findings, upon which
they were to rely heavily in reaching their decision, they stated that
at all levels of aggravation, "on average a white victim crime is 6 percent more likely to result in the [death] sentence than a comparable
black victim crime."[51] In the midrange cases, "on average, white victim crimes were shown to be 20 percent more likely to result in the
death penalty than equally aggravated black victim crimes."[52] This is
in fact not what the analysis showed at all; the appeals court majority
apparently mistook a *percentage-point* disparity for a *percentage* disparity. Consequently, they dismissed the statistical evidence on the
grounds that it showed a mere 6 percent disparity, which they held
to be within the discretionary bounds allowed to jurors.[53]

The Supreme Court granted McCleskey's petition for a writ of certiorari and heard oral arguments on 15 October 1986. One of the amicus briefs filed on McCleskey's behalf came from a group of leading
experts in social science and the law.[54] They upbraided the lower
courts for their handling of the statistical evidence, calling Judge
Forrester's critique "uninformed and indefensible"[55] and pointing
out the appeals court's "highly misleading" misstatement of the results.[56]

McCleskey's case was supported by other amici, including the International Human Rights Law Group, which argued that the imposition of the death penalty in a racially discriminatory fashion violates
widely accepted standards of international law.[57] The brief points out
that, although the United States has not ratified some of the applicable international agreements, a prohibition of state-sponsored discrimination is included in the Charter of the United Nations and the
Charter of the Organization of American States—both of which have
been signed and ratified by the United States, and both of which are
binding on the states under the supremacy clause of the Constitution,
which reads in part: "[A]ll treaties made . . . under the authority of
the United States, shall be the supreme law of the land; and the
judges in every state shall be bound thereby."[58] The Supreme Court
had recognized the relevance of international standards in previous
death-penalty challenges. In *Coker v. Georgia*, in which the Court
ruled the death penalty for rape unconstitutional, the opinion noted
that the vast majority of major nations did not allow capital punishment for rape.[59] However, the international-law argument, like the

constitutional claim, depended on the Court's acceptance of the evidence as showing discrimination.

McCleskey's attorneys went to considerable lengths in their written briefs to refute the various criticisms that had been directed at the statistical evidence by the lower courts. They also drew on prior discrimination cases in which the Supreme Court had relied on statistical showings of racial bias. But in a 5–4 decision, the Court upheld McCleskey's death sentence.[60] In evaluating the evidence, the majority applied an extremely demanding standard. The Court ruled against the Equal Protection claim of purposeful discrimination on the grounds that the studies failed to show that the prosecutor and jurors in McCleskey's particular case were racially prejudiced. Moreover, to demonstrate that Georgia's capital sentencing system violated the Equal Protection clause, McCleskey's attorneys would have to prove not only *that* the system was discriminatory, but that "the Georgia Legislature enacted or maintained the death penalty statute *because of* an anticipated racially discriminatory effect."[61] The studies were not designed to reveal such a legislative intent but only to determine if, overall, there was a measurable disparity in death sentencing by race of defendant or victim. The Court also rejected the Eighth Amendment argument, finding that any disparity shown by the statistical evidence fell within "a constitutionally permissible range of discretion" allowed to jurors.[62]

Three of the four dissenting justices filed opinions. Justice Brennan delivered a long summary of Baldus' findings and faulted the majority for its emphasis on the need to allow jurors discretion in sentencing, writing, "Discretion is a means, not an end."[63] Justice Stevens asserted that the disparity in sentencing demonstrated by Baldus and his colleagues "flagrantly violates the Court's prior 'insistence that capital punishment be imposed fairly, and with reasonable consistency, or not at all,' "[64] while Justice Blackmun observed that the Court seemed to be applying a lesser degree of scrutiny to allegations of discrimination in capital sentencing than to such allegations in the application of milder criminal sanctions.[65] All four dissenting justices agreed that the majority apparently intended to impose a crippling burden of proof on anyone claiming discrimination in criminal sentencing.[66]

Recommendations for Judicial Analysis of Statistical Evidence

The courts that ruled on the statistical evidence in *McCleskey* had available to them an analytical tool that might have provided a more reliable evaluation of the evidence that the courts produced. Michael Finkelstein proposed a set of four protocols for legal decision makers in administrative proceedings to follow whenever they relied upon the results of econometric models in reaching decisions.[67] These protocols are applicable in general, though doubtless not in some important details, to any statistical analysis employing quantitative models presented in legal proceedings. In a trial court judges may have less control over the form of the expert analysis. The protocols nevertheless can be adopted as well as is feasible within the constraints of time and procedure. The following discussion demonstrates how the Finkelstein protocols could have been adapted to the *McCleskey* proceedings.

The first protocol requires the decision maker—in a court proceeding, the judge—to specify the data that is most useful and important, to require analysis to begin with this data, and to employ other data only when necessary for purposes of accuracy and refinement.

In finding no proof of discrimination in death sentencing in *Smith v. Balkcom*, the Fifth Circuit did suggest the kind of data that is believed would establish discrimination. In the statistical study introduced in *Smith*, only one other variable besides race was controlled for: the presence or absence of a single statutory aggravating felony. The court criticized the statistical analysis as not controlling for racially neutral variables, thus implying that an analysis that did control for other variables would be acceptable.[68] Baldus and his colleagues undertook their analyses, in part, with *Smith* as a guidepost.[69]

In contrast to *Smith*, one searches the three levels of opinions in *McCleskey* in vain for a supportable statement of the data that would in principle be acceptable as proof of discrimination. This district court at least did set out its criteria for a valid study. Unfortunately, these criteria are over-broad and would exclude many major statistical studies that are scientifically accepted as proof. The Supreme Court's majority opinion implicitly accepted such severe criteria in approvingly citing the district court's criticisms of the studies presented in *McCleskey*.

The district court did define its criteria for factors other than race that should be controlled for in a convincing analysis. The researchers responded by analyzing the data using Judge Forrester's criteria, and they obtained race-of-victim results consistent with most of the other analyses of this effect in their studies.[70]

The protocol's requirement to begin with one set of data and add data only as required might have made the studies seem less opaque than they evidently did to the judges. A review of the several analyses by Baldus and his colleagues reveals a large number of models, types of analysis, and other variations in statistical treatment. Great care is required, even for the professional statistician, to follow the entire argument.

The second protocol requires that objections to a model should demonstrate the numerical significance of the objections whenever possible, and that the party objecting to a model supply a superior alternative analysis of the data. Requiring this protocol would have forced the state's experts to either drop may of their objections or else develop and refine them to show that they really did undermine the conclusions of Baldus and his colleagues. No court grappled with the constructive question of what model consistent with the data would in fact explain the sizable race-of-victim effect found.

Protocol three requires the decision maker to select a model that most usefully describes the data and to make findings on the basis of that model. Baldus has pointed out that, while the courts rejected the possibility of statistically determining and controlling for all the "unique" features that could properly inform a jury's discretion in death sentencing, they implicitly accepted the validity of just such statistical models as a basis for testing the uniform, non-arbitrary application of death-sentencing guidelines as required by *Furman*. If unique factors not susceptible to statistical analysis are so prevalent and important that they can prevent proof of discrimination in death sentencing cases—even when a disparate result is large—then they should also prevent any valid assessment of compliance with *Furman*. Thus, if the court endorses, implicitly or explicitly, statistical models that demonstrate the constitutionality of death-sentencing statutes, then it should not, under a broad reading of the third protocol, make a finding elsewhere that denies the usefulness of such a model.

Protocol four states that decision makers cannot reject findings from a model as inherently too vague or imprecise, while themselves reaching conclusions that are even more imprecise on the basis of the same data analyzed by the model. For example, the court of appeals found that the studies were sufficiently precise to confirm that the system was nondiscriminatory, yet found the studies incapable of handling myriad unique factors that could be present in every case.

Moreover, the district court found the *McCleskey* studies invalid, in part because of imprecision in establishing a race-of-victim effect, yet cited the studies as solid proof of the absence of discrimination against black defendants. The court interpreted a table from the statistical studies as showing that there was no statistically significant racial effect on the prosecutors' decision to seek or juries' decision to impose the death penalty.[71] Judge Forrester stated in a footnote: "As an aside, the court should think that this table should put to rest the sort of stereotypical prejudice against Southern jurisdictions typified in the petitioner's brief by reliance on evidence in the Congressional Record in the 1870s concerning the existence of a disregard by Southern officials for the value of black life."[72] Given the judge's overarching skepticism concerning the import of the statistical evidence generally, it is surprising that on this point the court is prepared to attach tremendous significance to them. Georgia's history of racial discrimination is undeniably real. Yet, aside from this comment, none of the court opinions made more than the most casual reference to that history, although it figured prominently in McCleskey's arguments and in the dissenting opinions.

Conclusions

The Supreme Court followed the court of appeals in assuming the validity of the studies and then finding the data unconvincing. The Supreme Court majority avoided the confusion between percentage difference and percentage-point difference, although the opinion did preserve the lower court's characterization of a "marginal disparity."[73] However, the justices focused on another issue: the fact that the statistical evidence did not *prove* racial prejudice accounted for the disparities in sentencing. "At most, the Baldus study indicates a discrepancy that appears to correlate with race. . . . Where the discretion that is fundamental to our criminal process is involved, we decline to assume that what is unexplained is invidious."[74] Thus, the majority accepted the researchers' results but not their conclusions. The disparity was recognized as real, but the magnitude was insufficient as a matter of law to implicate constitutional protections. The majority considered the reason for the disparity an open question. To the majority, the proposition that Georgia's prosecutors, judges, and juries sometimes were moved by racial discrimination was just a theory.

Justice Powell's opinion for the majority perhaps sheds some light on the failure of the statistical evidence to win a reversal. One of the Court's grounds for rejecting the statistical evidence was a form of slippery-slope argument:

McCleskey's claim, taken to its logical conclusion, throws into serious question the principles that underlie our entire criminal justice system. . . . [T]he claim that his sentence rests on the irrelevant factor of race could be extended to apply to claims based on unexplained discrepancies that correlate to membership in other minority groups, and even to gender.[75]

Justice Brennan commented in his dissent, "Taken on its face, such a statement seems to suggest a fear of too much justice."[76]

It is more likely that Justice Powell feared what the other judges who rejected the statistical evidence might have feared as well; they apparently felt that deciding a constitutional challenge solely on the basis of a statistical study would be tantamount to admitting that judges and juries are not competent to administer the criminal justice system, while statisticians are.[77] That a decision for McCleskey would have unleashed what Baldus and his colleagues termed "the invasion of the social scientists" seems unlikely, however. Performing statistical analysis on data collected in the field is expensive and time-consuming, and making the analysis stand up in court adds to the effort. Moreover, statistical methods are increasingly being used in many areas of the law and public policy making, and this has not led to the abdication of judges and politicians.[78]

Perhaps the most notable aspect of *McCleskey* is not that the Supreme Court rejected a statistically based claim of racial discrimination in criminal sentencing. As Professor Randall Kennedy observed in his commentary on the case, no criminal defendant has ever succeeded in overturning his or her sentence on the grounds that the sentence was discriminatory.[79] What distinguishes *McCleskey* is its illustration of the conflict between legal and social science analyses of social realities. The resolution of this conflict requires an understanding of social science methods and a sense of justice as well.

On April 16, 1991, the United States Supreme Court ended Warren McCleskey's search for judicial relief by sharply curtailing his ability and that of other death row inmates and state prisoners to file multiple federal court challenges to the constitutionality of their convictions or sentences. In *McCleskey v. Zant*[80] Justice Anthony M. Kennedy, speaking for six justices, said that only unusual circumstances should permit a prisoner's second or subsequent petition for habeas corpus—the means by which state prison inmates may bring their constitutional claims before federal courts. In the early morning hours of September 25, 1991, after it was learned that last-minute appeals had been denied, Warren McCleskey was electrocuted.

Notes

1. *Yick Wo v. Hopkins*, 118 U.S. 356 (1886) (facially valid ordinance held unconstitutional on grounds that more than 200 Chinese applicants for permits to operate laundries had been rejected while all but one white applicant had been accepted).
2. *Yick Wo v. Hopkins*, 118 U.S. 356 (1886); *Guinn v. United States*, 238 U.S.

347 (1915) (state law requiring potential voters to pass a literacy test but exempting those whose families were qualified to vote before 1866 is unconstitutional because law disenfranchises practically all illiterate blacks and practically no illiterate whites); *Gomillion v. Lightfoot*, 364 U.S. 339 (1960) (act changing city electoral boundaries so as to exclude 395 out of 400 black residents while excluding no whites is unconstitutional).

3. *Washington v. Davis*, 426 U.S. 229 (1976) (test administered to police recruits is not unconstitutional merely because blacks failed at higher rate than whites and proportion of blacks on the police force is lower than proportion in city at large); *National Educ. Assn. v. South Carolina*, 434 U.S. 1026 (1978) (revised qualifications for teacher candidates are not unconstitutional merely because they would disqualify 83 percent of black applicants and 17.5 percent of white applicants).

4. The studies are discussed below and also in *McCleskey v. Zant*, 580 F. Supp. 338, 350–380 (N.D. Ga. 1984); *McCleskey v. Kemp*, 753 F.2d 877, 886–887, 890–899 (11th Cir. 1985); id. at 914–917 (Johnson, J., dissenting); 481 U.S. 279, 286–288 (1987); id. at 325–328 (Brennan, J., dissenting).

The researchers have presented a detailed description and defense of their work in David C. Baldus, George G. Woodworth, and Charles A. Pulaski, Jr., *Equal Justice and the Death Penalty: A Legal and Empirical Analysis* (Boston: Northeastern University Press, 1990).

5. 481 U.S. at 291 n.7.

6. Id. at 338 (Brennan, J., dissenting).

7. Harvard Law Review Association, "The Supreme Court, 1986 Term: Leading Cases," *Harvard Law Review* 101 (November 1987): 158.

8. See, e.g., Randall L. Kennedy, "*McCleskey v. Kemp*: Race, Capital Punishment and the Supreme Court," *Harvard Law Review* 101 (1988): 1388–1443; Hugo Bedau, "Someday *McCleskey* Will Be Death Penalty's *Dred Scott*," *Los Angeles Times*, 1 May 1987, Sec. 2, 5; Anthony Lewis, "Bowing to Racism," *New York Times*, 28 April 1987, A13.

See also *Scott v. Sanford*, 60 U.S. (19 How.) 393, 426–427 (1856) (free persons descended from slaves are not U.S. citizens); *Plessy v. Feguson*, 163 U.S. 537, 550–551 (1896) (racial discrimination in public facilities does not violate Constitution); *Korematsu v. United States*, 323 U.S. 214, 219 (1944) (internment in concentration camps of American citizens of Japanese ancestry does not violate Constitution).

9. S.1696, 101st Cong., 1st Sess., 1989. The measure was defeated. See "Curbs on Execution Appeals Are Voted," *New York Times*, 25 May 1990, A19.

10. "Death Penalty Sentencing: Research Indicates Pattern of Racial Disparities," Report to the Senate and House Committees of the Judiciary, GAO/GGD-90-57 (February 1990), at 5.

The *McCleskey* study had the characteristics of studies judged by the GAO to be of "high quality." A study was considered high quality if: "it was characterized by a sound design that analyzed homicide cases throughout the sentencing process; included legally relevant variables (aggravating and mitigating circumstances); and used statistical analysis techniques to control for variables that correlate with race and/or capital sentencing." Id. at 3.

11. Comment by Daniel Popeo, director of the Washington Legal Foundation, reported in Kennedy, "*McCleskey v. Kemp*," p. 1389 n. 11 (note 8).

12. Amnesty International, *United States of America: The Death Penalty* (London: Amnesty International Publications, 1987), p. 9.

13. *Furman v. Georgia*, 408 U.S. 238, 292 (1972) (per curiam) (Brennan, J., concurring).

14. Id. at 364 (Marshall, J., concurring).

15. Amnesty International, *The Death Penalty* (note 12), p. 12.

16. Hugo Bedau, ed., *The Death Penalty in America* (Chicago: Aldine Publishing, 1964), p. 412.

17. See, e.g., 408 U.S. at 364 n. 152.

18. 408 U.S. 238 (1972) (decided with *Jackson v. Georgia*, No. 69–5030 [Sup. Ct. Ga.] and *Branch v. Texas*, No. 69-5031 [Crim. App. Tex.]).

19. *Gregg v. Georgia*, 428 U.S. 153, 181 (1976).

20. Id. at 162–168.

21. Id. at 155.

22. John Boger, telephone interview with author Dickinson, 2 August 1988.

23. 426 U.S. 229, 239 (1976).

24. *Bazemore v. Friday*, 478 U.S. 385, 400–401 (1985) (multiple regression analysis sufficient in principle to show employment discrimination under Title VII of Civil Rights Act of 1964); *Castaneda v. Partida*, 430 U.S. 482, 495–496 (1977) (underrepresentation of Hispanics in jury venire sufficient to show discrimination).

25. *Village of Arlington Heights v. Metropolitan Housing Dev. Corp.*, 429 U.S. 252, 266 (1976).

26. John Boger, telephone interview with author Dickinson, August 2, 1988.

27. The researchers present a detailed account of both studies in Baldus, Woodworth, and Pulaski, *Equal Justice* (note 4), pp. 40–80.

28. The Eighth Amendment prohibits "cruel and unusual punishments" and the Fourteenth Amendment provides in relevant part, "No State shall . . . deny to any person within its jurisdiction the equal protection of the laws."

The district court read Fifth Circuit precedent in *Spinkellink v. Wainwright*, 578 F.2d 582, 612–614 (5th Cir. 1978), as foreclosing McCleskey's Eighth Amendment claim, so the district court proceedings were limited to the Fourteenth Amendment Equal Protection claim. 753 F.2d at 885. McCleskey's attorneys raised both issues in the Court of Appeals and the Supreme Court. 753 F.2d at 890–891; 481 U.S. at 249.

29. Joint Appendix at 49.

30. John Boger, telephone interview (note 22).

31. Joint Appendix at 103.

32. Id. at 70–71.

33. Id. at 100.

34. See Baldus, Woodworth, and Pulaski, *Equal Justice* (note 4), p. 458:

[T]he State offered no substantive analysis of any type employing racial variables to refute petitioner's claims. Indeed, the State's principal expert testified that during the seven months in which he had possession of our data he never attempted to conduct a single analysis designed to measure racial effects in Georgia's capital-sentencing system after adjusting for aggravating and mitigating factors. The State's criticisms of our studies and Judge Forrester's opinion are based entirely on the speculation that the asserted deficiencies in the statistical procedures that we employed might be the actual source of the observed racial effects. [Citations omitted.]

35. Ibid., p. 66 (testimony of Dr. Richard A. Berk, Professor of Sociology and Director of the Social Process Research Institute of the University of California at Santa Barbara, former member of the National Academy of Sciences' Committee on Sentencing Research). *See also* Brief *Amici Curiae* for Dr. Franklin M. Fisher, Dr. Richard O. Lempert, Dr. Peter W. Sperlich, Dr. Marvin E. Wolfgang, Prof. Hans Zeisel and Prof. Franklin E. Zimring at 4.

36. *McCleskey v. Zant*, 580 F. Supp. 338, 350–380 (N.D. Ga. 1984).

37. Id. at 379.

38. Id. at 356.

39. Id. at 365–366.

40. Joint Appendix at 52–57.

41. Petitioner's Reply Brief at 29 n.10.

42. Baldus, Woodworth, and Pulaski, *Equal Justice* (note 4), p. 455.

43. 580 F. Supp. at 379.

44. Baldus, Woodworth, and Pulaski, *Equal Justice* (note 4), pp. 463–464.

45. The district court did reverse McCleskey's murder conviction on other grounds. 580 F. Supp. at 383. The state appealed this portion of the judgement, and the court of appeals reinstated the conviction. 753 F.2d 877 (11th Cir. 1985). The Supreme Court limited argument to the issues raised by the statistical study. 478 U.S. 1019 (1986).
Following the Supreme Court's ruling discussed below, McCleskey filed a second habeas corpus petition. The district court again granted relief, No. C87-1517A (N.D. Ga. Dec. 23, 1987), and the court of appeals again reversed. 890 F.2d 342 (11th Cir. 1989). The Supreme Court granted certiorari to review these later proceedings. 110 S. Ct. 2585 (1990).

46. *McCleskey v. Kemp*, 753 F.2d 877 (11th Cir. 1985).

47. Id. at 899.

48. Brief *Amici* for Fisher et al. (note 35), p. 16.

49. 580 F. Supp. at 375.

50. Brief for Petitioner at 14.

51. 753 F. 2d at 896.

52. Id.

53. Id. at 897.

54. Brief for Fisher et al. (note 35), p. 19, n.24.

55. Id. at 4.

56. Id. at 17.

57. Brief *Amicus Curiae* of the International Human Rights Law Group at 8.

58. U.S. Const. art. VI, sec. 2.

59. *Coker v. Georgia*, 433 U.S. 584, 596 n.10 (1977).

60. 481 U.S. 279 (1987). For a detailed analysis of the Supreme Court opinion, see Harvard Law Review Association, "Developments in the Law—Race and the Criminal Process," *Harvard Law Review* 101 (May 1988): 1603 (Part VIII, Race and Capital Sentencing).

61. 481 U.S. at 298 (emphasis in original).

62. Id. at 305.

63. Id. at 336 (Brennan, J., dissenting).

64. Id. at 366–367 (Stevens, J., dissenting).

65. Id. at 347–348 (Blackmun, J., dissenting).

66. Id. at 337 (Brennan, J. dissenting).

67. M. O. Finkelstein, "Regression Models in Administrative Proceedings," *Harvard Law Review* 86 (1973): 1442–1475.

68. 671 F.2d at 859, 860 n.33.

69. Baldus, Woodworth, and Pulaski, *Equal Justice* (note 4), p. 309.

70. Ibid., p. 323.

71. *McCleskey v. Zant*, 580 F. Supp. at 367. Baldus and his colleagues argue, contrary to Judge Forrester's characterization, that prosecutorial decisions are the principal source of race-of-the-victim disparities in capital sentencing. Baldus, Woodworth, and Pulaski, *Equal Justice* (note 4), pp. 401–403.

72. 580 F. Supp. at 368 n. 5.

73. 481 U.S. at 290.

74. Id. at 312–313.

75. Id. at 314–317.

76. Id. at 339 (Brennan, J., dissenting).

77. The *McCleskey* researchers made the following observation regarding the district court's treatment of the statistical evidence:

Even in 1987, Judge Forrester's hostility toward the studies we presented on Mc-Cleskey's behalf persisted. In the opinion vacating MeCleskey's murder conviction, he gratuitously remarked that the racial disparities we had estimated were the product of "arbitrarily structured little rinky-dink regressions that accounted for only a few variables. . . . They proved nothing other than the truth of the adage that anything may be proved by statistics."

Baldus, Woodworth, and Pulaski, *Equal Justice*, p. 367 n. 87 (quoting Mc-Cleskey v. Kemp, No. C87-1517A at 12 [N.D. Ga. Dec. 23, 1987]). The history of the subsequent proceedings in *McCleskey* is reviewed in note 45 above.

78. For an examination of this trend, see Stephen Fienberg, ed., *The Evolving Role of Statistical Assessments as Evidence in the Courts* (New York: Springer-Verlag, 1989).

Several books are available that explain statistical methods for use in litigation. See, e.g., Michael Finkelstein and Bruce Levin, *Statistics for Lawyers* (New York: Springer-Verlag, 1990); Wayne C. Curtis, *Statistical Concepts for Attorneys* (Westport, CT: Quorum Books, 1983).

79. Kennedy, "*McCleskey v. Kemp*" (note 8), p. 1402.

80. *McCleskey v. Zant*, No. 89-7024, 16 April 1991.

Chapter 12
A Statistical Analysis of Dutch Human Rights Case Law

Manfred Nowak and Herman von Hebel

The year 1980 may be regarded as a kind of dividing line between two periods in the attitude of Dutch courts towards international human rights treaties.[1] Until the late seventies such treaties, in particular the European Convention on Human Rights, had been treated by the courts as subsidiary law notwithstanding the already extremely favorable status of international law in the Dutch legal system since 1953.[2]

During the 1980s this situation changed fundamentally. Lawyers increasingly invoked treaty provisions before Dutch courts; and, in spite of the fact that the new Constitution of 1983 contained a comprehensive modern Bill of Rights, it was more and more the International Bill of Rights adopted by the United Nations and the Council of Europe which determined the human rights position of the Dutch people.[3]

There are different explanations for this changing pattern. First of all, the main emphasis of international human rights law has been moving simultaneously from promotion and standard setting to implementation and protection.[4] Special rapporteurs and working groups of the United Nations Commission on Human Rights investigate, in a public forum, serious human rights violations in a number of countries on the basis of the Universal Declaration of Human Rights of 1948 and specific procedural resolutions of the Economic and Social Council (ECOSOC). In addition, a growing number of binding international instruments adopted by the U.N. General Assembly have established independent expert bodies to supervise the domestic implementation of these universal conventions.[5] Although the international implementation of the European Convention by the European Commission and the European Court of Human Rights started as early as the late fifties, by the late seventies only very few cases had been decided by a binding judgment of the European Court. Since the eighties the Strasbourg Court has delivered, on the average, one judgment every month and in many individual cases it found violations of the European Convention by its States parties.[6]

This growing number of decisions by the European Courts, the United Nations Human Rights Committee, or similar bodies of supervision has, of course, had a significant impact on the jurisprudence of national courts in countries where human rights treaties are directly applicable in domestic law. The early eighties, therefore, opened a new period of national case law implementing international human rights provisions not only for the Netherlands, but also for Austria, for example. Although the European Convention had been fully incorporated into national constitutional law in 1958, it was only a few years ago that the Austrian Constitutional Court ended its reluctance to apply the Convention rights on an equal basis with the fundamental rights contained in the domestic Bill of Rights.[7]

Furthermore, with the exception of the Convention on the Elimination of All Forms of Racial Discrimination, all human rights instruments of the United Nations that provide for international implementation measures before independent expert bodies entered into force only during the late seventies and eighties. These and other factors justify restricting statistical analysis of Dutch human rights case law to the period since 1980. However, not all major human rights treaties have been ratified by the Netherlands. In particular, the U.N. Convention on the Elimination of All Forms of Discrimination Against Women 1979/81 (CEDAW)[8] and the U.N. Convention Against Torture and Other Cruel, Inhuman or Degrading Treatment or Punishment 1984/87 (CAT)[9] are still in the process of being ratified.

Consequently, the present statistical analysis applies to the following five conventions adopted by the Council of Europe and the United Nations respectively:

- the European Convention on Human Rights 1950/53, ratified in 1954 (ECHR)[10]
- the European Social Charter 1961/65, ratified in 1980 (ECS)[11]
- the U.N. Convention on the Elimination of All Forms of Racial Discrimination 1965/69, ratified in 1971 (CERD)[12]
- the U.N. Covenant on Economic, Social and Cultural Rights 1966/76, ratified in 1978 (CESCR)[13]
- the U.N. Covenant on Civil and Political Rights 1966/76, ratified in 1978 (CCPR)[14]

The present discussion starts from the hypothesis that the growing impact of international human rights law in the Dutch legal system will be reflected in a statistical analysis of domestic case law. It will be interesting to see whether the European Convention still occupies by far the most prominent place in Dutch case law, or whether U.N. instruments have already gained a similar significance. Another question which may be answered on the basis of statistical data is whether economic, social, and cultural rights (which form part of the national Bill of Rights in the Dutch Constitution of 1983) play the same role in domestic jurisprudence as do civil and political rights. For an evaluation of the substance of Dutch case law and the actual respect for human rights in Dutch society, the statistical analysis can, of course, provide no answers.[15] Nevertheless, some conclusions may be drawn and certain trends shown if the statistical data are interpreted in light of the legal and political context of human rights in the Netherlands.[16] Before we start to analyze statistical data, some preliminary remarks on the methodology and on the Dutch legal system seem appropriate.

Methodology

For reasons already explained, the period of this analysis covers the seven years from 1980 to 1986. Afterward, no complete set of relevant data is yet available. Although under the Dutch judicial system every court has to apply a self-executing provision of a human rights treaty,[17] we decided to restrict our analysis to the case law of the Supreme Court (Hoge Raad). Consequently, the total sample of our analysis encompasses all decisions which were handed down by the Supreme Court's chambers on civil, criminal, and tax law between 1980 and 1986. Out of these 18,551 decisions, a total of 325 refer to one or more provisions of a human rights treaty.[18] The Supreme Court normally refers to a human rights provision if it was invoked by the litigant. In exceptional cases—for example if a litigant only alleges a violation of his or her human rights without any reference to a specific provision—the Supreme Court may ex officio refer to a human rights treaty provision. The fact that a decision refers to an international convention as such does not give any indication whether or not the Supreme Court considered the allegation to be well-founded.

A litigant may invoke in one complaint any number of human rights provisions in any number of international instruments. Consequently, the total number of articles invoked may be much higher than the 325 cases. In fact, in these 325 cases one finds altogether

316 Manfred Nowak and Herman von Hebel

432 references to an international treaty, with a total of 552 references to specific articles.[19] These different numbers should be kept in mind when one draws comparative conclusions from the statistical data.

Domestic Status of Human Rights Treaties in the Netherlands[20]

Article 93 of the Dutch Constitution of 1983 provides that "provisions of treaties and of international institutions, which may be binding on all persons by virtue of their contents, shall become binding after they have been published."[21] This provision is based on the monistic view which considers international and national law as parts of one legal order. Consequently, the Netherlands is one of a few countries that apply international treaty law in the domestic legal order by way of adoption, that is to say without any further legislative act of explicit incorporation or transformation. However, not every provision of an international convention to which the Netherlands is a party forms part of its domestic legal order, but only one which by its content is "binding on everyone." Whether a provision is binding on everyone or not is decided by the courts when actually applying such a provision. As a general rule, only "self-executing" provisions are considered to be binding on everyone. A provision is regarded as "self-executing" if it is formulated in terms that are precise enough to allow for direct application and enforcement by courts or administrative agencies. A provision which needs further legislative or other concretization in order to be applied in individual cases lacks a self-executing character. The right not to be tortured or similar civil and political rights guaranteed by international instruments are today generally considered to be self-executing. The same cannot (yet) be said of economic, social, and cultural rights, the contents of which often explicitly refer to legislative and other measures to be adopted with a view to achieving progressively the full realization of such rights.[22]

A self-executing provision of an international human rights convention has not only a direct and binding effect in the domestic legal order of the Netherlands, but also precedence over domestic law. Article 94 of the constitution provides that "statutory regulations in force within the Kingdom shall not be applicable if such application is in conflict with provisions of treaties that are binding on all persons or of resolutions by international institutions." In other words, whenever the application of a domestic law, including acts of Parliament and even the Constitution itself, conflicts with an international human rights provision with direct effect in the Netherlands, the respective court is prohibited from applying this domestic regulation. A court has no formal power to nullify or repeal domestic law, but in practice a provision which has been found by the Supreme Court or another court of last instance[23] to be incompatible with an international obligation will not be applied subsequently by other courts until it is amended by parliament or another competent authority.

This comprehensive power of judicial review of domestic law in light of international treaty law may be surprising if one compares it with the rather limited impact of Dutch constitutional law. Parliament is, of course, bound to comply with all provisions of the Constitution, including its comprehensive Bill of Rights,[24] when enacting legislation, but the courts have no power of judicial review vis-á-vis the Constitution. Article 120 explicitly provides that "the constitutionality of Acts of Parliament and treaties shall not be reviewed by the courts." This somewhat odd system of hierarchy of norms and powers of judicial review may explain to a considerable extent why in fact the real Bill of Rights for the Dutch people is found in international treaty law rather than in the Constitution of the Netherlands.

Interpretation of the Statistical Data

Table 1 shows that less than 2 percent of all decisions of the Supreme Court dealt with human rights treaties during the period reviewed. Only during the last two years (1985 and 1986) of the period did the number of human rights cases increase both in absolute and relative

TABLE 1. Supreme Court Decisions with Explicit References to Human Rights Treaties, by Chamber, 1980–1986

	All chambers			Decisions with explicit references, by chamber		
Year	No. of decisions	With references	Percent	Criminal law	Civil law	Tax law
1980	2,132	27	1.3	21	5	1
1981	2,505	33	1.3	28	4	1
1982	2,789	36	1.3	25	11	—
1983	2,625	43	1.6	32	10	1
1984	2,948	35	1.2	29	6	—
1985	2,983	66	2.2	50	14	2
1986	2,569	85	3.3	63	20	2
1980–84	12,999	174	1.3	135	36	3
1985–86	5,552	151	2.7	113	34	4
1980–86	18,551	325	1.8	248	70	7

terms. The clear majority (76.3 percent) of all human rights cases was decided by the criminal law chamber of the courts, whereas the civil law and the tax law chambers dealt only with 21.5 percent and 2.2 percent of these cases, respectively. This result is not surprising since tax law cases normally do not raise human rights issues (apart from the right to property, and more recently, the requirement of the administration of justice under article 6 ECHR), and since the criminal law chamber has decided the majority (59 percent for the period from 1980 to 1986) of cases submitted to the Supreme Court.[25] In the criminal law chamber, 2.3 percent of the cases decided had reference to human rights treaties. Corresponding rates have not been calculated for the civil and tax law chambers or for any of the chambers by year because the necessary data on the total number of decisions by chamber and year were not readily available.

Table 2 shows that the ECHR and the CCPR were by far the most "popular" of all human rights treaties. More than 70 percent of all references (304 out of 432 references to a treaty, 391 out of 552 references to an article) related to the ECHR and slightly more than one fourth (116 references to a treaty, 145 references to an article) to the

TABLE 2. References to Treaties, References to Articles, and Violations Found, by Treaty, for the Period 1980–1986

| | Treaty[a] referred to: | | | All |
Item	ECHR	CCPR	Others	treaties
References to treaties	304	116	12	432
Percent of all decisions with references to treaty[b]	93.5	35.7	3.7	n.a.
References to articles				
Total number	391	145	16	552
Number per treaty reference	1.29	1.25	1.33	n.a.
Violations found				
Total number	35	2	0	37
Number per treaty reference	0.115	0.017	—	0.086
Number per article reference	0.090	0.014	—	0.067

[a] Treaties: ECHR = European Convention on Human Rights; CCPR = United Nations Covenant on Civil and Political Rights; Others = European Social Charter, United Nations Convention on the Elimination of All Forms of Racial Discrimination, United Nations Covenant on Economic, Social and Cultural Rights.
[b] Percentages based on the 325 cases with one or more references to treaties.

CCPR. In contrast, less than 3 percent of all references (12 references to a treaty, 16 references to an article) related to the ECS, the CESCR, or the CERD. This sharp contrast clearly reflects the difference between civil and political rights on the one hand, and economic, social, and cultural rights on the other hand. As in other western countries, the human rights concept in the Netherlands has traditionally been restricted to classical civil and political rights, whereas economic, social, and cultural rights are still widely regarded to be "non-self-executing." It is thus not surprising that the Supreme Court has not found even one single violation of a provision in ECS or CESCR. While one may detect a considerable increase in human rights cases during the last years, particularly between 1984 and 1986 (from 35 to 85), even the litigants themselves tend to invoke economic, social, and cultural rights less frequently than in 1980.

Although the CCPR entered into force only in 1978, the analysis does not reveal an increasing tendency of litigants to invoke the CCPR as compared with the ECHR. Notwithstanding the fact that the CCPR covers more rights than the ECHR, the latter still seems to be the convention most favored among Dutch lawyers.

The marginal role of the CERD cannot be explained in similar terms. In fact, the CERD is one of the older treaties: it was ratified by the Netherlands in 1971, contains primarily civil and political rights, and provides for the possibility of submitting an individual communication to the U.N. Committee Against Racial Discrimination in the event that a complaint before domestic courts should be rejected.[26] The major reason for the limited role of CERD in national case law must be sought in the fact that all the substantive provisions of this Convention have been transformed into provisions of the Dutch criminal code; the provisions of CERD need not, therefore, be directly invoked if a case of racial discrimination arises.[27] As a consequence, only one decision of the Supreme Court referred to the CERD, and no violation was established.

Tables 2, 3, and 4 establish several kinds of "input-output relationships" by comparing the number of human rights cases, references to treaties, and references to specific human rights provisions (which are normally allegations by the litigants that the right in question was violated) with the number of violations actually found by the Court. On the basis of these statistical data one certainly cannot conclude that the chances of lawyers to win a human rights case before the Supreme Court are very high. As shown in the next-to-last column of Table 3, the Court found violations in only 11.4 percent of these cases, about 1 case in 9. If violations are related to references to treaties and individual articles, the "success rates" are even lower, 8.6

TABLE 3. Number of Violations Found, by Year, 1980–1986

Year	Decisions with refs. to treaties	References to treaties	Total violations	Violations per decision	Violations per ref.
1980	27	34	1	.037	.029
1981	33	43	—	—	—
1982	36	55	6	.167	.109
1983	43	52	5	.116	.096
1984	35	44	3	.086	.068
1985	66	91	10	.152	.110
1986	85	113	12	.141	.106
1980–81	60	77	1	.017	.013
1982–86	265	355	36	.136	.101
1980–86	325	432	37	.114	.086

TABLE 4. Number of Violations Found, by Treaty, 1980–1986

Treaty	References to treaty[a]	Violations found	Violations per ref.
ECHR	304	35	.115
CCPR	116	2	.014
Others	12	—	—

[a] Decisions with references to one or more articles from the treaty shown. Some decisions have references to more than one treaty.

percent and 6.7 percent respectively, for the study period (Table 2). There was a distinct break in the case success rates between the first two years of the study period, during which only 1 violation was found, for a rate of 1.7 percent, and the subsequent five years, during which 36 violations were found, for a rate of 13.6 percent.

As shown in Table 4, all but two of the 37 violations found related to allegations based on provisions of the ECHR. The other two were based on provisions of the CCPR. No violations were found in the 12 cases with references to the other three treaties. As a result, the success rate (based on number of references to treaties) for the ECHR, 11.5 percent, was much higher than for the other treaties.

There may be various explanations for the low rate of violations found by the Court. As far as economic, social and cultural rights are concerned, the non-self-executing character of these rights could be the major reason.[28] Litigants often invoke provisions of the CCPR only after invoking similar or identical provisions of the ECHR; it thus may happen that the Supreme Court finds a violation of the

ECHR without further examining the case under the CCPR. In general, one has to keep in mind the difference between success rates based on cases and success rates based on references to treaties or to specific treaty provisions. Sometimes litigants refer in one case to a number of articles in two or more treaties, and the Supreme Court establishes the violation of one provision without further considering the other allegations. Hence, the complaint was successful, but the statistics only show that one article was found to be violated, while the other articles show no violation. Similarly, all cases which were referred back by the Supreme Court to one of the courts of appeal are statistically considered non-violations.[29] Notwithstanding these qualifications, the number of human rights violations found by the Supreme Court between 1980 and 1986 remains surprisingly low. Further in-depth research is needed to answer the question of whether these statistics reflect a rather cautious or conservative attitude of the Supreme Court towards international human rights instruments or the more encouraging possibility that human rights violations are rather scarce in the Netherlands.

The analysis of the statistical data on the precise articles of the ECHR and the CCPR which were invoked and found to be violated (Table 5) reveals some further interesting facts. Well over half (58.0 percent) of all references to human rights provisions concerned questions related to the administration of justice (equal access to the courts, right to a fair and public hearing, rule of law in civil and criminal procedure, minimum rights of accused persons in criminal proceedings, etc.) provided for in article 6 ECHR and article 14 CCPR. By far the most allegations in this broad category concerned the rights of accused persons to be tried without undue delay, which is guaranteed separately in article 14(3)c CCPR (64 out of 99 invocations of article 14), and in the context of the first sentence of article 6(1) ECHR.

The Supreme Court found, however, relatively few violations of these two provisions (5 violations of article 6 ECHR and one violation of article 14 CCPR). In fact, the success rate for these two articles was considerably lower than the success rate for some of the other articles shown in Table 5. Out of the 99 cases in which the litigants invoked article 14 CCPR, only 1 violation (1.0 percent) was established, and the 2.4 percent of violations of article 6 ECHR in respect to the number of references was only slightly higher.

The large number of cases in which violations of rights in the context of the administration of justice were asserted may be explained to some extent by the prominent role article 6 ECHR plays in the case law of the Strasbourg organs.[30] The jurisprudence of the European

TABLE 5. References to Articles of the ECHR and CCPR and Number of Violations Found, by Article, 1980–1986

Article number	Subject	References	Violations found	Percent
ECHR		391	35	9.0
3	Prohibition of torture	13	0	0.0
4	Prohibition of forced labor	7	0	0.0
5	Personal liberty	41	13	31.7
6	Administration of justice	212	5	2.4
7	No punishment without previous legislation	2	0	0.0
8	Privacy	48	11	22.9
9	Freedom of conscience and religion	6	0	0.0
10	Freedom of expression	20	0	0.0
11	Freedom of assembly and association	2	0	0.0
12	Marriage and family	5	2	40.0
13	Effective remedy	4	0	0.0
14	Prohibition of discrimination	22	4	18.2
18	Abuse of rights	1	0	0.0
25	Individual petition	1	0	0.0
1 Pr I	Enjoyment of possessions	3	0	0.0
2 Pr IV	Liberty of movement	2	0	0.0
3 Pr IV	No expulsion of nationals	2	0	0.0
CCPR		145	2	1.4
2	Effective remedy	3	0	0.0
7	Prohibition of torture	1	0	0.0
9	Personal liberty	4	1	25.0
12	Liberty of movement	3	0	0.0
13	Expulsion of aliens	1	0	0.0
14	Administration of justice	99	1	1.0
15	No punishment without previous legislation	1	0	0.0
17	Privacy	2	0	0.0
18	Freedom of conscience and religion	4	0	0.0
19	Freedom of expression	5	0	0.0
22	Freedom of association	2	0	0.0
23	Marriage and family	3	0	0.0
25	Political rights	1	0	0.0
26	Prohibition of discrimination	15	0	0.0
27	Rights of minorities	1	0	0.0

Court of Human Rights leaves open many questions which lawyers can then try to raise before national courts. Another explanation can be found in the restricted competence of the Supreme Court, which decides primarily in cases concerning disputes in civil and criminal law and procedure, whereas human rights violations by administrative agencies are often not dealt with by the Supreme Court but, for example, by the Judicial Division of the Council of State. The low "success rate" of these provisions can only be explained, however, by an extremely cautious attitude of the Supreme Court towards a more extensive interpretation of the rights contained therein.

On the other hand, we find a relatively high rate of violations for certain other provisions. More than one third of all 37 violations established by the Supreme Court (35.1 percent) concerned the right to personal liberty in article 5 ECHR (plus one violation of article 9 CCPR). The success rate of these two provisions combined amounted to 31.1 percent. Many of these cases concerned involuntary patients in psychiatric hospitals. Almost one third (29.7 percent) of all established violations related to the right to privacy and family life in article 8 ECHR, which was invoked by litigants even more often than the right to personal liberty (48 times), with a success rate of 22.9 percent. Surprisingly enough, its counterpart (article 17 CCPR) was only invoked twice, and without success. This sharp contrast may be attributed to the fact that the Strasbourg case law on the right to privacy, in particular with respect to the concept of "family life," is much further developed than that of the Human Rights Committee. The same holds true, in principle, for other rights, such as freedom of expression (article 10 ECHR and article 19 CCPR) or the prohibition of torture (article 3 ECHR and article 7 CCPR), which are couched in similar terms in both instruments.[31]

Finally, the allegation of violations of the right to marry and found a family as well as the prohibition of discrimination under the ECHR turned out to be rather successful. In 2 of the 5 cases concerning article 12 ECHR (40.0 percent) and in 4 of the 22 cases concerning article 14 ECHR (18.2 percent) a violation was found. The counterpart of the latter provision, article 26 CCPR, which contains not only a prohibition of discrimination related to the enjoyment of other rights of the respective convention, as in the case of article 14 ECHR, but also an independent right of equality before the law and equal protection of the law, was invoked in a total of 15 cases, albeit without success. Nevertheless, this comparatively high number of references indicates the growing significance of this provision. which was underlined by two landmark decisions of the Human Rights Committee in 1987 that found discrimination against women in the Dutch social security legislation.[32] These decisions, which were followed by Dutch courts,[33] even led to a serious public debate on the possibility of denouncing the CCPR in the Netherlands![34]

Conclusions

The statistical data available on the case law of the Dutch Supreme Court tell us some interesting facts:

- Fewer than 2 percent of all decisions of the Court deal with human rights
- The number of human rights cases submitted to the Court has been growing considerably since 1984
- The great majority of these human rights cases is decided by the criminal law chamber
- Litigants almost never invoke economic, social, and cultural rights contained in the ECS and the CESCR or provisions of CERD, and the Supreme Court has not yet found one violation of a provision of these three treaties
- More than 70 percent of all references to an international human rights provision, as well as 95 percent of all violations found, relate to the ECHR
- The success rate of alleging a violation of a specific provision of a human rights treaty is very low on the average (below 7 percent)
- More than half of all human rights cases before the Supreme Court concern questions relating to the administration of justice, but the success rate of these cases is below 3 percent
- More than one third of all violations found by the Supreme Court concern the right to personal liberty, and almost one third the right to privacy and family life

These conclusions, drawn exclusively from an analysis of rather simple quantitative data, form in our opinion a sound basis for in-depth research on one or the other questions which were raised but could not receive satisfactory answers during our statistical research.

Notes

1. Cf. Pieter van Dijk, "Domestic Status of Human-Rights Treaties and the Attitude of the Judiciary—The Dutch Case," in *Festschrift für Felix Ermacora: Progress in the Spirit of Human Rights*, ed. Manfred Nowak, Dorothea Steurer, and Hannes Tretter (Kehl-Strasbourg-Arlington 1988), pp. 631, 639ff.; Leo Zwaak, "The Implementation of International Human Rights Treaties in the

Dutch Legal Order," in *The Implementation of National Law of the European Convention of Human Rights*: *Proceedings of the 4th Copenhagen Conference on Human Rights, 28–29 October 1988*, Publications of the Danish Centre of Human Rights 11 (Copenhagen: Danish Centre of Human Rights, 1989), pp. 48–64.

2. See also Evert A. Alkema, "Fundamental Human Rights and the Legal Order of the Netherlands," in *International Law in the Netherlands*, ed. Haro F. van Panhuys, W. P. Heere, J. W. Josephus Jitta, Ko Swan Sik, and A. M. Stuyt, vol. III (Alphen a/d Rijn: Sijthoff and Noordhoff, 1980), p. 136.

3. See van Dijk, "Domestic Status of Human-Rights Treaties" (note 1), p. 649.

4. See Manfred Nowak and Leo Zwaak, "The International Protection of Human Rights," editorial *SIM Newsletter* (*SNL*) 6, No. 2 (1988): 2–4.

5. Cf. Manfred Nowak, "The Promotion and Protection of Human Rights by the United Nations," *SNL* 6, No. 2 (1988): 5–28.

6. Cf. Leo Zwaak, "The Protection of Human Rights and Fundamental Freedoms Within the Council of Europe," *SNL* 6, No. 2 (1988): 43–46 with further references.

7. For a comprehensive and critical survey of the Austrian case law to 1982 see Felix Ermacora, Manfred Nowak, and Hannes Tretter, eds., *Die Europäische Menschenrechtskonvention in der Rechtsprechung der österreichischen Höchstgerichte* (Köln: Karl Heymans Verlag, 1983), for the changing attitude during the last few years see Manfred Nowak, "The Implementation of the European Convention on Human Rights in Austria," in *Implementation of National Law* (note 1).

8. See Margaretha Wadstein, "Implementation of the UN Convention on the Elimination of All Forms of Discrimination Against Women," *SNL* 6, No. 4 (1988): 5–21.

9. See Manfred Nowak, "Die UNO-Konvention gegen die Folter vom 10.. Dezember 1984," *Europäische Grundrechte Zeitschrift* 12 (1988): 109–116; Herman Burgers and Hans Danelius, *The United Nations Convention Against Torture* (Dordrecht-Boston-London: Martinus Nijhoff, 1988); Manfred Nowak, "The Implementation Functions of the UN Committee Against Torture," in Nowak et al., *Progress in the Spirit of Human Rights* (note 1), p. 493.

10. See, among others, Pieter van Dijk and Fried van Hoof, *Theory and Practice of the European Convention on Human Rights* (Deventer: Kluwer, 1982); Jochen Frowein and Wolfgang Peukert, "Europäische Menschenrechtskonvention," *EMRK-Kommentar* (Kehl-Strasbourg-Arlington: Engel Verlag, 1985); Pieter van Dijk and Peter Leuprecht, *Digest of Strasbourg Case Law Relating to the European Convention of Human Rights*, 6 volumes (Köln: Karl Heymans Verlag, 1983–).

11. See Lammy Betten, "European Social Charter," *SNL* 6, No. 2 (1988): 69–82; David J. Harris, *The European Social Charter* (Charlottesville: University Press of Virginia, 1984); Theo Ohlinger, "Die Europaische Sozialcharta," in Nowak et al., *Progress in the Spirit of Human Rights* (note 1), p. 213; *The Future of European Social Policy: Views and Comments Expressed at the Conference on the Future of European Social Policy, Utrecht, 25–26 April 1989*, ed. Lammy Betten, David Harris, and Teun Jaspers (Deventer: Kluwen, 1989).

12. See Natan Lerner, "Curbing Racial Discrimination—Fifteen Years CERD," *Israel Yearbook on Human Rights* 13 (1983): 170–188; Theodor Meron, "The Meaning and Reach of the International Convention on the Elimination of All Forms of Racial Discrimination," *AJIL* 79 (1985): 293–319.

13. See Philip Alston, "Out of the Abyss: The Challenges Confronting the New U.N. Committee on Economic, Social and Cultural Rights," *HRQ* 9, No. 4 (1987): 332; Herman von Hebel, "The Implementation of the Right to Housing in Article 11 of the U.N. Covenant on Economic, Social and Cultural Rights," *SNL* 5, No. 20 (1987): 26–41.

14. See Louis Henkin, ed., *The International Bill of Rights* (Dordrecht: Martinus Nijhoff, 1981); Manfred Nowak, *CCPR-Kommentar, Knoomntar sum UNO Pakk über bürgerliche und politische Rechte* (Kehl-Strasbourg-Arlington: Engel Verlag, 1989).

15. See in this respect van Dijk, "Domestic Status of Human Rights Treaties" and Zwaak, "Implementation" (note 1). The Netherlands Institute of Human Rights (SIM) prepares, in cooperation with the TMC Asser Institute, a Digest on national case law relating to the European Convention and other human rights instruments; see also the regular reviews of the most outstanding domestic court decisions in the *NJCM-Bulletin*, the periodical of the Dutch section of the International Commission of Jurists.

16. For the possibilities and limits of improving the analysis of human rights with the assistance of statistical tools see Richard P. Claude and Thomas B. Jabine, eds., "Symposium: Statistical Issues in the Field of Human Rights," in *Human Rights Quarterly* 8, No. 4 (November 1986).

17. For a short introduction to the Dutch legal system refer to the next section.

18. See Table 1. For the selection of these 325 cases, the authors wish to thank the TMC Asser Institute for making their data available.

19. See Tables 2 and 3.

20. See, among others, van Dijk, "Domestic Status of Human-Rights Treaties" (note 1), with further references.

21. For the English translation see Gisbert H. Flanz, "The Netherlands," in *Constitutions of the Countries of the World*, ed. Gisbert H. Flanz and Albert P. Blaustein (New York: 1984). A similar provision was already inserted into the old Constitution in 1953.

22. See, e.g., articles 2 and 11 of the CESCR:
Article 2(1):

Each State Party to the present Covenant undertakes to take steps, individually and through international assistance and co-operation, especially economic and technical, to the maximum of its available resources, with a view to achieving progressively the full realization of the rights recognized in the present Covenant by all appropriate means, including particularly the adoption of legislative measures.

Article 11(1):

The States Parties to the present Covenant recognize the right of everyone to an adequate standard of living for himself and his family, including adequate food, clothing and housing, and to the continuous improvement of living conditions. The States Parties will take appropriate steps to ensure the realization of this right, recognizing to this effect the essential importance of international co-operation based on free consent.

23. For example, the Judicial Division of the Council of State (for administration law cases) or the Central Board of Appeal (for cases concerning social security).

24. Articles 1 to 23 of the Constitution 1983; for the English text see Flanz, "Netherlands" (note 21); for a commentary see Alis Koekkoek, Willem Konijnenbelt, and Frans Crijns,eds., *Grondrechten, commentaar op Hoodstuk 1 van de herziene Grondwet, aangeboden aan Mr. H.J.M. Jeukens* (Deventer: Kluwen, 1982); Peter Akkermans, ed., *De Grondwet: een artikelsgewijs Commentaar* (Zwolle: Tjeenk Willink, 1987).

25. Between 1980 and 1986 the criminal law chamber decided 11,016 (59 percent) out of a total of 18,551 cases.

26. As early as 1971, the Netherlands made the declaration under article 14 of CERD by which it accepted this optional procedure. This competence of the Committee became internationally effective, however, only on 3 December 1982. The Committee decided its first case under article 14 of CERD (*A. Yilmaz-Dogan v. The Netherlands*, Comm. No. 1/1984) on August 10, 1988: cf. the commentary of Manfred Nowak in *SNL* 6, No. 3 (1988): 62.

27. Cf. van Dijk, "Domestic Status of Human-Rights Treaties" (note 1), p. 643.

28. The statistical data do not show, however, whether allegations of violations of economic, social, and cultural rights were dismissed because of their non-self-executing character or on any other grounds.

29. Cf. van Dijk, "Domestic Status of Human-Rights Treaties," p. 643.

30. See, e.g., the survey of the comprehensive case law on article 6 ECHR in vol. 2 of the *Digest of Strasbourg Case Law* (note 10).

31. See, e.g., the respective chapters in Frowein and Peukert, *EMRK-Kommentar* (note 10) and Nowak, *CCPR-Kommentar* (note 14).

32. Cases of *Broeks* and *Zwaan-de Vries v. The Netherlands*, Comm. No. 172 and 182/1984; for the text of these decisions see the *11th annual report of the Human Rights Committee to the UN General Assembly*, U.N. Doc. A/42/40, 139 and 160.

33. See van Dijk, "Domestic Status of Human-Rights Treaties" (note 1), and Aalt Willem Heringa, "Article 26 CCPR and Social Security—Recent Dutch Cases Invalidating Discriminatory Social Security Laws," *SNL* 6, No. 1 (1988): 19.

34. See the petition of leading human rights scholars, "Petition to the Minister of Foreign Affairs of the Netherlands, Submitted by the Netherlands Jurists Committee for Human Rights," *SNL* 6, No. 1 (1988): 128.

Chapter 13
An Epidemiology of Homicide: *Ningún Nombre* Burials in the Province of Buenos Aires from 1970 to 1984

Clyde Collins Snow and Maria Julia Bihurriet

—of comfort, no man speak:
>Let's talk of graves, of worms, and epitaphs:
>Make dust our paper, and with rainy eyes
>Write sorrow on the bosom of the earth.
>Shakespeare, *King Richard II*

This report helps fulfill an elementary step in any homicide investigation: locating the body of the victim. In this case, the bodies are some of the thousands of Argentina's *desaparecidos*—men, women, and children who disappeared between 1976 and 1983 when the country was under Junta[1] rule. They were victims of the Junta's self-proclaimed "Dirty War" against what it perceived as a Marxist-inspired threat to overthrow the country.

The Junta's stated targets were members of two violent underground groups, the *Montoneros* and the *Ejército Revolucionario del Pueblo* (ERP), or People's Revolutionary Army. The Montoneros represented the radical left wing of Peronism. Reflecting the traditionally union-oriented populism of the Peronist movement, they were strongest in urbanized industrial centers and, accordingly, their operations followed the tactical textbooks of urban guerrilla movements—bombings, kidnappings, and assassinations. The ERP, in contrast, followed a more orthodox Marxist ideology. It was the armed wing of the *Partido Revolucionario de Los Trabajadores* (Revolutionary Workers' Party) that viewed its struggle as part of a broader international movement against capitalist imperialism. It sought its support from the impoverished peasantry of the northern rural areas and was particularly active in the subtropical province of Tucumán, where nearly inaccessible terrain gave cover to classical agrarian guerrilla operations.[2] Both groups, in an accelerating campaign of terrorism, had been responsible for perhaps 500 to 800 deaths during the early 1970s.[3]

The crimes of the Montoneros and ERP provided a convenient pretext for the Junta takeover. But, under the guise of combating these relatively small groups of avowed terrorists, the Junta broadened its definition of subversion to include anyone in disagreement with its totalitarian philosophy. Nowhere was the strategy of its campaign better defined than in the chilling words spoken in 1976 by General Iberico Saint-Jean, one of the principal combatants of the "Dirty War":

First we will kill all the subversives; then we will kill their collaborators; then . . . their sympathizers, then . . . those who remain indifferent; and finally we will kill the timid.[4]

In effect, the Junta declared war on Argentina's own citizens. Those caught in its net—terrorists and innocent alike—were denied their constitutional and human rights through abduction, detention in secret, torture and, eventually, extrajudicial execution. The process did not end with the death of the victim—extraordinary means were employed to destroy or conceal the body so no physical trace of the person's existence would remain. During those years in Argentina, the term "disappeared" had more than a figurative connotation.

The exact number of disappearances remains unknown but, in 1984, the Argentine National Commission on the Disappearance of Persons (CONADEP) documented 8,961 cases.[5] At the Commission's request, the senior author analyzed the age and sex statistics for a group of 7,385 desaparecidos whose cases had been reported by June 1984.[6] Although most were in their twenties and thirties, they ranged in age from newborn infants to septuagenarians; about one third were women.

More than the absolute numbers, the incidence of disappearances within the population provides some perspective on the scale and intensity of the "Dirty War." In eight years, nearly 9,000 of Argentina's 26 million citizens disappeared. In a country the size of the United

States, this would amount to about 77,000 disappearances—20,000 more than the 57,000 Americans who were killed in Viet Nam over a similar period.

The Process of Disappearance

Typically, there were four steps in the process of disappearance: 1) abduction, 2) detention, 3) execution, and 4) disposal of body. The kidnappings often occurred at night when groups of armed men broke into the victim's home. Handcuffed and hooded, the victim was forced into the trunk of an unmarked vehicle and driven to a "Secret Detention Center" (SDC). To date, investigators have been able to identify about 360 SDCs located throughout Argentina.[7] The majority were "Transient Centers" (TC), which frequently consisted of no more than a few holding cells in a local police station where the detainee was kept for a few hours or days pending transfer to a "Prisoner Assessment Center" (PAC). The PACs, usually located on military bases or in major police headquarters, were large facilities equipped with administrative offices, cell blocks, interrogation rooms, and torture chambers. Official and unofficial inquiries by families and friends of the disappeared were turned away with the reply that there was no record of the person being in custody.

Detainees were kept in the PACs for several weeks or months during which they were subjected to seemingly endless sessions of interrogation under severe torture. The CONADEP report contains hundreds of testimonies by survivors graphically detailing their nightmarish experiences in PAC torture chambers.[8] The most frequently reported form of physical torture was by electrical cattle prods applied to the mouth and genitals, but more bizarre methods were also employed. These sessions were monitored by military or police physicians to ensure that the victim did not succumb under torture[9]—an outcome that was considered "unprofessional." Often, whole families were abducted together and one spouse was forced to witness the torture of the other; children were also tortured in front of their parents. Female detainees were almost always raped, often repeatedly. An especially cruel fate awaited pregnant detainees—they were transferred to wards in military hospitals where they were treated relatively well until their infants were delivered. After delivery, the mothers were executed and their babies were sold on the black market or given to childless military or police couples.[10]

Disposal of Desaparecido Bodies as *"Ningún Nombres"*[11]

Various methods were used to dispose of the bodies of desaparecidos. Many were dumped from military aircraft over water or remote
land areas, others dismembered and cremated, and still others buried secretly in mass graves located on or near military reservations.[12]
It is doubtful that the remains of these victims will ever be found.
However, another common method of getting rid of the bodies
involved subverting the normal procedure of medicolegal death investigation so that the corpses were signed out as "unidentified,"
thereby paving the way for their burial in unmarked graves in public
cemeteries.

Under Argentine law, any victim of violent or suspicious death
must be examined by a police surgeon. The latter, usually a general
practitioner with little or no training in forensic pathology, makes a
determination of the cause of death. The results of his examination
are reported to the judge having jurisdiction over the case. Based
upon the pathological findings, along with evidence developed from
collateral lines of inquiry (scene investigation, witness statements,
etc.), the judge rules on the manner of death; that is, whether the
deceased died of natural causes or was a victim of an accident, suicide, or homicide.

An unidentified corpse is officially designated as an *Ningún Nombre*
(NN). Normally, an NN body is accorded a pauper's burial in a public
cemetery of the jurisdiction in which it was found. It is usually buried
in a largely untended part of the cemetery reserved for indigents. As
NN graves are unmarked, they can only be located by consulting the
cemetery's registry where they are recorded by grave number and
plot.

Many of the desaparecidos were buried as NNs. Typically, after
execution in or near the PACs where they had been held, their bodies
were dumped at night in vacant lots, alleys, or along country roads.
Passersby usually found them within a day or two and notified the
police. The latter, after a cursory scene investigation, took them to
the local judicial morgue where they were examined by a police surgeon. Apparently, some care was taken to dump them in jurisdictions
where the local police could be relied upon not to press their investigations beyond the barest limits required to cover themselves officially. Sometimes the killers acted more boldly; instead of dumping
the bodies, the execution squads took them directly to the morgue,
claiming they had been killed in shootouts with security forces or
during escape attempts. However the body arrived at the morgue,

the subsequent investigation of a desaparecido's death was perfunctory: routine police paperwork was completed, an autopsy duly performed, and a death certificate issued; but no serious attempt was made to actively pursue the case. Instead, the body was signed out as "unidentified," buried as an NN, and the investigation closed.

Ningún Nombre Burial Survey: Design and Response

In 1985, a survey of NN burials in cemeteries throughout the country was initiated by the Argentine Undersecretary of Human Rights. It had two purposes: 1) to provide an estimate of the number and location of NN graves which might be those of desaparecidos and 2) to provide a centralized, permanent registry of such graves useful in planning future medicolegal investigations of the desaparecidos' deaths. Such a registry would also be helpful to families of the disappeared seeking to trace the remains of their relatives.

Geographic and Demographic Factors[13]

This study is based on the data collected from the Province of Buenos Aires (PBA), the largest and most populous of Argentina's 22 provinces. The province is about the size of Arizona, and its eleven million inhabitants make up nearly 40 percent of the nation's total population. The provincial capital is La Plata, a city of nearly a half million located 59 kilometers southeast of the City of Buenos Aires, the national capital. The latter, with a population of about three million, is situated within the province as a federally governed, 77-square-mile enclave—the *Capital Federal* (CF). Both cities are major seaports, fronting on the broad estuary of the Rio de la Plata.

The Province of Buenos Aires is divided into 121 *departments* (governmental units corresponding to U.S. counties) and 4 small, independent *municipalities*.[14] The 19 departments clustered around the Capital Federal make up the densely populated urban area of Greater Buenos Aires (GBA), and their combined population of nearly seven million comprises 63 percent of the provincial total. Aside from those of Greater Buenos Aires and La Plata, only 3 other departments have more than 100,000 inhabitants: General Pueyrredon, Bahia Blanca, and San Nicolás. The first 2 are coastal cities south of Buenos Aires: San Nicolás is situated on the Paraná River 242 km upriver from Buenos Aires. The remaining departments are sparsely populated rural districts with an average population of about 31,000 inhabitants.

Geographic Distribution of Disappearances

Although the present study is limited to Buenos Aires Province, some insight is provided by the geographic distribution of disappearances within the country as a whole (Figure 1a). While disappearances occurred in Capital Federal and each of the 22 provinces, the pattern of distribution was far from uniform.[15] To a large extent, this pattern reflects the concentration of the military's principal targets, the Montoneros and ERP. Thus, nearly three quarters of the cases occurred in the Capital Federal (27%) and Buenos Aires Province (46%), where the Montoneros were strongest. Of the remainder, 24% were from six provinces of the northwestern interior which were ERP strongholds: Tucumán (8.6%), Córdoba (8.1%), Santa Fe (3.4%), Mendoza (2.2%), Salta (0.9%) and Jujuy (0.8%). Only 3.2% of all desaparecidos were reported from the remaining fifteen provinces.

While these statistics provide some idea of the scale of the Dirty War, a better picture of its intensity is given by relating the number of disappearances to population size. When measured by this index, sparsely populated Tucumán suffered most severely, with 88 disappearances per 100,000 inhabitants. Nearly matching it was the Capital Federal, with 80 disappearances per 100,000. The national average was 34 disappearances per 100,000 persons.

Figure 1b summarizes the disappearances statistics for Buenos Aires Province. More than half were from the cluster of 19 departments making up the densely urbanized district of Greater Buenos Aires. The Department of La Plata, the site of the provincial capital and one of the country's largest universities, was especially hard hit. There, about 910 cases occurred, amounting to 201 desaparecidos per 100,000 inhabitants—the highest disappearance rate recorded. About 350 occurred in General Pueyrredon, corresponding to a rate of 88 per 100,000. In only 3 other departments, Zarate, Bahia Blanca, and Campana, were there more than 50 disappearances. The remaining cases—7.8 percent of the total for the province—were distributed among 35 departments, leaving 66 departments with no reported disappearances.

In all, about 46 percent of the 8,961 disappearances reported to the CONADEP Commission occurred in Buenos Aires Province. Another 27 percent disappeared from the Capital Federal. While most of the latter were cremated in La Chacarita,[16] a large municipal cemetery in the city of Buenos Aires, many are known to have been transferred to PACs outside the Capital Federal. Smaller numbers abducted in other provinces were also transferred to PACs in Buenos Aires Province. Thus, altogether, it is probable that well over half of

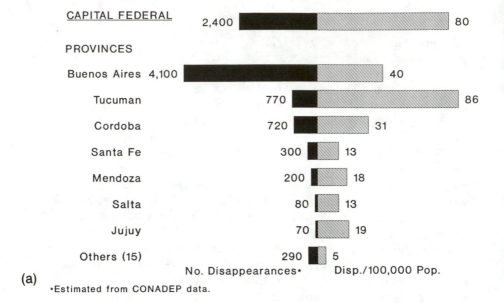

•Estimated from CONADEP data.

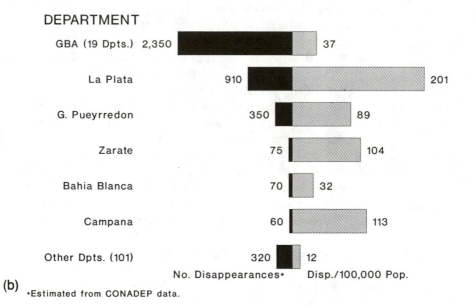

•Estimated from CONADEP data.

Figure 1. Geographic distribution of desaparecidos. (a) Argentina; (b) Buenos Aires Province.

Argentina's desaparecidos were killed in PACs within Buenos Aires Province. Those whose bodies were not disposed of by other means most likely lie buried as NNs in departments surveyed in this report.

Data Collection

This study is based on 1970–84 statistics on NN burials in Buenos Aires Province. These data were collected on questionnaires sent in 1986 to the superintendents of the 125 provincial departments. The superintendents were requested to provide the date of interment of each NN buried in cemeteries within their departments during the fifteen-year period covered by the survey as well as the decedent's sex, estimated age, and cause of death, if known. They were also asked to give the exact location of the grave, as indicated in the cemetery's registration records, and to indicate whether or not the remains had been transferred to an ossuary.[17]

Survey Response

Four departments have no public cemeteries. The cemetery records of 6 others could not be obtained because they had been previously sequestered by the courts and cannot be released pending the outcome of ongoing judicial investigations. Returns from 9 departments were not received in time to be included in this study. The report of one department, Quilmes, was rejected due to data irregularities. In this case, documentary evidence indicates that, although a large number of desaparecidos were buried in its principal public cemetery, these burials were not officially recorded.[18] The remaining 105 departments responded with completed questionnaires. When the 4 departments without public cemeteries are excluded, this represented a response rate of 86.8 percent.

Data Reduction

The data submitted from each responding department were tabulated as follows:

1. *Date of Burial*: month, day, year.
2. *Sex*: a. male, b. female, c. undetermined.
3. *Age* (yrs):   a. fetus, b. infant (< 3), c. child (4–13), d. adolescent (14–20), e. young adult (21–35), f. older adult (36 +), g. undetermined.

4. *Cause of Death*:   a. gunshot wound, b. cranial trauma, c. drowning, d. pulmonary, e. cardiac, f. accident-related causes, g. other, h. undetermined.
5. *Location*: a. original grave, b. ossuary, c. other.

Data Reliability

Readers familiar with the analysis of mortality statistics based on death certificates will be aware of the limitations and possible pitfalls of such an approach.[19] For example, the age of an unidentified body is, perforce, an estimate based on its general appearance. Depending upon the nature and degree of postmortem change, as well as the training and experience of the autopsy surgeon, such estimates may be wide of the mark by many years. When decomposition is advanced, even sex may be difficult to determine without the special expertise of a forensic anthropologist. Similarly, the cause of death, as entered on the death certificate, is often open to question. Even when a complete autopsy and toxicological study are performed by well-trained forensic specialists, the exact cause cannot be determined in some cases. With a few outstanding exceptions, Argentine police surgeons have little or no formal training or experience in forensic pathology and must often work in poorly equipped morgues. For this reason, many cases signed out as "cause undetermined" might have, in fact, been diagnosable, and some in which a cause is given were probably misdiagnosed. It is also possible that some police surgeons sympathetic to the Junta regime deliberately obscured or falsified their reports on the examination of desaparecido remains.

A related problem in evaluating the causes of death listed on the death certificates is the frequent failure of physicians to list both the *immediate* and *proximate* causes.[20] Thus, a victim of a gunshot wound of the head may die immediately from massive cerebral trauma or survive a few hours or days to succumb to some secondary or tertiary proximate cause such as hemorrhagic shock, aspiration of blood, or a complicating infection. Failure to fully document this chain of causes on the death certificate can lead to confusion in evaluating mortality statistics.[21] In such cases, the problem can only be resolved by a review of the original autopsy records or by interviewing the examining physician. Meanwhile, although the causes given on the NN death certificates must be taken at face value, those listing only proximate causes (e.g., "acute hemorrhage") that might obscure more immediate causes of violent death—particularly gunshot wounds—must be treated with caution.

Theoretical Considerations

The objective of this study is to identify those departments in which desaparecidos were buried as NNs. Our approach is based upon the assumption that, under normal circumstances, the incidence of NN cases is relatively constant within a given department. This "normal" incidence rate is determined by many factors. Among the latter, population size is undoubtedly the most important, but others such as standard of living, degree of urbanization, and the skills and resources of local forensic experts may also be significant. Acting together, these factors determine the overall incidence of NN cases. Minor fluctuations in the annual NN caseload can be attributed to chance, but larger ones would excite the curiosity of a statistician. Such major deviations could be caused by transitory events such as natural disasters resulting in a large number of unidentified victims. Long term changes might reflect shifts in the socioeconomic or demographic characteristics such as those mentioned above.

Like living groups, NN populations tend to show their own unique characteristics. Normally, in Argentina, as in other advanced nations, a high percentage of bodies signed out as "unidentified" are those of elderly indigents with no family ties. Within this group, males strongly outnumber females. Typically, they are transients who die of natural causes related to old age, exposure, malnutrition and, frequently, alcohol abuse. Significant changes in the normal age, sex, and cause-of-death profile of the NN population from a given department might thus signal the presence of unusual etiological factors. To look at these changes, we have divided the fifteen-year interval covered by this survey into two sub-periods, *Civil* (CIV)[22] and *Junta* (JUN), following the chronological scheme outlined below:

1. *Civil* (CIV): 1970–75 plus 1984, 7 years.
2. *Junta* (JUN): 1976–83, 8 years.
   a. *Early Junta* (JUN1): 1976–77, 2 years.
   b. *Later Junta* (JUN2): 1978–83, 6 years.

Prior to the initiation of the Junta's Dirty War, we would expect the NN population to display the normal pattern in terms of incidence and the age, sex, and cause-of-death profile described above. It can therefore serve as a control against which the NN statistics from the

JUN period can be tested. The subdivisions of the JUN period correspond to the course of the "Dirty War," which was conducted in two phases. During the first two years (JUN1), it was waged with extreme intensity; throughout the remaining years (JUN2), it was conducted with less force.

Our theory is that departments in which desaparecidos were buried as NNs should show significant changes during the period of Junta rule from the normal pattern of NN burials. These changes can be of three kinds: 1) increases in overall number of NN burials, 2) high proportions of the reported NN burials occurring during the First Junta (JUN1) sub-period and 3) shifts in the biological and pathological profile of the NN population in directions approaching the known characteristics of the desaparecido population in age, sex, and cause of death. Also, for reasons that will be discussed below, these departments should show a closer geographic relationship to PAC detention centers than those in which desaparecidos were not buried.

Statistical Model

To determine which departments showed significant increases in NN burials during the period of Junta rule, the following hypotheses were formulated:

$$H_1: JUN1n > CIVn$$

and

$$H_2: JUN2n > CIVn$$

where

$$n = \text{number of reported NN burials.}$$

To test these hypotheses, we have selected the chi-square test as a statistical model. The probability level of .05 or less is chosen to define statistical significance. Data were deemed sufficient for testing if the smallest expected cell was 5 or greater.

Since the CIV, JUN1 and JUN2 periods were of different lengths (7, 2, and 6 years respectively) the values of the expected frequencies were calculated as follows:

$$E_i = (Y_i/Y_t)N$$

where

E_i = expected frequency of period i,
Y_i = number of years in period i,
Y_t = number of years in total period tested,
N = total number of NN burials.

Nearly all departments displayed some growth in population during the 15-year survey period. Furthermore, there was a strong correlation between population size and the total number of NN burials in the 78 departments that reported at least one NN burial during the survey period ($r = .861$). To the extent that population growth would affect the number of NNs during the JUN period, it would result in higher chi-square values. If, in a given department the population effect were sufficient, it might raise the chi-square values beyond the .05 probability level and result in falsely accepting the hypothesis that the observed increase in NNs was due to desaparecido burials. To rule out this possibility, departments showing statistically significant outcomes in tests of H1 and/or H2 were retested by using *observed* cell values recalculated to eliminate the influence of population growth. To do this, the 1970–84 annual population of each department was first calculated from its 1970 and 1980 census figures (it was assumed that the growth was uniform and linear throughout the period). From these annual populations, the average population size of the department was then calculated for the CIV, JUN1 and JUN2 periods. The observed NN values for the three periods were then modified by the following formulas:

$$aO_{JUN1} = (P_{CIV}/P_{JUN1}) * O_{JUN1} \; ,$$

$$aO_{JUN2} = (P_{CIV}/P_{JUN2}) * O_{JUN2}$$

where

P = mean population of the period,
O = observed NN burials during period,
aO = adjusted value.

Hypothesis Testing

The total number of NNs reported in this series—4,297—included 131 aborted fetuses. As the latter were obviously not desaparecidos, they were eliminated prior to hypothesis testing, reducing the total number of cases subjected to analysis to 4,166.

Twenty-seven departments reported no NNs during the entire

fifteen years covered in this survey. Four others reported a combined total of 10 NN burials, but all occurred during the CIV period and could thus be eliminated as possible desaparecidos. The median population of this "ZERO" group was 12,794, and nearly all were located in the sparsely populated ranching areas in the western parts of the province. The most likely reason for the rarity of NNs in these rural departments is that, in small communities, the disappearance of a local resident is not apt to go unnoticed. Therefore, when a body is found, it is usually quickly identified unless it is that of a complete outsider. However, two departments in this group, Olavarria and San Nicolás, had populations significantly exceeding the group mean. They were also the only ones of the ZERO group in which PAC detention centers were located.[23] These findings suggest that their data should be considered questionable until they can be confirmed by a direct review of their cemetery and morgue records. Their elimination from the present study reduced the analysis group to 103 departments.

The numbers of NNs reported by 35 departments were insufficient to meet the criterion for chi-square tests (smallest expected cell ≥ 5). Collectively, this "INSF" group reported 138 NN burials or 3.3 percent of the total series. They tended to be somewhat more populous (median population = 19,831) than those of the group reporting no NNs, but most would still be classified as rural. Only one, Trenque Lauquen (pop. 31,449) in the extreme western part of the province, is known to have had a PAC detention center.[24] It reported 5 NN burials, only one of which occurred during the JUN period.

Despite its rural character, the number of NN burials in this group doubled during the JUN period (Table 1). When hypotheses H1 and H2 were tested on the grouped data, the results were significant for H1. This finding suggested that some of the departments in this group harbor desaparecido burials.

It appeared unlikely that the 35 departments of the INSF group, scattered throughout the entire province, would be statistically ho-

TABLE 1. Distribution of NN Burials in INSF Departments by Period and Chi-square Scores of Tests of Hypotheses H1 and H2

Group	Depts.	Total	CIV	JUN1	JUN2	H1	H2
All INSF depts.	35	138	46	30	62	13.09*	5.50
a. Bahia cluster	4	19	1	7	11	n.a.[1]	10.00**
b. Others	31	119	45	23	51	3.75	5.29***

—[1] not tested (least exp. < 5). * p <.005, (chi² > 9.21, 1 df).
** p <.001 (chi² >10.8, 1 df). *** p <.025 (chi² > 5.02, 1 df).

mogenous. Instead, it seemed more probable that the significant increases in NN burials during the JUN period were concentrated in one or more subgroups. When the geographic distribution of the departments was examined, it was noted that some were clustered around departments where PAC centers were located. This suggested that these PACs may have dispersed their victims over several adjacent departments. To examine this theory, we lumped the NN statistics of the departments within each cluster and tested hypotheses H1 and H2.

Of the eight clusters identified, only one showed a statistically significant increase in NN burials. It consisted of four departments adjacent to the department of Bahia Blanca where two PACs were located.[25] Although only 19 NNs were reported from the cluster, 18 occurred during the JUN period and, of these, 7 were in the JUN1 sub-period; expected cell sizes were still too small for testing H1 but the results for H2 were statistically significant (Table 1, row a).

When the "Bahia cluster" departments were subtracted from the INSF group, the grouped data of the remaining departments were not statistically significant for H1 but significant at the 0.02 probability level for H2 (Table 1, row b). This finding suggests that, within this group of 31 departments, at least a few desaparecidos were buried as NNs; however, the data are not sufficient to pinpoint the particular departments in which these burials occurred.

In fifteen departments there were no statistically significant differences between the CIV and JUN sub-periods (H1 and H2 rejected). Together, these "REJT" group departments reported 406 NN burials, 183 (44.6%) of which occurred during the JUN period. Like the departments of groups ZERO and INSF, those of this REJT group tended to be located in the interior of the province, yet the median population (35,576) was much higher.

In terms of population, one department of the REJT group, Bahia Blanca, appears anomalous. Its population of 219,199 significantly exceeds the mean (48,669.7) of the REJT group at the .005 probability level (Student's t = 3.817, 14 df). It was also the site of two PACS (see above). Furthermore, the four departments of the Bahia Cluster partially surround it. However, unlike the other three departments (Quilmes, Olavarria, San Nicolás) whose data were rejected as questionable, there is no reason to question the reliability of the Bahia Blanca statistics. To the contrary, the little evidence presently available suggests that few, if any, desaparecidos were buried as NNs in Bahia Blanca. First, in contrast to other urban centers, relatively few disappearances were reported from Bahia Blanca: only 32 per 100,000 inhabitants compared to the much higher rates in the Capital

Federal, La Plata, and General Pueyrredon (see Figure 1b). Second, it appears that many, if not the majority, of the abductees from this area were eventually transferred to PACs in or near the Capital Federal.[26] There is also reason to believe that the bodies of the relatively few desaparecidos who were killed in Bahia Blanca were either dumped at sea or, in a few cases, in the neighboring departments of the Bahia cluster.

Twenty-four departments yielded statistically significant results for H1, H2, or both (H1 and/or H2 accepted). Collectively, this "ACCP" group reported a total of 3,612 NN burials during the 15-year period surveyed. This amounted to 86.8 percent of all NN burials reported from the 103 departments of the analysis series. Part of this high proportion of cases is explained by population size. The median population of the departments of this group (107,674) strongly exceeds those of the ZERO, INSF, and REJT groups. All but 4 of these departments are located within the heavily populated area of Greater Buenos Aires and nearly all were in close proximity of at least one PAC (see below).

Effect of Population Growth

Between 1970 and 1980, the population of Buenos Aires Province grew from 8,774,529 to 10,865,408—an overall increase of 23.8 percent. However, due to heavy migration to larger cities,[27] growth within the province was not uniform. In the 103 departments analyzed here, those of less than 50,000 inhabitants grew an average of 10.2 percent during the decade. In contrast, the increase was 29.7 percent during the same period for departments with populations of 50,000 or more.

Since most of the departments which showed statistically significant increases in NNs during the JUN period also had large populations, it was important to ascertain the influence of population growth on the chi-square test results. When retested, the chi-square scores, as would be expected, were lowered and their concomitant probability levels reduced. Naturally, these reductions were greater in departments that experienced heavy population growth. However, all 24 departments of the ACCP group and the Bahia cluster of the INSF group still yielded significant results for H1 and/or H2. The only changes were in 5 departments that were previously significant for *both* H1 and H2 but, when retested, were significant for only one or the other of the two hypotheses. In summary, population growth does not appear to have been sufficient to account for the higher number of NNs in those departments where significant increases in such burials were observed.

For purposes of further analysis, the four groups of departments described above were reduced to two. The first group, "nSIG," consists of those that displayed no statistically discernible increases in NN burials during the period of Junta rule. It includes all of the departments of the ZERO and REJT groups. In addition, the departments of the original INSF group less the four making up the Bahia cluster were placed in this group, giving it a total of 75 departments. To form the second group, "SIG," the 24 departments of the ACCP group and the four making up the Bahia cluster were combined.

Results

As shown in Table 2, NN burials were nearly equally distributed between the CIV and JUN periods in the nSIG departments. In the SIG group, they nearly doubled during the JUN period.

The data are sufficient to show that the intragroup distribution of NN burials differs strongly in the nSIG and SIG groups. The next step in data analysis consisted of a further study of these intragroup distributions. This was done in order to see whether the SIG group departments conformed with the characteristics that we would expect to observe if they had, indeed, been used to dispose of the bodies of desaparecidos. These characteristics, as noted previously, should consist of parallels between the NN population of the SIG group and that of the desaparecidos in terms of 1) time and 2) place of death, 3) sex, 4) age, and 5) cause of death. These characteristics are treated individually below.

Temporal Distribution

The distribution of NN burials by year for the nSIG and SIG groups is shown in Figure 2a. While nSIG burials remained more or less constant throughout the survey, those of the SIG group more than

TABLE 2. Groups nSIG and SIG by Number of Departments, Median Department Population, and NN Burials by Survey Period

Group	No. of depts.	Median population	CIV	JUN	Total
nSIG	75 (72.8%)	17,673	278 (52.0%)	257 (48.0%)	535 (12.8%)
SIG	28 (27.1%)	70,321	1,227 (33.8%)	2,404 (66.2%)	3,631 (87.2%)
Total	103		1,505	2,661	4,166

doubled during 1976 and 1977, after which they dropped to near normal levels. To hold population differences constant, the rates of NN burials per 100,000 persons were calculated for each group (Figure 2b). In the nSIG group, the rate fluctuated between about 2 to 4 deaths per 100,000 during the entire period, peaking about 1975 to begin a slight but steady decline during the later years. SIG group rates during the CIV and latter part of the JUN periods were also fairly constant at about 4 to 5 deaths per 100,000 but more than tripled to about 14 per 100,000 during the JUN1 period of extreme repression.

If our theory is correct that the SIG departments are those in which substantial numbers of desaparecidos were buried, we should find a strong correlation between the temporal distribution of NNs from these departments and the number of disappearances reported over the same period. To study this relationship, we first needed to calculate the number of "Excess NNs" represented in the overall NN data.

As we have pointed out above, the normal NN caseload would be determined by a number of interacting demographic and environmental factors. It seems reasonable to assume that these factors would remain more or less constant throughout the fifteen years covered by our survey. To determine this baseline, we calculated regression of reported NNs on year for the CIV period. From the regression equation, we could predict the normal number of NNs expected in the SIG group departments during the JUN years. Subtracting these predicted values from the actual number of NNs reported during the JUN period provided an estimate of the number of Excess NNs. This procedure yielded an estimate of 940 Excess NNs during the overall JUN period; 791 (84.2%) of these occurred during the JUN1 period and the remaining 149 (15.8%) during the later JUN2 period (Figure 3a). In addition, there was a modest increase of 55 cases in 1975—the year immediately preceding the onset of Junta rule.

The course of the "Dirty War" is reflected in the statistics on disappearances. The picture emerges from a series of 7,385 cases from the CONADEP files analyzed by the senior author in 1984.[28] Prior to 1975, disappearances that were known or suspected to be politically inspired averaged about 10 per year. In 1970, the first year of the CIV period—when Argentina was still ruled by the military leaders of the Ongania regime—several left-wing armed political groups became active. These included the Montoneros and ERP, the two organizations which, in 1976, became the Junta's prime targets in the "Dirty War." They began a campaign of bombings, kidnappings, as-

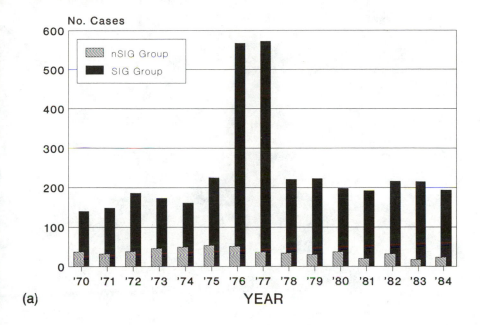

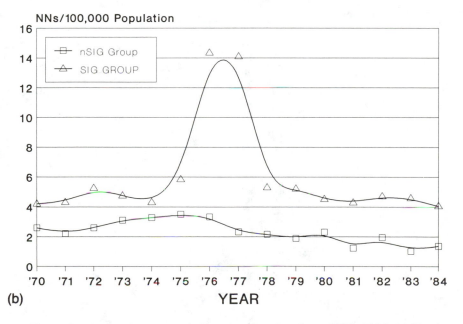

Figure 2. NN deaths reported, Buenos Aires Province, 1970–1984. (a) Total deaths; (b) deaths per 100,000 inhabitants.

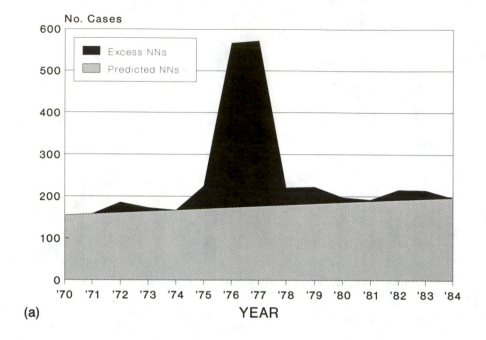

(a)

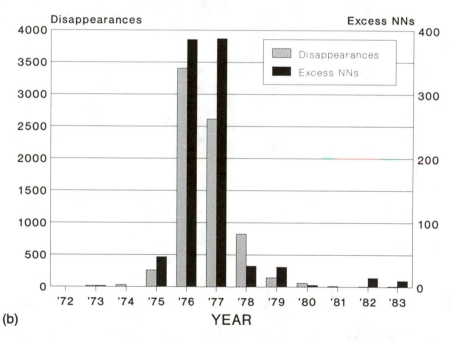

(b)

Figure 3. (a) Excess NN burials; (b) disappearances and excess NNs.

sassinations, and other acts of terrorism targeted primarily against military men, policemen, wealthy business leaders, and sometimes, even their families. They were taken on by ultrarightist groups, such as the paramilitary Argentine Anti-communist Association ("Triple A"), who employed equally violent tactics. While these right-wing, "counter-terrorist" groups operated unofficially, they were secretly subsidized by the military, and many of their people were, in fact, members of the armed forces or police acting in an "off-duty" capacity.

The result was a clandestine civil war between terrorists of the opposing groups. One tactic employed by both sides of this shadowy combat was the kidnapping and murder of members of the opposition whose bodies, often mutilated and showing signs of extreme torture, were found dumped in remote areas. Beginning with a few such disappearances in 1970, the number increased to about 20 per year by 1972.[29]

With the advent of Perón,[30] there was a temporary lull in this clandestine warfare as both sides paused to see in which direction—left or right—he would lead the country. Following his death and the advent of Isabel Perón to the presidency, there was a renewed surge in this underground warfare. It also appears that, during the final, chaotic months of her presidency, the military began to take a more active role in countering leftist terrorism. To some extent, this meant that the policemen and members of the armed forces on the counter-terrorist squads, while still operating covertly, were sanctioned to operate in an "on-duty" capacity. Some of the earlier clandestine detention centers were also established about this time. Reflecting this, the CONADEP files show a sharp increase in the number of reported disappearances during the six months prior to the Junta takeover on March 24, 1976. It is apparent that during these months the military developed and tested its operational plans and tactics for the full-fledged "Dirty War," perfecting a machine which, with terrifying efficiency, roared into action during the first hours of the Junta rule. In effect, on March 24 the mufti-clad death squads stepped into a closet and emerged in full uniform.

It is likely that a very high percentage of the pre-1976 abductees were Montonero or ERP members targeted in reprisal for their frequent assassinations of policemen, military servicemen, and, sometimes, even their families. When the Junta formally assumed power in 1976, the apparatus of repression was given full reign and disappearances skyrocketed so that the cases occurring in 1976 and 1977 comprised 81.5 percent of the sample. With the end of the most intense phase of the "Dirty War" in 1978, the number of disappearances dropped abruptly and continued to dwindle throughout the remaining six years of Junta rule.

The strong correspondence between the temporal distributions of Excess NNs and that of reported disappearances is shown in Figure 3b and by a high statistical correlation between the two variables ($r = .952$, $p < .001$, 13 df). During 1977, the second year of the JUN1 period, disappearances declined from the 1976 high of about 3,400 to about 2,600 cases; in contrast, the number of Excess NNs remained virtually constant. This relationship apparently reflects the overall lag time of several weeks or months between abduction and execution.

While the numbers are much smaller, the relationship between disappearances and Excess NNs during the JUN2 period is also interesting. Disappearances virtually ceased by 1981 and there was a similar decline in Excess NNs. However, in 1982 and 1983—the last two years of Junta rule, during which worsening economic conditions and the debacle in the Malvinas made it clear to the Junta leaders that their days of rule were numbered—there was a modest rise in the number of Excess NNs with no concomitant increase in disappearances. During this same period, the Junta leaders, concerned that they might eventually be called to account for their crimes, are known to have ordered the systematic destruction of material evidence.[31] This not only included documents such as lists and records of abductions and executions but physical evidence such as the detention centers which were often remodeled and converted to more innocuous uses and, in some cases, leveled completely. The modest upsurge of Excess NN burials reported during those same years suggests that, along with documentary and physical evidence, the few detainees who had managed to survive were also destroyed in order to eliminate future witnesses.

Geographic Relationships Between SIG Departments and PACs

According to Mittelbach,[32] 65 PACs (Prisoner Assessment Centers) were located in Buenos Aires Province and 11 in the Capital Federal. Although the Argentine Army had overall command responsibility for the conduct of the Dirty War, PACs were operated by all three military services and various civil police agencies. Some were located in federal or provincial penal institutions. A few had no known affiliation and were presumably operated by covert intelligence groups of the police or military. As shown in Figure 4a, nearly half of the known PACs were under police jurisdiction, making it clear that, during the period of Junta government, the civil police forces functioned as a "fourth arm" of the military.

Of the 76 Provincial and Capital Federal PACs listed by Mittelbach, the approximate periods of operation are known for forty-nine. The earliest two, "Pozo de Quilmes" and "El Banco," located in the departments of Quilmes and La Mantanza, respectively, opened in 1975. The last PAC, located in the Escuela Mecánica de Armada, near downtown Buenos Aires, was closed in 1983. The distribution of PACs by year is shown in Figure 4b. As might be expected, the general pattern corresponds closely to that of disappearances and Excess NNs (Figures 3a,b).

The journey of a typical desaparecido consisted of two legs: antemortem and postmortem. The antemortem leg began at the place of abduction and ended with death from torture or execution in or near a PAC. The postmortem leg covered the distance between the place of execution and the grave. Generally, the antemortem leg was much longer in both time and distance. As noted previously, detainees were taken first to Transient Centers which were widely scattered throughout the country. From these, they were transferred to the more centralized PACs and, often, through a series of PACs before finally being executed. Based on survivor accounts and other data, the general direction of flow was from outlying PACs to more central ones in or around the city of Buenos Aires. The transfers often covered several hundred kilometers. For example, we have previously noted that some abductees from the Bahia Blanca area were transferred to PACs located near Buenos Aires, a distance of around 600 kilometers.

The distance between execution and grave, in contrast, was apt to be relatively short. The extremes may be illustrated by two cases currently under investigation by the Argentine Forensic Anthropology Team (AFAT) and the senior author. The first involves the exhumation of a series of NN graves in the municipal cemetery of Avellaneda, a heavily populated department bordering the Capital Federal. The cemetery's records reveal that between 1970 and 1984, a total of 633 NNs were buried there. Of these, 244 (38.6%) were received during the CIV period. During the JUN period, 215 NNs (34.0%) were received during JUN1 (H1 accepted) and 174 (27.5%) during JUN2 (H2 rejected). From survivor interviews and documentary evidence, the AFAT team has been able to establish that nearly all of the desaparecidos buried in Avellaneda cemetery were executed at "Pozo de Bánfield," a PAC located 8 kilometers away in the neighboring department of Lomo de Zamora. Incidentally, among the list of possible

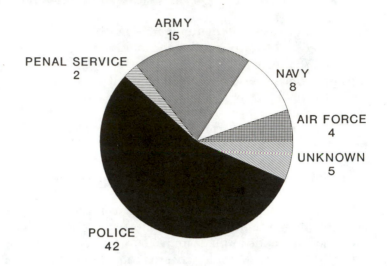

ARMY
15

PENAL SERVICE
2

NAVY
8

AIR FORCE
4

UNKNOWN
5

POLICE
42

(a)   • Data from Mittelbach, 1985.

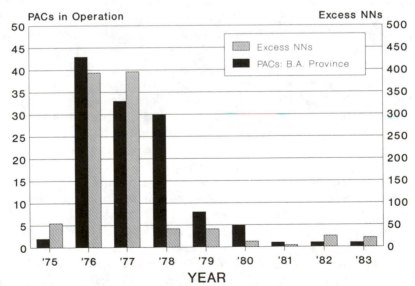

PACs in Operation

Excess NNs

Excess NNs

PACs: B.A. Province

YEAR

(b)   • Operational dates of 28 additional
PACs are not known. (Mittelbach, 1985).

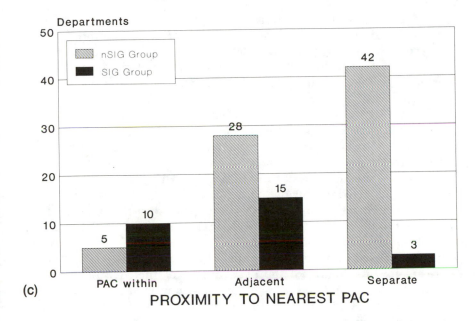

Figure 4. (a) Operational distribution of PACs, Buenos Aires Province and Capital Federal; (b) operating PACs and excess NNs; (c) geographic relationships of PACs to nSIG and SIG departments.

desaparecidos in this cemetery, a number disappeared from Bahia Blanca (see above).

The second case involves a group of 28 skeletons exhumed in 1986 by the senior author and the AFAT team in Derqui cemetery in the department of Pilar. They were found in a field near Derqui on August 20, 1976, and, after a perfunctory investigation by local police, signed out as unidentified and buried as NNs. Subsequent investigation established that they were detainees held in the secret detention center in the Security Headquarters of the Argentinian Federal Police in downtown Buenos Aires. They were removed from the detention center on the night of August 19, transported in police vehicles to the field where the bodies were found and executed on the spot. The distance between the detention center and the point of execution is approximately 46 kilometers.

These cases, as well as others, indicate that there was usually a fairly close geographic relationship between PACs and the cemeteries where desaparecidos were buried. Unfortunately, the evidence is not always as clear-cut as in the Avellaneda and Derqui cases. For instance, it appears that victims from a single detention center may have been distributed to several cemeteries and, conversely, one cemetery may have received desaparecido bodies from more than one center. However, the sparse data so far available indicates that bodies were usually dumped or taken directly to the morgues of departments within a radius of about 50 kilometers of the detention center.

If, as we have theorized, the SIG departments are those in which large numbers of desaparecidos are buried as NNs, we should expect them to show a closer geographic relationship to PACs than those in which no desaparecidos are buried. To study this relationship, we first mapped the locations of the 49 PACs known to have operated in Buenos Aires Province during the period of Junta rule. Each department was then assigned to one of three groups on the basis of its proximity to the nearest PAC: 1) PAC *within* department; 2) *adjacent* to another department within which a PAC was located; and 3) *separated* from nearest PAC by at least one other department. The difference in the distribution of the departments of the SIG and nSIG groups when classified in this manner is shown in Figure 4c. Twenty-five (89%) of the 28 SIG departments either contained PACs (36%) or bordered departments in which PACs were located (54%). In contrast, only 5 (7%) of the nSIG departments contained PACs and 42 (56%) were separated from the nearest PAC by at least one other department. Chi-square analysis of these data is significant (chi^2 = 22.67, p < .001, 2 df).

Sex of Desaparecidos and NNs

At the time the CONADEP data were analyzed, exact age data were available for only 5,849 individuals. Of these, 28.8 percent (1,687) were females. When the percentage of females is plotted against age (Figure 5a), there appears to be a gradual decline from about 40 percent female in the younger age groups to about 20 percent among the middle-aged, after which it again rises to reach about 30 percent among older individuals. Although the numbers at the extremes are quite small, this general trend probably reflects a real phenomenon in the pattern of disappearances. Most persons who were specifically targeted for disappearances were in their 20s and 30s and most were men. However, in many cases, in addition to the targeted victim, his or her whole family—including children and grandparents—were also abducted. Naturally, the sex ratio of these "non-targeted" family members would be closer to the 50:50 population norm. The fact that it does not quite reach this norm suggests that the abductors paid some deference to females in selecting family members for abduction; that is, younger girls and elderly women were less likely to be taken with the rest of the family.

Of the 3,270 NNs of known sex, 455 (13.9%) were females. There was a higher percentage of females reported from departments of the SIG group (15.4%) than the nSIG group (6.4%). When the sex distributions of the two groups are compared, this difference was found to be statistically significant (chi^2 = 21.72, p < .001, 1 df). The most likely reason for this is that women are more apt to be represented in the elderly, transient, and indigent population that normally supplies a high percentage of all NNs in more urbanized areas such as the majority of the SIG group departments.

Of more interest here is the intra-group distribution of the sexes by survey period (Table 3). Although both groups experienced some proportionate increases in female NNs during the overall JUN period, it was not statistically significant in the nSIG group. In the SIG group, the relative increase in the number of females was strongly significant during the JUN1 period but not for the JUN2 period. Figure 5b shows both the number of female NNs and the percentage of females reported annually in the SIG group during the period of the survey. Prior to the JUN period, the percentage of female NNs ranged from about 10 percent to 15 percent; during the JUN1 period it rose to about 20 percent and then declined to near normal levels during JUN2. This finding of a significant shift toward a greater proportion of females among the NNs of the SIG group thus supports the hypothesis that the departments were those in which large numbers of desaparecidos are buried.

TABLE 3. Distribution of NN Burials by Sex and Period, nSIG and SIG Department Groups

Group	Period	Female	Male	Percent female	Chi^2	p (2df)
nSIG	CIV	8	182	4.2		
	JUN: JUN1	5	46	9.8	2.465	
	JUN2	11	122	8.3	2.330	
Total		24	350	6.4		
SIG	CIV	104	726	12.5		
	JUN: JUN1	187	753	19.9	17.397	< .001
	JUN2	140	886	13.6	0.501	
Total		431	2365	15.4		

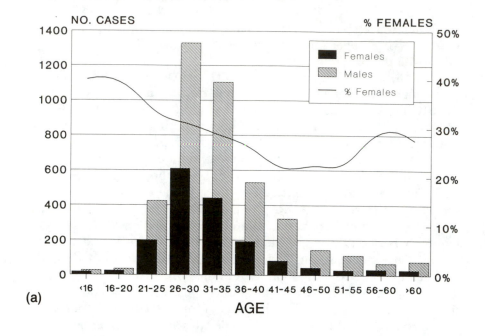

(a)

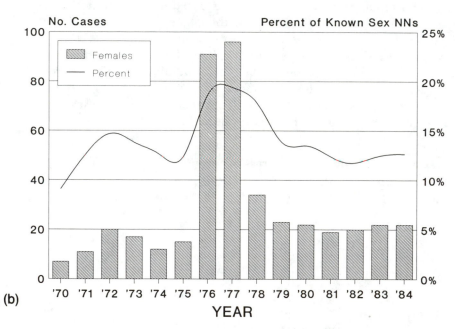

(b)

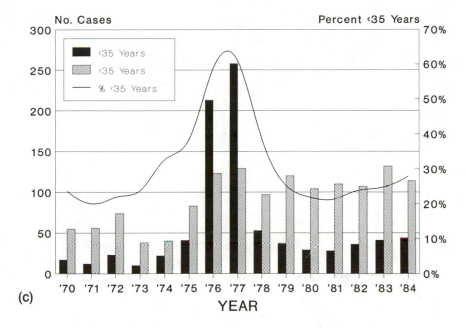

(c)

Figure 5. (a) Age and sex of desaparecidos, Argentina, 1973–1983; (b) SIG group, female NNs; (c) age of NNs in SIG group.

Age of Desaparecidos and NNs

Among 5,849 desaparecidos whose cases were reviewed in 1984, the mean age for both sexes was in the mid-twenties with males (28.7 yrs.) averaging about a year older than females (27.6 yrs.). The distribution is skewed toward younger individuals (Figure 5c) so that the median ages are about two years lower than the means in both sexes (females, 26.0 yrs.; males, 25.6 yrs.). Persons younger than 35 years made up 83.9 percent of the subseries.

As noted previously, we generally expect older persons to make up a high percentage of bodies that are eventually buried as unidentified. That this was true for the NN population in Argentina prior to the Junta takeover is shown in Table 4, which shows the distribution of age by survey sub-periods. During the CIV period, about 75 percent of all NNs were older than 35 at the time of death in both the nSIG and SIG groups. In the nSIG group, the proportion remained about the same during the JUN1 and JUN2 periods. However, in the SIG group, there was a fourfold increase in 20–35-year-olds during the JUN1 period and, also, a more modest increase of NNs in the 14–20-year-old category. Chi-square tests comparing the age

TABLE 4. Age Distribution of NN Burials by Period for nSIG and SIG Department Groups

Group			CIV		JUN1		JUN2	
Age		N	n	%	n	%	n	%
nSIG group								
< 35	b– 3	11	1	0.8	0	0.0	10	9.3
	4–13	1	1	0.8	0	0.0	0	0.0
	14–20	3	3	2.5	0	0.0	0	0.0
	21–35	41	22	18.6	5	16.7	14	13.1
> 35		199	91	77.1	25	83.	83	77.6
Total		255	118	100.0	30	100.0	107	100.0
SIG group								
< 35	b– 3	118	45	7.2	9	1.3	64	7.1
	3–13	14	4	0.6	3	0.4	7	0.8
	14–20	92	23	3.7	53	7.4*	16	1.8
	21–35	640	97	15.4	402	55.9*	141	15.7
> 35		1,382	460	73.1	252	35.6	670	74.6
Total		2,246	629	100.0	719	100.0	898	100.0

* $n < .001$ in chi² test comparing distribution of younger age group with "> 35 year" age group.

distribution of these two younger groups with those over 35 were significant at the 0.001 probability level (Table 4). In the SIG group, the proportion of younger individuals returned to normal levels during JUN2. Figure 5c shows the combined younger age groups and the "> 35 year" group plotted against year. The steep rise in younger NNs relative to older individuals is also shown by plotting younger NNs as a percentage of all cases. It is evident that, within the SIG group, there was a shift toward younger NNs during JUN1.

Causes of Death Among Desaparecidos and NNs

In the NN survey, the many specific causes of death listed in the cemetery records were lumped into several broad groups of related causes. This was done in order to minimize the time and effort on the part of the respondent and to facilitate initial data analysis. In the future, as specific cemeteries come under direct scrutiny, their death records can be reviewed in more detail prior to initiating large-scale exhumations of their NN burials. In this study, we will focus on two survey categories most likely to have been the cause of death in desaparecidos: gunshot wounds and cranial trauma. The latter category includes all causes involving head injuries ("cerebral hemorrhage," "cerebro-cranial destruction," "massive cerebral trauma," etc.).

According to the available witness evidence, while some desaparecidos succumbed under torture or died from other causes related to the physical neglect and mistreatment experienced during detention, the majority survived these ordeals to be finally executed. This is borne out by the several hundred known desaparecido skeletons examined to date by the senior author and the AFAT team. Within this series, all but three displayed clear-cut evidence of perimortem gunshot wounds—mostly to the head.

We have previously pointed out that many police surgeons listed only proximate causes in issuing death certificates of gunshot victims. This was particularly true of cases involving wounds of the head where proximate causes such as those mentioned above were frequently encountered. Therefore, we suspect that many of the NNs whose deaths are attributed to these causes were actually gunshot victims and, hence, very likely to have been executed desaparecidos. If departments of the SIG group were those in which desaparecidos were buried as NNs, we would expect to see an increase both in causes of death listed as gunshot wounds and in those due to cranial trauma during the period of Junta rule.

To test this hypothesis, we compared the incidence of deaths due to both these categories with a third survey category "Cardiac," which included all diagnoses related to either acute or chronic heart disease. The incidence of NN deaths attributed to heart disease showed a linear increase throughout the fifteen-year survey period ($r = .912$, 13 df). This steady rise in cardiac deaths among NNs is most likely a reflection of a similar trend in the general population.[33] It appears reasonable, therefore, to assume that the majority of cardiac-related deaths among NNs of the SIG group were from the subpopulation of "normal" NNs, that is, "non-disappeared." If the incidence of gunshot and cranial trauma cases within this group shows an increase *relative* to the incidence of cardiac deaths, it would help support the theory that these departments represent those in which substantial numbers of desaparecidos were buried. As a test of this hypothesis, chi-square tests were performed comparing the distribution of gunshot wounds and cranial trauma cases with cardiac cases during the CIV, JUN1, and JUN2 periods. The results are shown in Table 5.

Table 5 shows that cardiac-related deaths averaged about 75 percent of all cases of the three categories in the nSIG group throughout the survey period. Of the remaining cases in this group, deaths from cranial trauma made up about 20 percent and those from gunshot wounds slightly less than 5 percent during all three sub-periods of

TABLE 5. Distribution of Deaths Attributed to Gunshot Wounds, Cranial Trauma, and Cardiac Disorders Among NNs of the nSIG and SIG Groups

Cause of Death	N	CIV		JUN1		JUN2	
		n	%	n	%	n	%
nSIG group							
Gunshot wound	8	4	3.6	1	5.0	3	4.3
Cranial trauma	42	26	23.6	5	25.0	11	15.9
Cardiac-related	149	80	72.7	14	70.0	55	79.7
Total	199	110	100.0	20	100.0	69	100.0
SIG group							
Gunshot wound	334	23	5.5	286	52.8[a]	25	4.4
Cranial trauma	258	83	19.9	103	19.0[a]	72	12.8
Cardiac-related	931	311	74.6	153	28.2	467	82.8
Total	1,523	417	100.0	542	100.0	564	100.0

[a] Chi^2 comparing cause group with cardiac-related deaths during the CIV and JUN sub-periods significant at the .001 probability level with 2 df.

the survey. When compared to cardiac-related deaths, there were no statistically significant increases in these categories during either the JUN1 or JUN2 periods.

In the SIG group, the distribution of deaths by these causes was remarkably similar to those of the nSIG group during the CIV period. However, during the JUN1 period, deaths from gunshot wounds made up more than 50 percent of the reported NNs and a more modest rise was seen in cases of cranial trauma; in both instances, the increases relative to cardiac-related deaths were statistically significant. During the JUN2 period, the incidence of cases from both causes declined to about the same levels observed during the CIV period. Figures 6a,b show the annual distribution of NN deaths by gunshot wounds and cranial trauma in the SIG group by the number of cases reported and as ratios to the number of cardiac-related deaths.

Summary and Conclusions

In 28 (27.2%) of the 103 departments surveyed in this report, there were statistically significant increases in the number of NN burials during the period of Junta government. Nearly all the departments in this group were located close to the "Prisoner Assessment Centers" where it is known that most of the desaparecidos were executed. Within this group of departments, there was a shift toward a higher

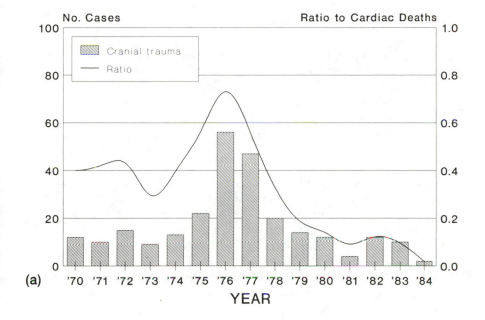

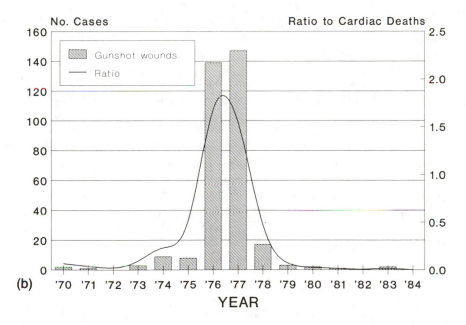

Figure 6. NN deaths in SIG group due to (a) cranial trauma; (b) gunshot wounds.

proportion of female and young NNs during the period of Junta government. These shifts were in a direction approaching that of the corresponding proportions for the desaparecidos, most of whom were in their 20s and about 30 percent of whom were female. In addition, the Junta period was marked by a distinct increase in the number of NNs whose deaths were attributed to gunshot wounds that were also the leading cause of death among the desaparecidos. Finally, the Junta period was marked by a strong correlation between the temporal distribution of NN deaths and reported disappearances.

Taken together, the above findings lead to the conclusion that these departments harbor a substantial number of desaparecidos buried as NNs. This number can be roughly approximated by subtracting the number of NNs that would normally be expected from the total observed during the period of Junta rule. Calculated in this manner, we conclude that between 900 and 1,000 desaparecidos lie buried in the cemeteries of these departments. This would amount to slightly over 10 percent of the nearly 9,000 persons reported to have been "disappeared" during the Dirty War.

Those desaparecidos whose bones are still in their original graves take on a particular significance in the ongoing judicial investigations of human rights violations under Junta rule. Unlike those disposed of by other means such as cremation or dumping at sea, they lie as well-preserved skeletons in individual graves which can be located by careful perusal of public cemetery records. Such graves, when excavated by using the same techniques long employed by archaeologists in exhuming prehistoric burials, yield a complete skeleton, including its dentition. When adequate antemortem data such as dental records and clinical x-rays are available for comparison, the victim can be positively identified. Evidence of the cause of death, such as bullet wounds, is often present. Ballistic evidence in the form of bullets, shotgun pellets, and cartridge cases may also be recovered. Signs of physical abuse and torture inflicted during the period of detention can sometimes be inferred from the presence of poorly healed or healing fractures. Taken together, such findings can help build a strong and objective body of evidence useful to the courts.

Notes

1. The Junta consisted of the Commanders-in-Chief (CIC) of the Army, Navy, and Air Force. During its eight-year reign, its composition changed from time to time. These changes were dictated, in part, by normal rotation of the CIC posts and, also, by forced resignations resulting from internal

power struggles. By 1983, when Junta rule ended, nine high-ranking officers had, at one time or another, served as their service arm's CIC and, hence, as members of the Junta.

2. Neither the Montoneros nor ERP were able to muster much support from the Argentine working classes. Instead, the majority of their recruits were university students, professors, lawyers, journalists, and other members of the intellectual elite.

3. Martin Edwin Andersen, "Dirty Secrets of the 'Dirty War'," *The Nation,* 13 March 1989; Ronald Dworkin, "Introduction" to *Never Again* (New York: Farrar Strauss and Giroux, 1986), English translation of CONADEP (Argentine National Commission on the Disappeared), *Nunca Más, Informe de la Comisión Nacional sobre la Desaparición de Personas,* ed. Ernest Sabato (Buenos Aires: Editorial Universitaria de Buenos Aires, 1984).

4. John Simpson and Jana Bennet, *The Disappeared and the Mothers of the Plaza* (New York: St. Martin's Press, 1985), p. 66.

5. CONADEP, *Nunca Más* (note 3); Estimates of the number of desaparecidos circulated during and immediately after the period of Junta rule ranged as high as 100,000. Somehow, the world press centered on the estimate of 30,000 and, today, this figure is still widely (and erroneously) cited as an "official" count. On the other hand, CONADEP's original listing of 8,961 disappearances documented by September 1984 is admittedly a minimum since, undoubtedly, some cases went unreported. However, it is significant that in the five years since the CONADEP report was issued, only 118 additional cases have surfaced, bringing the total to 9,079.

6. Ibid., pp. 293–302. On the authors' forensic work, see Christopher Joyce and Eric Stover, *Witnesses from the Grave, The Stories Bones Tell* (Boston: Little Brown and Company, 1991).

7. CONADEP, *Nunca Más,* pp. 54–223; Federico Mittelbach, *Informe sobre Desaparecidos* (Buenos Aires: Ediciónes de la Urraca, 1984).

8. CONADEP, *Nunca Más,* pp. 20–390 passim.

9. Cornelis A. Kolff and Roscius N. Doan, "Victims of Torture: Two Testimonies," in *The Breaking of Bodies and Minds: Torture, Psychiatric Abuse, and the Health Professions,* ed. Eric Stover and Elena O. Nightingale (New York: W. H. Freeman, 1985), pp. 45–57.

10. CONADEP, *Nunca Más,* pp. 299–323; Julio E. Nosiglia, *Botin de Guerra* [War Booty] (Buenos Aires: Tierra Fértil, 1985).

11. Best translated as "No Name," the Spanish equivalent of "John (or Jane) Doe."

12. CONADEP, *Nunca Más,* pp. 232–246.

13. Rep. Arg. Instituto Nacional de Estadística y Censos. *Censo Nacional de Población, Familias y Viviendas—1970* (Buenos Aires: Secretaria del Consejo Nacional de Desarrollo, 1971); Rep. Arg. Instituto Nacional de Estadística y Censos. *Censo Nacional de Población y Vivienda 1980* (Buenos Aires: Secretaria de Planificación, 1981); Provincial and departmental population figures given in this report represent estimates for the year 1977—the midpoint year of the fifteen years covered in this survey, 1970–1984. They were derived from the 1970 and 1980 official census statistics and assume linear growth during the decade.

14. Throughout the remainder of this report, the four independent municipalities will also be referred to as departments.

15. The figures given here for the number of desaparecidos in the

provinces and Buenos Aires Province departments are approximations extrapolated from a series of 5,083 CONADEP cases in which the place of disappearance was fully documented.

16. CONADEP, *Nunca Más*, pp. 238–239.

17. In Argentina, as in many Latin countries, families of the dead are required to pay an annual grave tax which goes toward the maintenance of the cemetery. If these payments are allowed to fall in arrears by more than five years, the bones are liable to disinterment and transfer to an ossuary. Having no known next-of-kin to pay their grave tax, NN skeletons are prime candidates for such secondary burials.

18. CONADEP, *Nunca Más*, pp. 228–229.

19. Alvan R. Feinstein, "Scientific Standards in Epidemiologic Studies of the Menace of Daily Life," *Science* 242 (1988): 1257–1263.

20. Lester Adelson, *The Pathology of Homicide* (Springfield, IL: Charles C. Thomas, 1981), 15–17.

21. For example, in one series of 124 cases from Boulogne Cemetery (Department of San Isidro) the senior author both examined the exhumed desaparecido skeletons and reviewed the original death certificates. Although over 90 percent of the skeletons showed clear evidence of death by gunshot wounds, in only about half of the cases was this indicated on the death certificates. Among the remainder, given causes included "massive cranial trauma," "acute hemorrhage," "cerebral hemorrhage," and "hypovolemic shock."

22. We have used the term *Civil* (CIV) to designate this period in order to distinguish it from the 1976–83 period of Junta rule. However, it should be noted that during the first years of the *Civil* period (1970–72), Argentina was governed by the military. They had taken power in June 1966 when, in a coup directed by General Juan Carlos Onganía, constitutionally elected President Arturo Illia was deposed. The military agreed to free elections in March 1973, and in the following May President Héctor Cámpora took office. A few months later, General Juan Perón was allowed to return from European exile and was elected to the presidency in September 1973. His second wife, Isabela, who was elected vice-president, assumed office upon Perón's death in July 1974. She governed until displaced by the military coup of March 1976.

23. CONADEP, *Nunca Más*, pp. 90–104 passim.

24. Ibid., p. 108.

25. Ibid., pp. 204–208.

26. Mercedes Doretti, personal communication, 1989.

27. Ricardo Gomez Insausti, "La Región Metropolitana de Buenos Aires: Una Desproporcionada Concentración" [The Metropolitan Region of Buenos Aires: a Disproportionate Concentration]. In *La Argentina: Geografía general y los marcos regionales*, ed. Juan A. Roccatagliata (Buenos Aires: Planeta, 1988), pp. 445–467.

28. Clyde Collins Snow, "Sex, Age and Other Statistical Characteristics of the *Desaparecidos*: A Report to Ing. Fernando Long," *Comisión Nacional sobre la Desaparición de Personas* (unpublished, 1984); This series consisted of those disappearances which had been reported to CONADEP by June 15, 1984. It comprises 82.4 percent of the 8,961 disappearances eventually reported. While not a random sample in the strictest sense, it is probably a fair representation of the total desaparecido population in terms of dates of disappearance, sex, and age.

29. David Rock, *Argentina 1516–1982: From Spanish Colonization to the Falklands War* (Berkeley: University of California Press, 1985), pp. 355–356.

30. General Juan Perón was first elected president in 1946. With his charismatic second wife, Eva, he evolved that peculiarly Argentine blend of populism, nationalism, and state socialism that is his political legacy. Eva died in 1952, shortly after his second election. Forced out by a military coup in 1955, he lived in exile until 1973 when he was once again allowed to return to Argentina. Choosing his third wife, María Estela Martínez de Perón ("Isabel"), as his running mate, he was, at the age of 78, overwhelmingly elected to his third term in 1973. While Peronism was rejuvenated, Perón was not, and he died seven months after taking office.

31. CONADEP, *Nunca Más*, pp. 9, 78, and 452–453.

32. Mittelbach, *Informe sobre Desaparecidos* (note 7), pp. 20–118 passim.

33. Irene Martinez, personal communication, 1989.

STANDARDS-BASED DATA

Chapter 14
New Patterns of Oppression: An Updated Analysis of Human Rights Data

David L. Banks

Banks[1] describes an application of statistical methods for exploratory analysis to human rights data collected by Gastil[2] and Humana[3] in 1983. Since then, both researchers have produced new sets of human rights ratings for all major nations, current as of January 1, 1986.[4] The primary purpose of this chapter is to extend the original analysis to their more recent data. A secondary purpose is to compare the 1983 and 1986 data and analyses with respect to both changes over time and the stability of interpretations. As with the original analysis, the human rights data are augmented by standard social and economic indices; this allows the investigation of societal factors associated with specific types of human rights behavior.

The major statistical techniques employed are variable clustering, hierarchical agglomerative cluster analysis, k-means cluster analysis, factor analysis, variable clustering, stepwise discriminant analysis, and classification and regression tree methodology. SAS procedures are used for the hierarchical agglomerative cluster analysis; CART[5] is used for the generation of the classification and regression trees. All other analyses use BMDP routines. Insofar as is reasonable, the software and methods correspond to those employed in the original analysis;[6] however, improved theory and better algorithms have suggested some changes. For example, work in Milligan and Cooper[7] suggests that the SAS procedure for hierarchical clustering offers more useful diagnostics than are provided by the BMDP software, so this study incorporates that analysis.

The first section of the chapter examines the nature of the data collected by both Gastil and Humana, at both time periods. It identifies nations that are not scored consistently and points up changes in the rating procedures between the 1983 and 1986 evaluations. It also describes the additional social and economic indices that have been combined with the human rights data. The following section develops a variety of cluster analyses of the human rights data and compares the results from different time periods and different clustering algorithms. A discussion follows on three different approaches to variable reduction. The emphasis is on discovering a smaller set of indexes that captures most of the information in the larger data sets. The next section presents several classification and regression trees and interprets the results. The last section summarizes the general conclusions of the entire chapter and places the results in the context of previous research.

The Data

Any attempt to measure freedom raises difficult problems at the boundaries of psychology, anthropology, and philosophy. Some argue that the concept of human rights is ethnocentric or idiosyncratic, while others assert that there is a reasonably consistent cross-cultural standard.[8] For statisticians, the key question is whether separate ratings are mutually consistent (i.e., replicable). If so, then there is some operational understanding of human rights that can be formally investigated. For this study, we compare the ratings of Gastil and Humana to check for consistency. The strong association discovered between the ratings indicates that both researchers are measuring essentially the same phenomenon, at least within the conceptual constraints of a common Western *Weltanschauung*.

Gastil is the former Director of the Comparative Survey of Freedom at Freedom House; this organization has been collecting and publishing human rights assessments since 1973. Their work has been criticized by Scoble and Wiseberg[9] and McCamant,[10] who maintain that the Freedom House ratings are biased in favor of Western capitalist democracies, and that their scores are not explicitly derived, but rather reflect a variety of implicit dimensions (e.g., severity of oppression, frequency of oppression, etc.). Despite this, most of the ratings have not aroused controversy and the accuracy seems sufficient for the corroborative use this study requires.

Humana has produced two sets of human rights ratings; the first contains ratings for 74 nations, and the second rates 89. His work is not subsidized by any group or government. The chief critics of his work are Stohl, Carleton, Lopez, and Samuels,[11] who consider his methodological training inadequate and his investigative techniques vague. But Humana's 1986 *World Human Rights Guide* responds to these points and provides greater detail on his methods. This additional background indicates that his work is not hopelessly naive and is quite possibly superior to that of Freedom House. His chief virtue is that he rates very specific freedoms, in contrast to Gastil's practice of making impressionistic ratings of political and civil rights.

The ratings given by Gastil and Humana are not directly commensurate. Gastil scores the nations on each of two seven-point scales, one pertaining to civil rights and one to political rights. Civil rights refer to freedom to practice religion, marry whom one wishes, join trade unions, travel within the country, and so forth. Political rights refer to voting privileges, active opposition parties, diverse representation, lack of excessive propaganda, and so forth.[12] In contrast, Humana's 1983 data set used forty different four-point scales, scoring the variety of freedoms listed in Table 1.

Notice that Humana does not rate the amount of leisure time, medical security, or guaranteed income, which many consider to be fundamental human rights;[13] even so, the scope is very broad. Also, some of Humana's scales appear binary (MILTSERV) or continuous (COSTFORCE), but the ratings nonetheless informatively use a four-point scale. For MILTSERV, he takes account of the duration of obligation and flexibility of service; for COSTFORCE, he divides the numbers into four ordered categories.

Humana's 1986 dataset is substantially similar to the 1983 dataset, with the modifications indicated in Table 2. Here the first 11 entries represent scales that were in the 1983 study but excluded in the 1986 study; the next 11 entries are new to the 1986 study. Otherwise, the scales are exactly as before.

The primary reason for changing the 1986 entries was to tie the types of freedom more closely to those set forth in the articles of the Universal Declaration of Human Rights.[14] This led to the deletion of ALCOHOL, CONCTOB, COSTFORCE, FORCE, MILTSERV, and WEAPON. Other freedoms were replaced by more specific descriptions; for example, WOMEN was replaced by LEGFEM and SOCFEM; DIVORCE was replaced by EQMARRY. These changes were undertaken in response to criticisms of the 1983 study;[15] however, these changes have slightly reduced the breadth of the 1986 survey as compared with the 1983 survey.

TABLE 1. Humana's 40 Rights/Freedoms in 1983

ABORTION:	Right to early abortion.
ALCOHOL:	Right to purchase and drink alcohol.
ANTIGOV:	Severity of punishment for nonviolent antigovernment activities.
ANYRELGN:	Freedom to practice any religion.
ASSEMBLY:	Right of peaceful assembly and association.
BANNDLIT:	Severity of punishment for possession of banned literature.
BOOK:	Freedom of book publishing.
BRTHCONT:	Right to use contraceptive pills and devices.
CAPPUN:	Prevalence of capital punishment by the state.
CONCTOB:	Severity of punishment for refusing compulsory national service.
COSTFORC:	Proportion of national income spent on police and military.
DETENTN:	Freedom from police detention without charge.
DIVORCE:	Right of divorce (for men and women equally).
ETHLANG:	Right to publish and educate in ethnic languages.
FORCE:	Ratio of police and military to citizens, on a four-point scale.
FREEART:	Freedom from state policies to control artistic works.
FREEINFO:	Right to seek information and teach ideas.
FREEMAIL:	Freedom from censorship of mail.
FREEPRESS:	Freedom from political press censorship.
FREEWORK:	Freedom from directed employment or work permits.
HOMOSEX:	Right to practice homosexuality between consenting adults.
INDCOURT:	Right of all courts to total independence.
KEEPCIT:	Freedom from deprivation of nationality.
MILTSERV:	Freedom from compulsory military service.
MIXMARR:	Right of interracial, interreligious, and civil marriage.
MOVEIN:	Freedom of movement within own country.
MOVEOUT:	Freedom to leave own country.
NOIDEOL:	Freedom from compulsory religion or state ideology in schools.
NOSEARCH:	Freedom from police searches of home without warrant.
POLTCOPP:	Right of peaceful political opposition.
PRVGUILT:	Right of assumption of innocence until guilt proved.
PUBTRIAL:	Freedom from civilian trials in secret.
PUNISH:	Freedom from corporal punishment by state.
QKTRIAL:	Right of accused to be promptly brought before judge or court.
SLAVLABR:	Freedom from serfdom, slavery, or forced child labor.
TORTURE:	Freedom from torture or coercion by state.
TVRADIO:	Freedom of radio and television broadcasts from state control.
UNION:	Right of independent trade unions.
WEAPON:	Lethality of weapons normally carried by civil police.
WOMEN:	Right of women to equality.

TABLE 2. Changes to Humana's 40 Rights/Freedoms in 1986

The following 11 variables appear in the 1983 data
but not in the 1986 data.

ABORTION: Right to early abortion.
ALCOHOL: Right to purchase and drink alcohol.
ANTIGOV: Severity of punishment for nonviolent antigovernment activities.
BANNDLIT: Severity of punishment for possession of banned literature.
CONCTOB: Severity of punishment for refusing compulsory national service.
COSTFORCE: Proportion of national income spent on police and military.
DIVORCE: Right of divorce (for men and women equally).
FORCE: Ratio of police and military to citizens.
MILTSERV: Freedom from compulsory military service.
WEAPON: Lethality of weapons normally carried by civil police.
WOMEN: Right of women to equality.

The following 11 variables appear in the 1986 data
but not in the 1983 data.

BALLOT: Right to multiparty elections by secret ballot.
MURDER: Freedom from extrajudicial killings or 'disappearances'.
EQMARRY: Equality of sexes in marriage and during divorce.
ETHEQ: Right of ethnic minorities to social and legal equality.
LEGALAID: Right of accused to free legal aid when necessary.
LEGFEM: Right of women to political and legal equality.
MEMBER: Freedom from compulsory membership in state parties.
MONITOR: Freedom to monitor human rights violations.
PAPER: Freedom for independent newspaper publishing.
PROPERTY: Freedom from arbitrary seizure of personal property.
SOCFEM: Right of women to social and economic equality.

A more general criticism is that neither Humana nor Gastil provides much detail on their coding protocol, partly to protect local informants and partly because the scoring entails subjective judgments and Delphi methods. Nonetheless, these datasets are the best available, and the broad agreement between them, as shown in Tables 3–6, suggests that their quality is good.

To measure Gastil and Humana's agreement in 1983, we sum Humana's variables ABORTION, ALCOHOL, ANYRELGN, BRTHCONT, ASSEMBLY, DETENTN, DIVORCE, ETHLANG, FREEART, FREEINFO, FREEWORK, HOMOSEX, MIXMARR, MOVEIN, UNION, PRVGUILT, SLAVLABR, NOSEARCH, and WOMEN to produce an index of civil rights comparable to Gastil's 1983 rating on civil rights. This sum excludes all of Humana's variables that are not clearly related to civil freedoms. Similarly, summing Humana's 1983 ratings on BOOK, FREEPRESS, FREEMAIL, INDCOURT, KEEPCIT, MOVEOUT, NOIDEOL, POLTCOPP, PUBTRIAL, and TVRADIO gives an index comparable to Gastil's 1983 score on political rights. The same approach is used for assessing agreement in 1986; the constructed index of civil rights replaces WOMEN and DIVORCE with LAWFEM, SOCFEM, and EQMARRY; the constructed index of political rights adds BALLOT and MEMBER. Of course, other sums or weightings will produce somewhat different results, but this is a crudely sensible way to compare the two sets of ratings.

In 1983, one finds that the correlation coefficient between the two scores on civil rights is .895 and the coefficient for the two scores on political rights is .900. In 1986, the correlation coefficient between the two scores on civil rights is .914; for political rights, it is .912. These numbers indicate that both Gastil and Humana reliably agree with each other and thus have some common concept of human rights that justifies additional analysis. Without such agreement, one would have to decide whether either scoring system had any validity; but since they do agree, this analysis can generally avoid second-guessing the accuracy of their judgements. Incidentally, the correlation between Gastil's two measurements is .948 in 1983 and .924 in 1986, which suggests that his scales are not truly distinct; more strongly, they tend to group into just two sets, those that are very free and those that are very unfree. Banks shows that this redundancy holds for all of Freedom House's ratings, starting in 1973.[16]

Despite the large values of the correlation coefficients, it is worthwhile to inspect the ratings for cases in which Gastil and Humana disagree. To identify such discrepancies, the indices of political and civil rights developed from Humana's variables were plotted in a histogram, then assigned to one of seven ordered categories according to natural breakpoints that separate the countries into groups. The *i*th largest category appears as column *i* in the following four tables. Notice that the sense of Humana's ordering is opposite that of Gastil; for Humana, low sums give low column numbers that correspond to unfree situations, whereas Gastil uses low numbers to indicate a high level of freedom.

Table 3 summarizes the agreement on civil rights in 1983. Visual inspection of distance from the table trend suggests there are nonconforming cases at (4,7) and (1,5) (here Gastil's rating is given first); these correspond to Ireland and Senegal, respectively. The disagreement on Ireland may be influenced by the fact that Humana is a

TABLE 3. Comparison of Civil Rights Ratings, 1983

Scale derived from Humana

0–39	40–50	50–54	55–59	60–64	65–69	69+	
0	0	0	0	1	0	13	1
0	0	0	0	0	3	8	2
0	0	1	3	1	1	0	3
0	0	1	1	2	1	1	4
0	3	7	2	5	0	0	5
1	6	1	3	0	0	0	6
3	6	0	0	0	0	0	7 Gastil's scale

TABLE 4. Comparison of Political Rights Ratings, 1983

Scale derived from Humana

0–11	12–16	17–21	22–26	27–31	32–36	37+	
0	0	0	0	0	3	18	1
0	0	0	0	1	3	4	2
0	0	2	0	3	1	0	3
0	1	0	0	3	0	1	4
0	1	0	8	1	1	0	5
3	2	6	1	2	0	0	6
3	4	2	0	0	0	0	7 Gastil's scale

citizen of the U.K., while Gastil is not; the disagreement on Senegal may indicate that Humana is paying attention to Senegal's position as an African advocate of human rights rather than to its actual performance.

Table 4 is similar to Table 3, except that it pertains to political rights in 1983. It highlights discrepant cases at (4,7), (5,6), (3,3), (4,2) and (5,2); these correspond to Senegal, Panama, Argentina, Malaysia, Turkey, and South Africa, respectively. Regarding South Africa, Humana's 1983 report emphasizes that the nation has two sets of human rights policies, depending on race; this may account for the disagreement in ratings. Regarding Argentina, Humana's rating was made immediately before the election of Alfonsín, while Gastil's appears to have been made afterwards. Regarding Panama, it put at least rhetorical emphasis on human rights and perhaps got credit by comparison with some of the other Central American nations. The bases for the other disagreements are unclear.

Table 5 pertains to civil rights in 1986. Cameroon at (7,4) appears odd.

Table 6 pertains to political rights in 1986. The only discrepancy is (6,6), which is Panama.

The tables suggest that Gastil and Humana are in broad agreement for all nations except Ireland, Senegal, Panama, Argentina, Malaysia, Turkey, and South Africa in 1983, and for all nations but Panama and Cameroon in 1986. Special caution will be used in treating these nations in subsequent analysis. Nonetheless, the general consistency in ratings between the two authors is quite strong.

As a further check on the accuracy of Humana's data, an informal experiment in the spirit of Themistocles was performed. (Herodotos[17] reports that after Themistocles' strategy won the battle of Salamis the Greek captains met to vote a prize to the person who most significantly contributed to the victory. Each captain had two votes; each voted for himself first, with Themistocles as second choice.) Six graduate students in statistics, one from each of Chile, China, Ethiopia, Mexico, Taiwan, and West Germany, were asked to evaluate Humana's 1986 ratings of all six nations. All but the West German decided that the aggregate ranking of their own country was too low, but that the other nations seemed correct (the West German agreed

TABLE 5. Comparison of Civil Rights Ratings, 1986

Scale derived from Humana

0–38	39–47	48–52	53–56	57–59	60–66	67+	
0	0	0	0	0	3	13	1
0	0	0	0	2	5	6	2
0	0	2	2	1	5	0	3
0	1	1	3	0	1	0	4
1	5	9	4	0	0	0	5
3	7	2	0	0	0	0	6
8	3	1	1	0	0	0	7 Gastil's scale

TABLE 6. Comparison of Political Rights Ratings, 1986

Scale derived from Humana

0–15	16–19	20–24	25–33	34–39	40–44	45+	
0	0	0	0	0	3	20	1
0	0	0	0	3	6	3	2
0	0	1	1	3	1	0	3
0	0	1	7	1	1	0	4
0	0	2	8	0	0	0	5
2	3	4	4	0	1	0	6
5	5	1	3	0	0	0	7 Gastil's scale

with all the rankings). Next, each was asked to criticize Humana's scores on specific freedoms; only two changes were suggested, and both acted against their native country. The Chinese student felt that Humana's rating of China as very free with respect to BRTHCONT was misleading; China enforces birth control, rather than permitting free choice. The Mexican felt that there was considerable pressure in Mexico to join the PRI, and so Mexico's rating on MEMBER should be reduced. The conclusion of this exercise is that Humana's ratings are broadly correct; also, people from strikingly different cultures seem to agree with line-by-line ratings, although they may place different emphasis on the importance of particular freedoms.

Finally, in order to provide some information about socioeconomic variables that might be associated with human rights behavior, Humana's 1983 and 1986 data sets were augmented by the 15 variables shown in Table 7. These variables are used only in the CART analysis that produced Figure 4, and in some inconclusive studies examined later in the chapter. A more thorough study should include many other such variables, but that effort would go beyond the scope of this project.

The data in Table 7 were derived from glosses in Humana's books[18] and two *World Almanacs*.[19] It should be emphasized that these data are not updated each year, but change only as survey or census data become available. Thus for many nations the almanacs record

TABLE 7. Socioeconomic Variables Added to Both 1983 and 1986 Data Sets

POP:	The population of the country, measured in millions.
LIFEEX:	The average life expectancy of inhabitants.
INFMORT:	The infant mortality rate per thousand.
INCOME:	The average income of the inhabitants, measured in dollars.
DENSITY:	The average number of people per square mile.
URBAN:	The percentage of the population living in cities.
ETH1:	The percentage of population belonging to the largest ethnic group.
ETH2:	The percentage of population in the second largest ethnic group.
REL1:	The percentage of population belonging to the largest religious group.
REL2:	The percentage of population in the second largest religious group.
LITERACY:	The percentage of population that is literate.
POLRGHT:	A seven-point subjective rating of political freedom.
CIVRGHT:	A seven-point subjective rating of civil freedom.
PARTY:	A four-point scale reflecting the number of active political parties.
FREETYPE:	Indicates membership in the 7 derived clusters.

no change over the time interval, and often the data are significantly outdated. Hence the analysis based on these data is intended as an example of a method rather than a serious investigation.

Clustering

This section summarizes several cluster analyses performed on the sets of 74 and 89 nations coded by Humana. Two principal strategies were available—hierarchical agglomerative clustering and k-means clustering. SAS routines were used for the hierarchical clustering,[20] and BMDP routines were used for k-means clustering.[21] It should be emphasized that there is no single correct clustering; rather, the advantage of cluster analysis is to point out patterns of national behavior that may provide insight into historical and societal factors that influence human rights. Therefore this section looks at several clustering algorithms; the results are in general agreement, but different algorithms are sensitive to different patterns. Ultimately, the reader must decide whether a particular cluster is plausible and informative.

In hierarchical clustering, the algorithm starts with all cases in different clusters and then successively links those clusters that minimize some measure of dissimilarity. The linking continues until there is a single cluster; there are many criteria for deciding which linkage best captures the number of clusters truly present in the data. In contrast, k-means clustering starts with all cases in a single cluster and successively separates the cases until a specified number of groups is obtained. Then it iteratively reassigns the cases to the nearest cluster center.

The SAS implementation of hierarchical clustering offers eleven linkage rules for building clusters and other options to fine tune the procedures. One option allows the algorithm to delete a specified percentage of the cases in order to reduce the influence of outliers, and another specifies the number of cases to use in a nearest neighbor density estimation subroutine. This study examined all linkage rules; each was considered with both 15 percent deletion and no deletion. Changing the number of cases used in nearest neighbor density estimation generally had little effect, so that option specified the default value of 2.

SAS offers three methods for deciding the correct number of clusters; for this study the cubic clustering criterion was most convenient. Milligan and Cooper[22] undertook a large-scale simulation study of 30 methods for estimating the number of clusters in hierarchical algorithms, and found that the cubic clustering criterion was sixth best.

In their study it gave the correct value 75 percent of the time; when wrong, it tended to slightly overestimate the number of clusters.

For the 1983 data (excluding the seven discrepant cases in Tables 3 and 4) with 15 percent deletion, seven of the linkage rules agreed in finding three clusters, and the cluster memberships were essentially the same for all of these measures. Table 8 shows cluster members for the AVE measure, which defines dissimilarity as the average of the distances from all members of one cluster to all members of another cluster. Milligan[23] reports that among hierarchical procedures, the AVE measure was best at cluster recovery in a simulation study that compared seven types of error perturbation.

These clusters might be broadly characterized as (1) western-style industrial democracies; (2) communist nations; and (3) non-communist developing nations. However, one would like to draw finer distinctions; also, it is not clear that deleting outliers is appropriate in this analysis. For example, South Africa might be viewed as a cluster of one, representing the last colonial-style government in the world; thus one may not want small clusters to be deleted rather than detected.

Without deletion, the number of clusters detected ranged from 4 to 12; the modal value was 7 with options AVE and SIN; three of the measures either did not converge or settled upon clearly foolish (e.g., order of input) solutions. Despite this lack of unanimity, it is worth looking at Table 9, which lists the cluster memberships for the AVE measure. One might characterize these clusters as (1) western-style industrial democracies; (2) communist nations; (3) stable, somewhat oppressive countries; (4) relatively progressive developing nations; (5) determinedly oppressive nations; (6) countries governed under a

TABLE 8. Clusters Formed for 1983 Data Using Cubic Clustering Criterion and SAS Proc CLUSTER; TRIM = 15, Method is AVE

CLUSTER 1:	Australia, Austria, Belgium, Canada, Denmark, Ecuador, Finland, France, Greece, Israel, Italy, Japan, Netherlands, New Zealand, Norway, Papua New Guinea, Peru, Portugal, Spain, Sweden, Switzerland, United Kingdom, United States of America, Venezuela, West Germany
CLUSTER 2:	Bulgaria, Chile, China, Cuba, Czechoslovakia, East Germany, Hungary, Iraq, North Korea, Philippines, Poland, Romania, Syria, Union of Soviet Socialist Republics, Viet Nam, Yugoslavia, Zaire
CLUSTER 3:	Algeria, Bangladesh, Colombia, India, Kenya, Mexico, South Korea, Sri Lanka, Sudan, Taiwan, Tanzania, Thailand, Zambia, Zimbabwe

TABLE 9. Clusters Formed for 1983 Data Using Cubic Clustering Criterion and SAS Proc CLUSTER; TRIM = 0, Method is AVE

CLUSTER 1: Australia, Austria, Belgium, Brazil, Canada, Denmark, Ecuador, Finland, France, Greece, Ireland, Italy, Japan, Netherlands, New Zealand, Norway, Panama, Papua New Guinea, Peru, Portugal, Senegal, Spain, Sweden, Switzerland, United Kingdom, United States of America, Venezuela, West Germany

CLUSTER 2: Bulgaria, China, Cuba, Czechoslovakia, East Germany, Ethiopia, Mozambique, North Korea, Poland, Romania, South Africa, Union of Soviet Socialist Republics, Viet Nam

CLUSTER 3: Argentina, Chile, Iraq, Philippines, South Korea, Syria, Taiwan, Turkey, Zaire

CLUSTER 4: Bangladesh, Colombia, India, Indonesia, Kenya, Malaysia, Mexico, Morocco, Nigeria, Sri Lanka, Sudan, Tanzania, Zambia, Zimbabwe

CLUSTER 5: Algeria, Hungary, Singapore, Thailand, Tunisia, Yugoslavia

CLUSTER 6: Egypt, Israel

CLUSTER 7: Pakistan, Saudi Arabia

state of emergency; (7) fundamentalist Islamic nations. Cluster 6 is a case of strange bedfellows, but both nations are operating under states of emergency that reflect internal unrest and external threat. If one uses a different measure of dissimilarity, then Cluster 6 sometimes merges with Cluster 1 or with Cluster 4.

For the 1986 data, a very similar picture emerges. The TRIM = 15 option together with the cubic clustering criterion gave three clusters, and the interpretations are essentially those of Table 8. In contrast, when TRIM = 0, the AVE procedures found 9 clusters as shown in Table 10. Generally speaking, one might characterize these clusters as (1) western-style industrial democracies; (2) orthodox communist nations; (3) stable, determinedly oppressive third world nations; (4) relatively liberal Islamic nations; (5) stable, moderately oppressive third world nations; (6) less orthodox communist nations; (7) relatively conservative Islamic nations; (8) relatively progressive third world nations, and (9) a unique case. SIN and other alternative measures of dissimilarity differ largely with respect to clusters 4, 7, and 9.

The BMDP k-means clustering algorithms offer five measures of distance and other options; they do not provide a criterion for choosing k, the number of clusters. Milligan[24] reports that k-means procedures are generally more robust than hierarchical clustering. The original study of Humana's 1983 data examined all the distance measures and values of k from 3 to 12, with particular attention to k

TABLE 10. Clusters Formed for 1986 Data Using Cubic Clustering Criterion
and SAS Proc CLUSTER; TRIM = 0, Method is AVE

CLUSTER 1:   Argentina, Australia, Austria, Belgium, Bolivia, Botswana,
Canada, Costa Rica, Denmark, Dominican Republic, Ec-
uador, Finland, France, Greece, Hong Kong, Ireland, Is-
rael, Italy, Jamaica, Japan, Netherlands, New Zealand,
Norway, Papua New Guinea, Panama, Portugal, Senegal,
Spain, Sweden, Switzerland, Trinidad, United Kingdom,
United States of America, Venezuela, West Germany

CLUSTER 2:   Bulgaria, China, Cuba, Czechoslovakia, East Germany,
Ethiopia, Iraq, Mozambique, North Korea, Poland, Romania, Union of Soviet Socialist Republics, Viet Nam

CLUSTER 3:   Chile, Haiti, Liberia, Philippines, South Africa, Zaire, Zimbabwe

CLUSTER 4:   Bangladesh, Egypt, Kuwait, Malaysia, Morocco, Nigeria,
Pakistan, Singapore, Tunisia

CLUSTER 5:   Algeria, Benin, Cameroon, Ghana, Kenya, Paraguay, Sierra
Leone, South Korea, Taiwan, Tanzania, Zambia

CLUSTER 6:   Hungary, Yugoslavia

CLUSTER 7:   Indonesia, Libya, Syria, Turkey

CLUSTER 8:   Brazil, Colombia, India, Mexico, Peru, Sri Lanka, Thailand

CLUSTER 9:   Saudi Arabia

between 6 and 8. Despite Milligan's results, the final clusters were not
entirely insensitive to the metric.

The most plausible clusters occurred with four metrics that evaluate the distance between case $\mathbf{x}_i$ and center $\mathbf{c}_j$ as

$$d_h(\mathbf{x}_i, \mathbf{c}_j) = \frac{1}{p}(\mathbf{x}_i - \mathbf{c}_j)^T \mathbf{M}_h^{-1}(\mathbf{x}_i - \mathbf{c}_j). \tag{1}$$

Here $p = 40$ is the number of variables and

$$\mathbf{M}_1 = \frac{1}{n-k}\sum_{j=1}^{k}\sum_{\mathbf{x}_i \in B_j}(\mathbf{x}_i - \mathbf{c}_j)(\mathbf{x}_i - \mathbf{c}_j)^T \tag{2}$$

is the matrix of pooled within cluster covariances. $\mathbf{M}_2 = \text{diag}(\mathbf{M}_1)$ is
the matrix of pooled within cluster variances; both matrices and clus-
ter centers change as the algorithm iterates.[25] $\mathbf{M}_3$ is the identity
matrix, which corresponds to Euclidean distance, and $\mathbf{M}_4 = \text{diag}(\sigma_1^2, \ldots, \sigma_{40}^2)$ is the matrix that standardizes each variable to have
unit variance. The fifth metric, based on Mahalanobis distance, did
not give reasonable results.

In order to combine the results of these k-means cluster analyses,
nations were grouped together if they appeared in the same cluster
in at least 8 of the 12 trials. This rule led to the results shown in Table

11. Eleven nations did not cluster consistently; these were Bangladesh, Brazil, Colombia, Ecuador, Indonesia, Iraq, Malaysia, Peru, Sri Lanka, Sudan, and Thailand. The South American nations swung between Clusters 4 and 5, and were almost sufficiently cohesive to form a separate group with Venezuela. Also, notice that the countries in Cluster 1 of Table 9 that clustered consistently split into Clusters 1 and 4 in Table 11. The k-means analyses are declaring a division based upon values of the variables MILTSERV and CONCTOB.

To characterize the groups in Table 11, Cluster 1 consists of western industrial democracies that do not require military service; Senegal, Panama, and Papua New Guinea are odd in this setting, but they were discrepant cases noted earlier (see "Data"). Clusters 2 and 3 are essentially communist nations (note that South Africa was also a discrepant case); the variable that best separates the two is KEEPCIT, which may reflect a policy difference in the treatment of dissidents. Cluster 4 is like Cluster 1, except as noted in the previous paragraph. Cluster 5 seems to pick out nations that have a commitment to improving human rights levels, but lack the requisite political tradition and socioeconomic stability. Cluster 6 represents fundamentalist Islamic nations, and Cluster 7 consists of relatively authoritarian regimes that show little concern for human rights issues.

Table 12 shows the results of a BMDP k-means cluster analysis for the 1986 data. The cubic clustering criterion in the hierarchical cluster analysis suggests that the number of clusters should be 8 or 9; both are examined and the results are very similar. To aid in comparing the k-means clusters with the hierarchical clusters, Table 12

TABLE 11. Clusters Formed for 1983 Data Using k-Means Clustering and BMDP Procedure KM with Options None, Var, Wvar, and Wcov

CLUSTER 1:	Australia, Canada, Ireland, Japan, New Zealand, Panama, Papua New Guinea, Senegal, United Kingdom, United States of America
CLUSTER 2:	Bulgaria, China, Hungary, Mozambique, North Korea, Viet Nam, Yugoslavia
CLUSTER 3:	Cuba, Czechoslovakia, East Germany, Ethiopia, Poland, Romania, South Africa, Union of Soviet Socialist Republics
CLUSTER 4:	Austria, Belgium, Denmark, Finland, France, Greece, Israel, Italy, Netherlands, Norway, Portugal, Spain, Sweden, Switzerland, Venezuela, West Germany
CLUSTER 5:	India, Kenya, Mexico, Nigeria, Philippines, Tanzania, Zaire, Zambia, Zimbabwe
CLUSTER 6:	Pakistan, Saudi Arabia
CLUSTER 7:	Algeria, Argentina, Chile, Egypt, Morocco, Singapore, South Korea, Syria, Taiwan, Tunisia, Turkey

TABLE 12. Clusters Formed for 1986 Data Using k-Means Clustering and
BMDP Procedure KM with Options None, Var, Wvar, and Wcov

CLUSTER 1:   Argentina, Australia, Austria, Belgium, Canada, Costa Rica,
             Denmark, Finland, France, Greece, Italy, Netherlands,
             Norway, Papua New Guinea, Portugal, Spain, Sweden,
             Switzerland, United Kingdom, Venezuela, West Germany
CLUSTER 2:   Bulgaria, Cuba, East Germany, Ethiopia, Iraq, Libya
CLUSTER 3:   Chile, Haiti, Liberia, Paraguay, Philippines, South Africa,
             Zaire
CLUSTER 4:   Bolivia, Botswana, Israel, Jamaica, Senegal, Trinidad
CLUSTER 5:   Algeria, Benin, Brazil, Cameroon, Hong Kong, Kenya, Ni-
             geria, Sierra Leone, South Korea, Taiwan, Tanzania,
             Zambia
CLUSTER 6:   Hungary, Indonesia, Kuwait, Pakistan, Saudi Arabia, Syria,
             Yugoslavia
CLUSTER 7:   Czechoslovakia, Poland, Romania, Union of Soviet Socialist
             Republics, Viet Nam
CLUSTER 8:   India, Morocco, Peru, Sri Lanka, Thailand, Zimbabwe
CLUSTER 9:   Dominican Republic, Ecuador, Ireland, Panama

summarizes the results for 9 clusters. As with the 1983 analysis, cluster membership varies with the choice of metric. This examination used the same four metrics as employed in the previous study and eliminated nations that did not cluster consistently for at least three of the four metrics. The countries that did not cluster consistently were Bangladesh, China, Colombia, Egypt, Ghana, Japan, Malaysia, Mexico, Mozambique, New Zealand, North Korea, Singapore, Tunisia, Turkey, and the United States of America.

One might characterize the clusters in Table 12 as (1) western-style industrial democracies; (2) repressive, generally third world socialist governments; (3) repressive, generally third world nonsocialist regimes; (4) generally third world nations with a demonstrated commitment to protecting human rights, but with various barriers to full realization of that goal; (5) generally third world nations that stand between the two previous clusters in terms of human rights; (6) generally Islamic governments (Hungary and Yugoslavia are on the boundary of the cluster); (7) generally industrialized socialist governments; (8) nations that have reduced human rights levels in response to internal threats; (9) Catholic nations that have relatively high human rights levels. Most of the unclassified countries swung between two of the clusters; for example, Japan and the United States twice grouped with cluster 1, and twice grouped with something like cluster 9.

One should be cautious in interpreting all these results. Cluster analysis is a highly exploratory procedure; what little formal basis it has is entirely rooted in normal theory. Fowlkes, Gnanadesikan, and Kettenring[26] have found that in nonparametric settings it is usually desirable to use some sort of variable selection procedure in conjunction with cluster analysis, but software for this is not yet available. Nonetheless, cluster analyses are widely used and often discover unanticipated patterns in the data that lead to better understanding.

In this study, the cluster analyses suggest several key patterns in classifying different sorts of human rights behavior. The western industrial democracies and the Communist nations nearly always separate cleanly. Other separations reflect the presence of mandatory military service, religious beliefs such as Islam and Catholicism, states of national emergency, and so forth. Results in the following sections examine the basis for these divisions more closely, using techniques of stepwise discriminant analysis and CART analysis. A variable clustering procedure and factor analysis also generate some insight.

Variable Reduction

Humana's 40 variables (which are slightly different in 1983 and 1986) each measure a different type of freedom. But some of these variables are strongly associated with each other, and some are quite difficult to assess. This section examines several methods for reducing the set of variables to a more manageable size; if possible, the retained variables should also be easy to measure. One wants to remove variables that are redundant but keep variables that help to categorize patterns of human rights behavior.

One approach for variable reduction is a cluster analysis of the variables rather than the cases. One starts with all of the variables, and at each step combines two variables or sets of variables that minimize some appropriate measure of distance. Two common measures of distance are defined in terms of the absolute value of the Pearson product-moment correlation. For example, if at some stage one has s sets of variables S_i, then the next step will union the two sets that attain

$$\min_{v \in S_i, w \in S_j} |corr(\mathbf{v},\mathbf{w})| \ . \tag{3}$$

Another distance measure combines the two sets that attain

$$\min_{i \neq j} \ \max_{v \in S_i, w \in S_j} |corr(\mathbf{v},\mathbf{w})| \tag{4}$$

Both methods act to cluster highly correlated variables into groups that have strong internal covariance. Variables with such a group tend to provide very similar information.

Banks[27] reports that for the 1983 data, the BMDP program 1M[28] finds the variable clusters shown in Table 13. Both of the above metrics were used, and they agreed on the low level linkages shown in the table. Higher level linkages were deemed too broad and were ignored. Variables that do not appear in Table 13 formed singleton sets. The mutual absolute correlations within each of the above groups are at least .8.

The analysis of the 1983 data was repeated for the 1986 data. Again, both distance measures were used. Table 14 shows the resulting low-level linkages common to both options. As before, the mutual absolute correlations within each of the above groups are at least .8. Also, variables that do not appear in Table 14 formed singleton sets.

In Tables 13 and 14, notice that variables that group together in the 1983 data are reasonably likely to group together in the 1986 data. The match is not perfect, but it suggests that there is some stability in the covariance of the indices over time, and encourages the hope that variable reduction can be made broadly practical. In applications, one would probably want to retain indices that seem conceptually different, even though they might be statistically associated.

Stepwise discriminant analysis is an alternative approach to vari-

TABLE 13. Groups of Variables Formed for 1983 Data Using BMDP Procedure 1M with Options Single and Complete

GROUP 1:   CONCTOB, MILTSERV
GROUP 2:   DETENTN, NOSEARCH, PRVGUILT
GROUP 3:   INDCOURT, PUBTRIAL
GROUP 4:   FREEART, FREEWORK
GROUP 5:   ANTIGOV, BANNDLIT
GROUP 6:   ASSEMBLY, BOOK, FREEINFO, FREEMAIL, FREEPRESS, POLTCOPP, UNION

TABLE 14. Groups of Variables Formed for 1986 Data Using BMDP Procedure 1M with Options Single and Complete

GROUP 1:   ASSEMBLY, BOOK, FREEPRESS, MONITOR, NEWSPAP, UNION
GROUP 2:   BALLOT, POLTCOPP
GROUP 3:   INDCOURT, PRVGUILT
GROUP 4:   DETENTN, NOSEARCH, STARCHAM
GROUP 5:   FREEINFO, FREEMAIL

able reduction that emphasizes the preservation of the information used in the cluster analyses described earlier. In stepwise discriminant analysis, one wants to discover classification rules that separate cases belonging to different groups. The classification rules are linear combinations of subsets of the available variables; if the value of the linear combination of a particular case's variables exceeds a certain value, then the rule classifies that case to a particular group. Most of the computational effort goes into determining the subset of the variables that enables one to build the most accurate classification rules. The entire algorithm is driven by a training sample, which includes both the variables and group membership information.

In this study we use BMDP procedure 7M[29] to pick the subsets of Humana's 40 indices that best separate the clusters identified by the prior analysis. There are two major problems in applying discriminant analysis:

1. The explanatory variables are being used twice; first they are used to develop the clusters according to the clustering algorithm, then the discriminant function algorithm uses them again as the training sample to rederive cluster membership in a different way. Almost certainly this results in estimates of the misclassification probabilities that are far too small.
2. Discriminant analysis is designed for the normal mixture model, which almost certainly does not apply to this kind of data. Although stepwise discriminant analysis is often robust to violations of this model, Goldstein and Dillon[30] offer several examples that show that incautious use of the technique can lead to foolish conclusions.

Nonetheless, it is informative to notice what variables the procedure chooses as being most influential in classifying the nations according to cluster membership for each of Tables 9 to 12. These results are summarized in Table 15. Notice that the variables used in both of the 1983 clusters (Tables 9 and 11) are very similar, whereas the variables selected for the 1986 clusters (Tables 10 and 12) are rather different. A partial explanation is that the number of clusters is greater for the 1986 data and this tends to muddle any sort of multivariate examination.

Jackknife techniques are one method for making a rough assessment of the error rates for classification rules based on stepwise discriminant analysis; bootstrap techniques are another.[31] Since the double use of the data has already violated basic assumptions that permit error-rate estimates, this study will not spend effort on what

TABLE 15. Variables Identified by Stepwise Discriminant Analysis BMDP Procedure 7M as Useful in Forming Clusters in Tables 9–12

TABLE 9:   ALCOHOL, DETENTN, FORCE, FREEINFO, FREEWORK, MIXMARR, TORTURE, TVRADIO

TABLE 10:   ANYRELGN, ASSEMBLY, DETENTN, FREEWORK, MIXMARR, MONITOR, MOVEOUT, MURDER, NOIDEOL, POLTCOPP

TABLE 11:   ALCOHOL, DETENT, FREEINFO, FREEWORK, KEEPCIT, MILTSERV, UNION

TABLE 12:   BALLOT, CAPPUN, KEEPCIT, MURDER, NOIDEOL, SOCFEM, TVRADIO

is probably a very misleading calculation. According to the most naive jackknife estimate, the worst case was for Table 9; the estimated probabilities of correct classification for each of the seven clusters were .96, .92, .89, .93, .5, .5 and 1.00. Even so, these estimates are clearly too optimistic; see Stone[32] for additional discussion of this sort of estimate.

As a final matter for investigation, one might look at a factor analysis or a principal components analysis of the data. Banks[33] found little of note in the 1983 data; principal components analysis of the 1986 data is similar, but a factor analysis does recover some interpretable structure. Using the BMDP procedure 4M with the quartimax option,[34] one finds that virtually all of the variables load heavily on the first factor; this suggests that the factor captures a very general type of freedom. For the second factor, LAWFEM, SOCFEM, DIVORCE, and MIXMARR all load heavily (the absolute factor loadings are all .45 or greater) and this suggests that the second factor reflects general sexual equality. On the third factor, BRTHCONT, PARTY, FREEART, and FREEWORK all load heavily; this seems to measure the pluralism of the society. The fourth factor picks up ETHLANG and ETHMIN, and the fifth factor picks up NOIDEOL. The fourth is clearly reflecting rights behavior towards minorities, and the fifth is probably spurious but may capture something about how governments approach legitimizing themselves.

Classification and Regression Trees

Classification and regression trees[35] offer an alternative to the discriminant analysis techniques, based on entirely different ideas. Discriminant analysis and factor analysis are rooted in multivariate normal theory, but the methods discussed in this section are nonparametric in character.

The applications in this section use classification and regression tree methodology to derive classification rules for determining membership in the clusters derived earlier. As before, the results will be too optimistic in terms of estimating the misclassification probabilities, since the clusters were derived from the same data that are used to form the training sample. Nonetheless, the methodology will identify important variables from an entirely different standpoint than that used in stepwise discriminant analysis.

CART is a package that implements the recursive partitioning ideas that underlie the classification and regression tree approach. It attempts to discover classification rules by examining each of the variables and then splitting the nations according to the variable that best separates the clusters. This leads to a tree diagram, with each branch point a division of the nations at that level into two sublevels that are more homogeneous with respect to group membership. Thus a variable may appear several times in the tree, and several terminal twigs may all indicate the same cluster. There is an extensive menu of options; these analyses use the Gini splitting criterion and take the prior probabilities of cluster membership to be equal rather than proportional to the representation in the training sample, but otherwise use the default options. See Banks[36] for more details.

Figure 1 shows the CART diagram obtained for the data in Table 11 under the original study. The CART diagram identifies UNION, FREEWORK, CONCTOB, KEEPCIT, and MILTSERV as the most useful variables, but one could use CONCTOB in place of MILT-SERV with almost equal success. To read this and subsequent diagrams, the convention is that at the node labeled UNION, a case goes left if its score on UNION is 3 or less, and right otherwise. At the FREEWORK node, a case goes left if its score on FREEWORK is 3 or less, and at node KEEPCIT it goes left if its score on KEEPCIT is 2 or less. If a nation goes left on each of those nodes, the last line of the diagram indicates that it is assigned to Cluster 3 in Table 11. Otherwise, it traces down a different path through the diagram and ends at a different terminal node corresponding to a different cluster assignment. Also notice that this diagram is relatively sparse, containing only five interior nodes.

The tenfold cross-validation estimate of the misclassification rate gave a total of 3 incorrect assignments out of 63. However, this is overoptimistic, since the same data were used to generate both the original clusters and also the classification and regression tree.

Figure 2 shows the CART diagram corresponding to the SAS clusters for the 1983 data shown in Table 9. Notice that it uses a smaller set of variables than was identified in the stepwise discriminant

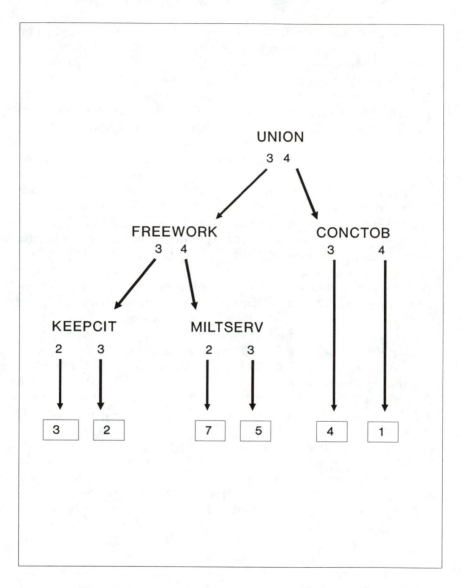

Figure 1. CART diagram for classifying nations into clusters shown in Table 11.

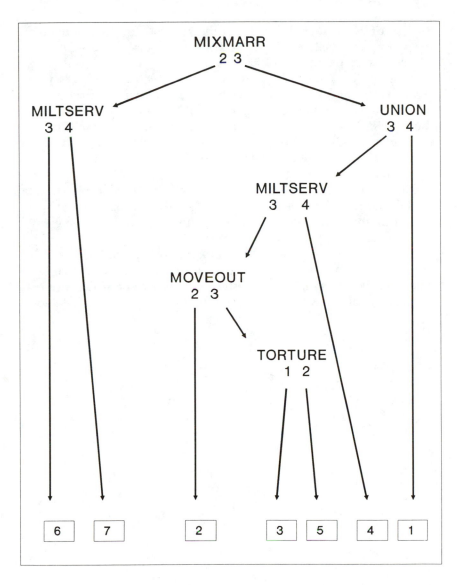

Figure 2. CART diagram for classifying nations into clusters shown in Table 9.

analysis of Table 15 and that two of the variables are considered necessary by both analyses. Tenfold cross-validation gave a total of 22 incorrect assignments out of 74 nations.

Figure 3 shows the CART diagram for the 1986 SAS clusters. Cluster 9, consisting of just Saudi Arabia, was omitted since the results were sensitive to small perturbations of its ratings. As with Figure 2, the CART diagram uses fewer variables than the stepwise discriminant analysis; three of those variables were selected by both algorithms. Tenfold cross-validation found a total of 24 incorrect assignments out of 88 nations.

One can perform a CART analysis on the clusters given in Table 12, but the resulting diagram is not persuasive. In part, this may be caused by the somewhat unsatisfactory links established in the clustering algorithm.

As a different question, one can look for social, economic, and demographic variables that enable one to develop cluster assignment rules. Banks[37] motivates this question and applies both stepwise discriminant analysis and CART analysis to the problem. Figure 4 shows

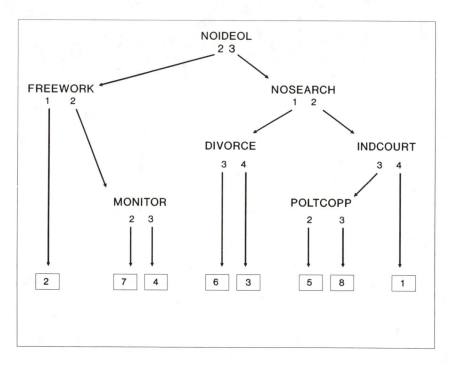

Figure 3. CART diagram for classifying nations into clusters shown in Table 10.

the results of the CART analysis; it uses only CONCTOB and the variables listed in Table 7 and attempts to produce classification rules that correctly assign nations to the clusters given in Table 11. CONC-TOB was added to the variables in Table 7 because otherwise it would be practically impossible to distinguish between Clusters 1 and 4. Tenfold cross-validation finds a total of 20 misclassifications out of 63 cases.

This study also examined the CART diagram that assigns nations to the nine 1986 SAS clusters according to exogenous variables. The diagram is not shown since the tenfold cross-validation estimate of the misclassification probabilities indicated that more than half of the cases are incorrectly assigned. Factors that may promote this poor performance are the increased number of clusters, the fact that MILTSERV is no longer available to clearly distinguish two very large clusters, the fact that much of the data gleaned from the almanacs is not current, and perhaps the unavailability of the rating on PARTY for 1986. However, the most serious flaw is that the very short list of social, economic, and demographic variables is not nearly comprehensive enough to honor the realities of national variability.

The basic conclusion of this section is that the CART methods used in the original study gave simple and sensible answers, but this does not happen as persuasively for the 1986 data. The failure may lie in the hope that classification and regression tree procedures offer a pertinent tool for understanding this kind of data, or it may lie in the choices made when focusing upon particular clustering algorithms. Additional study may clarify the importance of CART techniques for data of this kind.

Conclusions

It must first be emphasized that this study is entirely exploratory; there is no tractable statistical model that is appropriate to this kind of data. All of the patterns that have been noted may be spurious, and certainly they cannot be proven. Nonetheless, it is not unreasonable to think that some of the structure that has been detected offers reliable insight into human rights issues. Statistics is important to the social sciences largely because it is so robust to failures in classical modeling assumptions.

The examination in the first section shows by many methods that Humana and Gastil continue to corroborate each other, just as they did with the 1983 data. Their agreement in 1986 is closer than it was in 1983, and this may reflect improved methods on the part of Humana. In particular, Humana has fixed his survey firmly in time, and

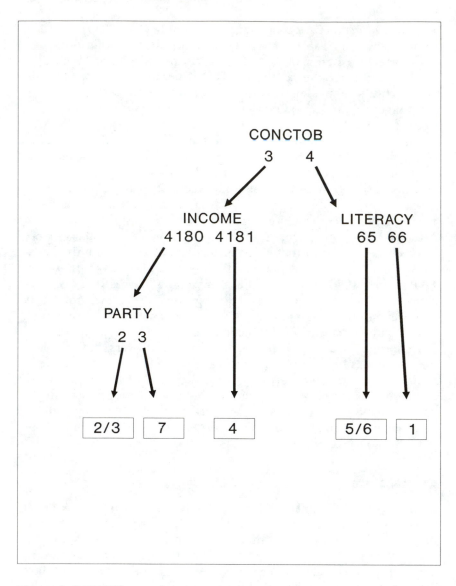

Figure 4. CART diagram for classifying nations into clusters shown in Table 11 using exogenous variables.

this avoids some of the difficulties and discrepant cases that were noted in the previous study. The central conclusion is that both authors have a common understanding of human rights, and this justifies using their ratings as a foundation for additional analysis.

The cluster analyses described earlier should not be taken dogmatically. The precise clusters obtained depend fairly sensitively on the clustering method employed. From the interpretative standpoint, this is not a significant drawback; the different methods are highlighting different aspects of a complicated phenomenon.

Using the TRIM option, virtually all of the clustering algorithms agree on three clusters; they identify one set of nations with high standards of human rights, another set with very low standards, and a third that is intermediate. Without the TRIM option, additional resolution appears, but often this implies a more narrow field of view. For example, Table 9 suggests that countries governed under a state of emergency show a common pattern of human rights behavior. Table 11 pertains to the same data but does not detect the state of emergency pattern; instead, it finds a pattern based upon mandatory military service. A similar case can be made for Tables 10 and 12. This suggests that multiple approaches in the analysis can discover important aspects of human rights that are not visible to a single procedure.

More pragmatically, the section "Clustering" helps to identify actions that may improve certain sorts of human rights patterns. Specifically, if negotiation and stability were to obviate the states of emergency in Egypt and Israel, then one might hope for improvement in the human rights arena. Similarly, the progressive third world nations should probably be handled very gently and possibly buffered from military and financial threats. One hopes that stable leadership and the passage of time may create a tradition of freedom that will reinforce their present direction.

The discussion on variable reduction examines various methods to reduce the number of human rights variables that one needs to monitor. Measurement is costly (at least for nongovernmental organizations), difficult, and controversial. It seems obviously desirable to avoid redundancy and to focus on a set of benchmark variables. The several methods examined all lead very specifically to substantial reductions of the data, and one need only decide what sort of information one wants to preserve.

The results of the CART analysis are disappointing. The early promise of CART methods for the 1983 data does not seem to be borne out in the 1986 data. Nonetheless, it may be that if different choices had been made at earlier points in the analysis, then CART diagrams may have produced more reasonable pictures.

Notes

1. David L. Banks, "Patterns of Oppression: A Statistical Analysis of Human Rights," *Proceedings of the Social Statistics Section of the American Statistical Association* (1985): 154–162.

2. Raymond D. Gastil, ed., *Freedom in the World: Political Rights and Civil Liberties, 1983–84* (Westport, CT: Greenwood Press, Freedom House, 1984).

3. Charles Humana, *World Human Rights Guide* (London: Hutchinson, 1983).

4. Raymond D. Gastil, ed., *Freedom in the World: Political Rights and Civil Liberties, 1985–86* (Westport, CT: Freedom House, 1986); Charles Humana, *World Human Rights Guide* (London: The Economist, 1986).

5. CART methodology is described in Breiman, Friedman, Olshen, and Stone's *Classification and Regression Trees* (Belmont, CA: Wadsworth, 1984).

6. Banks, "Patterns of Oppression" (note 1).

7. Glenn W. Milligan and Martha C. Cooper, "An Examination of Procedures for Determining the Number of Clusters in a Dataset," *Psychometrika* 50 (1985): 159–179.

8. This point is discussed in Eugene Kamenka, "The Anatomy of an Idea," in *Human Rights*, ed. Eugene Kamenka and Erh-Soon Tay (London: Edward Arnold, 1978).

9. Harry M. Scoble and Laurie S. Wiseberg, "Problems of Comparative Research on Human Rights," in *Global Human Rights: Public Policies, Comparative Measures, and NGO Strategies*, ed. Ved P. Nanda, James R. Scarritt, and George W. Shepherd, Jr. (Boulder, CO: Westview Press, 1981).

10. John G. McCamant, "A Critique of Present Measures of 'Human Rights Development' and an Alternative," in Nanda et al., *Global Human Rights*.

11. Michael Stohl, David Carleton, George Lopez, and Stephen Samuels, "State Violation of Human Rights: Issues and Problems of Measurement," *Human Rights Quarterly* 8, No. 4 (November 1986): 592–606.

12. A more complete description is in chapter 1 of Gastil, *Freedom in the World, 1985–86* (note 4).

13. M. S. McDougal, H. D. Lasswell, and L. Chen, *Human Rights and World Public Order* (New Haven, CT: Yale University Press, 1980).

14. Universal Declaration of Human Rights, adopted 10 December 1948, G.A. Res. 217A, 3 GAOR at art. 5, U.N. Doc. A/810 (1948).

15. In a personal communication, Charles Humana indicated that members of some European human rights organizations felt that the inclusion of MILTSERV and CONCTOB unfairly lowered their countries' standing. Others felt that human rights are properly defined only in terms of the Universal Declaration of Human Rights. See also Kenneth Bollen, "Political Rights and Political Liberties in Nations: An Evaluation of Human Rights Measures, 1950–1984," *Human Rights Quarterly* 8, No. 4 (November 1986): 567–591, and Gastil, *Freedom in the World, 1985–86* (note 4).

16. David L. Banks, "The Analysis of Human Rights Data over Time," *Human Rights Quarterly* 8, No. 4 (November 1986): 654–680.

17. Herodotos, *History*, Book VIII, paragraph 123, translated by A. D. Godley (Cambridge, MA: Harvard University Press, 1925).

18. See Humana, *World Human Rights Guide* (note 3) and Gastil, *Freedom in the World, 1985-86* (note 4).

19. H. U. Lane, *The World Almanac and Book of Facts 1982* (New York: Newspaper Enterprise Association, 1981); and H. U. Lane, *The World Almanac and Book of Facts 1986* (New York: Newspaper Enterprise Association, 1985).

20. W. S. Sarle, "CLUSTER Procedure," *SAS User's Guide: Statistics, Version 5* (Cary, NC: SAS Institute, Inc., 1985).

21. Laszlo Engelman and J. A. Hartigan, "K-Means Clustering," *BMDP Statistical Software*, ed. W. J. Dixon (Berkeley: University of California Press, 1983).

22. Milligan and Cooper, "Procedures" (note 7).

23. Glenn W. Milligan, "An Examination of the Effects of Six Types of Error Perturbation on Fifteen Clustering Algorithms," *Psychometrika* 45 (1980): 325–342.

24. Ibid.

25. Laszlo Engelman, "Cluster Analysis of Cases," in *BMDP Statistical Software* (note 21).

26. Edward B. Fowlkes, Ramanathan Gnanadesikan, and Jon R. Kettenring, "Variable Selection in Clustering and Other Contexts," in *Design, Data and Analysis*, ed. Colin Mallows (New York: John Wiley, 1987).

27. Banks, "Patterns of Oppression" (note 1).

28. John Hartigan, "Cluster Analysis of Variables," in *BMDP Statistical Software* (note 21).

29. Robert Jennrich and Paul Sampson, "Stepwise Discriminant Analysis," in *BMDP Statistical Software* (note 24).

30. M. Goldstein and W. R. Dillon, *Discrete Discriminant Analysis* (New York: John Wiley and Sons, 1978).

31. See B. Efron, "Estimating the Error Rate of a Prediction Rule: Improvements on Cross-Validation," *Journal of the American Statistical Association* 78 (1983): 316–331 for an overview of bootstrap, cross-validation, and resubstitution methods in this area.

32. M. Stone, "Cross-Validation: A Review," *Mathematische Operationsforschung und Statistik* 9 (1977): 127–139.

33. Banks, "Patterns of Oppression" (note 1).

34. James Frane, Robert Jennrich, and Paul Sampson, "Factor Analysis," in *BMDP Statistical Software* (note 21).

35. Breiman et al., *Classification* (note 5); and Milligan and Cooper, "An Examination" (note 7) are the key references in this area.

36. Banks, "Patterns of Oppression" (note 1).

37. Ibid.

DATA SOURCES

Chapter 15
A Guide to Human Rights Data Sources

Michael Cain, Richard P. Claude, and Thomas B. Jabine

This chapter provides a listing, in standard format, of 29 data bases that contain quantitative information on human rights and related topics. Our goal in providing this guide is to encourage human rights professionals to make greater use of existing data sources in their work, whether it be for analytical research, teaching, or advocacy. To this end, the guide provides a short description of the coverage and contents of each data source and information to help readers gain access to the data sources in which they are interested and obtain more detailed information about them.

We cannot claim that this guide provides exhaustive coverage of human rights data sources, however they might be defined. We began with a list of the sources familiar to us. The list was circulated to several human rights scholars for review, yielding some additional candidates for inclusion. For each of the sources on our list, we prepared a draft description, using the standard format, and sent the draft to the data base "custodian" for review and comment. Most of the data sources listed have had the benefit of this kind of review. There were a few for which we were unable to obtain a response from anyone responsible for the data base; however, we decided not to exclude any sources for that reason. We are very grateful to everyone who assisted in this undertaking, but we assume full responsibility for any errors remaining in the data base descriptions.

Scope

We gave much thought to the question of what kinds of data sources to include in this guide. As with most of the essays included in this volume, we focused here on data sources with information relevant to personal security and civil and political rights. Sources of statistical information useful for measuring the attainment of economic, social, and cultural rights are much more numerous and are generally better known to analysts. The United Nations and its specialized agencies and the World Bank provide a wealth of such data,[1] much of it available on electronic media for the convenience of users. Thus, the data are readily available for anyone who wants to analyze the performance of individual nations or to compare nations with respect to attainment of specific economic, social, and cultural rights for their citizens.

A few of the data sources included in the guide constitute exceptions to the above statement of scope. We have included descriptions of the Overseas Development Council's *Physical Quality of Life Index* (19),[2] the Population Crisis Committee's *International Human Suffering Index* (06), and Sivard's *World Military and Social Expenditures* (03), all of which represent serious attempts to assess the economic and social welfare of individuals in the nations of the world. These sources were included because of their broad worldwide coverage and because human rights researchers frequently use them to analyze the relationships between the enjoyment of civil and political rights and the level of economic and social development in different countries.

A second issue was the extent to which we should try to include single-country data sources, which are rapidly increasing in number. We did not have the resources to attempt full coverage, so we compromised by including, by way of illustration, a few especially interesting ones, including *Nunca Más: Report of the Argentine National Commission* (25), *Brasil: Nunca Mais* (26), two sources of data on South Africa (27,28) and one for the Philippines (29).

A difficult question of scope was where to draw the line between systematic compendia of statistics for defined time periods and geographic areas and reports which, although they contain some numerical information about human rights violations, present this information primarily in the context of a narrative report and do not make any claim to provide systematic coverage of all such events. We have included some data sources in the latter category, notably the U.S. State Department *Country Reports* (04), the *Amnesty International Reports* (01) and the *Human Rights in Developing Countries Yearbook* (24). At least the first two of these have been used by some researchers for comparative international analyses of human rights and associated phenomena, but potential users should be aware that the issuing organizations, especially Amnesty International, have strong reservations about their use for this purpose. They should exercise their judgment in deciding what uses of the data are acceptable.

Recent Additions

Our goal has been to include all important regional and international data sources that provide useful information about human rights in the civil, political, and personal security categories and to provide some illustrations of other pertinent types of data bases. We think it worthwhile to mention two new sources of data that have come to our attention too late to go through the process of developing a formal listing.

The Human Development Report (1991), published by Oxford University Press for the United Nations Development Program, was released in May 1991. The report ranks 130 countries according to a new Human Development Index, which is based not merely on gross national product, but on a combination of criteria that measure the quality of people's lives as well as their income. The 1991 *Report* included adopted human rights ratings based on Humana's data (07), and it expected that future reports will refine and improve the index.[3]

The American Society of International Law, based on a proposal developed by Amnesty International for the United Nations Special Rapporteur at the Centre for Human Rights in Geneva, is undertaking a feasibility study for an internationally accessible data base on states of emergency. Data base entries would provide information, in standard format, on the legal basis and actual use of emergency powers in selected jurisdictions in which there is a declared or non-declared state of emergency. It is likely that the data base will include simple statistics on the use of the relevant powers, such as internment without trial and special military or criminal tribunals.[4]

Sequence, Format, and Content

As indicated above, the data source descriptions are numbered serially, from 01 to 29. The listings begin with worldwide data sources, followed by regional and other multi-country sources, with single-country sources last.

Information about each of the twenty-nine data bases is presented in a standard format consisting of twelve categories. The categories are designed to: identify the data base and its developers and spon-

sors; describe its purposes and content; identify the principal sources
of information contained in the data base; list publications that describe the data base or make use of the information in it; and tell
potential users of the data base how to obtain access to it. If the title
of a category is followed by "NA," we were unable to obtain any information relevant to that category.

Following is a description of the kinds of information provided in
each of the twelve standard categories:

1. Data base name. For most entries, the data base name is the same
one assigned by the person or organization responsible for the data
base. However, for some entries, we have shortened the name or provided one which we think identifies the aim or scope of the data base
more clearly.

2. Organization. In this category, organization refers to either an
original or current institutional sponsor of the data base or an organization with which the author is currently affiliated. This ambiguity
is necessary because the development of some data bases required the
initial assistance of several institutions, which sometimes changed
over time. For some entries, there is no institutional sponsor; for
these entries we give the name of the organization with which the
author is currently affiliated.

3. Contact person(s). This category refers to individuals who are
knowledgeable about the data source. In most instances, the persons
listed verified the details contained in our draft listing. For most entries, the contact persons are either the original compilers of the data
base or professionals who are currently affiliated with the organizational sponsor of the data base. Most entries provide the address and
phone number of at least one contact person at the time this listing
was published.

4. Purpose. This category usually refers to the original intent of the
author or organization in creating the data base.

5. Geographic coverage. Listings have worldwide, regional, other
multi-country or single-country coverage. Whenever an entry is identified as having multi-country coverage, we specify the number of
countries included in the coverage. For some entries the geographic
coverage has varied from year to year; in these instances, to the extent possible, we have provided some indication of changes over time
in the number of countries included in the data base.

6. Frequency. For regularly published reports, this category specifies
the time interval between reports. We also specify the first year

published information was available. For ad hoc reports, years of publication are given. For onetime reports, a reference date or time period is given.

7. Content. This category distinguishes between data bases, such as the U.S. State Department *Country Reports*, that are primarily in narrative form and those that include statistical data in individual or aggregate form. For the latter type of data base, this category specifies the units of observation (events, persons, countries, etc.) and the key variables (type of violation, demographic characteristics of persons, country rankings or scores, etc.) that are contained in the data base for these units.

8. Primary sources of information. This category refers to the publications or other sources of information most frequently relied upon to develop the data base. For some data bases (such as Amnesty International or the U.S. State Department *Country Reports*) the sources are diverse and cannot be fully documented.

9. Description of methodology. This category usually contains a reference to direct the reader to the most complete published statement of the techniques and methods used in developing the data base. For some entries, we also provide a brief description of the techniques used.

10. Published data. This category lists any books, articles, or reports which contain either analyses, summaries, or listings based on the data source.

11. Other means of access. Some data bases are stored on nonprint media, such as magnetic tape, microfiche, or diskette. If the data base is available to the public in one of these forms, we give the name and address of the organization to contact.

12. Derivative uses. This category refers to known secondary applications or uses of the data source. For example, some other data bases may include variables developed from the listed data source. For widely used data bases such as Amnesty International or the U.S. State Department *Country Reports*, we have arbitrarily limited the number of derivative uses cited.

Quality of Data

The inclusion of a data source in this guide does not constitute a guarantee that it is appropriate and of adequate quality for a particular application. We have included, for each data base, a brief description of its sources of information and method of compilation, plus references, whenever available, to more detailed information on methodology. The chapters in Parts I to III have much to say about the quality of data in general and some of them comment on the quality of particular data sources included in this guide (see especially Goldstein in Part I; Bollen, Innes, Pritchard, and Lopez and Stohl in Part II; and Banks in Part III). Thus, we leave it to potential users of a data source to review the available information about its quality and decide whether it is adequate for their purposes.

Some Comments on the Data Sources Included in the Guide

Of the 29 data sources listed, 20 have worldwide coverage. Three provide data for all or most of the Latin American countries and one is for a small group of developing countries that receive aid from Nordic countries. Each of the five remaining sources provides data for a single country.

For the analyst who wants to study changes over time, data sources that provide information annually or more often are perhaps the most useful. Among the data sources with worldwide coverage, the following publish new information annually:

No.	Name	Year first published
01	Amnesty International Reports	1962
02	Comparative Survey of Freedom	1973
03	World Military and Social Expenditures	1975
04	U.S. State Department *Country Reports*	1976
18	Journalism Morbidity Survey	1982
05	Persecution of Human Rights Monitors	1987

Two of the single-country data sources (28 and 29) publish monthly information, probably because they are action-oriented advocacy groups whose effectiveness depends on getting information about human rights abuses before the authorities and the public as rapidly as possible.

Some of the other worldwide data sources include data for extended periods, but are not reissued annually. Sources with coverage over an extended period include: the Conflict and Peace Data Bank (10), with events data for 1948 to 1978 (and being updated through 1989); the Cross-National Time Series Data Archives (11), with annual data for 1950 to 1984; and the *World Handbooks of Political and Social Indicators II and III* (13 and 14), which provide annual events data for 1948 to 1977.

The data available from the listed sources can be classified into three broad categories: information about individual events; counts of events and other kinds of aggregate data; and scores or rankings based on expert judgments.

Information about individual events sometimes identifies specific victims, such as persons illegally detained, by name, for example as in the Amnesty International Reports (01). Some events, such as suspension of publication of an opposition newspaper, are actions by national governments. Another type of event, affecting substantial numbers of persons, is an episode of genocide or politicide, which is the basic unit for which information is provided in the data base Genocides and Politicides Since 1945 (15).

Many of the data sources include counts of events and other kinds of aggregate data. Counts may be converted to rates, using population as a base. For example, Seymour's Indices of Political Imprisonment (20) provides categorical ratings of countries, based on the number of political prisoners per million population, as of a specified date. Different statistics based on counts can be combined to form an overall score or index, as in the Physical Quality of Life Index (19), which combines data on infant mortality, life expectancy, and literacy to form an overall index.

Several of the data sources include scores, scale values, or rankings of countries based on expert or informed judgments concerning the extent to which the countries provide specific rights or groups of related rights to their citizens. For some data sources this is the only type of information presented. Freedom House's *Comparative Survey of Freedom* (02), for example, scores each country on two variables, political rights and civil liberties, using a seven-point scale. Humana uses a similar approach for his *World Human Rights Guide* (07), but scores countries on each of 40 different rights, using a four-point scale.

Some publications, such as the Amnesty International Reports (01) and the U.S. State Department's *Country Reports* (04), present narrative evaluations of country performance on specific rights, without any attempt to provide numerical scores or rankings that can be used for comparative analysis. Some researchers have used these narrative evaluations to develop country scores for use in comparative international analyses, despite the sponsors' assertions that the information is not intended to be used in that way.

Many data sources include data in more than one of the three major categories. The kinds of information provided in each data source will be found in its listing under the heading "Content."

Most of the data sources have been developed and disseminated by universities or nongovernmental human rights organizations. As might be expected, the former tend to be research-oriented and the latter are more often by-products of case work activities or are designed for advocacy and educational purposes. Three of the sources listed are issued by or directly sponsored by one or more national governments: the U.S. State Department *Country Reports* (04), *Human Rights in Developing Countries* (24) and *Nunca Más, Report of the Argentine National Commission* (25).

For many users, especially researchers, the most convenient data sources are those that are available to them on electronic media. As indicated in the individual listing under "Other means of access," several of the data bases listed are available on tape from:

Inter-University Consortium for Political and Social Research
Institute for Social Research
P.O. Box 1248
Ann Arbor, MI 48106   Tel. (313) 763-5010

Notes

1. One example is the annual statistical compilation *Social Indicators of Development*, published for the World Bank by the Johns Hopkins University Press, Baltimore.

2. Numbers in parentheses are the numbers of the listings in this guide.

3. "Measuring Human Development and Freedom," United Nations Development Program, *Human Development Report* (New York: Oxford University Press, 1990), pp. 13–21.

4. American Society of International Law, "Proposed International Database on States of Emergency," *Human Rights Advocacy Interest Group Newsletter* 1, No. 2 (June 1990): 2–3.

Index to Data Sources Listed

No.	Name of data source	Organization or individual
01	Amnesty International Reports	Amnesty International
02	Comparative Survey of Freedom	Freedom House
03	World Military and Social Expenditures	World Priorities, Inc.
04	Country Reports on Human Rights Practices	U.S. State Department
05	Persecution of Human Rights Monitors	Human Rights Watch
06	Human Suffering Index	Population Crisis Comm.
07	World Human Rights Guide	Charles Humana
08	Freedom in National Press Systems	Raymond Nixon
09	Status of International Human Rights Instruments	United Nations
10	Conflict and Peace Data Bank	Ctr. for Internat. Dev. & Conflict Mgmt.
11	Cross-National Time-Series Data Archive	SUNY at Binghamton
12	Dimensionality of Nations Project	Univ. of Hawaii, Manoa
13	World Handbook of Political and Social Indicators II	Virginia Polytechnic and State Univ.
14	World Handbook III	Same as 13
15	Genocides and Politicides	U.S. Naval Academy
16	Global Survey of Minorities at Risk	Univ. of Maryland and Univ. of Colorado
17	World Directory of Minorities	The Minority Rights Group
18	Journalism Morbidity Survey	Freedom House
19	Physical Quality of Life Index	Overseas Devel. Council
20	Indices of Political Imprisonment	James Seymour
21	U.S. Assistance and Human Rights Policy in Latin America	Univ. of North Carolina
22	Survey of Latin American Political Democracy	Univ. of Missouri, Saint Louis
23	Violence and Repression in Latin America	University of Denver
24	Human Rights in Devel. Countries	Chr. Michelsen Institute
25	Nunca Más: Report of the Argentine National Commission	Argentine Nat. Commission on the Disappeared
26	Brasil: Nunca Mais	Archdiocese of Sao Paulo
27	Detention & Torture in South Africa	University of Cape Town
28	Human Rights Update, South Africa	Human Rights Commission
29	Reports of Task Force Detainees of the Philippines	Task Force Detainees of the Philippines

Individual Listings

Serial number: 01

Data base name: Amnesty International Reports

Organization: Amnesty International Publications
1 Easton Street
London WC1X 8DJ
United Kingdom

Contact person: Gillian Hoffmann
01-833-1771

Purpose: Annual reports place on public record the work of Amnesty International to prevent human rights violations and help victims in over 125 countries. Amnesty International seeks "to identify and free prisoners of conscience, to secure prompt and fair trials for political prisoners and to end torture and executions throughout the world."

Geographic coverage: Worldwide. The coverage of Amnesty Reports has grown to over 125 countries in 1988.

Frequency: Annual since 1962.

Content: The annual report documents, for each country, the detention of political prisoners who are held without being given the chance to defend themselves in a fair and open trial. It describes torture and ill-treatment in detention centers, prisons, and military camps. It records the taking of life by the state in executions and political killings. Although some statistics are given throughout the reports (usually on political killings or illegal detentions), generally speaking, the reports are narrative essays on human rights abuses in particular countries. Amnesty clearly states that statistical or other generalized comparisons cannot adequately measure the full impact of human rights abuses and should not be used as the basis for developing comparative and international statistical data presentations. The Amnesty International statement of principles in this regard states:

Amnesty International is often asked to compare the human rights records of different countries. It does not and cannot do this. Government secrecy and censorship obstruct the flow of information from many countries and impede efforts to verify allegations. Statistical or other generalized comparisons can never measure the impact of human rights abuses on the victims, their families, and the societies of which they are part. Comparisons of governments' human rights practices can be manipulated and misused for political ends. (*Amnesty International Reports, 1987*, p. 2)

Primary sources of information: Diverse

Description of methodology: NA

Published data:

1. Results published annually in *Amnesty International Reports*, Amnesty International Publications, London.

Other means of access: A collection of published and unpublished materials in Amnesty International's Research Archives is available on microfiche from IDC:

> Inter Documentation Company AG
> Industriestrasse 7
> 6300 Zug Switzerland.

The microfiche collection is annually updated, and a cumulative inventory on microfiche lists all individual documents in this collection. Annual reports are also separately available on microfiche from IDC.

Amnesty International's Research Archive includes a wide variety of reports on human rights. For example, Amnesty issues single country reports which focus on different topics in human rights of immediate relevance to that country. They also issue special reports on different topics including torture, the death penalty, political killings, and disappearances.

Derivative uses:

1. James D. Seymour, "Indices of Political Imprisonment," *Human Rights Quarterly* 1, No. 1 (January–March 1979).

2. Neil J. Mitchell and James M. McCormick, "Economic and Political Explanations of Human Rights Violations," World Politics 40 (July 1988): 476–98.

3. David Carleton and Michael Stohl, "The Foreign Policy of Human Rights: Rhetoric and Reality from Jimmy Carter to Ronald Reagan," *Human Rights Quarterly* 7, No. 2 (May 1985).

Serial number: 02

Data base name: The Comparative Survey of Freedom

Organization: Freedom House
48 East 21st Street
New York, NY 10010

Contact person: Joseph E. Ryan, Director
Comparative Survey of Freedom
(212) 473-9691

Purpose: The central purpose of the Survey is to provide an annual review of the status of political rights and civil liberties in the countries of the world.

Geographic coverage: Worldwide. All independent nations and related territories (167 and 56, respectively, in the 1989–90 survey).

Frequency: Annual since 1973 (semiannual reports issued in 1973 and 1974).

Content: Each country is scored on two variables—political rights and civil liberties—using a seven-point scale.

Primary sources of information: Media reports in English.

Description of methodology: An up-to-date description of the survey methods is provided annually in the January-February issue of *Freedom at Issue*.

Published data:

1. Results published annually in January issue of *Freedom at Issue*, published by Freedom House.

2. Data and analysis published in book form: Raymond D. Gastil, ed., *Freedom in the World: Political Rights and Civil Liberties*, by Freedom House for 1978, 1979, and 1980 and by Greenwood Press, Westport, CT for 1981, 1982, 1983–84, 1984–85, 1985–86, 1986–87, and by the University Press of America, 1987–88, 1988–89 and 1989–90.

Other means of access: Survey data for 1972–76 are available on magnetic tape from ICPSR (see introduction to this chapter). Data for selected years during the period from 1973 to 1982 appear in Georg P. Muller, *Comparative World Data: A Statistical Handbook for Social Science* (Baltimore: Johns Hopkins University Press, 1988). The handbook covers the decades of the 1970s and includes data for a total of 51 variables (two from *The Comparative Survey of Freedom*) for 128 countries. The data for the 51 variables are available on diskettes.

Derivative uses:

1. The International Human Suffering Index, 1987, issued by the Population Crisis Committee, Washington, DC.

2. David L. Banks, "The Analysis of Human Rights Data over Time," *Human Rights Quarterly* 8, No. 4 (November 1986): 654–680.

3. David L. Banks, "Patterns of Oppression: A Statistical Analysis of Human Rights," *Proceedings of the Social Statistics Section of the American Statistical Association* (1985): 154–162.

4. David Carleton and Michael Stohl, "The Foreign Policy of Human Rights: Rhetoric and Reality from Jimmy Carter to Ronald Reagan," *Human Rights Quarterly* 7, No. 2 (May 1985): 205–229.

5. Kenneth Bollen, "Political Rights and Political Liberties in Nations: An Evaluation of Human Rights Measures, 1950–1984," *Human Rights Quarterly* 8, No. 4 (November 1986): 567–591.

6. Hans S. Park, "Correlates of Human Rights: Global Tendencies," *Human Rights Quarterly* 9, No. 3 (August 1987): 405–413.

7. "Population Pressures: Threat to Democracy, 1989," issued by The Population Crisis Committee, Washington, DC. (For their full address see Serial Number 06 below.)

Serial number: 03

Data base name: World Military and Social Expenditures

Organization: World Priorities Inc,
Box 25104
Washington, DC 25140

Contact person: Ruth Leger Sivard
(202) 965-1661

Purpose: ". . . provides an annual accounting of the use of world resources for social and military purposes and an objective basis for assessing relative priorities."

Geographic coverage: Worldwide. In the 1987–1988 edition, 142 countries are contained in the data base.

Frequency: Annual since 1975. In "Notes on the Data," in the 1987–1988 edition, Sivard mentions that the statistical tables, although prepared in 1987, are sometimes from 1984 or 1980 data, which is the latest year for which adequate worldwide coverage was possible. Projections to 1984 were necessary for some of the social statistics, while military, population, and GNP data were generally available through 1985 and 1986.

Content: In the statistical annex, Sivard provides three tables that provide a comparative analysis of selected military and social trends. The first table provides a measure of military and social trends for the world (all nations included), developed and developing countries, measured at five-year intervals from 1960 to 1970 and annually thereafter. The military trend variable includes military expenditures measured as a percent of GNP, per capita and per soldier, as well as expenditures on arms exports and imports. The social trend variable includes measures of GNP, foreign economic aid given, population, number of physicians, teachers, and military personnel. The second table provides a country by country measure of selected public expenditures and human resources. Public expenditures include expenditures on military, arms imports, international peacekeeping, education, health, and foreign economic aid given and received. Human resources include the number of members of the armed forces, physicians, and teachers. The third table shows the country rank on a per capita basis for selected indicators of economic and social development.

Primary sources of information: The various data sources used in the statistical tables are listed under separate topics. Two principal sources of information are organizations in the United Nations and the U.S. Government. Various nongovernmental international organizations are also mentioned.

Description of methodology: In the section entitled "Notes on the Data," Sivard provides a brief description of definitions and data sources used in her tables. The section also contains some warnings on the limitations of these data sources.

Published data:

1. Results published with analysis by Ruth Leger Sivard, *World Military and Social Expenditures*, 12th ed. (Washington, DC: World Priorities Inc., 1987).

Other means of access: NA

Derivative uses:

1. George Thomas Kurian, *The New Book of World Rankings* (New York: Facts on File, 1984).

Serial number: 04

Data base name: Country Reports on Human Rights Practices

Organization: U.S. Department of State
2201 C Street, NW
Washington, DC 20520

Contact person: George Lister
Bureau of Human Rights and Humanitarian Affairs
(202) 647-2741

Purpose: Report submitted to the Congress by the Department of State in compliance with Sections 116(d)(1) and 502(b) of the Foreign Assistance Act of 1961, as amended. The legislation requires human rights reports on all countries that receive aid from the United States and all countries that are members of the United Nations.

Geographic coverage: Worldwide. The first report reviewed only 6 nations. The second report, for 1977, covered 82 nations. The third report reviewed 105 countries and the fourth report in 1979 reviewed 115 countries. In 1989, the report covered 170 countries.

Frequency: Annual since 1976.

Content: Narrative reports on all countries, although many reports contain specific numbers of different kinds of human rights violations. Each narrative report contains two very general headings entitled **Respect for Human Rights** and **Economic, Social, and Cultural Situation.** Under the first heading there are four sections, each divided into several subsections. The first section, "Respect for The Integrity of the Person," includes specific subsections on freedom from: (a) political killing; (b) disappearance; (c) torture and cruel, inhuman or degrading treatment or punishment; (d) arbitrary arrest, detention, or exile; (e) denial of fair public trial; (f) arbitrary interference with privacy, family, home or correspondence. The second section, "Respect for Civil Rights," includes specific subsections on (a) freedom of speech and press; (b) freedom of peaceful assembly and association; (c) freedom of religion; (d) freedom of movement within the country, foreign travel, emigration, and repatriation. The last two sections under the general heading of **Respect for Human Rights** are "Respect for Political Rights: The Right of Citizens to Change Their Government" and "Governmental Attitude Regarding International and Nongovernmental Investigation of Alleged Violations of Human Rights." This is followed by a brief description of the economy, health care, and education, a survey of working conditions, rights of women, and where applicable, the treatment of ethnic or national minorities, under the general heading **Economic, Social, and Cultural Situation.**

Primary sources of information: The *Country Reports* are based on information available to the United States Government. Sources include American officials, officials of foreign governments, private citizens, victims of human rights abuse, congressional studies, intelligence information, press reports, international organizations, and nongovernmental organizations concerned with human rights. Much information is not attributed to specific sources. For a broad, public discussion of the quality of the *Country Reports*, see House Committee on Foreign Affairs, Subcommittee on Human Rights and International Organizations, *Review of U.S. Human Rights Policy Hearings*, 98th Cong., 1st sess. (Washington, DC: U.S. Government Printing Office, 1984).

Description of methodology: Appendices A, B, and D of the *Country Reports* (1985). See also Judith Innes de Neufville, "Human Rights Reporting as a Policy Tool: An Examination of the State Department *Country Reports*," *Human Rights Quarterly* 8, No. 4 (November 1986).

Published data:

1. Annual data published in a report to the Committee on Foreign Affairs, House of Representatives and the Committee on Foreign Relations, U.S. Senate by the Department of State. *Country Reports on Human Rights Practices for 1989* (Washington, DC: U.S. Government Printing Office, 1990).

Other means of access: NA

Derivative uses:

1. Charles Humana, *World Human Rights Guide*. See listing 07 below.

2. David Carleton and Michael Stohl, "The Foreign Policy of Human Rights: Rhetoric and Reality from Jimmy Carter to Ronald Reagan," *Human Rights Quarterly* 7, No. 2 (May 1985).

3. "Population Pressures: Threat to Democracy, 1989," issued by The Population Crisis Committee, Washington, DC. (For their full address see listing 06 below.)

4. David L. Cingranelli and Thomas N. Pasquarello, "Human Rights Practices and the Distribution of U.S. Foreign Aid to Latin American Countries," *American Journal of Political Science* 29, No. 3 (August 1985): 539–563.

Serial number: 05

Data base name: Persecution of Human Rights Monitors

Organization: Human Rights Watch
485 5th Avenue
New York, NY 10017

Contact person: Aryeh Neier, Executive Director
(212) 972-8400

Purpose: Human Rights Watch believes that its most important task is to protect those who monitor human rights abuses by their own governments. The dissemination of the information they collect enables the international community to make informed judgements about human rights conditions in different countries.

Geographic coverage: Worldwide. Sixty-two governments included in the report.

Frequency: Annual. First report issued 1987.

Contents: Reports on the persecution of "human rights monitors" and those who are persecuted "because of their connections to human rights monitors." Individuals are listed by name, organization, and country, along with brief descriptions of their human rights activities as well as the date and circumstances of their persecution. The 1988 report lists some 750 cases of persecution either by governments or by some other type of armed group. The 750 cases include fifty reports of killings and three cases of "disappearance" (taken into custody by military or security forces).

Primary sources of information: Affiliated NGOs.

Description of methodology: NA

Published data:

1. *The Persecution of Human Rights Monitors* (Washington, DC: Human Rights Watch, 1988).

Other means of access: NA

Derivative uses: NA

Serial number: 06

Data base name: The Human Suffering Index

Organization: Population Crisis Committee
1120 19th Street, N.W.
Washington, DC 20036

Contact persons: Sharon L. Camp and J. Joseph Speidel
                         (202) 659-1833

Purpose: Attempts to rate and measure the differences in living conditions between countries.

Geographic coverage: Worldwide. 130 countries are included in the index.

Frequency: Plans to update every 5 years.

Contents: Each country is scored on ten variables: (1) Per Capita Gross National Product in U.S. Dollars, (2) Average Annual Rate of Inflation, (3) Average Annual Growth of Labor Force, (4) Average Annual Growth of Urban Population, (5) Infant Mortality Rate per 1,000 Live Births, (6) Daily Per Capita Calorie Supply as Percent of Requirement, (7) Percent of Population with Access to Clean Drinking Water, (8) Energy Consumption Per Capita in Gigajoules, (9) Adult Literacy Rate, (10) Personal Freedom/Governance. This last variable relies on the 1987 Freedom House "Political Rights" variable in *Freedom at Issue*.

Primary sources of information: Most of the data are from the World Bank, the United Nations, and United States government sources.

Description of methodology: Assigns each country a score from zero to ten, for each of the ten variables. The overall rating for a country, the human suffering index number, is determined by summing its scores on the ten variables. The highest possible score for a country is one hundred, which represents the greatest suffering or misery, and the lowest score is zero, which represents the least human suffering. For further information, see item 1 below.

Published data:

1. Sharon L. Camp and J. Joseph Speidel, "The International Human man Suffering Index" (Washington, DC: Population Crisis Committee, 1987).

Other means of access: NA

Derivative uses: NA

Serial number: 07

Data base name: World Human Rights Guide

Organization: None

Contact person: Charles Humana
38 Greyhound Road
London WG 8NX

Purpose: Assesses the human rights performance of countries based on a questionnaire covering 40 human rights drawn from United Nations treaties. "The work seeks to measure the results with a view to establishing a percentage rating on the overall aggregate."

Geographic coverage: Worldwide. Assesses the human rights performance of 120 countries.

Frequency: 1983, 1986. To be repeated at 2- or 3-year intervals, support permitting.

Content: The *World Human Rights Guide* scores 90 countries on each of 40 human rights. Humana divides these rights into five general categories: **Freedom To, Freedom From, Freedom For or Rights To, Legal Rights, Personal Rights.** The results form the basis for a human rights percentage rating. The remaining thirty countries are evaluated on their human rights performance in narrative form. Each of these countries is then assigned a ranking of "good, fair, poor, or bad."

Primary sources of information: Besides information obtained directly from government responses to questionnaires, Humana lists a variety of sources which include the United Nations, the World Bank, Amnesty International, the U.S. Central Intelligence Agency and the U.S. State Department *Country Reports*. Since there are no notes on these sources, it is difficult to assess whether they are of primary or secondary importance in establishing the human rights scores of countries.

Description of methodology: Each of the 90 countries is graded according to a four-point scale (0–3) on 40 human rights. Those human rights which violate the person directly are further weighted by a factor of three. Percentage ratings for each country are obtained by dividing the number of points a country receives by the maximum number of points possible. The maximum number of points a country can receive is 162.

Published data: The following organizations have published either the 1983 or 1986 edition of the *World Human Rights Guide* by Charles Humana

1. Buchet-Chastel, 18 Rue de Conde, Paris 75006 (1985, 1988).

2. Economist Publications, 40 Duke Street, London W1 (1986).

3. Facts On File, 460 Park Avenue South, New York, NY 10016 (1986).

4. Hutchinson and Company, London (1983).

5. Pan Books, Cavaye Place, London SW10 (1987).

6. Pica Press, New York, NY (1984).

Other means of access: NA

Derivative uses:

1. David L. Banks, "Patterns of Oppression: A Statistical Analysis of Human Rights," *Proceedings of the Social Statistics Section of the American Statistical Association* (1985): 154–162.

2. David L. Banks, "Patterns of Oppression: An Exploratory Analysis of Human-Rights Data," *Journal of the American Statistical Association* 84, No. 407 (September 1989): 674–681.

3. Courses on educational psychology by K. Sebaly, Kent State University.

4. Included in schools' human rights courses in France, Norway, Australia, and other countries.

5. United Nations Development Program, *Human Development Report 1991* (New York: Oxford University Press, 1991), pp. 13–21.

Serial number: 08

Data base name: Freedom in National Press Systems

Organization: None

Contact persons: Raymond B. Nixon

Peter Galliner
International Press Institute
Mangoldveg 2
8142 Vitikonwaldegg
Switzerland

Purpose: A comparative analysis of national press systems intended to determine the degree of correlation between press freedoms in national press systems and other variables such as literacy rates and per capita income.

Geographic coverage: Worldwide. The first study covers 85 countries; the second covers 117 countries.

Frequency: Two studies completed, in 1959 and in 1964.

Content: In the first study, countries are classified into one of four categories which range from authoritarian press systems (with strong controls over all mass media) to intermediate press systems (with some authoritarian controls) to free press systems. Another separate category classifies communist press systems. In the first study, three experts, including Nixon, scored each of the 85 countries in the study using a nine-point scale. Correlations between each country's press freedom score, literacy rate and per capita income are presented. In the second study, five experts used the same nine-point scale, but with slightly different verbal descriptions of the scale points, to assign scores to 117 countries. A similar analysis correlates press freedoms with the same variables plus some additional ones.

Primary sources of information: Various United Nations Publications, UNESCO, and the International Press Institute Survey.

Description of methodology: Simple analysis of variance between each country's press freedom score and other quantitative variables.

Published data:

1. Raymond B. Nixon, "Factors Related to Freedom in National Press Systems," *Journalism Quarterly* 37 (Winter 1960): 13–28.

2. Raymond B. Nixon, "Freedom in the World's Press: A Fresh Appraisal with New Data," *Journalism Quarterly* 42 (Winter 1965): 3–5, 118–119.

Other means of access: NA

Derivative uses:

1. Rudolph J. Rummel, *The Dimension of Nations* (Beverly Hills, CA: Sage Publications, 1972).

Serial number: 09

Data base name: Status of International Instruments on Human Rights

Organizational sponsors: United Nations Center for Human Rights
Geneva
Switzerland

Netherlands Institute of Human Rights
Boothstraat 6
3512 BW Utrecht
Netherlands

Contact person(s): NA

Purpose: Updates the status of international human rights instruments.

Geographic coverage: Worldwide.

Frequency: United Nations reports annually for 1978–1983 and 1987. The Netherlands Institute reported once in 1989.

Content: The United Nations report lists twenty-two human rights instruments and the status of each state with respect to that instrument. The Netherlands Institute lists twenty-seven human rights conventions and the status of each state with respect to that convention.

Primary sources of information: NA

Description of methodology: NA

Published data:

1. *Human Rights: Status of International Instruments* (New York: United Nations, 1987).

2. "State of Ratifications of Major Human Rights Conventions," appendix V, *Netherlands Quarterly of Human Rights* 7, No. 3 (1989): 361–375.

Other means of access: NA

Derivative uses: NA

Serial number: 10

Data base name: Conflict and Peace Data Bank (COPDAB)

Organization: Center for International Development and Conflict Management
Mill Building
University of Maryland
College Park, MD 20742

Contact person: Dr. John L. Davies, Research Coordinator
Center for International Development and Conflict Management
(301) 314-7703

Purpose: COPDAB is a computer-based library of daily international and domestic events/interactions. This global data set is intended to make reliable event records readily accessible for researchers, teachers, and policy professionals. It is currently being adapted for use with microcomputers and specialized COPDAB software for data selection, graphic display, and analysis.

Geographic coverage: Worldwide. Events data for 135 nation states, currently being expanded to include 139 states and over 250 nonstate actors from 1979.

Frequency: Onetime, 1948–1978, currently being updated to 1989.

Content: The COPDAB library contains approximately 500,000 event records to 1978. An event statement is a brief verbal description of some domestic or international act which a nation initiates or receives, as summarized from a public source. Each events record contains the following elements: **Date; Actor** (who initiated the event); **Target** (to whom the event was directed); **Source** (where the event description was gathered); **Activity** (the verbal or physical act initiated); **Summary** (information regarding the substance of the event); **Issue Type** (whether economic, political, military, cultural, etc.); **Level of Cooperation Conflict** (15-point scale). More detailed summaries, source, and coder referencing are included from 1979.

Primary sources of information: The events data come from about 70 "reputable public sources," including international and regional news services and archives.

Description of methodology: See item 4 under "Published data."

Published data:

1. Edward E. Azar, "The Analysis of International Events," *Peace Studies Reviews* 4, No. 1 (1970).

2. Edward E. Azar and Joseph D. Ben-Dak, eds., *Theory and Practice of Events Research* (New York and London: Gordon and Breach Science Publishers, 1975).

3. Edward E. Azar and S. Lerner, "The Use of Semantic Dimensions in the Scaling of International Events," *International Interactions* 7 (1981): 361–378.

4. Edward E. Azar, *Codebook for the Conflict and Peace Data Bank* (University of Maryland Center for International Development and Conflict Management, 1982).

Other means of access: ICPSR (see introduction to this chapter).

Derivative uses: There have been many derivative uses of COPDAB data. Listed here are several recent applications.

1. W. J. Dixon, "Reciprocity in US-Soviet Relations: Multiple Symmetry or Issue Linkage?" *American Journal of Political Science* 30 (1986): 421–445.

2. J. Faber, "Measuring Cooperation, Conflict, and the Social Network of Nations," *Journal of Conflict Resolution* 31 (1989): 438–464.

3. Ruth Leger Sivard, *World Military and Social Expenditures*, 12th ed. (Washington, DC: World Priorities Inc., 1987).

4. M. D. Ward and L. L. House, "A Theory of the Behavioral Power of Nations," *Journal of Conflict Resolution* 32 (1988): 3–36.

Serial number: 11

Data base name: Cross-National Time-Series Data Archive

Organization: SUNY at Binghamton
Political Science Department
Binghamton, NY 13901

Contact person: Arthur S. Banks
(607) 777-2000

Purpose: Intended as a research and reference tool in comparative politics. Summarizes a large amount of information "in a form that should enable the trained reader to discern new relationships among political phenomena" and "to assist the reader in discovering patterned co-occurrences and inter-relationships in political institutions, structures and behavior."

Geographic coverage: Worldwide. 115 countries.

Frequency: Onetime. Contains annual indicators for 1950 through 1984.

Content: Of the fifty-seven variables measured in the earliest published work (1963), only a small subset are relevant to civil and political human rights. **Freedom of the Press** (13) measures nations according to a four point scale, ranging from complete freedom of the press to strict censorship or control. The **Constitutional Status** variable (26) assigns nations to one of three categories: constitutional government, authoritarian government, or totalitarian government. **Freedom of Group Opposition** (30) measures nations according to a four-point scale ranging from groups free to enter politics to no groups tolerated in political activity. Published information from a later work (1971) contains some other potentially useful measures of political rights including: Openness of the nominating process (segment 19 field 4), selection process for effective executive (segment 21 field 6), selection process for legislative body (segment 22 field 5), and the effectiveness of the legislative body (segment 22 field 4). Freedom of group opposition (segment 19 field 6) is also continued in this later data base publication. Each of the 1971 measures rates nations on a three- or four-point scale.

Primary sources of information: The appendices to the publications provide lists of sources, which include United Nations reports, books, periodicals, encyclopedias, almanacs and newspapers. Primary sources of information for each variable are footnoted in the section of the publication where the data for that variable are presented. For further information, see the chapter by Bollen in this volume.

Description of methodology: The units of analysis are countries or, according to Banks' more precise specification, "independent polities." Raw values are assigned to each country for each of the 57 variables using a nominal or ordinal scale. A total of 194 dichotomous variables are then constructed, using various combinations of these raw values. The dichotomous variables are used for a variety of country cross-tabulations.

Published data:

1. Arthur S. Banks and Robert B. Textor, *A Cross Polity Survey* (Cambridge, MA: MIT Press, 1963).

2. Arthur S. Banks, *Cross-Polity Time-Series Data* (Cambridge, MA: The MIT Press, 1971).

3. Arthur S. Banks, *Cross-National Time-Series Data Archive User's Manual* (Binghamton: State University of New York at Binghamton, 1979).

Other means of access: NA

Derivative uses:

1. George Thomas Kurian, *The New Book of World Rankings* (New York: Facts on File, 1984).

2. Rudolph J. Rummel, *National Attributes and Behavior* (Beverly Hills, CA: Sage Publications, 1979).

Serial number: 12

Data base name: Dimensionality of Nations Project (DON)

Organization: University of Hawaii at Manoa
Department of Political Science
2424 Maile Way
Honolulu, HI 96816

Contact person: Rudolph J. Rummel
(808) 948-8358

Purpose: "The major concern of the DON project has been to develop a theoretical, empirical, and quantitative framework for understanding the nature of war and violence, and for contributing to their resolution."

Geographic coverage: Worldwide. Data are reported on 72 nations for 1950, 82 nations in 1955, 87 nations in 1960, 107 nations in 1963, and 113 nations in 1965.

Frequency: Onetime. Data reported for the years 1950, 1955, 1960, 1963, and 1965.

Content: The DON project collected data on 236 attributes for each nation. Of these 236 attributes, 91 are reported in published form. Of these 91 reported attributes, at least 7 are relevant to political or civil rights. **Freedom of Political Opposition** (14) rates countries according to a three-point scale. Zero is assigned to nations that do not permit political opposition, one is assigned to nations that have restricted political opposition allowed, and two is assigned to nations that permit most political opposition. **Purges** (24) refers to the number of any systematic jailings or execution of elites with a ruling regime or opposition movement per year. **Demonstrations** (25) refer to the number of publicly reported demonstrations of at least one hundred people per year. **Emigrants to Population** (45) is a simple ratio of emigrants to the total population (in thousands). **Number of**

Political Parties (65) lists the total number of political parties with membership greater than one percent of the population. The **Electoral System** (81) variable rates countries on a three-point scale, according to the degree to which political parties can compete in the general election process. The **Censorship Score** (87) rates countries on a three-point scale according to the extent of government control of the nation's press.

Primary sources of information: United Nations statistical sources, U.S. Government sources, the New York Times, Facts on File, World Encyclopedia of the Nations, and many other sources.

Description of methodology: See items 1 and 3 under "Published data."

Published data:

1. Rudolph J. Rummel, *The Dimension of Nations* (Beverly Hills, CA: Sage Publications, 1972).

2. Rudolph J. Rummel, *The Dimensionality of Nations Project* (Ann Arbor, MI: ICPSR Codebooks, 1976).

3. Rudolph J. Rummel, *National Attributes and Behavior* (Beverly Hills, CA: Sage Publications, 1979).

Other means of access: All data are available on tape through the ICPSR (see introduction to this chapter). Also see ICPSR Codebook, Item 2 above, listed under "Published data."

Derivative uses:

1. R. J. Rummel, *Field Theory Evolving* (Beverly Hills, CA: Sage Publications, 1977).

2. R. J. Rummel, *Understanding Conflict and War,* vols. 1–5 (Beverly Hills, CA: Sage Publications, 1975–81).

Serial number: 13

Data base name: World Handbook of Political and Social Indicators II

Organization: Virginia Polytechnic and State University
          Political Science Department
      Blacksburg, VA 24061

Contact persons: Charles Lewis Taylor
Chair, Political Science Department
Virginia Polytechnic and State University

Michael C. Hudson

Purpose: ". . . attempts to compare nations on a great variety of politically relevant indices . . . to present some of the data necessary for the further development of a science of comparative and international politics and to illustrate some of the means of analyzing the data."

Geographic coverage: Worldwide. Political events data and country indicators for 136 countries.

Frequency: Onetime. Presents data for 57,268 events occurring during the period 1948 to 1967.

Content: Contains national aggregate data for each country. There are 56 tables and 107 time-series analyses, of which only a few are directly relevant to human rights research. **Press Freedom** reproduces data from Ralph Lowenstein's *World Press Freedoms*, which scores nations on an eight-point scale, ranging from positive four, the greatest amount of press freedom, to negative four, the least press freedom. Countries are also ranked according to their score. **Electoral Irregularity** ranks countries and election dates into three categories concerning the fairness of the election. Taylor and Hudson note that the judges for this variable may have unduly penalized single party systems. **Protest Demonstrations** is an annual events count that includes the number of nonviolent gatherings of people organized to protest the policies, ideology, or actions of a regime, government, or political leaders. **Deaths from Domestic Violence** refers to the number of persons killed in events of domestic political conflict annually. This does not include assassinations or political executions which are scored separately on the data tape. **Governmental Sanctions** are actions taken by the authorities to neutralize, suppress, or eliminate a perceived threat to security, the regime, or the state itself. Annual number of events is given for each country.

Primary sources of information: Most events reports were obtained and coded from newspapers or press services.

Description of methodology: See item 2 below.

Published data:

1. Charles Lewis Taylor and Michael C. Hudson, *World Handbook of Political and Social Indicators II* (Ann Arbor, MI: Inter-University Consortium for Political Research, 1971).

2. Charles Lewis Taylor and Michael C. Hudson, *World Handbook of Political and Social Indicators*, 2nd ed. (New Haven, CT: Yale University Press, 1972).

Other means of access: The most complete events file, the daily file, is available on tape from the ICPSR (see introduction to this chapter).

Derivative uses:

1. Ralph Lowenstein, "Press Freedom as a Barometer of Political Democracy," in *International and Intercultural Communications*, ed. Heinz-Dietrich Fischer and John Calhoun Merrill (New York: Hastings House, 1976).

Serial number: 14

Data base name: World Handbook of Political and Social Indicators III

Organization: Virginia Polytechnic and State University
Political Science Department
Blacksburg, VA 24061

Contact persons: Charles Lewis Taylor
Chair, Political Science Department
Virginia Polytechnic and State University

David Jodice

Purpose: "This book provides a record of political protest and violence, state coercive behavior, and formal governmental change and elections in the major countries of the world. These data are useful for the description of political processes in diverse societies and for the analysis over time and across countries of political change and instability."

Geographic coverage: Worldwide. 136 nations.

Frequency: Onetime. Presents country indicators and data for 30,065 events occurring during the period from 1948 to 1977.

Content: This data base was designed to extend and elaborate some of the series already available in *World Indicators II* as well as present some new ones. It updates to 1977 the **Protest Demonstration** and **Government Sanction** variables and reproduces selected years of political rights and civil liberties measures by Gastil. It also includes a measure of **Political Executions**, an event in which a person or group is put to death under orders of the national authorities while in their custody. Researchers should be aware that subtle differences exist in the coding of events between *World Indicators II* and *World Indicators III*. Some variables from each data set have the same name but contain different information.

Primary sources of information: Most events reports were obtained and coded from newspapers or press services.

Description of methodology: See item 1 below under "Published data."

Published data: The following book presents a selected subset of data on 136 countries:

1. Charles Lewis Taylor and David Jodice, *World Handbook of Political and Social Indicators III*. 3rd ed. (New Haven, CT: Yale University Press, 1983).

Other means of access: The complete data set is reported in both daily and annual format in the archival data tapes available from the Zentralarchiv fur Empirische Sozialforschung in Cologne and the ICPSR (see introduction to this chapter).

1. Zentralarchiv fur Empirische Sozialforschung
   Universitat zu Koln
   Bachemer Str. 40
   D-5000 Koln 41
   Federal Republic of Germany

Data for riots, protest demonstrations, and political strikes for the 5-year period 1970–1974 appear in Georg P. Muller, *Comparative World Data: A Statistical Handbook for Social Science* (Baltimore: Johns Hopkins University Press, 1988). The handbook includes data for a total of 51 variables (three from this source) for 128 countries. The data for the 51 variables are available on diskettes.

Derivative uses: NA

Serial number: 15

Data base name: Genocides and Politicides Since 1945

Organization: Political Science Department
U.S. Naval Academy
Annapolis, MD 21402

Contact person: Barbara Harff
(301) 267-2430

Purpose: This global survey of episodes of massive state repression "is part of larger comparative study whose objective is to test and refine theories about conditions leading to genocides and politicides."

Geographic coverage: Worldwide. Episodes in 32 countries.

Frequency: Onetime. Covers episodes occurring in the period 1945–1985.

Content: Contains data for each of 44 episodes. Each episode is classified by a typology which distinguishes between two types of genocide (in which victim groups are defined in terms of communal characteristics) and four types of politicide (in which victim groups are defined in terms of their political status or opposition to the state). Data for each episode include the country, type, and duration of the episode, a name for each of the victimized groups, and the number of victims.

Primary sources of information: Historical and journalistic accounts; reports from various advocacy organizations.

Description of methodology: See item 1 under "Published data."

Published data:

1. Barbara Harff and T. R. Gurr, "Research Note. Toward an Empirical Theory of Genocides and Politicides: Identification and Measurement of Cases Since 1945," *International Studies Quarterly* 32, No. 3 (September 1988).

2. Barbara Harff and T. R. Gurr, "Genocides and Politicides Since 1945: Evidence and Anticipation," *Internet on the Holocaust and Genocide* 13 (December 1987).

3. Barbara Harff, "State Perpetrators of Political Mass Murder Since 1945," paper presented at the Conference on State Organized Terror: The Case of Violent Internal Repression, Michigan State University, November 2–5, 1988.

Other means of access: NA

Derivative uses: NA

Serial number: 16

Data base name: A Global Survey of Minorities' Rights at Risk

Organizations: University of Maryland
Government and Politics Department
Lefrak Hall
College Park, MD 20742

University of Colorado at Boulder
Political Science Department
CB 333
Boulder, CO 80302

Contact persons: Ted Robert Gurr and James R. Scarritt
(301) 405-4121 (Gurr)

Purpose: This data base is part of a more general research effort aimed at developing and coding information on minorities' involvement in conflict, concentrating on the period since 1945. It focuses on minorities that are subject to conditions that impair or threaten to impair their survival rights. Survival rights are identified by the authors as rights to political security and economic subsistence. Two related indicators are used to determine whether a minority's survival rights are at risk: the existence of malign differential treatment by the larger society (in the form of political or economic discrimination) and/or the pursuit of more favorable differential treatment that aims at promoting group interests (as sought by separatists and by advantaged minorities).

Geographic coverage: Worldwide. The study covers all 126 countries with populations over one million in the 1980s. The initial data set identifies 261 communal groups in 99 of these countries.

Frequency: Onetime. The population and status of communal groups are recorded for the 1980s. A subsequent version of the data set will include more comprehensive and discriminating codings of group status and demands and codings of their involvement in open conflict from 1945 to 1989.

Content: Each of the 246 communal groups (or minorities) is listed in the published data base by name and country of residence with estimates of its absolute and proportional population and categorical codings of its type, status, and geographic dispersion. These data are summarized in three tables. The first table analyzes minorities in each of the eight world regions: the number of countries in the region with minorities at risk, the number of groups at risk, and the total population of minorities at risk, expressed in absolute terms and as a percentage of total regional population. The second table summarizes information on the types and status of minorities in each region: advantaged minorities (n = 28) have disproportionate political power or material advantage; separatist minorities (n = 72) pursue greater autonomy (or have done so at some time since 1945); while 185 groups now or in the recent past have been subject to discrimination. (Some groups are both separatist and subject to discrimination.) The third table lists countries with more than twenty-five percent of their populations at risk.

Primary sources of information:

1. Ted Robert Gurr and Erika B. K. Gurr, "Group Discrimination and Potential Separatism in 1960 and 1975," In *World Handbook of Political and Social Indicators III*, 3rd ed., vol. 1, by Charles Lewis Taylor and David Jodice (New Haven, CT: Yale University Press, 1983), pp. 50–57, 66–75.

2. Georgina Ashworth, ed., *World Minorities* (volumes I, II, and III published in London: Quartermaine House Ltd., for the Minority Rights Group, 1977, 1978, and 1980, respectively for each volume).

3. *Minority Rights Group Reports*, Nos. 1–80.

4. *Cultural Survival Quarterly*, various editions and special reports of Cultural Survival, Inc.

Description of methodology: See item 1 listed below.

Published data:

1. Ted Robert Gurr and James Scarritt, "Minorities' Rights at Risk: A Global Survey," *Human Rights Quarterly* 11, No. 3 (August 1989).

Other means of access: Copies of the *Minorities Coding Sheet: Short Form* which is being used for in-depth coding are available from the Center for International Development and Conflict Management, University of Maryland, College Park, MD 20742. A version of the updated data set will eventually be available on disk from this source.

Derivative uses:

1. Barbara Harff and T. R. Gurr, "Victims of the State: Genocide, Politicides and Group Repression since 1945," *International Review of Victimology* 1, No. 1 (1989): 23–41.

Serial number: 17

Data base name: World Directory of Minorities

Organization: The Minority Rights Group
379-391 Brixton Road
London, SW9 7DE
United Kingdom

Contact person: Alan Phillips, Executive Director
02-79-442601

Purpose: Provides a listing of ethnic, linguistic, and religious minorities and indigenous peoples and nomadic tribes.

Geographic coverage: Worldwide.

Frequency: Onetime

Content: The minorities listed in this directory are mainly "larger minority groups" who have been considered minorities for at least 40–50 years; therefore some smaller and newer minority groups are excluded. Individual entries have been grouped into 11 world regions: North America; South America; Central America; Eastern Europe; U.S.S.R.; Western Europe and Scandinavia; Middle East and North Africa; Sub-Saharan Africa; South Asia and East Asia; South-East Asia; and Oceania. Each entry provides: alternative names of the minority group, its location, its current population (total and as a percent of the region it inhabits), its religion, and its language. Each entry includes a narrative report on social and political characteristics of the minority group and the region it inhabits.

Primary sources of information: Most of the information contained in the *Directory* comes from the Minority Rights Group's own reports (see item 2 under "Published data"). Some information came from reports published by other nongovernmental organizations, whose names are listed in the Preface (pp. xv) of the *Directory*.

Description of methodology: NA

Published data:

1. Patrick Thornberry, ed., *World Directory of Minorities* (London: Longman, 1989).

2. Georgina Ashworth, ed., *World Minorities, Volume 1* (London: Quartermaine House, Ltd., 1977).

3. Georgina Ashworth, ed., *World Minorities, A Second Volume* (London: Quartermaine House, Ltd., 1978).

4. Georgina Ashworth, ed., *World Minorities in the Eighties* (London: Quartermaine House, Ltd., 1980).

Other means of access: NA

Derivative uses: NA

Serial number: 18

Data base name: Journalism Morbidity Survey

Organizational sponsor: Freedom House
48 East 21st Street
New York, NY 10010

Contact person: Leonard R. Sussman
(212) 473-9691

Purpose: Viewing the free flow of information as a human right, the purpose of the Journalism Morbidity Survey is to monitor the treatment of journalists worldwide, spotlighting hindrances to their professional activities.

Geographic coverage: Worldwide. The 1989 survey listed 1,164 cases in 84 countries.

Frequency: Annual, since 1982.

Content: For each year of coverage, statistics are given for the number of journalists killed, kidnapped and disappeared, arrested and detained, and expelled. Other statistics concerning specific types of coercion of the press are given for 1988 and subsequent years.

Primary sources of information: Freedom House correspondents, Committee to Protect Journalists, Observatoire de l'Information and others.

Description of methodology: An up-to-date description of the survey methodology is provided annually in the January-February issue of *Freedom at Issue*.

Published data:

1. Leonard R. Sussman, *Power, the Press and the Technology of Freedom: The Coming of Age of ISDN* (New York: Freedom House, 1989).

2. Leonard R. Sussman, "Journalism Morbidity Table," *Freedom At Issue*, January–February 1990 (New York: Freedom House, 1990).

Other means of access: Xerox University Microfilms
Ann Arbor, MI

Derivative uses: NA

Serial number: 19

Data base name: Physical Quality of Life Index (PQLI)

Organization: Overseas Development Council
1717 Massachusetts Avenue, NW
Washington, DC 20036

Contact person: Mr. Stuart Tucker
(202) 234-8701

Purpose: The PQLI attempts to measure the performance of the world's poorest countries in meeting the most basic needs of people. It measures basic needs by focusing on some of the most immediate indicators of human welfare.

Geographic coverage: Worldwide. Provides an index for 150 countries.

Frequency: Onetime. Based on data gathered between 1970 and 1975, although some country indices are based on older information dating from 1947 to 1969.

Content: The PQLI is based on three indicators: infant mortality, life expectancy at age one, and literacy. Individual countries are evaluated on a scale from zero to one hundred for each indicator. The PQLI value for each country is presented along with other information in three tabular appendices. Appendix A compares the PQLI number assigned to countries within four different categories of GNP. Appendix B lists each country according to its PQLI rank and

GNP rank. Finally, Appendix C lists PQLI indicators by sex for seventy-four countries for various years between 1947 to 1973.

Primary sources of information: United Nations statistical sources, the World Bank, as well as some others. See Appendix A in the work listed under "Published data" below.

Description of methodology: The PQLI indicator for literacy is measured as a percentage of the population over fifteen years of age who are literate. This percentage corresponds directly to the PQLI literacy indicator. The PQLI indicator for infant mortality, which is scaled from zero to one hundred, is based on infant mortality rates ranging from 7 (100) to 229 (0) per thousand live births. This means that a 2.22 decrease in the infant mortality rate will show up as a one-point increase in the PQLI infant mortality indicator. Similarly, the PQLI indicator for life expectancy at age one is based on years of life expectancy at age one, ranging from 38 years (0) to 77 years (100). This means that an increase in life expectancy of 0.39 years will result in a one-point increase in the PQLI life expectancy indicator. The overall PQLI is the unweighted mean of the three indicators.

Published data:

1. Morris David Morris, *Measuring the Conditions of the World's Poor: The Physical Quality of Life Index* (New York: Pergamon Press, published for the Overseas Development Council, 1979).

Other means of access: NA

Derivative uses:

1. Han S. Park, "Correlates of Human Rights: Global Tendencies," *Human Rights Quarterly* 9, No. 3 (August 1987): 405–413.

Serial number: 20

Data base name: Indices of Political Imprisonment

Organization: None

Contact person: James D. Seymour
SPEAHR
P.O. Box 1212 Cathedral Station
New York, NY 10025

Purpose: Attempts to summarize, using information on "political imprisonment," the degree to which Article 19 of the Universal Declaration of Human Rights has been respected throughout the world.

Geographic coverage: Worldwide.

Frequency: Onetime. Reference date is January 1, 1977, or as close to that date as possible.

Content: Categorical rating of each country, according to the number of political prisoners held per million of population.

Primary sources of information:

1. *Amnesty International Reports: 1977.* Also relies on the 1975 and 1976 Amnesty Reports.

Description of methodology: See item 1 below.

Published data:

1. James D. Seymour, "Indices of Political Imprisonment," *Universal Human Rights* 1, No. 1 (January–March 1979).

Other means of access: NA

Derivative uses: NA

Serial number: 21

Data base name: U.S. Foreign Assistance and Human Rights Policy in 23 Latin American Countries

Organization: Institute of Latin American Studies
Hamilton Hall
University of North Carolina
Chapel Hill, NC 27599-3205

Contact person: Lars Schoultz
(919) 962-0422

Purpose: "The purpose of this paper is to analyze two related aspects of comparative human rights behavior: the comparative level of human rights violations among twenty-three Latin American nations; and the comparative level of financial support of human rights violations in Latin America by the Administrations of Presidents Ford and Carter."

Geographic coverage: Twenty-three Latin American countries.

Frequency: Onetime. Covers the period 1975 to 1979.

Content: The relationship between U.S. foreign assistance and human rights behavior was measured by two variables. One variable, foreign assistance, was measured in terms of absolute levels of aid to countries. The other variable, human rights behavior, was measured by surveying a group of experts knowledgeable about international human rights. The experts were asked to rank "the level of human rights violations by each Latin American government in 1976." Countries were then assigned a rank order according to the mean expert assessment of the level of human rights violations in each country.

Primary sources of information: U.S. aid data were obtained from U.S. government sources, and human rights data were compiled from 38 responses to a questionnaire that was sent to 91 human rights experts.

Description of methodology: Simple comparison between aid levels and mean evaluation of human rights behavior using ordinary least squares regression and first- and second-order correlations.

Published data:

1. Lars Schoultz, "U.S. Foreign Policy and Human Rights Violations in Latin America: A Comparative Analysis of Foreign Aid Distributions," *Comparative Politics* 13, No. 2 (January 1981): 149–170.

2. Lars Schoultz, "U.S. Policy Toward Human Rights in Latin America: A Comparative Analysis of Two Administrations," in *Global Human Rights: Public Policies, Comparative Measures, and NGO Strategies*, ed. Ved P. Nanda, James R. Scarritt, and George W. Shepherd, Jr. (Boulder, CO: Westview Press, 1981).

Other means of access: NA

Derivative uses:

1. William C. Wipfler, "Human Rights Violations and U.S. Foreign Assistance: The Latin American Connection," in *Human Rights and U.S. Foreign Policy*, ed. Peter G. Brown and Douglas MacLean (Lexington, MA: D. C. Heath & Co., Lexington Books, 1979).

Serial number: 22

Data base name: Survey of Latin American Political Democracy

Organization: None

Contact persons: R. H. Fitzgibbon and K. F. Johnson
Kenneth F. Johnson
University of Missouri at St. Louis
8001 Natural Bridge Road
St. Louis, MO 63121

Purpose: A limited polling of specialists to provide data to measure the degree of democracy attained in twenty Latin American nations.

Geographic coverage: Twenty Latin American nations.

Frequency: Every five years from 1945 to 1980.

Content: Based on the responses from a questionnaire sent to a panel of Latin American experts, each country is given a rating on fifteen indicators of democracy. Several of these indicators may be considered measures of political or civil rights, such as: (1) Freedom of the press, speech, assembly, radio, etc., (2) Free and honest elections, (3) Freedom of party organization, (4) Respect for the decisions of the judiciary.

Primary sources of information: Survey questionnaires completed by expert respondents.

Description of methodology: Continuing with Fitzgibbon's initial research from 1945 (See item 1 under "Published data"), a panel of Latin American experts was asked to evaluate twenty nations according to fifteen different criteria. The responses of experts were then used to construct a rating for each country. Experts were polled every five years. For a complete description of the methodology, see item 2 under "Published data."

Published data:

1. Russell H. Fitzgibbon, "Measurement of Latin-American Political Phenomena: A Statistical Experiment," *American Political Science Review* 45 (June 1951): 517–523.

2. Kenneth F. Johnson, "Measuring the Scholarly Image of Latin American Democracy, 1945–1970," in *Statistical Abstract of Latin America*, ed. James A. Wilkie (Los Angeles: University of California, 1976), p. 17.

3. Kenneth F. Johnson, "The 1980 Image-Index Survey of Latin American Political Democracy," *Latin American Research Review* 17, No. 3 (1982): 193–201.

Other means of access: NA

Derivative uses: NA

Serial number: 23

Data base name: Violence and Repression in Latin America

Organization: Graduate School of International Studies
University of Denver
Denver, CO 80210

Contact persons: Ernest A. Duff and John F. McCamant (Denver)

Purpose: Violence and repression vary considerably in Latin America and are caused by conditions common to these countries and their societies. The purpose of this study, therefore, is to isolate these common characteristics and show how they explain almost all variations in violence and repression when it occurs in that region.

Geographic coverage: Twenty Latin American nations.

Frequency: Onetime. Annual data for 1950 through 1970.

Content: Both violence and repression are measured annually for each of the twenty Latin American countries. The **repression variable** is constructed using four (highly correlated) indicators which are scored according to a four-point scale. The four indicators are: suspension of constitutional guarantees; arrests, exiles and executions (of political opponents); restriction on the organization of political parties; and censorship of the media. The four indicators are averaged to create a measure for that year. The authors note that "on three of our [indicators] the determination is made on the basis of assessing the situation rather than in counting repression occurrences or events." The **violence variable** is constructed by scoring events of armed and unarmed violence for each year. Armed violence includes the number of days of reported armed opposition; the casualties per ten million of the population, and the number of participants per one million of the population. Each of these categories is measured according to a nine-point scale, assigned a weight depending upon the category, and then averaged. Unarmed violence includes the number of days of reported unarmed opposition and the number of participants per one million of the population. These categories are then measured in the same way as the armed violence categories. Both armed and unarmed scores are standardized and then added to create the yearly violence measure for each country. The authors explain variations in both repression and violence variables by two different multiple regression equations.

Primary sources of information: Many sources of information are informally mentioned, and the authors include a bibliography at the end of their book. (See item 1 listed under "Published data" below.) Nevertheless, the exact set of sources used for constructing their indices of repression and violence cannot be precisely determined from their descriptions in the text.

Description of methodology: Each Latin American country is assigned a violence number and a repression number for each year. The variation which occurs in violence and repression for countries is explained by appeal to several multiple regression equations. Using a stepwise multiple regression procedure, three variables are used to predict violence, and two variables are used to predict repression. These equations are then illustrated with empirical cases.

Published data:

1. Ernest A. Duff and John F. McCamant, *Violence and Repression in Latin America: A Quantitative and Historical Analysis* (New York: The Free Press, 1976).

2. Ernest A. Duff and John F. McCamant, "Measuring Social and Political Requirements for System Stability in Latin America," *American Political Science Review* 62 (December 1968): 1125–1143.

Other means of access: NA

Derivative uses: NA

Serial number: 24

Data base name: Human Rights in Developing Countries

Organization: Christian Michelsen Institute
Danish Center of Human Rights
Norwegian Institute of Human Rights
Abo Akademi Institute for Human Rights
Netherlands Institute of Human Rights, Utrecht
Human Rights Research and Education Centre, Ottawa

Contact person: Mr. Tor Skalnes
Chr. Michelsen Institute
Fantoftvegen 38
N-5036 Fantoft Bergen
Norway

Purpose: To guide the allocation of development assistance by monitoring human rights performance in countries receiving aid from five donor countries: Norway, Denmark, the Netherlands, Finland, and Canada.

Geographic coverage: International. The 1988/89 report included thirteen countries: Bangladesh, Botswana, India, Kenya, Mozambique, Nicaragua, Pakistan, the Philippines, Sri Lanka, Suriname, Tanzania, Zambia, and Zimbabwe. Eleven of these countries were included in the 1987/88 report and ten in both previous reports.

Frequency: Annual since 1985.

Content: Narrative reports on countries receiving development assistance, although most reports contain specific numbers on different kinds of human rights violations. Each report begins with three tables entitled **Fact Sheet, Economy and Development Aid**, and **Social Indicators**, respectively. There are six narrative sections in each report: **Summary; The Government position on human rights; System of governance and the right to participation; Civil rights; Socio-economic rights;** and **Equality, non-discrimination, rights of peoples and minorities.** The section on **Civil rights** contains subsections on: Life, liberty, and integrity of person; administration of justice; and freedom of movement.

Primary sources of information: A variety of government and international sources are listed, including "first hand information such as fact-finding missions carried on by the authors and well-checked reports from various local and international NGOs and inter-governmental organizations."

Description of methodology: The 1989 *Yearbook* was prepared by a project group of 19 independent researchers in different disciplines, following guidelines prepared by participating institutes. See the introduction to the 1989 *Yearbook* and the chapter by Kathleen Pritchard in this volume.

Published data: The first edition of this yearbook, item 1, was a pilot project in Norwegian only:

1. *Menneskerettighetene i Norges hovedsamarbeidsland 1985* (Bergen/Oslo: Christian Michelsen Institute/Det norske menneskerettighetsprosjektet, 1985).

The second edition was published in both Norwegian and English:

2. Skalnes, T. and Egeland, J. (eds.), *Human Rights in Developing Countries 1986: A Yearbook on Countries Receiving Norwegian Aid,* Christian Michelsen Institute (Oslo: Norwegian University Press, 1986).

The first collaborative report was issued by the three institutions including Christian Michelsen Institute, Danish Center of Human Rights, and the Norwegian Institute of Human Rights.

3. Bard-Anders Andreassen and Asbjorn Eide, eds., *Human Rights in Developing Countries 1987/1988* (Akademisk Forlag, Copenhagen: 1988).

The next collaborative report was issued by the five institutions mentioned above.

4. Manfred Nowak and Theresa Swinehart, eds., *Human Rights in Developing Countries, 1989 Yearbook* (Arlington, VA: N. P. Engel, 1990).

Other means of access: N. P. Engel Verlag
P.O. Box 1670
Gutenbergstr. 29
D-7640 Kehl am Rhein
FEDERAL REPUBLIC OF GERMANY
Fax 07-8510-4234

Derivative uses: NA

Serial number: 25

Data base name: Nunca Mas: Report of the Argentine National Commission

Organization: Argentine National Commission on the Disappeared (CONADEP)
Buenos Aires, Argentina

Contact person: Guillermo Frugoni Rey
Undersecretariat for Human Rights
Ministry of Interior
Balcarce 26
Buenos Aires, Argentina

Purpose: A report to the people of Argentina on the so-called "Dirty War" carried out by the Argentine military dictatorship. The principal aims of the Commission included: the recording of depositions from witnesses; the identification of secret detention camps; finding the methods of disappearances; investigating crimes committed concerning the property of the disappeared; clarifying events relating to the disappearance of persons in Argentina; and investigating their fate or whereabouts.

Geographic coverage: Argentina.

Frequency: Onetime. Covers the period from 1976 to 1982.

Content: Based on the work of the National Commission on the Disappeared, *Nunca Más* details the abuses of human rights of so-called subversives by the military in Argentina. Although the report contains some statistics, it is primarily a narrative description of the extent and nature of the repressive apparatus and the victims who suffered either torture or some other violation of their political and civil rights during this time. The report also describes the role of the judiciary during the repression.

Primary sources of information: Depositions from relatives of the disappeared in 7,380 case files, testimonies of people released from secret detention centers, and statements by members of the security forces who had taken part in the acts of repression.

Description of methodology: See part 4, "Creation and Organization of the National Commission on the Disappeared," in the work cited below.

Published data:

1. *Nunca Más, The Report of the Argentine Commission on the Disappeared* (New York: Farrar Straus Giroux, in association with Index on Censorship, London, 1986).

2. *Nunca Más, Informe de la Comisión Nacional sobre la Desaparición de Personas,* ed. Ernest Sabato (Buenos Aires: Editorial Universitaria de Buenos Aires, 1984).

Other means of access: NA

Derivative uses: NA

Serial number: 26

Data base name: Brasil: Nunca Mais (Never Again)

Organization: The Archdiocese of São Paulo
São Paulo, Brazil

Contact persons: Cardinal Paulo Evaristo Arns
Archbishop of São Paulo

Dr. Jaime Wright

Joan Dassin, Representante
Fundacão Ford
Praia do Flamengo 100, 12 andar
CEP 22210 Rio de Janeiro, RJ
Brasil

Purpose: A report on violations of political and civil rights as well as rights concerning the integrity of the person, under the Brazilian military regime.

Geographic coverage: Brazil.

Frequency: Onetime. Covers the period 1964 through 1979.

Content: The project archive, entitled "Project A," includes the military court proceedings of 707 complete trials held in Brazilian military courts from 1964 through 1979 and fragmentary records for dozens of others. The archive also includes 120 different statistical tables on the treatment of individuals in the Brazilian military judicial system. There is a listing of the 17,420 people who in some way were caught up in the military justice system. This listing contains four subsections: those charged and taken to court; those charged but not taken to court; witnesses who were arrested; and others required to give depositions. There is a listing of individual torturers as well as lists of bureaucrats who sanctioned or participated in violations of individual rights. Project A includes some 2,700 pages of testimony, given by 1,843 political prisoners, which document 283 types of torture.

Primary sources of information: Records and documents from Brazilian military court proceedings.

Description of methodology:

1. Lawrence Weschler, "A Reporter At Large (Brasil: Nunca Mais)," parts I and II, *New Yorker*, May 25, 1987 and June 1, 1987.

Published data:

1. Joan Dassin, ed., *Torture in Brazil*, trans. Jaime Wright (New York: Vintage Books, 1986).

2. Joan Dassin, ed., *Brasil: Nunca Mais* (Petropolis: Editora Vozes Ltda., 1985).

3. *Perfil dos Atingidos*, projeto "Brasil: Nunca Mais" (Petropolis: Editora Vozes Ltda., 1988).

Other means of access: A copy of Project A is currently housed at Columbia University in the City of New York, Law School Library, International Law Section, 435 West 116th Street, New York, NY 10027-7297.

Derivative uses: NA

Serial number: 27

Data base name: A Study of Detention and Torture in South Africa

Organization: University of Cape Town
Department of Psychology
Rondebosch 7700
South Africa

Contact person: Don Foster
02-1-650-3435

Purpose: A study of the legal, historical, and psychological aspects of detention in South Africa. This study provides detailed information on conditions, events, and actions surrounding periods of detention. It analyzes reports by former detainees of their psychological states and symptoms during and following detention.

Geographic coverage: South Africa.

Frequency: Onetime, covering the period 1975 through 1984.

Content: The study analyzes 176 cases of detention in South Africa. All detainees in the study were interviewed and the information they provided was coded. The results are presented in frequency tables covering the following areas of detention: pre-detention aspects, patterns of arrest, general patterns of detention, physical conditions of detention, conditions of interrogation, contact during detention, incidence of physical torture, claims regarding psychological torture, reported health problems during detention, and reported problems on release from detention.

Primary sources of information: Intensive personal interviews with 158 former detainees on a country-wide basis. (Some individuals in the study were detained more than once.)

Description of methodology: For a detailed description of the interview procedures, see item 1 under "Published data," especially chapter 5.

Published data:

1. Don Foster, "Social Science and Apartheid: Research on Detention and Torture in South Africa," presentation to American Association for the Advancement of Science, Philadelphia, May 26, 1986.

2. Don Foster, *Detention and Torture in South Africa* (Cape Town: David Philip Publisher, 1987).

3. Don Foster, Diane Sandler, and Dennis Davis, "Detention, Torture, and the Criminal Justice Process in South Africa," *International Journal of the Sociology of Law* 15 (1985–1986): 105–120.

4. Don Foster, "Political Detention in South Africa," *International Journal of Mental Health* 18, No. 1 (1989): 21–37.

Other means of access: See the Appendix of Foster (1987). Although the questionnaires are stored at the University of Cape Town, the material is, according to Dr. Foster, "too sensitive for general use."

Derivative uses: NA

Serial number: 28

Data base name: Human Rights Update of South Africa

Organization: Human Rights Commission (HRC)
PO Box 32723
Braamfontein 2017
Johannesburg, South Africa

Centre for Applied Legal Studies (CALS)
University of Witwatersrand
WITS 2050
Johannesburg, South Africa
01-1-716-5666

Contact persons: Dr. Max Coleman (HRC), formerly Director
Detainees' Parents Support Committee (DPSC)
Professor John Dugard, Director (CALS)

Purpose: *Human Rights Update* monitors and publicizes information on human rights violations by the South African Government. The publication of *Human Rights Update* was largely the result of the banning of the Detainees' Parents Support Committee in February 1988. Before it was banned, the DPSC published reports on detentions, deaths in detention, new security measures, and political trials in South Africa.

Geographic coverage: South Africa.

Frequency: Quarterly, beginning April 1988. Similar information was published by the Detainees' Parent Support Committee (DPSC) before it was banned by the South African government. The DPSC published a monthly report beginning August 1981.

Content: *Human Rights Update* contains current information on emergency regulations, bannings under security legislation, attacks on individuals and property, political trials, executions, deaths in detention and policy custody, and detentions. Some information contained in *Human Rights Update* is primarily narrative in form; however, many published lists and tables in the *Update* could be used for statistical analyses. Their "Fact Papers" in part accomplish this. Fact papers focus on particular topics already reported on in the *Update*; for example, "Banning of Organizations," which lists organizations banned or restricted under different statutes for the period from 1950 to 1988. It also presents the number of organizations banned from 1950 to 1988 by region and the proportion of different types of organizations affected. "Detention of Individuals" presents tables on the number of detainees each year by the reason for detention and graphs from 1986 to 1988, showing the daily number of detainees, detention exceeding 30 days, and estimated total of all detentions. "Deaths in Detention" presents various statistics on the number of deaths in detention.

Primary sources of information: NA

Description of methodology: NA

Published data:

1. *Human Rights Update.* A quarterly report by the Human Rights Commission of South Africa in association with the Centre For Applied Legal Studies.

2. "Fact Paper," published irregularly by Human Rights Commission of South Africa.

3. "DPSC Report." A monthly report issued by the Detainees' Parents Support Committee.

Other means of access: NA

Derivative uses: NA

Serial number: 29

Data base name: Reports of the Task Force on Detainees of the Philippines (TFDP)

Organization: The Research, Documentation, and Information Desk of the Task Force Detainees of the Philippines, National Center.

Contact person: Sister Cres Lucera
Human Rights Update
Sisters Formation Institute
214 N. Domingo Street
Cubao, Quezon City
Republic of the Philippines

Purpose: Originally, TFDP sought to document and systematically report on the adverse consequences for human rights of martial law imposed by President Ferdinand Marcos (1972–1983). Human rights violations have persisted beyond the Marcos regime and during the incumbency of President Corazon Aquino. Accordingly, TFDP reports continue to be published internationally and presented to the Human Rights Commission of the Philippines, established by the Constitution of 1987.

Geographic coverage: The Philippines.

Frequency: Irregularly from 1976 to 1986. Monthly since 1986 in *Philippines Human Rights Update*.

Content: TFDP "works for the promotion and observance of both civil/political rights and economic/social/cultural rights . . . but constrained by its resources to addressing the more basic rights (mainly civil and political rights)." The Philippine situation is "complicated by armed conflict between government troopers and rebels," and thus TFDP reports also reflect violations of Hague and Geneva conventions and other provisions of humanitarian law. TFDP has consistently documented incidents of "salvaging"—a term that connotes surreptitious murder, massacres involving the murder of several persons in one incident, and "strafings," or random firing incidents that typically kill several persons. Since 1977 TFDP has published annual comparative statistics on the number of persons arrested, persons salvaged, victims of involuntary disappearances, and cases of massacres and "frustrated massacres." Reporting on the last category could be understated in the pre-1985 period.

Primary sources of information: Direct field reporting by church and TFDP groups that compile data in documentation centers throughout the archipelago and then send them on for assessment and aggregation to the National Center.

Description of methodology:

1. "Practical Human Rights," *Philippine Human Rights Update* 2, No. 4 (international edition, August 15–September 14, 1987): 4–5, 21–22.

Published data:

1. Association of Major Religious Superiors, *Political Detainees in the Philippines* (Manila: 1976).

2. "The Human Rights Record of the Aquino Government in its First 1,000 Days of Office," *Philippine Human Rights Update* 3, No. 11 (international edition, November 15–December 14, 1988): 8–17.

Other means of access: NA

Derivative uses:

1. Canada-Asia Working Group, *Submission to the 42d Session of the United Nations Commission on Human Rights: Philippines, etc.* (Ontario, Canada: Canadian Inter-Church Coalition on Asian Concerns, 1986).

2. Commission of the Churches on International Affairs, *Philippines: Testimonies on Human Rights Violations* (Geneva: World Council of Churches, 1986).

3. Richard P. Claude, "The Philippines," in *International Human Rights Handbook*, ed. Jack Donnelly and Rhoda Howard (Boulder, CO: Westview Press, 1987), pp. 279–299.

Contributors

David L. Banks	Department of Statistics Carnegie Mellon University, Pittsburgh, Pennsylvania
Maria Julia Bihurriet	Subsecretariat of Human Rights Ministry of Interior, Argentina
Kenneth A. Bollen	Department of Sociology University of North Carolina, Chapel Hill
Michael Cain	Department of Government and Politics University of Maryland, College Park
Richard P. Claude	Department of Government and Politics University of Maryland, College Park
Glenn Dickinson	Urban Morgan Institute for Human Rights University of Cincinnati, Cincinnati, Ohio
William B. Fairley	Analysis and Inference, Inc. Philadelphia, Pennsylvania
Judith Dueck	HURIDOCS Task Force Leader Winnipeg, Manitoba, Canada
Robert Justin Goldstein	Department of Political Science Oakland University, Oakland, California
Ted Robert Gurr	Department of Government and Politics University of Maryland, College Park
Barbara Harff	Department of Political Science U.S. Naval Academy, Annapolis, Maryland
Judith Eleanor Innes	Department of City and Regional Planning University of California, Berkeley
Thomas B. Jabine	Statistical Consultant Washington, DC

George Lopez   Institute for International Peace Studies
                               University of Notre Dame, Notre Dame, Indiana

Manfred Nowak   Verwaltungsakademie des Bundes
                               Vienna, Austria

Kathleen Pritchard   Department of Political Science
                               Marquette University, Milwaukee, Wisconsin

Jose Quiroga   School of Public Health
                               University of California, Los Angeles

Randy B. Reiter   University of California, San Francisco

Douglas A. Samuelson   College of Engineering
                               Memphis State University, Memphis, Tennessee

Clyde Collins Snow   Office of the Oklahoma State Medical Examiner

Herbert F. Spirer   Department of Information Management
                               University of Connecticut, Storrs

Michael Stohl   Department of Political Science
                               Purdue University, West Lafayette, Indiana

Herman von Hebel   Netherlands Institute of Human Rights

M. V. Zunzunegui   School of Public Health
                               University of California, Berkeley

Index

University of Pennsylvania Press
Pennsylvania Studies In Human Rights

Bert B. Lockwood, Jr.,
Series Editor
Professor & Director, Urban Morgan
Institute for Human Rights, University of Cincinnati College of Law

Advisory Board

Marjorie Agosin
Philip Alston
Kevin Boyle
Richard P. Claude
David Weissbrodt

Iain Guest, *Behind the Disappearances: Argentina's Dirty War Against Human Rights and the United Nations.* 1990.
Thomas B. Jabine and Richard P. Claude, editors. *Human Rights and Statistics: Getting the Record Straight.* 1992.
Abdullahi Ahmed An-Na'im, editor. *Human Rights in Cross-Cultural Perspectives: A Quest for Consensus.* 1992.

This book was set in Baskerville and Eras typefaces. Baskerville was designed by John Baskerville at his private press in Birmingham, England, in the eighteenth century. The first typeface to depart from oldstyle typeface design, Baskerville has more variation between thick and thin strokes. In an effort to insure that the thick and thin strokes of his typeface reproduced well on paper, John Baskerville developed the first wove paper, the surface of which was much smoother than the laid paper of the time. The development of wove paper was partly responsible for the introduction of typefaces classified as modern, which have even more contrast between thick and thin strokes.

Eras was designed in 1969 by Studio Hollenstein in Paris for the Wagner Typefoundry. A contemporary script-like version of a sans-serif typeface, the letters of Eras have a monotone stroke and are slightly inclined.

Printed on acid-free paper.